SHOT
IN THE
HEART

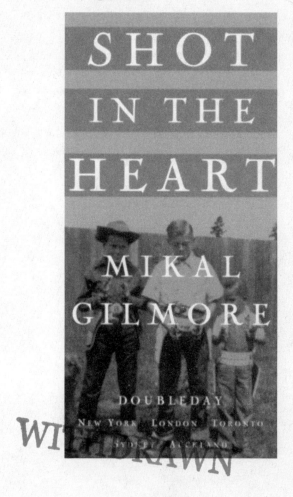

SHOT IN THE HEART

MIKAL GILMORE

DOUBLEDAY
New York London Toronto
Sydney Auckland

ANCHOR BOOKS
DOUBLEDAY
NEW YORK LONDON TORONTO
SYDNEY AUCKLAND

An Anchor Book
PUBLISHED BY DOUBLEDAY

a division of Bantam Doubleday Dell Publishing Group, Inc.
1540 Broadway, New York, New York 10036

ANCHOR BOOKS, DOUBLEDAY, *and the portrayal of an anchor*
are trademarks of Doubleday, a division of Bantam Doubleday Dell
Publishing Group, Inc.

Shot in the Heart *was originally published in hardcover by*
Doubleday in 1994. The Anchor Books edition is published by
arrangement with Doubleday.

We gratefully acknowledge permission from the following:

"Valley of Tears" by A. Domino and D. Bartholomew.
Copyright © 1957 (Renewed 1985), c/o EMI UNART
CATALOG INC. Reprinted by Permission of CPP/Belwin,
Inc., Miami, Florida. All Rights Reserved.

Lines from Harry Crews's "Fathers, Sons, Blood"
reprinted by permission of John Hawkins.
Copyright © 1993, Poseidon.

Lines from *Reasons for Moving Darker: The Sargentville*
Notebook by Mark Strand. Copyright © 1973 by Mark
Strand. Reprinted by permission of Alfred A. Knopf.

Book design by Marysarah Quinn

The Library of Congress has cataloged the Doubleday hardcover edition as follows:

Library of Congress Cataloging-in-Publication Data
Gilmore, Mikal.
Shot in the heart / Mikal Gilmore. — 1st ed.
p. cm.
1. Gilmore family. 2. Murder—United States—Case studies.
3. Violence—United States—Case studies. I. Title.
HV6529.G55 1994
364.1'523'0973—dc20   93-45627
CIP

ISBN 0-385-47800-3
Copyright © 1994 by Mikal Gilmore
All Rights Reserved
Printed in the United States of America
First Anchor Books Edition: September 1995

5   7   9   10   8   6   4

This book is dedicated to my brother, Frank Gilmore, Jr.
He endured much to help me tell this story.

There's something the dead are keeping
back.

— ROBERT FROST

THE DREAM

I HAVE DREAMED A TERRIBLE DREAM.

In this dream, it is always night. We are in my father's house—an old charred-brown, 1950s-era home. Shingled, two-story, and weather-worn, it is located on the far outskirts of a dead-end American town, pinioned between the night-lights and smoking chimneys of towering industrial factories. In front of the house, forming the border to a forest I am forbidden to trespass, lies a moonlit stretch of railroad track. Throughout the night of the dreams, you can hear a train whistle howling in the distance, heralding the approach of a passenger car from the outside world. For some reason, no train ever follows this signal. There is only the howl.

In the house, people come and go, moving between the darkness outside and the darkness inside. These people are my family, and in the dream, they are all back from the dead. There is my mother, Bessie Gilmore, who lived a life of bitter losses, who died spitting blood, calling the names of her father and her husband—men who had long before brutalized her hopes and her love—crying to them for mercy, for a passage into the darkness that she had so long feared. There is my brother Gaylen, who died young of old wounds, as his new bride sat at his side, holding his hand, watching the life pass from his sunken face. There is my brother Gary, who murdered innocent men in rage against the way life had robbed him of too much time and too much love, and who died when a volley of bullets tore his violent, tortured heart from his chest. There is my brother Frank, who turned increasingly quiet and distant with each new death, who was last seen walking down a road nearby the night-house of this dream, his hands rammed deep into his pockets, a look of uncomprehending pain seizing his face. And there is my father, Frank Sr., who died from the ravages and insults of cancer. Of all the family members, he is in these dreams the least, and when he is there, I end up feeling guilt over his presence: I am always happy to see him, it turns out, but nobody else is. That's because, in the dreams, as in life, there is the fear that my father will spread anger and ruin too far for his family to survive, that he will somehow find a way to kill those who have already been killed, who have already paid dearly for his legacy. When he appears, sometimes the point of the dream is to convince him that the *only cure for all the bitterness, for all the bad blood, is for him to return to death. Lie down, Father, we say. Let us bury you again.*

Finally, there is me. I watch my family in these dreams and seem always to feel apart from the fraternity—as if there is a struggle here for love and participation that, somehow, I always fail. And so I watch as my brothers come and go. I look out the windows and see them move in the darkness outside, through the bushes, across the yard, toward the driveway. I watch cars cross the railway tracks. I watch them come and take my brothers and deliver them back, and I know they are moving to and from underworlds that I cannot take part in, because for some reason I cannot leave this house.

Then, one night, years into these dreams, Gary tells me why I can never join my family in its comings and goings, why I am left alone sitting in the living room as they leave: It is because I have not yet entered death. I cannot follow them across the tracks, into the forest where their real lives take place, he says, until I die. He pulls a gun from his coat pocket. He lays it on my lap. There is a door across the room, and he moves toward it. Through the door, there is the night. I see the glimmer of the train tracks. Beyond them, my family. "See you in the darkness beyond," he says.

I do not hesitate. I pick the pistol up. I put its barrel in my mouth. I pull the trigger. I feel the back of my head erupt. It is a softer feeling than I expect. I feel my teeth fracture and disintegrate and pass in a gush of blood out of my mouth. I also feel my life pass out of my mouth, and in that instant I feel a collapse into nothingness. There is darkness, but there is no beyond. There is never any beyond, only the sudden, certain rush of extinction. I know that it is death I am feeling—that is, I know this is how death must truly feel—and I know that this is where beyond ceases to be a possibility.

I have had this dream more than once, in various forms. I always wake at this point, my heart hammering hard, hurting for being torn back from the void that I know is the gateway to the refuge of my ruined family. Or is it the gateway to hell? Either way, I want back into the dream, but in those haunted hours of the night, there is no way back.

I HAVE A STORY TO TELL. IT IS A STORY OF MURDERS: murders of the flesh, and of the spirit; murders born of heartbreak, of hatred, of retribution. It is the story of where those murders begin, of how they take form and enter our actions, how they transform our lives, how their legacies spill into the world and the history around us. And it is a story of how the claims of violence and murder end—if, indeed, they ever end.

I know this story well, because I have been stuck inside it. I have lived with its causes and effects, its details and indelible lessons, my entire life. I know the dead in this story—I know why they made death for others, and why they sought it for themselves. And if I ever hope to leave this place, I must tell what I know.

So let me begin.

I AM THE BROTHER OF A MAN WHO MURDERED INNOCENT MEN. His name was Gary Gilmore, and he would end up as one of modern America's more epochal criminal figures. But it wasn't his crimes—the senseless murders of two young Mormon men on consecutive nights in July 1976—that won him his notoriety. Instead, what made Gary famous was his involvement in his own punishment. His murders took place not long after the United States Supreme Court had cleared the way for the renewal of capital punishment, and Utah—the place where he had murdered—had been among the first states to pass legislation restoring the death penalty. But practicing it was another matter. When Gary received his death sentence in the fall of 1977, nobody had been executed in America in more than a decade, and despite its new laws, the country still didn't have much taste for legal bloodshed. All that changed with Gary Gilmore.

On November 1, 1976, Gary refused his right to appeal his sentence and insisted that the state go ahead and meet the date it had set for his death. Immediately he hit a national nerve, and nearly every day and night for the next few months he made headline news. There were arguments, delays, and intrigues; there was even a love story. But through it all, Gary remained fierce and unswerving in his determination to die—he even tried his own hand at it twice—and he had put the State of Utah and death penalty advocates in a difficult, unexpected spot. He made them not just his allies, but he also transformed them into his servants: men who would kill at his bidding, to suit his own ideals of ruin and redemption. By insisting on his own execution—and in effect directing the legal machinery that would bring that execution about—Gary seemed to be saying: *There's really nothing you can do to punish me, because this is precisely what I want, this is my will. You will help me with my final murder.*

And the nation hated Gary; not for his crimes, but because, in his indomitable arrogance, he seemed to have figured out a method to win, a way to escape.

Many people, of course, already know this part of the story. It was major international news for several months in 1976 and 1977, and it was later the subject of a popular novel and television film, Norman Mailer's *The Executioner's Song*. If you've read that book or seen the film, you know the story of Gary's last few months: the trusts he betrayed, the love he lost, the lives he destroyed, and the self-negation he sought. What is less generally known, and what has never been much documented, is the story of the *origins* of Gary's violence—the true history of my family and how its webwork of dark secrets and failed hopes helped create the legacy that, in part, became my brother's impetus to murder.

These parts of the story were never told because, quite simply, nobody would ever talk about them. During the last few weeks of Gary's life, Larry Schiller—who had secured the rights to Gary's life story and who would later conduct most of the interviews for *The Executioner's Song*—tried to get Gary to talk openly about the realities of his childhood and family life. Schiller sensed that something horrible had happened in that past, but Gary insisted this was not the case, and he often met these questions with mockery or anger, even until the last hours of his life. Months later, Schiller and Norman Mailer would spend numerous hours interviewing my mother, Bessie Gilmore, trying to explore the same necessary territory: Had something happened in Gary's childhood that later turned him to the course of murder? Schiller and Mailer tried their best but, more often than not, my mother answered their inquiries with maddening riddles and outright avoidance. There were large, dark parts of the family's past that she would not deal with, and that she preferred to cloak in the guise of mystery. Something to do with my father: how he had lived his life and how he had treated his sons. Whatever happened in those long-ago days, neither Gary nor my mother would reveal it, and both of them went to their graves keeping a tight hold on their secrets. It was as if they would rather die than give up the past.

I also would not discuss the details of my family's past. In fact, I would spend the next fifteen years of my life trying my best to distance myself from my family and what I saw as its terrible history and luckless destiny. I used to tell myself that whatever ran in Gary's blood that turned him into a killer did not also run in my blood, and that whatever turned my family's hopes to wreckage would not also devastate my life. I was *different* from them, I knew. I would escape.

I now know better. To believe that Gary had absorbed all the family's dissolution, or that the worst of our rot had died with him that morning in Draper, Utah, was to miss the real nature of the legacy that had placed him before those rifles: what that heritage or patrimony was about, and where it had come from.

PART ONE

MORMON

GHOSTS

"[T]here are transgressors who, if they knew themselves, and the only condition upon which they can obtain forgiveness, would beg of their brethren to shed their blood, that the smoke thereof might ascend to God as an offering to appease the wrath that is kindled against them, and that the law might have its course."

— BRIGHAM YOUNG,
Journal of Discourses

Even when the Mormons built ghosts, they built for the ages.

— WALLACE STEGNER,
Mormon Country

CHAPTER 1

BROTHERS

ONE BY ONE I HAD WATCHED THEM ALL DIE. First, my father. Then my brothers Gaylen and Gary. Finally, my mother, a bitter and ravaged woman. In the end, there was just me, the youngest, and Frank, the oldest. Then one day, when the pain of the family's history had become too much to bear, Frank simply walked into a shadow world and could not be uncovered, no matter how hard I sought him. Or maybe I just didn't seek hard enough.

That was over a decade ago. In the time that followed I believed I was no longer tied to the wreckage that had been my family's spirit, and whatever devastations might come in my life, at least now they would be my own. I told myself I was finally alone: free to pursue my own family dream.

One day, though, that dream dissolved into a nightmare. When that happened, I began to understand that I hadn't avoided my family's ruin after all. Indeed, it felt like our ruin might be endless and that the only way to stop it might be to stop the legacy itself—and the only way to do that was to crack open its god-awful secrets, if I could find them.

And so now I want to go back into my family—back into its stories, its myths, its memories, its inheritance. I want to climb back into the family story the same way I've always wanted to climb back into that dream about the house where we all grew up. Climb back in and find out what made the dream go bad, and what made it destroy so many lives.

It's as if the structure of my family's past has taken on the dimensions of a mystery for me. I want to see if, by examining our history, I can discover somewhere within it a key—an event that might explain what produced so much loss and violence. Maybe if I could discover some answers, I might be able to bargain my way out of any further loss.

So back I go, afraid in part that I might never know the truth, afraid also that I might find too much. I know this much: We all paid for something that had happened long before we were born, something that we were not allowed to know. In the end, perhaps it will all remain a mystery that nobody may touch at the heart.

THE FAMILY I GREW UP IN was not the same family my brothers grew up in. They grew up in a family that was on the road constantly, never in the same place longer than a couple of months at best. They grew up in a family where they watched the father beat the mother regularly, battering her face until it was a mortified, blue knot. They grew up in a family where they were slapped and pummeled and belittled for paltry affronts. They grew up in a family where they had to unite in secret misadventures just to find common pleasures.

In the family I grew up in, my brothers were as much a part of its construction as my parents. They were part of what I had to experience, to learn from. They were part of what I had to overcome and shun. They gave me something to aspire to: the chance to escape their fates. In fact, one of the ways my family best served me was by teaching me that I did not want to stay bound to its values and its debts or to its traditions.

In any event, I grew up in a world so entirely different from that of my brothers, I may as well have grown up under another surname. Obviously, I should be thankful for those differences, but of course things never work quite that smoothly. The misery of my brothers' childhood is so distinct from the misery of my own childhood, it's almost impossible for me to feel delivered from their hell, anymore than I feel saved from World War Two merely because I didn't have to live through it.

You could find much of the truth about these two families—the family of my brothers and the family I grew up in—by flipping through the pages of our main photo albums. Those pages are made up almost entirely of pictures of my brothers, and in most of those photos my brothers appear together in one configuration or another. Pictures of Frankie and Gary as babies, holding each other's hands and smiling delightedly at the camera; pictures of them standing together, in their matching army and navy outfits during the war years, or in matching slacks, with suspenders, white shirts, and wide ties, when the family lived in the deserts of Arizona. After Gaylen was born, it was pictures of the three of them. Three boys, dressed in authentic cowboy gear, standing with gleaming toy guns in their hands, all trying to look ominous, like little brother outlaws. By the time you page through the books to the time of my childhood, you will find only a few photos of me with any of my other brothers—mostly as we were lined up single file on Christmas mornings in front of the tree, looking like heartsick convicts. Just as notably, there are only two or three pictures of me by myself in those main family albums, in contrast to the numerous solo portraits of my brothers.

These pictures make plain a certain truth: My brothers and I did not inhabit the same time and space. We did not know each other. We barely belonged together. I remember playing a bit with Gaylen when I was a child, because he was the one closest in age to me, and I remember Frank Jr. taking care of me, taking me to movies, looking after me, loving me. Contrary to my mother's memories, I don't recall doing much of anything with Gary until years later, when we were both adults. For all of two or three days.

Mostly, I remember playing by myself, with my own toys. I liked guns and Western scenarios, just like my brothers—though they all forbade me to touch any of their fancy-ass silver-plated pistols that I envied so much. But more than guns, I liked castles. I had a fine model set of King Arthur's castle, complete with a drawbridge and turrets. But I didn't like—in fact threw away—the cheap plastic figurines of knights that came with the package. I had seen a much nicer-looking set of metal knights and horses, in fearsome-looking action positions, made by a ritzy English company called Britains. They were hand-painted, they were gorgeous, and they were expensive, and I more or less made my mother buy them for me. If my brothers could have their pearl-handled six-guns, I could have my ornate knights. I loved placing those knights inside the castle walls, pulling up the drawbridge, keeping them in the fortress where no harm could come to them. I never let my brothers touch my cavaliers in armor—not that they wanted to.

IT'S POSSIBLE MY BROTHERS and I may have played together more than I recall, but only a few incidents involving the four of us stick out in my mind. One time, we were all in the backyard of our home in Portland, Oregon, and my brothers were tossing darts at a board they had hung on a tree. I loved watching them and I wanted to throw the darts too, but they weren't about to have a clumsy little kid cluttering up their sport. Of course, I persisted. Pouted, probably. Finally one of them—Gary, if I remember right—relented. "Okay," he said, "if you want to play darts, we'll play darts. Here's how we do it." He took me over and stood me in front of the target. "We see who can get their darts closest to *you*."

I should have run, but I didn't. I was glad to be included. Gary tossed the first dart, and it landed about six inches from my foot. Frank Jr. lobbed another, and it hit a couple inches closer. Gaylen tossed his, and it ended up maybe less than an inch from one of my feet. I was starting to feel less like I wanted to be included. The next dart—tossed by Gary— did the trick. It hit my right shoe, went through the top, through the toenail of my big toe, and stuck upright. My brothers looked panicked, and I started to cry. My mother came outside, saw the dart sticking out of my foot, the sheepish look on my brothers' faces, and was not pleased.

Later, I took a revenge of sorts. On a beautiful summer afternoon, Gary was sitting on our front porch with a couple of his girlfriends, and my brother Frank was there too, with a girl. Again, I wanted to be in- cluded, and again I was told to go away. I went to the side of the house, got one end of the long garden hose, dragged it to the front porch. I handed the nozzle to Gary, who was sweet-talking a honey-blond-haired young woman, and said: "Here, hold this. I'll be right back." He wasn't paying much attention to what I said. He sat there, holding the hose, talking to the girls.

I ran to the back and turned the hose faucet on full blast. As I'd hoped, the spray got Gary right in the face—*hard*—and soaked his clothes. I could hear his howl in the backyard, and I could hear the girls' laughter. I ran and hid in some brier bushes behind our house, and I didn't come back for hours. When I did, Gary was still looking dour. "I'll never forgive you," he said.

———

I STUDY THOSE PICTURES of my brothers. I have more hard feelings about those photos than any other items in our family scrapbook. I look at the three of them, their guns pointed at the camera, and I can feel the world they shared together, the world they belonged in. It isn't the toughness of their stance—their romance as little boy outlaws—that calls out to me. Instead, what strikes me about these photos is how much my brothers smiled when they were together—how happy they seemed in that world of theirs. I don't remember people in my family smiling that much when I was a child, but then, there's a lot about those years I don't remember that well. Those smiles are like a mystery: They tell me there was a whole life my family lived that I still know nothing about—a life that, even to this day, nobody talks about.

For all the hell my brothers may have gone through, they were, at least for a time, real brothers. I look at the faces in those pictures, and I hate them. I don't want to, but I do. I hate them because I wasn't included in their picture. I hate them for not being a part of their family, no matter how horrible its costs.

CHAPTER 2

BLOODLINES

I TRY TO REMEMBER MY MOTHER. I shut my eyes and make myself recall her face from my earliest memories, when my father was gone much of the time, and my brothers had not yet drifted into lives of serial disaster. She smiled a lot in those days; every morning I awoke to a face that seemed to take delight at my awakening. Then I see her face from a few years later. It was different by then, full of hot anger, and sometimes alive with a dangerous insaneness—a face that could not help displaying the costs of a history of endless disappointments. I grew afraid of her face during that time—in part because my father told me I *should* be afraid of it—and that only made matters worse.

The truth is, Bessie Gilmore had plenty to be angry about. My father had taunted and berated and beat her for years, and my brothers had already turned our house into an address of neighborhood notoriety. But the anger began earlier than that. Much earlier.

In the end, my mother is the person I would spend the most time with in my family, and as I grew older I believed I identified with her experience of sorrow and loneliness, her sense of being a maddened outcast. But now, I reach this place where I must begin to reconstruct her for this story, and I am surprised to learn that perhaps I never really understood the depths or the sources of her damage at all. The rest of us in the family were men; I know well our particular meannesses, our fitful and plundering moods. To a certain extent, I even understand the violence that ran through our lives — at least I understand how one can hate the world for its refusals, and how one can want to punish or destroy anything or anybody that might savor a happiness that we will never have. But when I try to imagine the reality of my mother's heart, and its endless hatred and fear and hurt, I grow afraid. I'm afraid that the deepest parts of our hearts are inherited, and that my mother's was a heart of prophecy. In the end, I am only able to enter her memory when I imagine the damnation she felt in her youth and the bereavement she felt in her later years. It's as if I only understand the painful brackets of her life: the fright she grew up in, the fright she died in.

But I also know this: It was my mother who did her best to instill in me a sense that I might succeed in this world — in other words, that I might escape the tradition of our family — and it was she, perhaps more than any other person, who helped enable me to accomplish that dream. It is probably true, in fact, that she sacrificed some of the health and security of her later years so that I might realize that success. In turn, I learned how to forsake her, just as I learned how to forsake everybody else in my family. She wanted me to survive our bad legacy, to be her best work, and yet in order to do that, I felt I had to leave her behind, and of course that hurt her. You cannot move into a new world and still stay bound to the demands of the old world, and I figured I was somebody who was always headed for new worlds.

But I wasn't the only one that my mother had hopes for. I suspect that she saw Gary as her work as well: Perhaps he was the one who might act out her rage for her, and avenge all the years of abuse and exclusion she had suffered during life in Utah. If ever a mother had a son who might pay back the legacies of her past, then that alliance was Bessie and Gary Gilmore. I remember my mother once telling me: "Gary was the criminal. I'd like you to be the lawyer. Your brothers will need a good and caring legal mind."

She said this without demand, but also utterly without humor or irony.

TO EXPLAIN WHY BESSIE GILMORE might have wanted to punish her kin and homeland, I should begin by telling a bit about the people and history she grew up with. My mother was born into the world of early twentieth-century Mormon Utah—a place that, in many respects, was dramatically different from the America that surrounded it. The Mormons had long possessed a strong and spectacular sense of otherness and unity: They saw themselves not only as God's modern chosen people, but also as a people whose faith and identity had been forged by a long and bloody history, and by outright banishment. They were a people apart—a people with its own myths and purposes, and with a history of astonishing violence.

My mother remembered hearing the legends of her people—their miracles and persecutions—throughout her childhood, and she passed these same tales along to me and my brothers in our childhoods. Chief among these stories were accounts of Mormonism's early struggle for survival—in particular the powerful and haunting story of the church's martyred founder, Joseph Smith, Jr. Smith was a man with a remarkable imagination and vision—indeed, he was among the most innovative mythmakers in the nation's history—and he was also a man who managed to turn his most personal obsessions into a complex, epic mix of theology and folklore. Smith would build nearly his entire complex theology on what was essentially a dilemma of bloodline: how one might redeem the dreams and debts of one's heritage, or else perish as the result of unfinished curses. By the time this question reached my own family, it had become a matter of fatal consequence.

Smith's most lasting work, of course, was the Book of Mormon. First published in the late 1820s, the Book of Mormon has managed a staying power matched by only a handful of other American texts and novels from the same period, and for over a hundred and sixty years, it has been a central factor in helping to establish Mormonism as one of the fastest growing religions in modern history. The origins of the book are as fascinating as they are controversial: Smith claimed that the book had been transcribed from a set of ancient golden plates that had been presented to him by an angel of God named Moroni. Upon these plates was written the history of America's ancient inhabitants and their dealings with the God of Israel—in effect, Smith was claiming to have discovered a long-lost, sacred complement to the Bible's Old and New Testaments. The book had—and still has—a tremendous impact on the minds of many Americans, and it is not hard to understand its almost primal appeal. Once you strip away all the Book of Mormon's pretenses of scriptural import, what you have is nothing more nor less than a lusty tale of America's favorite subject: families and murder.

Written—or at least narrated by Smith to his transcribers—in a voice that sought to emulate the King James translation of the Bible, the Book of Mormon tells the one-thousand-year chronicle of a Jewish tribe, the family of a righteous man and prophet named Lehi, who took his kin and friends and fled Jerusalem in the year 600 B.C., during a time of the city's corruption. Under the direction of God, Lehi and his sons built a ship and sailed to a new land, where Lehi taught that the greatest purpose in life—the single path to redemption—was to win God's love by obeying his laws. But there had always been a rivalry in Lehi's tribe, and at the time of the old prophet's death, when he appointed one of his younger sons, Nephi, as the family's rightful patriarch and seer, the development was met with great resentment by the older sons, Laman and Lemuel. Soon, Laman and Lemuel swelled in their anger toward their father's legacy, as well as toward the piety of Nephi and his Old World god. They threatened to overtake their brother and his followers, until Nephi was forced to remove his tribe from his brothers' dynasty. God was enraged by Laman and Lemuel's rebellion, and because of their pride and blood-thirstiness he struck them with the curse of red skin and proclaimed that all their descendants would have to carry this blemish—and the knowledge of God's disfavor—as payment for their fathers' sins. Thus began the schism between the Nephites and the Lamanites, which formed the central historical dynamic for the Book of Mormon.

Over the next millennium, the posterity of these two families warred almost constantly, one side paying the cost for having descended from righteous blood, and the other doomed to living out the disobedient and murderous legacy of their evil forefathers. Later, in the book's most daring moments, Jesus Christ visits these peoples, following his crucifixion and resurrection, and administers to them the doctrines of salvation and the counsel of peace. But peace does not hold for long. Violence returns, and killing grows rampant. At the book's close, there is only the voice of one man, Moroni, the last survivor of the Nephites. He ruminates over the history of his fallen people and their last battles, which began in a city called Desolation. At the end of the battles, the bodies of the Nephites lay in thousands, across the bloodied landscape of a dying nation, and the few children who survived were forced to eat the flesh of their fathers. Finally, there is nothing left for Moroni to do except wait for the Lamanites, who are in effect his estranged brothers, to find him and slay him.

Murder and ruin are written across the breadth of Joseph Smith's pre-American panorama, and because violence always demands an explanation or solution, the Book of Mormon's unexamined greatest revelation is a truly startling one: As Moroni looks at the blood-reddened land around him, and as he reviews the full reach of the history that led to this mass extinction, it is plain that the force behind all these centuries of destruction is none other than God himself. It is God who brought these wandering people to an empty land, and it is God who established the legacies that could only lead to such awful obliteration. God is the hidden architect of all the killing at the heart of America's greatest mystery novel, the angry father who demands that countless offspring pay for his rules and honor, even at the cost of generations of endless ruin.

The single strongest instance of blasphemy in the Book of Mormon occurs when a charismatic atheist and Antichrist named Korihor stands before one of God's judges and kings and proclaims: "Ye say that this people is a guilty and a fallen people, because of the transgression of a parent. Behold, I say that a child is not guilty because of its parents."

For proclaiming such outrageous words, God strikes Korihor mute, and despite Korihor's full-hearted repentance, God will not allow him forgiveness. Korihor is left to wander among the people of the nation, begging for mercy and support, and the people take him and stamp upon him, until he lies dead under their feet.

THE BOOK OF MORMON'S VISION OF AMERICA as a land that had always known destruction would in effect become his most haunting work of prophecy. Violence and fear would follow Joseph Smith and his people until his own bloody death years later, and even after that, murder would have a way of staying in the Mormons' history.

Despite all this, thousands of men and women flocked to Smith and his beliefs. Joseph would eventually name his new religion the Church of Jesus Christ of Latter-Day Saints, and its followers, the Saints. But his enemies—drawing on their hatred of the Book of Mormon—called them the Mormons.

My mother's Mormon pedigree stretched back to these early times, along all the paths of her ancestry. Most of these men and women came to the American Mormon community from the poverty of England, on the promise that they were journeying to the new Promised Land. What they found instead was a land full of fear and violence. By the mid 1830s, the Mormons had already been forced from several settlements, including the large communities they had built in Kirtland, Ohio, and Independence, Missouri. Their farms had been burned, their men and children murdered, their women raped—sometimes under the direction of state militiamen. Much of the enmity was ascribed to what many Americans viewed as the Mormons' odd beliefs and troubling mode of community— the Saints were said to be practicing polygamous marriages (which turned out to be true), and believed in a system of plural deities and multiple heavens (which also turned out to be true). But what seemed to disturb— or stir—people most was the character of Joseph Smith himself. He was an alluring man, but also a proud and ambitious one. Speculation was rampant among politicians and newspapermen that Smith had a meticulous plan to conquer America's middle states and build a Mormon Empire, based on a religious government, with Smith at its head. By the 1840s, Smith had been tarred and feathered, shot at, jailed and threatened with military execution, and had been called, by many men, "the most dangerous man on the American frontier." One state governor— Lilburn Boggs, of Missouri—had even decreed that the Mormons had become an official enemy, and should be driven from the land, or exterminated. The Mormons left and built a new city-state called Nauvoo, across the river in the western part of Illinois. Under Smith's direction, Nauvoo would become one of the largest and most wondrous cities in the Midwest—but ironically, that development only tended to make matters worse for Smith and his followers. The Mormons were already seen as a kingdom within a state—an accomplishment unparalleled in America's growth—and by 1844 the people of Illinois had come to fear Smith and his Mormons as the Missourians had. When it was rumored that Smith's personal bodyguard—a legendary Western gunfighter named Orrin Porter Rockwell—was responsible for shooting Missouri's former governor, Lilburn Boggs, in the back of the head (miraculously, Boggs lived), the dream of Midwestern empire was effectively over.

After a few more troubling incidents, Illinois exploded in rage at Smith, and Governor Thomas Ford insisted that the prophet turn himself over to civic authorities to stand trial. Smith surrendered himself to the authorities, and was held in jail—along with his brother Hyrum and a few other church leaders—in a small town called Carthage. There was no criminal charge at first, but soon one was formed: treason against the state—a crime punishable by death.

Governor Ford had guaranteed the Smiths' safety if they surrendered, but the militia assigned to protect them was the Carthage Greys—a troop that, on Joseph's appearance in the town, had assured him that they would see him dead before they would see him free again. On the late afternoon of June 27, 1844, a small force was guarding the Carthage Jail when a mob of a hundred men approached. The mob and the guardians were friends and part of the same militia, and so there was no real resistance offered the attackers. Several men entered the jail and rushed up the stairs to the room where Joseph and Hyrum were held. The mob-members fired musket shots through the door into the room, and a bullet caught Hyrum in the face. Four more shots ripped through him before he fell to his brother's feet, dead. Joseph had a pistol which a friend had slipped him earlier. He fired all six bullets back through the door. Three of the shots wounded some attackers, slowing the assault long enough for him to rush to the window to escape. He swung one leg out, and when he looked down, he saw nothing but bayonets and rifles. According to most accounts, it was there, as Joseph Smith was perched on the moment where he could see the full cost of his vision, that bullets riddled him from the doorway and from the crowd below. He cried, "Oh Lord, my God!" and toppled from the window to the ground. The mob outside gathered around him, some of them kicking and jeering at him, until they were satisfied he would never rise again, and then they fled.

That's the story I have heard all my life about the martyrdom of Joseph Smith. There were other witnesses, though, who told a different story about Smith's death, and for many years after the event, I learned recently, it was their version that was widely accepted as the true one. According to the earlier account—which had been supported by Mormon witnesses and the later confession of a mob member—this is what happened in Joseph Smith's last living moments in Carthage:

He made it to the window, then two shots hit him and he fell outward, to the waiting mob. One of the men in the crowd picked Joseph up and propped him against a well curb, a few feet from the jail. A militia colonel ordered four men to shoot him. They stood about eight feet from Joseph, and at the same moment, they fired their bullets through his heart. Joseph Smith fell on his face, and his blood poured into the land of the country whose secret history he had once tried to divine. He lay there for a long time alone, dying.

He was no blood relation, but I feel more kinship to Joseph Smith—the damnation he feared, and the long-coming doom that finally swallowed him—than I do any of my true forebears. I feel for him as a brother.

THE KILLING OF JOSEPH SMITH WAS MEANT TO END MORMONISM, but instead, it changed its course. Within a few months of the assassination the surviving church rallied around a new prophet and president, Brigham Young—a less visionary theologian than Smith, but a smarter leader and more gifted autocrat. The Mormons remained in Nauvoo for two more years—long enough to make it temporarily the largest city in Illinois. But pressures for the Mormons to move continued and so did the mob assaults, and after Young heard a rumor that federal troops were preparing a campaign to destroy the Saints, he decided that the only way for his people to survive America was to leave it. In February 1846, Young and the Mormons began the long pilgrimage to find a new home beyond the nation's borders. Eighteen months later, they settled in the Great Salt Lake Basin, in a land that they called Deseret (taken from the Book of Mormon's term for the honey bee—which is to say, the industrious worker who knew how to work in a like-minded community). This new home was to be, in part, the fulfillment of Joseph Smith's dream of a Kingdom of God on earth—and, in fact, it became the only religious nation ever established within America's borders. In this millennial land called Deseret—later to be called Utah—the Mormons would be free from the fearful vigilante armies that had made them, along with the Cherokees, one of the only populations ever to be driven from the United States under the threat of extinction, and in this promised place, they would defend themselves from any oppressors who might follow them.

Shortly after settling in Salt Lake, Brigham Young sent out word that all Saints in any land who could make the journey should migrate to the Great Basin, and help the church establish and populate colonies for its long-awaited empire. This was the decree that brought my mother's final Mormon forebear, Francis Kerby, into the Utah Valley, where years later, according to one story, he would come face to face with a terrible and disillusioning reality.

Not long ago, I found a microfilmed copy of Francis Kerby's old handwritten journal (like so many Latter-Day Saints' chronicles, it has been preserved in the invaluable archives of the Mormon Family History Library, in Salt Lake City). Of all our ancestors, Joseph Kerby (who was my grandmother's grandfather, on her paternal side) left the most detailed personal record—at least, up to a certain time and place. Kerby was born in 1821, into an aristocratic family of devout, long-standing members of the Church of England, who resided on the Channel Islands, off the coast of France. In 1849, when he was twenty-eight years old, Francis and his wife, Mary LeCornu Kerby, heard the preachings of a Latter-Day Saint missionary, read the Book of Mormon, and converted to the Mormon religion. Kerby's parents were stunned and outraged, and though they never completely severed their ties with their son, they grew distant from his concerns and would later leave him and his children little or none of their wealth. Almost immediately, Kerby went on to a fairly stellar career in the British Mormon world, and within days of his conversion, he had accepted a church leader's suggestion and started keeping a journal of his daily and weekly activities. It is a document that is, at once, both tedious and fascinating to read. Like many Mormon journals, Kerby's diary—which was kept from 1849 to 1893—is brimming with mundane ecclesiastical detail, and not much else. If Francis Kerby ever had an argument with his wife, or ever had a row with a neighbor—or, for that matter, ever got sick, heard a good joke, or noted a passing moment of history—he did not record it in his journal. Instead, he related page after page of church activities, including dinners with distinguished Mormons and accounts of his attendance at various LDS functions.

On January 1, 1857, Francis Kerby and his wife and children sailed to America, and three years later they joined the last of the Mormons' handcart expeditions to Utah (the handcarters literally walked their way across America, pushing and carrying carts that held their possessions). After his arrival in Utah, Kerby was apparently never the same man. Whereas in England he had kept a meticulous and proud list of all his ecclesiastical activities—and, in fact, had held high rank among the church's U.K. clergy—after he got to Utah, he was less interested in keeping track of his life within the church, and seemingly less interested in church activity itself. Indeed, the final thirty-three years of his diary notations consists almost exclusively of remarks about marriages, births, and deaths. There are no long passages in those last pages about his beliefs and devotions, as there had been during his English career.

My mother had a theory about what happened to Francis Kerby: She thought he had a crisis of faith. "He was never the same man after the Mountain Meadows Massacre happened," she once said. "He couldn't believe that the Mormons would have done such a thing, and after he learned the truth about it he never had the same heart for the church he had once loved."

THE MOUNTAIN MEADOWS MASSACRE HAD TAKEN PLACE IN 1857
—the same year that Francis Kerby had arrived in America—but the
roots of the tragedy reach back into Mormonism's earlier years, when
Joseph Smith began to conceive a theology that might prove as merciless
and bloody as the history he had envisioned for the Book of Mormon.
More particularly, the event's proper history probably began during the
Nauvoo era, when Smith first promulgated a principle that was to become known, infamously, as Blood Atonement. Aside from the practice
of polygamy, no other Mormon teaching has proven as complex or controversial as Blood Atonement. In its most widely understood sense—and
in Joseph Smith's original precept—the tenet runs like this: If you take a
life, or commit any comparable ultimate sin, then your blood must be
shed. Hanging or imprisonment would not suffice for punishment or res-
titution. The manner of death had to be one in which your blood spilled
onto the ground, as an apology to God.

In recent years, mindful of its historical image as a vengeful people,
the Mormon Church has gone to pains to disavow this interpretation.
The real principle of Blood Atonement, the modern theologians claim, is
a matter of redemption, not vengeance. Jesus Christ atoned for the sins
of the world by the shedding of his own blood; if you believed in Jesus
as the Son of God, and if you followed his teachings and obeyed his laws,
then you would be purged of sin through his blood. However, there are
some sins that are so grave—and murder is one—that if you commit these
deeds, you have placed yourself beyond the power of Christ's atonement.
The only hope for redeeming such sin is to have your own blood shed—
and even that may not be enough to earn forgiveness in the next world.
But for this form of Blood Atonement to be properly carried out, we
must all wait for a better world when the civil and spiritual laws are
administered by the same government, and such a time has not yet come.

That's the official account, but the legends of the West told a different
story. According to some observers—including former governors and jus-
tices of the Utah territory, and a few confessors and witnesses—Blood
Atonement was indeed practiced by the Mormons, and it was applied to
a wider range of sins than simple murder. Some of the offending crimes
that might merit death are not hard to imagine: There were numerous
rumors in the mid to late 1800s about men who had strongly offended
Brigham Young, or who had violated Mormon oaths of truth and secrecy,
and ended up lying along some remote roadside, or buried in nameless

graves, with bullets through their heads. But there were also other offenses that might invite death. Among them, according to some writers,
were adultery, incest, whoredom, rape, thievery, hopeless mental illness
(which in its more dramatic forms was sometimes read as a sign of de-
monic possession), and flagrant and persistent disobedience of one's parents. At midnight, the stories went, a committee of Mormon elders,
dressed in black, would visit the offender at his home and would lead
him or her to a freshly dug grave site. Some prayers would be offered as
the condemned kneeled by the grave, and then someone—perhaps the
wronged husband or father, or a righteous church leader—would lean
over and cut the offender's throat, holding him or her by the head, so
that the dying person's blood would empty onto the ground.

Did any acts of Blood Atonement ever really occur in Mormon Utah?
Church historians have denied the rumors for over a century now and,
indeed, there are no proven cases of Mormon authorities ever having
sanctioned any acts of execution or bloodletting under the church's aus-
pices. But it is also true that many Danites—the Mormons' band of secret
protectors, police, and avengers—were guilty of a sizable number of
shootings and murders in the Utah area, without being tried or apparently even chastised for their deeds. Obviously, given the unscrutinized
and theocratic rule that the Mormons enjoyed in large parts of the Utah
territory during the early years of its settlement, it is possible that executions and assassinations may have been conducted with such ironclad and
sacred secrecy that history may never retrieve the truth. As Wallace Stegner wrote in *Mormon Country*: "[I]t would be bad history to pretend that
there were no holy murders in Utah . . . , that there was no saving the
souls of sinners by the shedding of blood . . . , and that there were no
mysterious disappearances of apostates and offensive Gentiles."

The legends of Blood Atonement also served both a mythic and moral
purpose. On one level, the spread of these stories illustrated two harsh
facts. To the extent that the stories were spread by anti-Mormons, they
illustrated how America regarded the Saints as demons who had turned
their religion into a system of ritualistic outrages. To the extent that the
stories were perpetuated by Mormons themselves, they demonstrated
how the bitterness of their history had turned them into a hard people,
and how that hardness and meanness had now spilled over into the land
that they were settling. In addition, the rumors about Blood Atonement
helped the Mormons keep their own people in line. My mother recalled
hearing terror tales about old Utah's secret Danites and their midnight
deeds for years. She also remembered that these fables were often told to

children, in tones that implied that maybe the Danites and their rites of Blood Atonement weren't altogether banished in early twentieth-century Utah.

But the Mountain Meadows Massacre was not a myth and it was not a rumor. It happened, and its horror has been well-documented, even confessed to. Briefly, here is what took place:

In September 1857, a wagon train of Arkansas emigrants, known as the Baker-Fancher party, was making its way through southern Utah, en route to California. Unfortunately, they were journeying through the region shortly after the Mormons had received word that federal troops were marching their way. The intent of these troops, Brigham Young had decided, was hostile—he had long been expecting a showdown between the Saints and the nation that had expelled them—and as a defense strategy, Young had enlisted several of the local Indian tribes to help repel the U.S. invasion.

When the Baker-Fancher party arrived at the southern outpost of Cedar City, the Mormons in the region viewed the group with frightened suspicion: Perhaps the emigrants were, in fact, an advance party for the U.S. troops. It hardly helped matters when a few of the emigrants—later dubbed the "Missouri Wildcatters"—boasted that they had been among the militiamen who had slaughtered Joseph Smith a few years before and that, as soon as they reached California, they would raise forces to come back and help exterminate the surviving Utah Saints. The Mormons that these Missourians chose to infuriate were Mormons who remembered well what it was like to be driven from their homes by violent mobs, and they decided that these people would not leave their land to bring back new armies to kill them. They held a meeting and discussed whether to treat the emigrants—who were resting for a few days at a watering hole known as the Mountain Meadows—as enemies of war. The Mormons dispatched a messenger to Brigham Young in Salt Lake City, asking his counsel. Young replied that these visitors were definitely *not* a part of the federal campaign, and that they should be allowed to pass unharmed. By the time the messenger arrived back in Cedar City a few days later, nearly the entire Baker-Fancher party had been slaughtered. When Brigham Young heard about the massacre, he wept over the realization that his people could commit such an atrocity.

The news of the Mountain Meadows Massacre spread rapidly, and soon became a chief weapon in the U.S. war against the Mormons. Finally, eighteen years after the event, the man who had been reported to have been the commander of the slaughter—a prominent Mormon named John D. Lee, also a famed member of the Danites—was arrested, and in the course of two trials, Utah and the nation began to get a better picture of what had really happened at Mountain Meadows. Lee had been the area's Indian agent at the time, and according to the accounts of local tribesmen, he had approached them with reports that the Baker-Fancher group was poisoning the Indians' stock and planning greater violence. Lee himself testified that it was the Indians who had felt injured by the actions of the emigrants, and that they had threatened Lee that if he did not help deliver the wagon train party to the Indians' justice, then the Mormons would be endangered as a result. In any event, shortly after the messenger had left to consult Brigham Young, a group of Mormons and Indians carried out an attack on the Baker-Fancher party. The battle went on for days, and as a way of ending it, Lee told the tribesmen that if they would allow the women and children to escape unharmed, the Mormons would allow the slaughter of the migrant men. The Indians, Lee said, agreed, and he then convinced the Baker-Fancher group that if its survivors would surrender, they would be allowed to leave the area. Lee marched the male emigrants out of the encampment first, and a signal was given the Indians to begin their killing. But as soon as the slaughter started, the assailants lost control, and when the bloodbath was over, over one hundred men, women, and children lay dead in the Utah dirt. Many of them had been killed with unnecessary brutality.

Lee was found guilty for his part in the slaughter by an all-Mormon jury and was sentenced to death.

JOHN D. LEE WOULD NOT BE THE FIRST MAN to be legally executed in the Utah territory, but no man before him and no man after him—until my brother, one hundred years later—had such a keen understanding of the meaning of Utah's death penalty. In the early 1850s, when the Mormon-dominated territorial legislature was drafting a criminal code, it designed a punishment for first-degree murder that would specifically satisfy the doctrine of Blood Atonement: Those who were condemned to death could choose between the options of being shot to death by a firing squad or being beheaded (the latter choice was eliminated in 1888, because—not surprisingly—nobody ever opted for it). Or, for those who were a little less anxious to have their blood shed, or who might simply be non-Mormon, there was always the possibility of a non-enlightened death: a simple hanging. As it turned out, a fair amount of blood ended up getting spilled. From the late 1840s to 1977, roughly fifty men were executed in Utah: eight by hanging, one reportedly by disemboweling, two by undocumented means; the remaining thirty-nine were shot by firing squads. Obviously, several other states—notably, ones in the South—executed greater numbers of men during the same period. None, though, would put to death so many by a means that so pointedly resulted in the spilling of blood, and no other state in the Union had a capital punishment code that prescribed its methods of death according to religious doctrine.

When Lee was given the choice of the mode of execution, he chose according to his faith: He chose to be shot.

On March 23, 1877, Lee was taken to the site of the Mountain Meadows Massacre. "I do not fear death," he said that morning. "I shall never go to a worse place than I am now in." Then, after he denounced Brigham Young for leading the Mormons astray from the teachings of Joseph Smith, Lee added: "I have been sacrificed in a cowardly, dastardly manner. I cannot help it. It is my last word—it is so." (Later, after hearing a report of Lee's words, Brigham Young—in the manner of the Book of Mormon's Lord God—cursed Lee and all his generations to come.)

Lee sat back down on his coffin and spoke his final words: "Center my heart, boys. Don't mangle my body."

The executioners obliged the request. They fired their bullets in close formation through John D. Lee's heart, and he fell back across his coffin. His blood spilled into the Utah soil, where the blood of the massacre's victims had spilled a generation before, and then his body was placed in the wooden casket and given to his family for burial.

The whole affair had been another violent turning point in the Mormon world. The massacre had been disgraceful, and so was the way that Lee was used to relieve the Mormon structure of its culpability in the matter. (Eighty-four years later, the church finally cleared Lee's name and reinstated him to full membership, with restoration of his former blessings.)

After Mountain Meadows, Mormons had to face that murder was everywhere in God's promised lands—in the America forsaken, and the kingdom to come. The blood would not stop spilling, and now the chosen people found its stain on their own hands.

CHAPTER 3

THE HOUSE ON

JORDAN LANE

THESE WERE THE LEGENDS THAT MY MOTHER HEARD growing up in Mormon Utah, and they were part of the inheritance that she passed along to us. And then there were the stories of her own family.

MY MOTHER'S MOTHER, MELISSA KERBY, WAS THE GRANDDAUGHTER of Francis Kerby and the great-granddaughter of Emanuel Masters Murphy. By the time of Melissa's generation, both the Murphy and Kerby clans had settled into the Provo region of Utah, about fifty miles south of Salt Lake City. Provo was the second city that Brigham Young ordered organized in the region in the late 1840s and, more than most Mormon Utah colonies, it had a violent history. It was named after a man named

Etienne Provost, whose exploration party had been slaughtered by the Snake Indians on the Jordan River, many years before. In its first decade or so, Provo saw a fair amount of battles with local Indians over land use and cattle grazing—though it was the Indians, more often than not, who paid with their lives for these skirmishes.

Utah's first recorded execution—an unofficial one—took place in the Provo area. A bold and nasty-tempered Ute Indian named Patsowits (or Pat Souette, as the Mormons spelled it) had killed a local settler in 1850 and then went on to kill several of the Mormons' cattle and horses. He also threatened to kill a local chief for acquiescing to the Mormons' land-grab. He was captured by two Ute Indians. Anxious to improve relations with the new settlers, the Utes turned Patsowits over to local Mormon authorities, who, in a particularly novel twist on Blood Atonement and frontier justice, disemboweled the Indian, then filled his abdomen with rocks and tossed him into a lake.

Between all the Mormon superstitions and various Indian tales, Provo came to be known as a haunted place. There were stories about ghosts who moved through the hills and around the farms at night: the spirits of men who had lost their land and their lives to the Mormons and their strange new rituals.

This is the area where my grandparents were born and where my mother and her brothers and sisters were born and raised. My grandmother Melissa Kerby came from nearby Wallsburg in 1880, the daughter of Joseph Kerby and Mary Ellen Murphy. Joseph Kerby was a talented artist—he was best known for taking his canvas and tools and isolating himself in one of Utah's canyons for days at a time, painting majestic mountain views. He was also a man given to frequent depression and abrupt mood changes, and his need for solitude was often hard on his family. When Melissa was nine, her father sent her to nearby Heber, to cook and keep house for three men who worked for him. She later said that she was lonely and homesick the whole time, and it was in one of these periods of isolation that Melissa began to write as a way to stave off the boredom. It was a habit she would never give up; she wrote an incessant outpouring of poems, plays, letters, stories, and journals, and she committed herself to daily writing of one sort or another until the last day of her life.

While Melissa's poems and church-aimed writings were full of typical Mormon pieties, her short stories were something else. Sometimes she wrote first-person accounts about a young woman whose father was lonely and tormented—a man who forced his daughter to stay home, to look after him and keep the world out, while he drank himself into deeper shame and unconscious violence. He would beat his daughter and wreck his house, but the anguish he showed afterward always won his daughter's pity and her pledge never to abandon him to himself. Some of her other stories were about a young woman who needed to win the love and devotion of the young men around her—sometimes two or more at a time—and who would then invariably reject the men and break their hearts. It is tempting to infer facts about Melissa Kerby's young life from these stories, but I have no way of knowing if such an interpretation would hold. All I know from family legend is that Melissa was supposed to have been attractive when she was young and had several male pursuers and, yes, she reportedly broke a few hearts before she met the man she could not spurn.

Melissa Kerby found that man in William Brown, a shy and gangling fellow who was six years her junior, and apparently no match for her intelligence. Will's father, Alma, had lived in Provo all his life, working as a blacksmith and a railroad man. Alma married Mary Ann Duke in 1875 and, in ideal Mormon tradition, they had ten children; Will was the fifth born. In his middle adult years, Alma slipped under the wheels of a moving train at Provo's train yards and lost a leg. After his accident, he reportedly became a hard, madly authoritarian man. In his worst bouts of rage, Alma Brown would pull off the wooden leg he now wore and would beat his wife Mary Ann with it in front of the children. Sometimes he did it until she would drop unconscious, and at least once or twice he beat her terribly enough to send her to the hospital for a few days. One time, when he was young, Will tried to intervene and stop the beating; he found the wooden leg turned against him, and he ended up in the hospital with his own leg badly injured. The Browns would later tell the story that Will's horse had fallen on him. Will learned to obey his father without resistance after that, and he learned to keep his feelings quiet.

By the time Melissa met Will, Alma's fearful days were past; in fact, the old man would die just a week or two before the young couple's marriage. When the two met, Melissa was the belle of the local church ward. She directed the ward's plays, had been named the ward poet and the president of the Young Ladies' Association, and had even been chosen the local Goddess of Liberty for Provo's big July 24th pageant (the annual celebration of the day the Saints arrived in the Salt Lake Valley). Will had a part in a play she was directing for the event, and there was something about his shyness, the broken way he tried to speak his lines, that appealed to her. Maybe there was something in his loneliness that she identified with. In any event, this was a man's heart that she could not bring herself to break.

On December 4, 1907, after a year and a half of courtship, Will Brown and Melissa Kerby were married in Provo. The money side of things ran against them from the start. With his father dead, it had fallen to Will to continue the support of his mother and siblings and the maintenance of their farm, in addition to looking after his own new family. What's more, Mary Duke Brown insisted that her children stay as close to her as possible. With such obligations, a man couldn't make much of a living or afford much of a home, and so, after their wedding, Will and Melissa took the only course they saw open: They moved in with Will's mother and devoted their time to her farm. According to my mother, Mary Brown was a hard taskmaster. It was as if she'd been waiting all those years for Alma Brown to die so she could try on his role for size.

In 1908, Melissa and Will had their first child, a boy named George. Two years later, they had another baby, a daughter named Patta, but the birth had been hard on Melissa, and she almost died. Will decided that the crowded living conditions at his mother's farm, plus the strain of looking after two children, would likely be too much for Melissa. He told his mother that the time had come for him and his wife to build their own home. Mary Brown didn't like the idea of losing her son entirely to a life of his own, and so she made him an offer. Up Jordan Lane a ways, where the road curved around to a hill crest that sat across from the Wasatch Mountain Range and overlooked the entire Provo Valley—an area appropriately called Grandview—there was a nice bit of farmland that Mary and Alma had owned for years and had once hoped to move to. She would give her son and his wife the best acre and a quarter of that land, on the condition that Will would continue to run her own farm for her and would promise that, as soon as his children were old enough to lift a pail and dig dirt with their hands, they too would help on her farm. Will knew that this was a chance to get some of the best high-level farmland in the Provo area. He agreed to his mother's terms, and within a short time he had built a two-room house on the land at the top of Jordan Lane, for him and his wife and children to live in.

A year after Patta, Melissa bore her third child, a girl named Mary, and then, on August 19, 1913, my mother, Bessie Brown, was born. In the next few years, five more Brown children would be born: Mark, Alta, Wanda, and a pair of twins, Ada and Ida. One by one they all crammed into the two-room house on Jordan, nine children in all, and when everybody finally started to push against each other, Will added two more rooms to the house—including a bedroom for him and his wife, and another room for all the girls. Out in back of the house, past a couple of large trees, Will built a storage and work shed, where the boys slept at night. Next to the shed, he built a large, simple barn. Will and Melissa's home was now a modest farm, but it would never come to much—in large part because Will and his children were working his mother's farm down the road more than they worked their own.

Like many of the small farms in Provo, Will's farm yielded enough fruits and vegetables to keep his wife and children fed, but rarely more. For milk, there was also a family cow—an animal named Bessie. My mother hated that cow with a vengeance. It was bad enough she had to share the bossy's name. What was worse, she was told the cow had held the name first—which led to an endless run of bad jokes about how she had been named after the damn thing. Years afterward—and up until the time of her death—my mother waged a campaign to disprove the charge that she shared a forename with the family cow. "My real name was *Betty*, not Bessie," she would say. "It's short for Elizabeth. I was named after the Queen of England." I never thought to ask her which Queen Elizabeth she meant, but I'm willing to bet it was the modern one—who wasn't born until 1926, thirteen years after Bessie Brown.

As the years went along, the Brown children were left to raise themselves much of the time. In addition to working his mother's farm, Will had taken on a job as the janitor at the local school, and he also became the Grandview Hills Watermaster, in charge of the water flow for the area's irrigation canals. Plus, he did blacksmith work whenever there was a call for it. Meantime, Melissa became more and more flustered by having so many children to look after. In addition, after the twins' birth, Melissa's hearing began to fade. In short, there was too much family, too many obligations, and too little time. Will and Melissa had given birth to so many children because, as Mormons, they were obliged to. However, they weren't prepared to give the children a lot of individual time. They made it understood: The children had to work hard and help take care of each other. And if anybody strayed too far from an acceptable range of behavior, if anybody became too defiant or rebellious or violated the values of their community or church, they would be thrown out. That was how it had to be.

WHEN I WAS A CHILD, I USED TO FIND IT ENCHANTING that my mother had grown up on a farm. Apparently my mother did not feel the same. "I *hated* working on the farm, getting my hands dirty," she said. "I had *pretty* hands. I couldn't see ruining them, picking cucumbers and bush beans, just to keep mean old Grandma Brown happy. She wouldn't even say thank you." As much as she could, my mother skipped out on the farm jobs, under one ruse or another. She had a hiding place on Grandma Brown's farm, where she had found a small quicksand pit. She would spend hours there, sinking twigs and stones, and sometimes her sisters' dolls. The pit seemed to be bottomless.

Other times, Bessie would take off across Jordan Lane, down the hill into the valley, where some Gypsies kept a seasonal encampment. Nobody would follow her down there. "The Gypsies steal children," her mother warned her. "But don't worry: They only steal beautiful children." Most of the time, though, Bessie tried to stick close to her father, playing around him, watching him as he would hammer horseshoes on his anvil and then nail the shoes to the animal's hooves. She liked to watch his big hands and his steady concentration as he worked. Bessie decided that she must be Will Brown's favorite daughter and that he would give her anything she wanted. One day she tested this belief. The first thing Bessie saw every morning, as she looked out the Browns' front door, was the line of the Wasatch Mountains—a long, towering ridge that looked like it had been lifted from the earth to protect God's people from the land outside. One mountain in particular stood out from the rest. This was the mountain where Brigham Young University eventually built a large Y, made of bright white stones; on nights when the school's football team was victorious, the players would climb the mountain and plant lighted torches into the stones, making a fiery Y that could be seen throughout the valley. Bessie loved that mountain more than anything else about Utah. She spent hours staring at it, talking to it, giving it her secrets. Truth be told, she probably prayed more ardently to that mountain than she ever did to her people's God. Finally, she decided that, like her father's love, the mountain was a prize that belonged solely to her heart.

"Dad," she said one afternoon, watching her father work at his anvil, "can I have that mountain? Can I claim it for my own?"

Her father stopped the pounding of his hammer long enough to glance up at the mountain, then shrugged. "Sure, I don't see why not," he said, and went back to his hammering.

"Okay, mountain," Bessie said, "you're mine."

A few weeks later, Bessie was playing in the barn, close to her father as he worked, when she came across an old wooden box, nailed shut. "What's in there?" she asked.

Her father walked over and pried the nails off the box. "Open it and see," he said.

My mother opened the box and inside she saw the wooden leg that Alma Brown had once used to beat his wife and son. Bessie screamed and slammed down the lid and started to cry. Will Brown, standing next to her, roared with laughter.

I WAS THE ONLY PERSON IN MY FAMILY WHO HAD NEVER spent time on my mother's farm. My brothers had lived there several times over the years with my mother, during my father's various absences, and they knew its temper and history almost as well as she did.

Then, one day in early 1959, my mother received word that her father had suffered a stroke and might not live much longer. My mother had not been back home since my birth, and she decided that I should make the train trip to Utah with her and see the home of my grandparents.

I was eight at the time, and even now it surprises me how much I can recall from that journey. I remember my mother's older brother George—from whom I gained my middle name—meeting us at night at the old train station. He seemed shy and funny, a slender, elderly man with a mustache, dressed in a flannel shirt, a heavy cap with earflaps, and a winter coat. He took us to a well-weathered station wagon, and as we drove up into the foothills above Provo, George told Bessie that she should be prepared to speak loudly and directly to their mother. By this time, Melissa's hearing was almost gone, and some days even her hearing aid hardly helped.

We pulled into a long, rough driveway that took us past a small house and into the backyard. In the moonlight, I could make out the barn and large trees that I already felt anxious to make my own. We entered the house by the back door, into a kitchen that looked as if it still had the same flowered wallpaper and old-fashioned wall telephone that had been there in my mother's youth. In the kitchen's corner, in a rocking chair, sat my grandmother, her head tilted in sleep, her reading glasses halfway down her nose. She did not know we were in the room until George shook her gently by the shoulder. Her eyes jumped open, with that instant look of terror and grief that comes to those who awaken to a painful reality, and then she saw my mother. Melissa leaped to her feet and hugged her daughter instantly. It was a quick reconciliation, and perhaps for both of them it momentarily overcame the years of hard distance. They talked into the night, while George showed me around the farmyard in the dark.

When it was time to sleep, Melissa led us to the bedroom where Bessie and her sisters had slept for years. I lay awake for hours, excited about being in Utah. I tried not to move, because my mother was a light sleeper. After a time, I became aware that she was crying. I looked over at her. She had her back to me, but I could tell that she had her hand cupped over her mouth, and she was sobbing a desolate, uncontrollable sob that I had never heard from her—or from anybody—before. Something about it told me to leave her alone. I figured she was crying because her father was near death, and perhaps that's what it was, though it's just as likely it was the memories that this place stirred for her.

By the time I awoke the next morning, my mother was already up. I found her outside, in the front yard. She was staring at the mountain that she had claimed for her own, years before. After seeing it again recently, I understood better her fondness for it. It is a proud and isolated thing, like Bessie Brown herself.

"Is that your mountain?" I asked.

"Yes, that's my mountain. I've been talking to it. I know how to hear the things it says, and this morning it is telling me that my father is not going to live."

"Oh, Mother, he'll be fine," I said, even though I knew that she was likely right. This was to be my first encounter with death, and I felt both exhilarated and frightened by its nearness. It would not be long before death's excitement wore off for me and its fearfulness increased.

"No," she replied. "He's not going to be all right. This time he's going to die." She folded her arms across her breast—a familiar gesture when she had decided to close off a discussion—and stood looking at the mountain a few moments more. Then she moved away from me, her eyes watching the ground as she walked around to the back of the old house. I did not follow her. I just stood, watching my mother's mountain, trying to figure out how you talked to such a thing and how you could hear its revelations.

The rest of that day and most of the next were spent meeting my Utah family—mostly aunts who were sugar-sweet on the outside, but who seemed awfully fussy about table manners and dinner prayers. I also didn't get along particularly well with most of my cousins. They seemed prissy and mean at the same time—in the way that only well-bred Mormon children can seem—and I remember getting in a fight or some sort of jabbing bout with one of them. The exception to all this was the family of my mother's favorite living sister, Ida. Generations before, when Melissa began to feel overwhelmed by nine children, she had assigned the care of Ada to Mary, and Ida to my mother. Mary prodded Ada to be competitive with her twin, and told Ida that she was the uglier of the two (or so my mother claimed). In turn, Bessie became protective of Ida and dressed her in pretty clothes and bought special ribbons for her hair. Many years later, the relationship between my mother and Ida would take on its own difficulties — in part because Ida had made a stable marriage to a good, sober man, and her children were loving and respectful, and prone only to unspectacular trouble. By contrast, my mother had married a drunk who left her regularly, and her children were . . . well, we were bad news, no matter how you sliced it.

But during our visit to Utah, these differences were never mentioned. In fact, some of the old affections and allegiances seemed to get resurrected. When Bessie and Ida saw each other they couldn't stop talking and laughing and crying, and on our second day there, Ida insisted that we move to her house, where she lived with her husband, Vernon Damico, and their daughters. Vern was a tall, husky man who walked with a limp — the by-product of an old war wound. He ran a popular shoe store on Provo's Center Street, where I spent my happiest hours in Utah, watching his big hands as they soled shoes, probably in much the same way my mother once had studied her father in his work. Vern was a good man to have as an uncle: He was big, warm, protective, and good-humored. Also, he had a handsome mustache that caused him to resemble the comedian Ernie Kovacs. I didn't know it then, but the mustache had been grown to cover a cleft palate. Vern had borne a lot of grief and nastiness because of that particular birth defect, and as a result, he had grown up rough. But I never saw any of that roughness in him. I just saw the first man who would make me wish for a different father.

Vern and Ida also had two teenage daughters, Brenda and Toni. I may have been only eight at the time, but I already knew cute and sexy when I saw it, and Brenda and Toni fit that bill in an unmistakable manner, though there was nothing showy or inappropriate about it. They were sweet and concerned, and they were the only women who would ever feel like sisters to me. I felt safe at Ida and Vern's house. I remember thinking: This would be a good family to stay with. That same thought, I later learned, had also occurred to my brothers many times over the years, and eventually it led to horrible consequences for us all.

On the third or fourth night of our Provo visit, I was sitting on the front porch of my grandparents' house with my mother and grand-mother. The BYU football team had won a game earlier that evening, and the players had made the trek to light up the Y on the side of Bessie's mountain. My mother was thrilled that I got to witness this ritual. We sat there and watched the burning Y until it faded into a bare glow. A few minutes later, from down the road in the direction of Mary Brown's old farm, we saw something white emerge from the darkness and move our way. As it quickly got closer, it seemed to float about a foot off the ground. Above its white form—which now looked like a gown, rippling in the night breeze—we saw two eyes, looking our way, glowing. Bessie and Melissa stood up at the same moment. "It's the ghost," my grand-mother said, and my mother took me by the shoulders and steered me into the house. I wanted to go closer—I had never seen a ghost before; I wanted to see what it would do if you moved its way—but Bessie and Melissa would not allow it. So I watched for a while from the front win-dow. After we moved inside, the apparition stopped advancing toward the house. It moved back and forth across the road several times, like it was waiting for something to happen, or like it was studying us. Then, after a minute or two, it took off, moving quickly back into the night it had come from. Later, when I told my father about the ghost, he laughed. "That was no ghost," he said. "It was probably just a neighborhood dog that had pulled an old white shirt off a laundry line and was looking for somebody to show it off to. What you saw were the silly superstitions of old Mormons."

THE NIGHT AFTER THE APPEARANCE OF THE GHOST, my grandfather Will Brown died at age seventy-three. At his bedside were his church bishop, his wife, and all his living children. I don't remember feeling much about his passing at the time—after all, I never got to meet the man—but thirty-some years later, when I read Melissa's final journals, I came across a simple passage that broke my heart. Melissa's last few note-books were tedious as hell to read—page after page after page about knitting doilies for grandchildren, or cooking roasts for guests, or dusting knickknacks. Even her reportage of her husband's stroke was dully mat-ter-of-fact. And then, noting Will Brown's final night, Melissa wrote five words about his slip into darkness: "Watched him die. So hard." After reading those words, I never took those people's feelings lightly again.

Will Brown's funeral was reportedly one of the biggest that Provo had witnessed in years. Apparently, everybody had revered the old school janitor. For some reason, all the grandchildren—and various other tots—were seated in the first few rows of the church, right in front of my grandfather's open casket. It was the first time I had ever seen a dead person up close. I studied Will Brown's white hair, trying to feel something. Mostly, I just felt horrified at having to look at a dead man. There was something unreal about staring so long at death, something that felt forbidden, like looking at raw sex—except death, I later realized, was far nastier.

Later, a long line of limousines and cars rode out to the Provo City Cemetery. We stood around a freshly dug empty grave, and my grandfather's coffin rested alongside the deep hole. Wreaths had been draped across the casket and, one by one, Will Brown's children approached the coffin and added single flowers to the pile. When my uncle George's turn came, he seemed to fumble, looking for a place to put his flower. Finally he dropped it on the pile, and the boutonniere glided gracefully into place alongside the other flowers. It seemed to me at the time as if my grandfather had reached up from death and pulled the rose down to him. I have thought about that image many times over the years, and it has appeared frequently in my dreams.

As we were walking away from the grave, I stepped accidentally on a headstone. Then, deliberately, I stepped on another and another. Maybe I was trying to dispel some of the fear I felt, being so close to the dead. I don't really know. It was a childish and irreverent thing to do, and it was met with disapproving gasps from my aunts and cousins. The next thing I knew, one of the stern Mormon patriarchs had grabbed and whirled me around and was sticking a finger in my face. "Never disrespect the dead, young man," he told me, poking his finger. "*Never*. Remember that you live in their debt."

CHAPTER 4
ALTA AND THE
DEAD INDIAN

NOT LONG AGO I PAID A REPEAT VISIT of sorts to the Brown farm.

My cousin Brenda took me on a drive up around the Grandview area, which is now filled with nice, clean, box-style houses. What was once Jordan Lane is now Jordan Avenue, and at the end of the avenue is the property that was once owned by my grandparents. It now belongs to a cousin—the son of one of my mother's sisters—and he (or somebody) has sequestered the land behind a fence and posted a sign: DEAD END, PRIVATE PROPERTY. There's something unreal about the barrier: It's a dead end where there really shouldn't be one; you get the feeling that what's been sealed off here isn't property so much as history—a past that's better forgotten. At the same time, there's no history visibly apparent. Everything that was once here has been transformed or razed, turned into modern urbanity, and modern mundaneness. Of course, you can't exactly fault anybody for that. Who would want to live in or preserve an old two-room shack farm merely because their grandparents lived there? Who would want to keep an artifact of past poverty and fragmented family hopes intact as an unvisited and unloved museum? Yet in another way, none of this transformation matters: It still felt like a place where loss was lived out over the course of nearly a century. Some things don't leave the air just because the land has been changed.

Brenda and I parked out front, where some boys tinkered on a car, and since we were on what was essentially private property we gradually invited some curious looks. Brenda asked for her cousin, and he came out, acting polite, but also wary—perhaps not exactly thrilled to find me, a bad reminder of a horrible history, on the edge of his front lawn. We talked nicely and emptily for a few minutes, but there was no invitation to come in and see what had been done with the farm, or to look about the old property. After a bit, Brenda said our good-byes and we got back in the car to drive on. As we left, Brenda pointed out a patch of ground right before the property, just at the place where the land begins to tip and run down over the steep hill to the valley below. "That's where it happened," she said, and I knew immediately what she meant. It is the spot where, over sixty years before, tragedy entered and filled the Browns' life with a suddenness and horrific impact that was never forgotten, and never eradicated. In the light of the setting sun, it almost looked as if there was still a patch of blood on that spot—blood that cost so much hope and, in my mother's mind, announced such unshakable ruin that no amount of time or weather could ever fade it out.

AS THE YEARS PROGRESSED, THE BROWN CLAN BROKE DOWN into two camps: the good children and the rebellious ones. In the former group were those who were diligent farm workers, and who were obedient to their parents and church leaders—such as Mark, Mary, and Wanda. In the latter camp were those who made a point of having a will and pride of their own, like George and Patta, and, in time, my mother. Somewhere in between these two factions was Alta, who had been born five years after Bessie. Alta was the dividing line between the family's older and younger children. She was also a dividing line in other ways.

In the photos I have seen of her, Alta looks plain and stoic, like so many of the serious-faced children of pioneer stock. But in her eyes you could see an unmistakable, active intelligence. She looked like someone who could outsmart anybody around her without making the slightest show of it. That's probably why she became everybody's favorite of the Brown children—well-liked enough that her death was headline news in Provo. In her parents' eyes, Alta was the ideal child: She was humble and obedient—did what she was told without resentment—and brought home good reports from her teachers at school and church. But according to my mother, there was something more to Alta than that. She knew how to play the surfaces, how to appear as if she was giving people what they wanted, yet behind that pose of compliance, Alta led her own life. Like Patta and my mother, she pretty much did what she wanted, but in secret, without the defiance the others flaunted. Whereas Bessie and Patta might stay out late against their parents' instructions—bringing holy hell on their heads when they got home—Alta would wait until after her parents were asleep, then sneak out and meet her sisters, or a boyfriend. It was easy to do; Melissa's deafness was already bad enough that she couldn't hear the window opening and closing in the next-door bedroom.

Even though my mother was half a decade older, she felt closer to Alta than any of her other sisters, and Alta felt the same bond—or so Bessie later claimed. They would tell each other their best guarded secrets, and though Bessie could not emulate Alta's social finesse, she admired it. "Alta was the best of us," my mother said. "She was the one who showed the most promise. We never got over losing her. We were less of a family after that."

IN THE WEEKS BEFORE HALLOWEEN IN 1929, when Alta was twelve and Bessie sixteen, the two girls, along with the rest of their family, sat in Sunday School one afternoon while the bishop railed against the danger of Ouija boards and other spiritualist trappings. The Mormons had a special calling to be on guard against spiritualism, the bishop said. More than most people, the Saints understood that spirits were real. It had been a spirit, after all, in the form of the Angel Moroni, who had led Joseph Smith to the golden plates at the start of their religion, and in the generations since, spirits had made themselves manifest to the Mormons a thousand times, in a thousand ways. But some spirits, the bishop warned, were like some people: troubled and ignoble. They might reach for the living through such means as Ouija boards or séances, but any such occult connection would be the work of Satan. Once such a spirit was in a person's life, it could lead him or her wayward—to unredeemable sins, or even a horrible death. The bishop personally knew of young

Mormon men who had gone astray. They had tried to contact the dead, but they had raised something evil instead, and one or two of them had been found nailed to the wall, their hair turned shock-white, a Ouija board under their feet.

Have fun with Halloween, concluded the bishop. Dress up and scare yourselves silly. But remember that you are Saints, and Saints do not invite Satan's spirits into their home.

A week or so later, Bessie, Alta, and the others were down on Provo's Center Street, shopping for decorations for a Halloween party, when Bessie found a Ouija board in a five-and-dime store. She bought it, hid it in her shopping bag with some other items, and sneaked it home. Late that night, after the parents had gone to sleep, Bessie and Alta lit a candle in the girls' bedroom. They sat cross-legged next to each other on the floor and put the Ouija board on their knees. The others sat up in bed to see what they were doing. Patta joined Bessie and Alta, but Mary was indignant. "What are you doing?" she said. "You know what the bishop said. Do you want to bring the devil into our house?"

Wanda started to whimper. "I'm going to go tell Mother."

Bessie glared up at her. "You'll do no such thing, unless you want a good slapping."

Bessie turned back to Alta and Patta. The three of them placed their fingertips on the heart-shaped planchette that rested on the board. Their sisters stood around watching, frightened and transfixed at the same time. "What do we say?" asked Patta.

Bessie looked at Alta and shrugged. Alta shut her eyes tight, tilted her head back, and intoned: "Is there anybody there?"

The room was quiet. Everybody watched the planchette. After a few moments it began to move, with the girls' fingers resting on it. Slowly, jerkily, it inched to the Ouija board's corner, to the word YES.

Bessie, Patta, and Alta looked at each other, eyes wide. They'd made contact. No prayer had ever been answered so quickly or so palpably.

Alta closed her eyes again and asked: "Who are you?"

More quickly this time, the planchette moved over the board's single letters, spelling out its reply: I-A-M-A-D-E-A-D-I-N-D-I-A-N.

"A dead *Indian*?" said Bessie.

At that point, the girls heard a ghostly wail that scared the hell out of them all. It was Wanda, trembling and crying. Before anybody could stop her, she bolted out of the room, screaming.

Melissa may have been hard of hearing, but not that hard. She stormed into the bedroom and saw the Ouija board on her daughters' laps. "What," she said, "have you brought into my house?"

Nobody said a word.

Melissa turned on Alta. "I might expect this from Patta and Bessie," she said. "They like to flirt with wickedness. But you *know* better, Alta. How could you take part in bringing evil into our home? Don't you know you are mocking God? Don't you know the price of mocking God?"

Alta looked stricken. "I'm sorry, Mother. We were just making a game out of it. We'll put it away."

"No," said Melissa. "You'll do more than that: You'll take it outside and put it in the incinerator and burn it, this instant. *You* will do it, Alta. And you'll do it alone." Melissa stood and watched her daughter slip into her clothes. Then she followed Alta out of the bedroom, slamming the door behind her.

As soon as she was gone, Bessie turned on Wanda. "Tattletale."

Wanda started to whimper again. "Leave her alone," Mary said to Bessie. "You asked for this trouble, bringing that infernal thing in here."

A half hour later, Alta returned. As they were all falling asleep, she whispered to Bessie: "Mother went back to bed. I hid the Ouija board in the barn."

THE OUIJA BOARD INCIDENT HAD BEEN GOOD FOR A FEW DAYS of misery and preaching around the Brown home. The guilty took their chastisements silently, with only Alta showing convincing remorse.

Halloween night arrived. The Browns went to a costume party at the Grandview church ward, and everybody danced and laughed until they were giddy and tired with the silliness of it all.

At about two that morning, Alta and Bessie sneaked out their bedroom window to the barn. It was a silent autumn night. Bessie lighted a kerosene lamp and Alta dug out the Ouija board. It was time to get back to their spirit.

Alone in the barn, Bessie and Alta sat with the board on their knees, their fingers on its planchette, and they made the same inquiries as before. Again, the words spelled out under their fingers: "I-AM-A-DEAD-INDIAN. I-WAS-KILLED-BECAUSE-I-KILLED-A-MAN. HE-STOLE-FROM-ME. I-WANT-BACK . . ."

Bessie and Alta heard the barn door creak. They saw a figure move through it and into the dim light. It was their father. Bessie might have been relieved, but by this time she had already learned some hard lessons about her father. Will Brown was a nice man until you made him angry. Then he was not a nice man at all.

He walked toward them. "Are you conjuring spirits in the middle of the night?" he asked. "Are you my children, or have you already given yourselves to the devil?" Will picked up an ax. He took the Ouija board from their hands and hacked it to pieces. "If I ever find you worshiping the devil again," he said, "I'll give you to the Danites."

That was the end of Ouija boards in the Brown household. In the weeks that followed, Bessie and Alta tried a time or two again to contact the spirit, holding hands in the dark, in secluded places far away from home. But nothing ever happened. No voices answered, no images materialized. They might as well have been praying.

CHRISTMAS CAME AND WENT, AND THEN CAME THE NEW YEAR. In the second week of 1930, Provo awoke to a snowfall that spread across its valley and mountains. It snowed the rest of the week.

One night, after the day's snow had fallen, a white horse wandered into the backyard of the Provo farmhouse. Since Grandview was a small community, everybody knew everybody else's horses as well as they knew each other's children, and the Browns knew nobody who owned such a lovely, ghostly-looking mare. Bessie and her sisters went outside to stare at the animal, and Alta wandered over and petted its mane. When Melissa saw her daughters with the strange horse, she ordered them inside. She tried to shoo the animal away, but it just looked at her.

The horse stood there for hours staring at the house, shimmering in the winter moonlight. When Will Brown arrived home from his job at the school, he chased the horse away. Later that night, my mother heard her parents talking. "You know what it means when a white horse comes to visit," my grandmother said. "It means someone in this house will die."

"I'm not sure," Will said, "that I've ever known the Lord to work that way."

Early the following Sunday evening, a neighbor was using his horse to pull a sled around Grandview, and he offered the Brown girls a chance to pile on the sled for a ride. Alta and Wanda ran to find their mother and ask if it was okay to ride down the street on the sled. Melissa knew the man, and she knew the horse—a calm, friendly animal—but she shook her head. "I don't have a reason to say no," she said, "but I'm going to tell you no. I just have a funny feeling." The girls were disappointed but they didn't argue back. After Melissa had returned to her work, Alta went and got Bessie. "Come on, Bess," she said. "We can sneak down around the bend and ride the sled back up the hill. Mother will never know."

For once, Bessie's intuition matched her mother's. "No," she said. "I don't think it's a good idea."

Alta turned to Wanda. "Will you come with me?" Wanda hesitated. She wasn't accustomed to disobeying her mother. But then, what was the wrong in a sleigh ride? The two girls ran out of the front yard and down the hill, out of sight of the farmhouse.

Bessie stood on the front porch, watching Ada and Ida as they tried to build a snowman, waiting for the sled to come by. A few moments later, the horse came around the bend, galloping steadily. Alta was lying flat, holding on to the sled, with Wanda piled on top of her. As the horse pulled up in front of the house, something spooked it. The man riding it tried to calm it down. Then it reared again and threw the sled into the air, tossing the girls in an arc against a utility pole. Wanda hit the pole hard on her left shoulder and everybody in the yard heard a crack. Alta hit the pole face first, with a terrible impact, and fell to the ground.

Somebody ran inside and found Melissa, who came hurrying to the road to find two of her daughters spilling blood on the snow. Wanda was unconscious, apparently dead, but Alta was scrabbling on the ground, trying to turn over. Melissa kneeled down beside her and placed Alta's head on her lap. The front of Alta's skull had been broken in; Melissa could see bone. "Oh, Mama," said Alta, "I'm so sorry. I should have listened to you." And then Alta began to cry. There was so little bone support left in her face that the crying forced her eyes from their sockets, until they rested on her cheeks. Melissa stayed in the snow, rocking her favorite daughter back and forth, petting her hair, until the life left her.

Bessie's younger brother, Mark, saddled up a horse from the barn and rode down to the church to find his father. By the time Will and Mark arrived back at the Brown home with the bishop and a doctor, the two girls had been moved inside the small front room. The doctor looked at Alta and pronounced her dead. He examined Wanda more closely. "This one," he said, "is still alive. But she might not be for long if we don't get her to a hospital."

Wanda recovered from the accident, but she was partially paralyzed on her left side for the rest of her life.

A few days later, when the time had come to bury Alta, the ground was frozen over. The coffin had to be left beside the burial place, waiting for the ground to thaw. For the next couple of days, the Brown children would make the trek to the cemetery and sit around the coffin, praying for their dead sister's soul.

A few weeks later, there was a final haunting. "The sisters were in their bedroom at night," my cousin Brenda told me, "when they saw a white light in the dark room. The light came closer and closer to their bed. It was Alta. She sat down on the bed with the girls and told them she was all right, that she wasn't in any pain and she was very happy. She wanted to make sure the girls knew that. She loved them. Then the light dimmed and she was gone, but the girls could see the indentation on the bed where she had sat."

Nobody ever figured out what had spooked the horse in that winter dusk time, but my mother knew: She believed it was the demon of the dead man that she and Alta had conjured, and now he was the ghost that would haunt her family.

MANY YEARS LATER, WITHOUT KNOWING ANY of the details of this story, I asked my mother if I could have a Ouija board. It was during the time after my father's death—a period in which I was reading nothing but Edgar Allan Poe, Bram Stoker, and Victorian ghost stories. The macabre and supernatural comforted and enthralled me in ways that I could not explain and that my mother could barely tolerate. She denied my request, and, as she had done all those years before, I went out and bought my own Ouija board and sneaked it into the house. The only problem was, I could never get my brothers to try it with me, and so, like a fool, I'd sit around by myself, with the board on my knees, asking it questions and waiting for the planchette to move under my fingers. I don't remember ever getting much from the spirits in return.

One afternoon, my mother found me concentrating over the board, and she became livid. "I want you to get that goddamn thing out of my house immediately, and *never* bring it back here. And I want you to stop reading all those morose books about ghosts and horror and evil. I do not intend for all my sons to grow up to be monsters." And then she wept, so long, so loud and pitifully, that I left the house, just to get away from the sound of her crying.

PART TWO

THE BLACK SHEEP

AND

THE DENIED SON

Children begin by loving their parents; as
they grow older they judge them;
sometimes they forgive them.

— OSCAR WILDE,
The Picture of Dorian Gray

CHAPTER 1

THE

BLACK SHEEP

FOR MOST OF HER LIFE, BESSIE GILMORE SPOKE of her father as an ideal. He was a quiet and modest man who would make any sacrifice for a friend or family member in need, without asking anything in return. He was a deep-loving father, who worked long hours to keep his children clothed and in school, and who taught them to think charitably of neighbors and strangers alike.

In her last few years, though, my mother's portrayal of Will Brown changed drastically. This was in the period following Gary's execution, when she retreated more and more into the terrain of the past. It became one of the reasons I began to call or visit her less: All she could talk about was the milestones of our collective tragedy. I suspect that by this time the chain of all the disappointments and deaths had made her crazy, and she felt driven to reexamine each link in her mind, looking for the key to where everything had gone wrong—not unlike what I've been doing these last few years. Or maybe she had come to suspect that the whole story had been fated from the start, and she couldn't stop dwelling on the cruelty of a joke that keeps you waiting over a lifetime for a punch line of hope or deliverance that never arrives. In any event, as my mother replayed her past, she began telling remarkably different stories about her youth than she had told before.

In particular, she told stories about her father. As the Brown children grew older, my mother said, Will Brown's temper grew shorter and took on a frightening resemblance to his own father's legendary explosiveness. The two children he selected as the most frequent targets of his anger were my mother and her older brother, George. I'm not sure what the main quarrel was between George and his father, though I do know that George became regarded by both his family and the Grandview community as the odd character among the Browns. Apparently he had always been a bit shy and awkward (much like his father had been in his youth, which may have been part of what Will could not tolerate), and some of the neighborhood children teased him for his homely looks and gawky manner. Consequently, George spent a lot of time alone and, like his grandfather Joseph Kerby, used his solitude to develop his artistic skills. He painted rich, naturalistic views of the Provo landscape, and he also carved handsomely detailed bows for archers throughout the state.

Sometimes, though, George's isolation seemed to drive something wild in him. On these occasions, he would strip off his clothes and lay them in a tidy pile in the Browns' front yard, then take off running down Jordan Lane. Once or twice he made it all the way to Provo's Center Street, running naked among the pop-eyed Mormons, until the police would pick him up and hold him for Will Brown to come and retrieve him. Invariably, these events would be followed by Will beating George, though frequently the beatings happened for no reason better than Will's own fury. On these occasions, Will dragged George to one of the large trees in the backyard and tied him to its trunk with a strong rope. Then he took a strap and lashed his screaming son until the boy passed out from the pain and humiliation. Occasionally, the beatings grew so fierce that Bessie or Mark would run next door, where Will's older brother Charley lived, and beg him to come over and drag Will off George. At such times, Charley was the only person in the world who could come safely between Will Brown and his rage.

The beatings continued until the 1940s, when George and Mark went off to fight in the Second World War. George was among the American troops who helped liberate the Nazi concentration camps in Germany, and he was also stationed in France for a short time. Within a few days after his return from the war, George got on the wrong side of his father's temper. Will threw a fist at his son, but George caught it and twisted his father's hand. "You will *not* hit me again," George told him. According to my mother, Will Brown never hit George or anybody after that.

All the years of outrage and madness left their mark on George. He never dated, he never married, and for all the hurt he had suffered at home, he never ventured outside of the family. In a trunk in his room, George kept a collection of photos he had brought home from the war. Some were pictures he had taken of the corpses and emaciated survivors left in the concentration camps. The others were pornographic postcards that he had bought on the streets of Paris. Sometimes, George would coax his nieces and their friends into his room. Then he would lock the door and not let them out until they had looked at both sets of photos. It was an odd choice of images to show children—pictures of the modern world's most horrific murders, mingled with pictures of forbidden pleasures. No doubt something about the juxtaposition titillated Uncle George, though something about the mix also told the whole sad story of what had been done to his life.

George never left the farm. He inherited it after his mother died, and he lived there by himself, until his death in 1974. He lay dead for three days before he was found alone in his bed, near the trunk where he kept his pictures.

ACCORDING TO MY MOTHER, THE DAY SHE FIRST CAME TO HATE Will Brown was the day of an execution. It's an interesting story, so mired in fear and improbability that I'm no longer sure what its real meaning might be. Still, the story should be told, if only because it's one that had consequences.

Sporadically, Utah's executions had been public or semi-public affairs. At times, hundreds had assembled for these events; sometimes thousands. On a few occasions, fathers and mothers would bring their families to witness the deaths and to attest to the merciless cost of violating God's most precious laws. For a child growing up in early twentieth-century Utah, the atmosphere surrounding these events could be a fearful thing. My mother used to tell us that she hated hearing people talk about an impending execution, that she would cover her ears and try to shut out the awful news and the grim but excited way that her father and other churchmen would discuss the event. On the day of the actual execution, she said, she would get up before dawn and hide in a dark recess in the family's barn, sometimes staying there all day until night came, so she could miss the worst of the news and talk.

One time, though, she wasn't so lucky. On one summer morning, my mother said, around the time of one of her youthful birthdays, Will Brown woke her and loaded her and her brothers and sisters into the family wagon and drove them in the darkness to a meadow not far from the state prison. There, she claimed, they watched as a fated man was led up the stairs to the noose and the executioner. She said that she could not watch the hanging itself, that she shut her eyes tight and buried her face into her father's side. But she heard the trapdoor crack open, and she also heard the horrible snapping sound a split second later, when the man's weight hit the end of the rope's length and his neck was broken. Then she heard something worse; she heard cheers and applause. As the family moved away from the site, she stole a look back and saw the man's body dangling and swaying. She saw men on the meadow around her, holding the hands of their children, pointing at the corpse, admonishing their brood to remember this moment and this lesson.

Certainly, Bessie Brown remembered it. Indeed, something about the Mormons' attitude toward the death penalty caused my mother to start to hate her own people—or at least to hate the beliefs that would allow them to participate in these ceremonies. In any event, she hated executions. When I was a child, and we were living in Portland, Oregon, she would follow the news of impending executions with a fearful anxiety. She would write letters to the governor, arguing the morality of the death penalty, and asking the state to commute the condemned person's sentence. And she would have me join her at the dining table and write my own letters to the governor. Since, as she once explained to me, these killings were the only killings that we *knew* were going to occur—the only killings, that is, that had a schedule to follow—then they were also the only killings we might possibly prevent. I think she truly believed the morality of that argument, but more than anything, she never got over the horror behind the idea of a public audience watching a man's death. She believed that the men who took their families to watch these executions were, in some ways, worse even than the murderers. After all, such men made their children participants in a killing.

I heard my mother's stories about Utah's executions many times over the years—I suppose we all did—but it wasn't until the last time I saw her alive that she amplified her tale and revealed an important hidden detail. On that Christmas Day, a few months before she would die, my mother told me that she had not managed to keep her face buried in her father's side after all on the morning of the hanging. Instead, right before the trapdoor was pulled, her father had grabbed her by the hair and yanked hard, forcing her to watch the man as he dropped into death. She said that on the ride back, she decided that she would never forgive her father and that she would live a life to spite his hard virtue. As she told me this, she wore a look of perfect hatred on her face—her eyes were wide with the inflamed stare of one who has had to see things that one should never have to see. By the time her account ended, the dreadfulness of what she had told me made me share her hatred, and I felt like her memory of the event had in fact become my own. Her tale also made me wonder: If my mother's father had *not* forced this fatal vision on her, would Gary still have ended up the violent man he became? Had some horrific fate been born in that moment, and had it found its final, awful consequences some fifty-odd years later in the murders that my brother would commit, and in his own blood being spilled on the land that had raised my mother?

It was not until a year or two ago, after I started working on this book and was doing some reading in the history of Utah's death penalty, that I learned something even more disturbing: These stories that my mother told could not have been true; she could never have witnessed what she claimed to witness. There were no semi-public executions in Utah after about 1919, when my mother would have been six years old, and it is not likely that any children or families had been present at these events for several years before that. More important, as far as I have been able to determine, there were no hangings at all in Utah during my mother's childhood and youth. About twelve executions took place in that period—including the world-famous 1915 death of union activist Joe Hill, whom we also heard much about in our home—and all these sentences had been carried out by firing squads, behind the walls of Utah's Sugarhouse Prison, before invited assemblies of witnesses.

I think about my mother's tales, and I know now that it was remarkable and terrible to tell these things to children or young men. On one level, of course, I am struck by the impact that such legends must have had on us. I think these images helped to instill a sense of otherness—not to mention a sense of doom—in our hearts. I think we felt we were hearing not just a story of the distant past in a cruel place, but that we were also hearing something about our own predestination. Or, to put it differently, there was no way you could hear such a story as a child and want to be any part of the world that gathered together to put a man to death. The only place left for you in the story was to be the condemned man or the child forced to behold his fate; my brother Gary chose to be one, and I guess I chose to be the other. I know I could never have chosen to be among the executioners. In any event, I grew up in a family where the noose worked as a talisman; it hung over our heads not so much as a deterrent but as a sign of destiny. As a result, the ideal of ruin was a family covenant. Nobody ever said as much out loud, but then, nobody had to.

I try to imagine what was in my mother's heart to make this ideal such an intrinsic part of our mythology. What had really happened to her that gave her such an overpowering fear of Blood Atonement, and how did it happen that her fear would be transformed into a near prophecy of how her favorite son would die? Sometimes we tell lies about our past—maybe a claim to achievement, maybe a claim to crime—as a way of heightening our importance, and sometimes we tell our fictions as a subterfuge to keep our deepest secrets hidden. I believe that when my mother told us the story of the hanging in Utah, something else was at work for her: I think she was probably trying to convey to us the harshness of growing up amid such an unforgiving land and its people. And I also believe that she could have been trying to tell us about other ways that her father may have visited ruin and violence upon her—ways that she might not have been able otherwise to talk about, or that perhaps she could no longer bring herself to remember.

WHAT MIGHT THOSE WAYS HAVE BEEN? I don't really know for sure. I have only guesses and rumors to offer. In one way or another, the problem probably had to do with sex. When she was still a child, Bessie was regarded as one of the Browns' prettiest daughters. She liked dressing in graceful outfits and putting large bows in her beautiful, black hair; apparently, she made a dainty little sight at church dances and picnics. In those days, Will had been proud of Bess. Some thought he was even a bit possessive of her. But when Bessie turned older, her prettiness started to become a liability in the Brown home. According to some folks, Bessie began to take on airs. She acted as if she were the child of a rich family— as if she were simply too good to do the hard farm work that the others had to do. She didn't like blistering her fine hands—it made it hard to wear her rings—and she hated getting her hair dirty. Said it spoiled the nice clothes she was making for herself to wear to church balls, and to the weekend dances at Provo's Utahna Dance Hall. Worse, Bessie started acting as if the house rules no longer applied to her. She liked staying out later than the others, and she liked the attention of boys—especially the older ones who attended Brigham Young University. This last item was particularly hard on Bessie's father. It was said of Will Brown that he loved his daughters and did not want to lose them. For his taste, Bess was moving too quickly into dating.

Whereas the other Brown children learned how to make a peace with their parents' house rules—or to sneak around them without getting caught—Bessie liked to make a point of flouting authority. Of course, this was seen as a bad example for the other children. Then, after Alta's death, Bessie got worse. It seemed to others in the family as if some restraint inside Bess had died along with her sister. It was like she had turned her mourning into outright rebellion—or as if she held her parents or the farm itself to blame for what had happened that day. She started staying out later, and when she came home, the fights with her parents got louder and nastier. Will and Melissa accused her of immoral behavior with the boys she dated. Bessie never came out and said it was true—it probably wasn't—but she liked the leverage the suspicion gave her, the way it drove her parents nuts when she said, "Wouldn't *you* like to know?" Still, it was a dangerous game. Short of murder or betraying one's testimony of God, there was no greater sin in the Mormon world than sexual vice. By taunting her parents on this point, Bessie was risking exclusion from the family. A generation or two before, she might have been risking the discipline of the Danites.

One night, in fact, Bessie came close to such a judgment. For a couple of weeks she had been dating a young man from Salt Lake. He was rumored to be a drinker and somebody who led a fast life. This was in the middle of Prohibition, and though Provo had a speakeasy or two, no Mormon family could afford to have its daughter found in one. Bessie's parents told her that she should no longer see this young man, and that he wasn't welcome at their house. But Bessie kept seeing the boy anyway, and in the period of a single week she came home past her parents' curfew on three occasions, resulting in the ugliest arguments anybody had ever witnessed in the Brown household. On the fourth occasion, Bessie was standing on the front porch of her house at about 3 A.M., giving her boyfriend a good-night kiss, when the door was flung open. Will Brown stood there with a shotgun, and he leveled it at his daughter. His face was full of fear and insanity. "I'm going to blow your whore soul to hell,"

Will said, and pulled back the hammer on one of the barrels. At that moment George stepped up from behind his father and grabbed the rifle. "You aren't shooting anybody," he said. In the fight that followed, George and Bessie got whipped badly by their father, while the other children stood around crying, begging for the violence to stop. Meantime, Bessie's boyfriend got his little Mormon ass the hell *off* the crazy Brown farm, never to bring it back.

I HAVE A HANDFUL OF PICTURES OF MY MOTHER TAKEN, I believe, by my Uncle George, in about 1933, when Bessie was around twenty years of age. I never saw these photographs while my mother was alive—they were given to me by Larry Schiller, who interviewed my family extensively, a short time after her death. The first time I saw them they bothered me so much that I put them away immediately and didn't pull them out again for years. It took me a while to figure out my reaction. I had never before seen my mother's image when she was a young woman. The face is unmistakably hers, and yet it appeared so different, stripped of everything that age and pain and the experiences of death would later bring to it.

My mother was always a courageous woman—even on those days when the world utterly terrified her—for without courage she could not have endured what she endured until the end of her life. She was not, however, always a hopeful woman. In fact, I don't recall ever seeing un-adulterated hope in her expression the entire time I knew her. So what shocked me about these pictures was that there was hope in her face on the day that they were taken. Not a bounty of it (not as much as there was pride), just enough to make plain what the lack of it for nearly fifty years can do to a person's look. Seeing these pictures, I realized that my mother could have died with a different face. That not only made me feel a new sadness for her, it also made me worry about my own face in its closing days.

My mother had a way of looking at a camera that could tell you everything about how she was looking at life. In my favorite of these pictures, Bessie Brown is seated in a chair. She is looking toward her left, in a three-quarter profile, one leg crossed elegantly over the other, her hands meeting calmly in her lap. She is wearing a simple, floor-length white dress—it fits perfectly and looks stunning—and around her neck rests a string of pearls. She has tied her long black hair up in back, and wears the rest of it in a flourish of curl that emphasizes her intelligence as much as her beauty.

The picture was taken outdoors. Bessie is seated in a chair on the farm, in front of her favorite mountain. Next to her stands a woman (a sister or a friend) holding a purse. She looks fine, but the picture belongs to Bessie, who knows the wonderful incongruity of her own pose: the exquisite beauty in a rustic setting. There's a faint smile on her face. It says she knows too much about herself, and about life, to stay in this setting. It is a small smile, bemused and a bit impatient, and in her eyes there is the steady, dark stare of hope.

In 1933, despite everything that had already happened, my mother had not yet learned to hate what a camera could reveal about her mind and soul.

THE PHOTOGRAPH TURNED OUT TO BE BESSIE'S FAREWELL to the Brown farm. As my cousin Brenda once told me, "Your mother had a longing for the finer life." In this case, the finer life meant Salt Lake City, fifty miles to Provo's north. In the mid 1930s, Bessie left home and moved to Salt Lake with three friends. They all rented an apartment not far from the city center, and all four took housekeeping jobs. They hadn't been there a month when one of the women returned to her family's home in Provo and told her folks she didn't like the way Bessie and the others were living in Salt Lake. They had all quit their jobs, she said, but nobody had trouble paying the rent.

The Browns didn't hear much from Bessie for a while, and they never made the trip up north to see her. Occasionally, Bessie would go back home, mainly to see her youngest sister, Ida. When she did, she made a point of wearing her fine new clothes and her new jewelry. She now wore a ring on each finger. Her parents asked her how she could afford such things, and she told them she had taken a job modeling jewelry. They had trouble believing her, and then the fights would start again. Finally, Bessie would stomp out in a rage, and her father would go down the hill to a tavern in the valley. Will Brown, the good Mormon patriarch, was learning how to drink.

RUMORS FOLLOWED BESSIE LIKE AN UNWANTED DOG. In 1936, she disappeared for a while. Later, there was talk that she had hitchhiked to California with a friend, and while she was there, she had fallen deeply in love with a serviceman. But the romance went bad, and Bessie came home, brokenhearted and compromised. After that, she lived by herself and began to keep a distance from her old friends.

All the gossip had its effect on her. Insofar as the rumors were a kind of judgment, a dismissal of her worth and goodness, Bessie felt deeply hurt and enraged by all the talk. But on the surface, she managed to wear her image with the pride of the outcast. She had too much dignity to surrender to the displays of repentance and humiliation that her parents and others wanted from her. All she could do was push on, the wayward daughter, moving into a prohibited frontier.

Bessie Brown was about to become the first child in three generations of her family's lineage to leave the refuge of Mormon Utah.

CHAPTER 2
THE
DENIED SON

I AM GOING TO MAKE A CONFESSION.

I never knew anything about how my parents met, or much about the early life of my family, until after my brother Gary had died. I suppose it says something about my detachment, but all I really knew much about were the family's legends of mystery and death. I knew about the violence of Mormon history, and about the haunted death of Alta, because these were stories my mother told me, time and again. I knew also that my father had a shadowy past—that his own father had wronged him beyond repair, and he had fled some deadly secret for nearly half a century—because these stories, too, were part of our active mythology.

But what I did not know, and what nobody ever told me, was this: I did not know how my parents came to know each other, or how they came to love each other (I never even actively *thought* they had once loved each other, since all I ever saw between them was distance or anger). I did not know what went on in the years that my brothers were born; I knew the names of various towns the family had lived in, but almost nothing about the family's life in those places—why my parents moved so frequently, and to such far-flung locales, or what my father did to support everybody in those towns. Mostly, I did not know if my family had ever been a real family. Had my father played sports with his sons? Had they all gone to church together, or to movies or a picnic on the weekend? Did my parents read stories to my brothers when they were small? (I don't remember anybody ever reading to me.) Did these people love each other—was there any cohesion to the unit beyond the habit of fear or the power of hatred?

The first glimpse I had of what that life may have been like was in 1979, when Norman Mailer's *The Executioner's Song* was published. Larry Schiller and Mailer had interviewed my mother at great length about Gary's childhood—a core period of the family's past—and in the book's latter half, Mailer laid out an intriguing sketch of the family's background. In a few pages he revealed more than I had been told in twenty-five years. To be honest, though, almost none of it sank in for me. The first few times I read the book, I let my eyes skim over those passages. I didn't linger on the details of my father's earlier marriages, or the mention of his criminal trouble, and I didn't accommodate any of it to the landscape of my own memory. It seemed too much like somebody else's world—a world you might read about in a book.

When the time came to try to dispel the secrecy of my family's past for the purposes of this story, Schiller was enormously generous, and offered to loan me the tapes of the interviews that he and Mailer had conducted fifteen years before with my mother and my brother Gary. Somehow, hearing about the family's hidden past in my mother's voice helped make that past palpable for me. I had not heard her voice, of course, since she had died; I had *never* heard her voice tell stories like these. But for every new revelation, there were now many new questions. Schiller and Mailer tried their best, but as often as not, my mother answered their inquiries with maddening riddles and outright avoidance.

At one point, Schiller asked her why she feared telling him and Mailer too much. With my father and Gary dead, he said, who was there left to protect by preserving old secrets? She replied that she was doing it for me. "Mikal doesn't know any of these things," my mother said. "I'm afraid he'll hate me when he learns all this. Or I'm afraid he'll hate his father, which would be horrible. He was the only one of the boys who ever truly loved his father, and I would hate to take that love away from him."

With the help of Schiller and Mailer's tapes, and with the invaluable assistance of a few other people—primarily my brother Frank, after I finally found him—the true story began to take shape for me. Or at least some of it did. For better or worse, much of the truth of our past was lost for good when my parents and brothers died.

THIS, THEN, IS HOW MY MOTHER MET MY FATHER:

It was summer, 1937. By this time, Bessie Brown was living alone in a small hotel room in downtown Salt Lake City. She made enough money to support herself with a little housework, and with part-time hand-modeling of jewelry for ads.

In those days, as today, Salt Lake City was the largest and liveliest city in Utah. Still, when it comes to Utah, *lively* is a relative term. There is more to do in Salt Lake than in much of the state, provided you do most of it before nightfall. When my mother lived there, as a twenty-four-year-old woman, she found the city's streets impossibly wide and the blocks eternally long. Since she had little money, Bessie walked those streets every day. She would walk up to the old library, across from the county courthouse, and she would sit in its reading room, where she liked to pore over books about astrology and medical science, and other matters that she had learned little about back in Provo. Some days, she walked over to the city's vast Liberty Park. She sat near its lake, watching couples ride in blithe circles in paddleboats, or she bought popcorn or bread slices and fed the ducks. She liked the ducks because they seemed to know their place. They would pay attention to you but never try to get too close.

Most of the city closed at dusk, and as the sun started to set, Bessie would walk the many blocks back to her hotel room. Sometimes she would have dinner with a girlfriend or take in a dance at a local ballroom, where touring big bands sometimes played.

Largely, though, this was a season of being alone. Bessie was a little wary of men after the debacle in California. She was in no hurry for true love, and unlike most young Mormon women, she was not anxious to find herself a husband.

One of Bessie's best friends during this time was a woman named Anita, a waitress at a local seafood restaurant. Anita had just come out of a bad marriage and was a serious drinker, which made for natural limitations in the relationship. Bessie was no drinker—she didn't like the dizzy, stupid feeling it gave her the one or two times she'd had a few drinks—but she also didn't have much appetite for judging another person's weaknesses. Anita wasn't the most high-class person, but Bessie liked her just the same. Maybe she felt a little sorry for her.

One day, Bessie met Anita at the Utah Hotel, just off Temple Street, where Anita lived with her boyfriend, a man she called Daddy. The two women were supposed to go shopping, but Anita had already had a few drinks that morning—actually, one too many. "Look, Bessie," she said. "Look at the typewriter my Daddy gave me." Anita lifted the typewriter proudly, but it fell from her hands and broke on the floor. Just then, Daddy walked in. He was a well-dressed man, in his late forties—Bessie recognized his pride immediately—and he was not looking pleased. Anita tried to sputter an apology and an introduction to Bessie at the same time. Daddy glanced momentarily at Bessie and said: "Hello. I'm Frank Gilmore." To Anita, he said: "I asked you not to touch my typewriter. Now you've broken it. This is it. Pack your things and leave."

Bessie saw that this was no time to stick around. "I'll talk to you later, Anita," she said, and left. Bessie could hear Anita crying by the time she got to the elevator.

A FEW DAYS LATER, BESSIE WAS WALKING along Temple to the library when she ran into Frank Gilmore. He was standing in front of the Utah Hotel, wearing a brown sport coat and a string tie over a sky-blue shirt. A dirty-white fedora hat covered his slightly longish, graying hair. Bessie hadn't heard from Anita since the scene in the hotel room and was a little concerned. "Hey," she said, "did you and Anita ever make up?"

"No, no, no," said Frank. "She's probably got somebody else by now." Frank looked at Bessie for a long second, then said: "Care to get a cup of coffee?"

They went to a diner around the corner and had a cup of coffee, then another. Bessie told Frank a little about herself, and in turn learned a little about him. He was an ad salesman for *Utah Magazine* and had been a salesman all around the country. Someday, he said, he wanted to have a magazine of his own. He had a confident, intelligent way of talking, Bessie thought, plus he was deeply attractive. The thought came on Bessie suddenly that she liked this man. She remembered an old saying: You meet the right man and you throw caution to the aside. Sitting there in the Salt Lake diner, drinking coffee with Frank Gilmore, Bessie thought: Here's a man I might be willing to throw caution aside for.

Frank must have sensed something about the thought, because he found a way to drop a bombshell into the conversation. He said: "I'm getting married tomorrow."

Bessie sat there, stunned. Here she was, liking a man who only three days before had broken up with one of her best friends, and who was already preparing to marry another woman. She had never experienced anything like it before.

Bessie didn't ask for any explanations, and Frank Gilmore didn't offer any. He wasn't that way.

"Congratulations," she said.

ALMOST A YEAR LATER, BESSIE RAN INTO FRANK AGAIN, standing in front of the same hotel. "Well, how's your marriage?" she asked.

"Oh, that didn't last," Frank said. "It broke up." He shrugged like it was already a forgotten mistake. Then he smiled at her. "I was planning on going to a movie tonight," he said. "Would you like to join me?"

Bessie thought about the first boy who had ever caught her fancy, an Italian kid by the name of Joe, who worked at a candy factory with her back in Provo. To Bessie he was perfection: tall, with a good build and brown eyes. Working on the assembly line, where several people worked together, wrapping the hot candy and placing it in packages, Bessie saw a cute little routine develop. Every once in a while, one of the girls would "accidentally" leave one of her tools on the factory belt and then act flustered. When the tool got down to Joe at the end of the belt, he would retrieve it and graciously bring it back to them. Bessie decided to try the same trick. One day, she shoved her candy pan onto the belt and let it get away from her. When Joe brought it back to her she was so self-conscious she couldn't even look at him and couldn't say thank you. She spent the rest of the day hating herself. After that, she decided: If I want to win a fellow over, I'm going to look at him and smile; I'm going to really make him think he is outstanding and something very special and wonderful. No more do I just take my pan and walk away and ignore him.

Standing outside the Utah Hotel, Bessie Brown gave Frank Gilmore her best smile. "I'd love to go to the movie with you," she said.

ACTUALLY, BESSIE DIDN'T MUCH LIKE GOING TO MOVIES. Something about the vast darkness of a theater reminded her of a tomb. But she felt better about the experience, sitting next to Frank. He was a strong man, and she felt less afraid of the darkness with him close by. Years later, she would remember that feeling and wonder where it had gone.

On their second date, a night or two later, Frank took Bessie to a bar. Bessie didn't drink, but Frank did. He began to talk a bit about his past. Not too much—just enough to let her know that he was a man who had led an interesting life.

Apparently he had grown up around show business and had worked as a performer himself. In 1910—before Bessie had even been born—Frank had been a clown and tightrope walker in the Barnum & Bailey Circus, and he had gone by the name of Laffo the Clown. He would wobble his way across the tightrope humorously, like a drunk. Other times, Laffo would build a tower of precariously balanced chairs and then, in his drunken manner, scale the chairs to the top, where he'd do a handstand. One night, the real Laffo was really drunk. He got to the top of the chair pyramid and one of the chairs at the bottom slipped. Frank had taken many falls over the years and knew how to land and roll so as to avoid injury. But this night the liquor slowed his reflexes and he came down on his left leg and ruined his ankle. By the time the fracture had healed, the circus had found a new aerialist clown and Frank's tightrope days were over. So he tried a new stint: lion tamer. He liked working with the big cats, he liked rubbing their fur and feeling their taut muscles. But when one nasty-tempered leopard took a swipe at him and left a scar across his cheek and forehead, Frank decided that the cats were undependable partners, and he left the circus.

A few years later, Frank told Bessie, he moved to Los Angeles, where he worked in silent movies as a stuntman. He had been a stand-in for Harry Carey and Francis X. Bushman ("They were both sons-of-bitches," Frank said), and he had also done some work for Hollywood's first big cowboy hero, Tom Mix. He and Mix became good friends, Frank said, and good drinking pals. One night Frank was driving and Mix was drinking—or maybe it was the other way around. Anyway, whoever was driving piled the car into a pole in the Hollywood Hills. Mix escaped injury, but Frank ended up in the hospital. When he came to, he found his leg hurt again, and he also found he only had half his teeth left—the ones on the right side of his face. After that, Frank decided he had seen enough of Hollywood. He went on to other places and other things.

If Bessie had been thinking about the stories Frank Gilmore told about himself, she might have noted a few things. For one, most of his tales ended in disaster, often brought on by drunkenness. She also might have noted that, since Frank was now about forty-seven, his tales only accounted for a small portion of his life, and they seemed to zigzag clear across the map of America. There was still a lot of Frank Gilmore's past she knew nothing about, and that he seemed in no rush to fill in. Even at his most drunk, he only told so much about himself, and when he was sober, he told almost nothing. Or maybe Bessie *did* note his vagueness and felt relieved by it. After all those years of Mormon genealogy—all the family legends memorializing pioneer ancestors who probably, behind all the inflated and pious myths, were really hard-asses and sons-of-bitches—maybe Frank Gilmore's reticence about his own history came as a welcome contrast.

In any event, Frank was utterly unlike any other man Bessie had ever known. Clearly, he was an older man, but in some ways Bessie thought he was younger in spirit than she was. He had seen plenty of life—he was experienced and worldly—but at the same time, Bessie felt that Frank Gilmore was still searching the world to find his place in it. More than anything, she felt like searching the world with him.

One night when they were coming out of a movie, Frank turned to Bessie and said: "Why don't we go out to Sacramento? You can meet my mother and we can get married while we're out there."

She noticed he didn't exactly get down on his knees. Too vain a man for that. But she remembered the lesson of the candy pan. "Okay," Bessie said. "That would be fine."

SO BESSIE WENT WITH FRANK TO SACRAMENTO, and it was one surprise after another. Soon as they hit town, Frank got them a room at the Semoh Hotel, across from one of the large city-center parks. He was anxious to go see his mother, who was staying at the Ladies' Cottage—a rest home at the Sacramento County Hospital. On the way over, Frank explained a couple of things. His mother's name was Fay Ingram. Like Frank, she had once worked in show business. The last time he saw her, she was married to a local psychologist, but Frank heard that he had since died.

"How long has it been since you've seen her?" asked Bessie.

"Eighteen years." Again, he said it like there was no reason to explain or apologize.

At the hospital's gift shop, Frank bought a box of chocolates and some white roses, and then took Bessie with him up to Fay's floor. He opened the door to his mother's room, walked in and said, "Hey, lady, I've got a package for you."

Fay was seated in a wheelchair, at a card table, working on a letter. She was a small lady in her late sixties, with cloudy-white hair and vivid blue eyes. Like Frank, she seemed both old and young at the same time, and like Frank, she immediately came off as imperial as hell. Fay glanced at the man who had just walked into her room, took off her reading glasses, and said, with little apparent emotion: "Where the hell have *you* been these last eighteen years?"

Frank smiled and laid down the flowers and candy. "Oh, here and there," he said.

Fay saw Bessie. "And who's this? Your new wife?"

"She will be," said Frank.

Frank made arrangements to get Fay out of the Ladies' Cottage. He rented her a handsome Victorian house on P Avenue, not far from his hotel, and he told her that, in time, he and Bessie would come and live there with her. In the process of moving Fay into her new home, Bessie learned something Frank hadn't told her: Fay was a practicing psychic and fortune-teller, and to hear her tell it, she was a damn good one. She could get spirits to materialize, make noise, show their forms, and communicate to the living a comforting knowledge of the afterlife. Also, she knew how to reach a troubled spirit and help resolve its pain, so it would no longer be earthbound. "Promise me," said Bessie, "that you won't ever do any of that around me. I've had bad experience with spirits. They give me the creeps."

It turned out that Fay was also a licensed minister in the Spiritualist Church of California, which gave her the authority to perform marriages. She wanted to be the one to marry her son to his new bride. Bessie was a little uneasy with the idea. How would *this* look back home: bad Bess, married to a man twice her age by his witchy mother? Still, she didn't want to hurt Fay's feelings. She agreed to the idea and told herself that at the first opportunity she would get Frank to remarry her with a proper minister or justice of the peace. On Frank and Bessie's second night in Sacramento, after settling Fay into her new residence, the old woman married her son and his new bride. Lit some candles, said a few words, offered an incantation, and that was it. No licenses, no blood tests, no papers. (I have never been able to find an official record of the marriage in Sacramento County, or any place else in California.)

The two hadn't been married but a few minutes when Fay turned to Frank and said: "You know, Robert's living not far from here. He tried to find you once or twice over the years. I thought you would have asked about him by now."

Frank said nothing in reply. Instead, a bitter look crossed his face.

"Who is Robert?" my mother asked.

Frank and Fay exchanged a glare. After a moment, Frank said: "He's my son."

"Your *son*?"

"Yes, from an earlier marriage."

"How old is he?"

Frank turned to Fay. "I don't know, how old *is* he?"

"Robert is now nineteen," said Fay, showing all her lovely teeth in a big smile.

"When did you last see him?" asked Bessie.

"Well, about eighteen years ago. I brought him here after my marriage was over. That woman wasn't fit to raise him. I asked Fay to look after him for a while."

"When it was obvious you weren't coming back," said Fay, "I adopted him. His name is now Robert Ingram."

Frank signaled that he'd had enough of the discussion. "Tell Robert where I'm staying," he told Fay. "Tell him to come by sometime."

Then Frank took his new bride back to the Semoh Hotel. The marriage had begun.

SEVERAL HOURS LATER — AT ABOUT 4 A.M. — Frank and Bessie were enjoying the first sleep of their marriage when there was a knock at the door. Bessie felt Frank tense up beside her. "Who is it?" he said.

"It's Robert."

Frank seemed relieved, but also annoyed. "Goddamn, what are you doing here this time of the night?"

Bessie said, "Oh, get up and let him in."

Frank got up, opened the door, and looked at his son. Bessie, lying in bed, looked at him at the same time. Robert had dark brown, curly hair and, like Fay and Frank, bright blue eyes. She thought to herself: This is the best-looking man I have ever seen in my life. This must be what Frank looked like twenty-five years ago. One handsome fellow.

Frank said, "Well, let's walk down to the park and get acquainted. We'll wait out here in the hallway while Bessie gets dressed."

The three of them sat down on a bench in the park. The conversation was awkward at the start. Robert told Frank that he had run away once at age fourteen to find Frank and had been arrested and returned to Fay. Frank didn't say anything in reply. After a bit, Robert turned to Bessie and said, "You remind me of my girlfriend. You have beautiful hair." It was more of a compliment than she had ever got out of Frank. Bessie liked Robert right away.

Frank and Robert sat there, trying to get acquainted, but Frank acted like he was bored. As it grew light out, Robert asked Frank if he knew how he could find his mother.

"No," said Frank, "and I wouldn't tell you if I did. She was no damn good."

That was the end of their first visit. It would never be a close relationship. Bessie suspected that Frank was making Robert continue the payment for whatever the boy's mother had done, eighteen years before.

AFTER THEIR FIRST FEW COMMUNICATIONS, IT WAS APPARENT that some old discomforts still lingered between Frank and Fay. It seemed to Bessie that Frank probably loved his mother a great deal—he spoke of her in the most praising and longing of terms—but when he was actually in Fay's company, the climate could be tense and chilly. In turn, Fay often taunted her son with her coyness and with ceaseless demands. Also, Bessie noted, when the four of them—Frank and Bessie, Robert and Fay—were together and company would come over, Fay would always introduce Robert as her son, and Frank as simply Frank Gilmore. Fay seemed to save her real fondness for Robert and Bessie. About the only time the guard ever dropped between her and Frank was when the two of them would share a bottle of whiskey. This was something Bessie was learning about Frank: He could drink at great length, and when he did, he was an impressive drunk. He was funny and told colorful stories, and Bessie learned to keep her ears open when Frank and Fay drank together. She heard scandalous tales about show business and circus performers at those times. In particular, she heard a lot about the famous late magician and escape artist Harry Houdini. It was apparent that Fay had known him well—had, in fact, helped him at an early stage of his career—but felt wronged by something he had later done to her. Bessie figured it had something to do with Houdini's exposé of spiritualist charlatans. Whatever it was, Frank shared his mother's hatred for the dead man. The two of them would get drunk and call Houdini the worst names. It was their strongest bond.

FRANK AND BESSIE HADN'T BEEN MARRIED FOR LONG when Frank announced abruptly one day that he had to go out of town on some business and might be gone for a while. When Bessie asked him where he was going and what the business was, Frank acted too rushed to explain. "I owe a man some work," was all he would say. "I want you to stay here and take care of Fay."

That was the first disappearance. Frank had simply packed a bag and was gone within the hour. Later departures would have less forewarning. Here was Bess, five hundred miles from home, looking after a nice but strange old woman whom she barely knew, and who had a penchant for bossing people around. Bessie had too much defiance in her to succumb to somebody else's royal highness act. The first time Fay gave her a command, Bessie said, "Look, that might work with Frank and Robert, but it doesn't wash with me. I know you're in a wheelchair, but that doesn't make me your servant." Something about the remark seemed to draw Fay's respect. After that, the two of them got along fine.

Frank's absence stretched on for a couple of weeks, and Bessie began to grow concerned. Also, a bit angry. She asked Fay if she knew where Frank had gone and how she might reach him. Fay studied Bessie with her sharp blue eyes as if she were appraising the young woman's mettle. Then Fay said: "Tell me, Bessie how long was it you knew Frank before you decided to marry him?"

Bessie got the hint. Maybe she should have learned a bit more about the man and his history before deciding to spend a life with him. Bessie explained that Frank had always been tight-lipped about his past, that it had even come as a surprise to learn he had a living mother. Fay just sat there, watching Bessie silently as she spoke, not volunteering anything. Bessie decided to take a more direct approach.

"Tell me about Frank's first wife," she said. "Why did she give up Robert to him?"

Bessie said it with such genuine innocence, it caught Fay off guard. "Frank's *first* wife?" she said, laughing. "Oh, honey, he really *hasn't* told you much, has he? As far as I can tell from my count, you are likely Frank's sixth or seventh wife, but then you have to remember I lost track of him quite a few years ago, and he hasn't really filled me in on all his in-betweens. Also, Robert wasn't Frank's first child—more like his fifth. Frank has left families scattered all over the nation."

Fay went on to tell her about Frank's marriage to Robert's mother, but Bessie was dazed enough only to remember a few particulars. The woman's name was Nan, and Frank had married her about 1919, in Chicago. She was a real beauty, Fay had heard, and she came from a prominent Illinois Mormon family. She might not have married Frank, but he got her in trouble, and even though Frank was not a Mormon, Nan's parents insisted she marry him to try to make up for her sin. For a time, Frank—who had been raised a staunch Catholic by Fay—even thought about converting to Mormonism. He occasionally went to Sunday School with Nan, and even read that god-awful Book of Mormon, said Fay. In 1920, Frank and Nan had a son and named him Robert. Frank loved the boy, Fay said, but only because he loved the mother so much. Fay had never known a woman to get to her son like Nan. His letters were filled with praise and hope.

Then, the letters stopped coming. Fay wrote to his Illinois address, but the letters were returned. One day a few months later, there was Frank at her door, with Robert, not even a year old. Frank was a mess. Hadn't shaved in days, been drinking, and needed to borrow some money. Seemed he owed a man who helped him get to Sacramento. Then Frank told Fay the story. He came home early one day from his job as a newspaper ad salesman and found his beautiful Nan in bed with a church elder. He beat the man up bad—Frank was a mean fighter; he could knock a man across a room easily—and then he took the baby Robert and walked out on his home. That was the last that Frank or the boy would ever see of Nan. Brought the child to Fay. That was his punishment on his wife. For that matter, Fay was a bit surprised to see Frank show up years later with Bessie, another Mormon woman. "Last time I saw him," she said, "he had a powerful hatred for the Mormons."

But, asked Bessie, didn't the police ever try to find Frank and Robert? Didn't they know where Fay lived?

"No," said Fay, "I don't think so. You see, he didn't use the name Frank Gilmore during that marriage, so they didn't really know who to look for. Hell, Frank's lived under more names than he's had wives. In fact," added Fay, smiling, "I do believe that you may be the only woman he has ever married under the name he was raised with. Though, I might add, Gilmore isn't his real name either."

"What *is* his real name?"

Fay studied Bessie's face for many moments before answering.

"Weiss," she said finally. "But don't ever tell anybody I told you that. Don't even tell Frank."

Now the questions poured out of Bessie. Who had been Frank's other wives? And what were these other names that he used? Where did they come from, and why did he use them? Fay's face shut down momentarily as Bessie rattled off her questions. The old woman was aware she might be on the verge of saying too much. "I'll tell you a few things," she said. "I figure you're entitled to that much. But there are some things about Frank's life and affairs that I will never tell you, no matter how much you want to know. You'll have to get those secrets from your husband."

Fay was willing to let Bessie in on some of Frank's other names—she figured the couple would be living under those names soon enough anyway. Frank, she said, had made equal use of such forenames as Frank, Francis, Franklin, Harry, and Walter. His last names had included Ingram, Seville, Sullivan, Lancton, LaFoe, Collier, and Coffman; he had even sometimes used his real name of Weiss, though Fay had always discouraged that. As to why he had chosen the other names, Bessie would have to ask Frank. And then there were the wives and the children. Frank's first son, called Christopher, had been born in Baltimore, in 1914 (a year after Bessie). He was born illegitimate—as far as Fay knew, Frank's only illegitimate child—and had been adopted by a good Baltimore family. Even though the boy was adopted, Frank still kept contact with him over the years and so did Fay. Christopher now worked in show business and wrote Fay occasionally. He had even come to visit her. It was through Christopher, she said, that she managed to keep loose track of Frank in the years after he abandoned Robert.

A couple of years after Christopher's birth, Frank had a brief, stormy courtship with a famous opera singer in New York, which resulted in a briefer, stormier marriage, and a fast, nasty annulment. Then there had been the marriage to Nan, and after Frank showed up with Robert, he stopped contacting Fay. A few years later she learned from Christopher that, in 1928, under the name Walter Coffman, Frank had married a seventeen-year-old woman named Barbara Solomon, in Greenville, Alabama. They'd had two children, a boy and a girl. After that, Fay thought there might have been a family in Seattle, under the name Lancton, and probably at least one or two childless marriages. As far as she knew, Frank always legitimately married and divorced the women—Robert's mother, Nan, being a possible exception in the divorce department. At the same time, since he never married any two women under the same name, Fay wasn't sure what difference all the niceties made, though they seemed to matter to Frank.

But the marriages, said Fay, were only a part of Frank's story. "You have picked an interesting man to marry," she told Bessie. "Nobody has ever held him for very long. But I have a better feeling about you than the others."

WHEN IT CAME TIME FOR FAY TO TALK ABOUT HER OWN PAST, Bessie found the old woman could be just as reticent and mysterious as her son. Fay claimed she had been born in French Canada and that her father had been a descendant of the royal French House of Bourbon. In the 1870s, according to Fay, circumstances had forced her parents to move their family to Lincoln, Nebraska, and change its name to Lancton. Fay would not say what the original family name had been or what had caused the move. Like Bessie, Fay had several sisters, and they had all tired of small-town life. In the late 1880s, they had put together a song and dance act and hit the road. In early 1890, they performed at the Chicago World's Fair as Iva and the Lancton Sisters. It was there, said Fay, that she had met the man who would be Frank's father—a man who had gone on to great fame. Fay would not reveal his identity. "If I told you who it was," she said, "it would shock you." Fay had briefly loved the man but then soon hated him forever. After she became pregnant with his child, he disavowed knowledge of her, and she returned to Lincoln, disgraced, and delivered Frank, on November 23, 1890.

"Where did the name Gilmore come from?" asked Bessie.

"A man I knew back in Nebraska."

Suddenly Bessie remembered one of the few things Frank had ever told her about his father: He said that he had been killed by a blow to his stomach. Was that the man named Gilmore, or was that Frank's real father?

"I'm surprised Frank told you that," said Fay. "No, that was not Gilmore. He wasn't in our life for long, and I have no idea what became of him. The man who was killed from being hit in the belly was Frank's real father. And that's all I'm going to say on that."

In the mid 1890s, Fay's family left Nebraska and moved to the East. Fay put Frank in an Eastern boarding school and joined her sisters on-stage again for a while. They played around Boston and New York, but eventually the act split up, and Fay followed a bad love affair to the West Coast. She settled in Sacramento in the 1920s, she said, because the city had been a haven for the Spiritualist and Theosophy movements, which Fay became active in. Then she married a man named William Ingram, one of the city's prominent psychologists, and worked for him as his aide. After Ingram died a few years back, Fay continued to see some of his patients. In time, she found herself drifting back into Spiritualism. She believed that what really troubled many people was lack of a connection with the other side—that is, with those who had gone on to the spirit world, by way of death. It could bring great healing to both the living and the departed if they could establish communication through a medium such as Fay. "For example," said Fay, "I can see that there is a gentle spirit who is around you at all times. She is here even as we speak. I sense that she works to protect you from a darker spirit that also lurks nearby, and often tries to get closer to you."

"That," said Bessie, "is enough of that. I don't care what you do for a living, Fay, but if you want me to stay here with you, don't bring any spirits knocking against my walls in the dark. I will leave faster than you can believe. When it comes to these matters, I have decided to stay a coward for the rest of my life."

Fay agreed not to meddle between Bessie and her attendant spirits.

ALL THE BUSINESS ABOUT FRANK'S FAMOUS FATHER had left Bessie intensely curious, and something in Fay's mess of hints and detail had clicked for my mother. She knew this much: Frank's real surname, according to Fay, was Weiss, and his father had been killed by a stomach injury. Armed with this information, and her suspicions, Bessie visited the Sacramento Public Library one afternoon and did a little reading. It didn't take much to give her what she wanted. In 1874, the celebrated magician Harry Houdini—the man so despised by Frank and his mother—had been born as Ehrich Weiss. He later changed his name to Houdini as a tribute to the famed French magician Robert Houdin. In 1926, during a tour, Houdini—who was then forty-eight—allowed an overzealous fan to deliver some hard blows to his midsection as a proof of the magician's undiminished stamina and strength. The blows did severe damage that could not be repaired, and on October 31, 1926, Houdini died of an advanced form of peritonitis.

According to this information, Bessie surmised, Harry Houdini had been Frank Gilmore's real father.

When Bessie told Fay what she had learned, Fay confirmed her suspicions. Years before, Fay said, after Houdini's rise to fame, she had contacted the magician and tried to establish Frank's claims to paternity. But Houdini, who was bitterly disappointed that his own wife could not have children—and in no mood for a scandal—refused Fay's request. Still, she had let her son know who his father was; she thought it only fair. "That," said Fay, "is the great tragedy of Frank's life. The anger of the man is that he can never claim who he truly is."

It was this bitter knowledge that his own father had refused him, said Fay, that had turned Frank into a restless man, bound for trouble, and unable to stay true to his own children. "If you have children with him, Bessie, make him stay true to them. That's the only thing that will ever bring him peace. It's too late for him to be Houdini's son. The only thing he can do now is to be a father to his own sons."

CHAPTER 3

FAY'S SECRET

FOR YEARS, FAY HAS FASCINATED AND PERPLEXED me as much as anybody in my family's history. Clearly, she was a woman who knew the effective force of mystery. The mystery of a powerful past that owns your destiny without giving up its own secrets. The mystery of the world of death.

Fay sowed her lore well. We heard her legends about Houdini's patrimony and our lost royal lineage throughout our youths. Along with the tales of Mormon ancestors and Blood Atonement, Fay's mysteries were an important part of our sense of where we had come from. There were secrets and debts in our past, there were birthrights that had been stripped from our hands, there were ghosts on our heels, there was a darkness in the marrow of our history. A darkness that we could not fully understand, except to know that it was the oldest and truest part of ourselves.

In a way, whether any of these tales were true or not hardly mattered. We believed these claims about our lives, and so we acted upon them. Still, when I began this task, I hoped to find as much truth about these legends as I could. I must admit, Fay was adept at covering her tracks— she managed to hide most of her life story and significant parts of her son's story. But she left one small piece of evidence behind. I suspect it may be one of the sad keys to the whole fucking tragedy.

HERE IS WHAT I HAVE LEARNED ABOUT FAY'S WORLD, and the circumstances of my father's birth:

On November 7, 1869, Fay's mother, a seventeen-year-old woman named Josephine St. Louis, married a man named Lewis Lavois, a twenty-seven-year-old shoemaker, in Marlborough, Massachusetts. Both of these people were born in French Canada, but their French origins are largely untraceable. If there's any royal connection in either lineage, it's as good as lost. I have never found a birth record for Fay—who reportedly was born January 8, 1871—in either Canada or Massachusetts, though it is probable she was born in the latter place.

Fay's family next turns up in the 1880 U.S. Census, in Lancaster County, Nebraska. By this time, they have a new surname, Lancton, and the father is now listed as Peter, a forty-six-year-old carpenter. One experienced genealogist who helped me trace these histories believes that the Lewis Lavois who disappeared from Massachusetts in the 1870s and the Peter Lancton of Nebraska in the 1880s (also listed as Peter Lancto in some accounts) were different people. For one thing, Lancton is listed as being ten years older than Lavois. I'm not so sure. Given Fay's claim that the family had undergone some sort of identity change—and that there was never any mention of a second father—I'm not so sure that Lavois and Lancton weren't the same man. In any event, this much is certain: In Nebraska in 1880, Josie was living with a man named Peter Lancton, and that is the surname that the family would remain known by.

The Lanctons, like the Browns, were basically poor with several children. They moved frequently during their Lincoln years, usually around the fringes of the city, from one small home to another. Driving through their old neighborhoods recently, I discovered that probably little had changed about the dismal area in which they once lived. It would be a stultifying environment for a young person in any era, then or now. To survive it, you would either have to be as dull as the land around you, or you would need an imagination that could transcend its flatness.

Here's where Fay's story starts to break down: From what I can tell, she never went with her sisters to perform at the Chicago World's Fair in 1890. Instead, on July 31, 1886, Fay—who was known in Lincoln as Fannie—had married a man named Harry Noole Gilmore, in Omaha, Nebraska. Harry, who was born in Illinois, would not prove a man of significant means. According to the Lincoln City Directory's listings for this period, Harry and Fannie spent much of their time living with her family. Sometimes Harry worked as Peter Lancton's carpenter's assistant, and sometimes he worked as a Lincoln City streetcar driver.

A little over a year after their marriage, on August 26, 1887, Fannie and Harry had their first child, a boy named Clarence. Then, on October 31, 1890, Harry and Fannie's young son Clarence died, and was buried at Lincoln's Wyuka Cemetery. Three weeks after the burial, on November 23, 1890, my father, Frank Harry Gilmore, was born. Or at least I have to assume that is when he was born. Since Nebraska did not keep birth records during this time, I have never been able to locate a birth certificate, or a baptismal or christening record, for Frank Gilmore.

There isn't much left to the Nebraska story after that. In early 1893, Fannie sued her husband for divorce—an event novel enough to be noted in the *Nebraska State Journal*, under the headline: "Divorce Market Good." The February 28, 1893 story read: "Fannie Gilmore wants the district court to give her a divorce from Harry Gilmore, and to that end she filed a petition yesterday. She states that Harry married her at Omaha, in July, 1886, and that ever since that time, he has neglected to provide any support for her. She adds that she has been compelled to eke out a living by manual labor, and by the assistance which relatives rendered her. The court is requested also to give Mrs. Gilmore the custody of her child."

Following the divorce, Fannie and her son moved back in with her parents. In 1896, the Lanctons moved to the East, where the sisters worked together for a few years, dancing and singing on the Northeastern vaudeville circuit. Meantime, Harry Gilmore appeared in the Lincoln City Directory until 1895, as a bellboy at the Lincoln Hotel. That was the last anybody heard of him until June 11, 1911, when this item appeared in the *Nebraska State Journal*: "SCOTTS BLUFF, NEB. JUNE 10—Harry Gilmore, 40 years old, died at the Scotts Bluff hospital yesterday of typhoid fever. Nothing could be found in his effects that could give a clue who his friends or relatives are, or where he came from. He has been working at the sugar factory and the boys at the factory will have charge of the funeral tomorrow."

After the 1890s, Fay vanished from the family's records, or from any recorded history for many years after that. The next anybody heard of her was around 1920, when she was in Sacramento, conjuring up spirits under the name Baby Fay LaFoe. Frank Gilmore, meanwhile, went on to lead his own life of hidden history.

THAT IS THE TRUE STORY OF MY FATHER'S ORIGIN, as far as I have been able to determine. I do not believe that he was the illegitimate son of Harry Houdini, though I suspect that my father believed it. If he ever remembered his real father, or knew anything about Harry's lonely fate, Frank Gilmore never mentioned it. At the same time, not all of Fay's stories were fictions. There's enough truth in her narrative of the Lanctons' early years, for example, to give a hint of possibility to some of her mysteries. Plus, her accounts of Frank's various marriages and surnames all proved truthful.

Which only makes Fay's fictions all the more troubling. Why would she have invented the legend of an illegitimate birth for her son, and why would she have kept that myth alive for the rest of her life? Obviously, the cost to Frank Gilmore was immense, and the cost did not end with him. I've thought at times that Fay might have devised the story to redeem her own disappointments. Maybe the marriage and its failure had been too banal for a person with an imagination as large and hungry as Fay's. Maybe she needed a bigger failure to live up to—like the lost love of a great celebrity, who had fathered her bastard son. Maybe she simply enjoyed the importance that such a story gave her—and perhaps she recognized, years later, that the story had now become her best shot at being remembered past her own death.

Perhaps, but then maybe it was something else.

Not long ago, I visited the Wyuka Cemetery, just outside Lincoln, where my father's older brother, Clarence, was buried at age three. Wyuka is one of Nebraska's oldest large cemeteries; it has been receiving the dead and their mourners for over a century. It is laid out like a mosaic. Narrow driveways wind around a vast patchwork of lots and gardens, each of them an island of graves. Clarence's grave lay on the far side of the cemetery, in one of its oldest sections. I parked my car near that section early on a winter morning. It was bitterly cold—there was a blizzard watch on the news that morning—and a haze hung over the ground that made it hard to read the markings on the old, timeworn tombstones. I searched for some time before I found it: a small, isolated plot lying next to an empty patch of ground, surrounded by the grave colonies of full families. On a stone lying flat on the earth was all that was left of the Lanctons' history in Nebraska, and of my father's first family. The stone read: OUR BABY.

I stood there and looked at it for as long as I could take the cold. I tried to imagine what it was like when Fay and Harry buried their son here. Maybe the marriage was already bad, and maybe the child's death had killed whatever hope had been left for the young couple. I thought of it this way: You have a child, you love it, you put something of the best of yourself and your hope into your efforts for that child. And then the child dies—your hope is wiped out, and your hurt is endless. On top of that, three weeks later, you have another child—the child that would be my father—and the hope and love are supposed to begin again. But what if they don't—what if it's too soon? What happens if the emotions that are invested in that child are *not* emotions of reborn hope but, instead, feelings of great fear and grief, or even resentment? When Fay looked at her new son, so soon after putting her first child in the ground, did she feel comforted by the baby's face? Or did she feel there was too much risk in loving this child as she had loved the first? Or did she just *hurt* too damn much over Clarence to give Frank the sense of love and security a young baby requires?

Whatever the answers, the Gilmores' marriage did not hold. Within a few years it was finished and Fay was gone and Harry was forgotten. I don't think Fay kept Frank Gilmore close to her heart and life after Nebraska. Instead, she sent him off to a sequence of boarding schools and only shared a home with him occasionally. Better to keep a child distant than to love and bury him. Frank Gilmore was denied all right—by everybody. He grew up without a father and without a mother. Thirty years later, when he brought Robert to Fay's door, he might well have been saying: *Here, I've brought myself back to you.* And then Frank pushed his son away, into the hands of the mother who had once pushed Frank away.

That helps explain the distance between Fay and Frank, but why the Houdini rumor? I'm not sure. Maybe Fay *did* have an affair with him. Perhaps she knew him at some point and felt betrayed by something he had done. What could be a better revenge than the scandal of a bastard son? And maybe by making Frank believe the legend, she was just trying to bury the truth of her own sad past a little deeper.

I took another look at Clarence's headstone and thought: I am probably the only person who has ever visited this particular grave in the last hundred years. That idea was enough to fill me with such immediate despair, I got back in my car and drove away from the site as fast as the narrow roads would take me. Just before I left the graveyard, I stopped at the main office and asked about the empty plot next to the baby's grave. It seemed odd to find a vacant grave, in the portion of a cemetery that had been filled for nearly a century. The kindly old man at the desk pulled out some ancient books, ran his fingers along the ledgers, and then told me: "That plot belonged to a man named Harry Gilmore. He was Clarence's father, and bought the grave site for himself a few years after he had buried the child. But he never came back, and he was never buried there."

Nobody is laid to rest next to Clarence Gilmore's grave. He stays there alone, a little secret, left behind.

MAYBE AT THIS POINT BESSIE should have said to herself: Oh-oh— looks like I've married into a family with more problems than the one I just fled. But she didn't. Bessie stayed, despite all the terrible secrets, and all the frightening prospects. She even stayed once the drinking and beatings and disappearances began in earnest.

She had her reasons.

And we—the sons—are the result of that decision.

CHAPTER 4
YEARS OF
WANDERING

During Frank's absence—which had now gone on for a month —Fay's psychic business got up and running again. Much of this work was what Fay called "daytime spiritualism": card reading and fortune-telling for those who were worried in love or desperate in business. These clients needed assurance and counseling as much as anything, and Fay was savvy at providing it. In the evenings, Fay did the serious stuff: séances, summonings, materializations. These were the occasions when she gathered those who were anxious to contact a loved one who had gone on the dark side of the veil. Usually, Fay attracted about a dozen people for these sessions, though sometimes she had as many as forty participants sitting in her parlor. Most of these were older folks, around Fay's age. They were eager to reconcile painful misunderstandings with people they had loved and lost. Or they were desirous of the departed one's crucial advice on one secular matter or another. Or they simply wanted some sign that there was life and deliverance beyond death. They found these signs in Fay's living room, under her guidance. Familiar voices came out of the dark, or from Fay's mouth, in those moments when she would allow herself to be a conduit for the dead. The hands and breaths of the dead brushed up close against the faces of the living, and strange sounds thumped along the floor and the walls. Sometimes, luminous faces floated in the dimness, like an apparition breaking free into the real world.

My mother would not stick around when Fay invoked the spirits. She was uncomfortable with the atmosphere in the house at those times, plus she was uneasy with what these events implied. Either Fay's clients were pathetic and needful people who were being duped, or Fay was the genuine article—somebody who could reach into God's proper realm and talk to the dead—and for Bessie, the latter notion was more disturbing than the first. On the nights of the séances, Bessie would often go visit Robert, who lived in a small room a few blocks away. She had come to like this son of Frank's, who was now nearly a man in his own right. He was shy and polite, and damn handsome to boot. Plus, the longer Frank's absence stretched on, the more she began to feel she had in common with Robert, since they had both, in a way, been abandoned by the same man. Bessie could tell there was a deep and confused hurt in Robert. He had been raised in a world of weird psychic shadows, and he had hungered to be claimed by his father. But all he knew of his dad was that he was a man who had grown up in vaudeville and the circus, and who could not come for Robert because some great mystery kept him away. But the idea of the secret mystery didn't help Robert much. The truth was, Frank Gilmore had found it terribly easy to leave his son, without once calling or writing him. Robert still wanted to get close to his father, but he wasn't finding it easy.

Bessie and Robert spent many evenings talking about these and other matters, while the spirits held court in the night at Fay's house.

HALFWAY THROUGH FALL, after a six-week absence, Frank returned home. Bessie saw him coming up the walkway to Fay's and, despite all her agitation, something in her heart surged. He had a way that got to her, something that told her he was the only man she was ever going to really love. Still, she had to let him know that she wasn't happy being left behind, and that she had learned a few details about his life. She told him that Fay had told her about his other wives and many names. She told him that she had figured out that Ehrich Weiss was his father.

Frank took all this in without showing much in return. Just like his mother, Bessie thought.

"What else did Fay tell you?" Frank asked.

"Nothing else. She told me that if I wanted to know any of your other secrets, I'd have to ask you."

Frank seemed relieved by that. He gave my mother a look that told her that revealing anything more was the last thing on his mind.

Bessie decided to push a little. "Frank, where did you go? What were you doing?"

"If I thought it was any of your damn business," Frank said, "I would have told you already. Maybe it's better if you not know everything. Think of it that way."

There was one thing, though, she had to know: Did he have other families in other places? Did he still see any of his other wives or support their children? "I can take a lot of things, but if you are still seeing other women, I'll leave you."

Frank laughed and lifted her chin tenderly. He looked into Bessie's green eyes and said: "Believe me, you're more than enough for me. Besides, a man would have to be a damn fool to have more than one wife at the same time. Hell, *I'm* not a Mormon. Don't worry, I don't see any of those other women anymore. Once in a while I get in touch and see one of the kids. That's about it."

Bessie didn't know why, but she believed him.

FRANK SURE HAD MADE SOME MONEY while he was away, and he wasn't shy about spending it. He took Bessie downtown, bought her new clothes and new rings, and gave Robert the money for a used Ford he had wanted. Then he paid up Fay's rent for the next six months and gave her an envelope with some more cash and told her to use it to live on. He said he was feeling restless and wanted to take Bessie to see some of the country before they started having kids. Told Fay they'd be back in a few months. To Bessie, he explained that he didn't feel like sticking around Fay's supernatural antics. He had seen plenty of such stuff over the years, and he had nothing but contempt for all the fools who took her mumbo jumbo to heart. It was all a lot of bunco, he said. Fay installed switches under the table and carpet, he explained, that she could throw with her hands and feet and make things happen in the dark.

Bessie wasn't so sure. She knew from her faith that there was only a thin veil that separated the living from the dead. The departed were always close by—closer than you might believe, Bessie said. Besides, how could Fay accomplish all those tricks when she was confined to a wheelchair?

Frank laughed. "She doesn't need that damn thing," he said. "It's just part of the act. Plus, it's a good way to get people to wait on her."

Bessie decided Frank was kidding. She had seen how helpless Fay was in her chair, and she had seen how dead her legs were. There was little doubt that Fay was a paraplegic.

Anyway, Frank and Bessie moved on. Frank bought a new wood-paneled station wagon Pontiac—he would always have a great weakness for woodies—threw a few items in a couple of suitcases, and drove the two of them back to Utah. He wanted to collect some money that his employer at *Utah Magazine* still owed him, and Bessie thought it was time for her family to meet her husband. She had written them from Sacramento, telling them she had married. Her husband, she wrote, was a successful advertising salesman, and he had once worked in silent movies and the circus. She didn't tell them any of the other stuff—for example, about his being almost twice her age or that he'd had a half dozen other wives and children. She figured she would keep that information to herself, for fear it would become neighborhood scuttlebutt. A couple of weeks later she got back a brief but pleasant letter from her mother. "We had been a little worried about you since you left Utah, but we were happy to receive your news," Melissa wrote. "As you know, it is only through marriage that a woman can come into the full presence of God and the glory of the celestial kingdom, and we are glad that you have taken this important step. Please come and see us when you get back. We'd like to meet your Frank."

Right from the start, the visit did not go well. Both Melissa and Will were upset to see Bess with a man so much older than she—a man only four years younger than her father. Melissa didn't say as much to my mother's face, but she let on to her sisters, and the word got back to Bessie. Also, there was something about Frank that just rubbed her parents the wrong way—it was as if they could smell criminal written all over him. Will, in particular, was disappointed that Bessie had married such a character. "This is a man," he told her one day as they walked in the backyard, "who has been in prison. Why didn't you tell us that? Why would you marry a man like this?"

"He has *not* been in prison," Bessie said, the old anger returning to her face. "Frank's had a hard life. He was abandoned by his father at birth and his mother had to work in show business to keep him in school. He was forced to fend for himself a lot over the years, and he had to grow up tough. But my husband is not a criminal. How *dare* you say that."

Bessie's protests, though, didn't count for much. The Browns didn't warm to Frank, and her younger sisters seemed almost terrified of him. More than ever, Bessie felt the judgment and scorn of her family. In fact, she felt it descend on her in the worst possible way. In the Mormon world, there was nothing more important than the bond of marriage—it was the rock on which you built your family, and it was a key element to eternal blessings. Bessie was now made to feel that she had failed in this matter of utmost consequence. She believed that the disdain she was now experiencing had nothing to do with Frank Gilmore. She could have married Franklin Roosevelt and it would have made no difference. The whole message she had got from her family for years, she thought, was that she was worthless—she counted for nothing in their world, and in God's estimation. Now, it was as if that message were being sent with the finality of condemnation.

As Bessie and Frank drove away from the Provo farm, Bessie sat in the front seat of the Pontiac with both hands cupped over her face, crying as hard as she had ever cried. She felt like she didn't care if she never saw any of those people again. Frank put his arm around her and drew her close to him, pressing her head to his shoulder. "What the hell can you expect," he said, "from a bunch of damn Mormons."

THAT WAS WHEN THE WANDERING STARTED. In the next few months Bessie would see small towns and back highways all over Southern California, Nevada, Arizona, and Colorado. They would move into a place, spend a couple of weeks, then move on. Rarely did they stay anyplace for as long as a month or two. And when the time came to leave, it was almost always in a hurry. Frank would tell Bessie not to bother with packing the things they had accumulated. It was always just get in the car and go. "We'll buy new things in the next place," he would say. He wasn't about to be slowed down by possessions.

As it turned out, there were often good reasons for moving on quickly. Frank's main career, Bessie began to see, was scamming. The first thing he would do when they hit a town was get a phone installed in their hotel room or apartment, under one of his names. Then he would make the rounds to various businesses, selling advertising for a forthcoming magazine or specialty publication. He would show a sample of what the magazine would look like, leave a business card, then go back to the hotel and wait for the merchants to call and place their ads. Sometimes, he'd have Bessie answer the phone, posing as his secretary. "Hello, this is Mr. Collier's office." Or: "Hello. Miller Publications. Frank Collier's office." Then Frank would return to the merchants, collect the material for the ads, and full payment or partial payment for the ad. The publication, of course, would never materialize. Frank would take the money and move on. This approach to ad-selling was called "hundred-percenting," because the seller took all the profit and ran.

Activities like that were reason enough for putting a few hundred miles between yesterday and tomorrow, but the scams weren't the only thing that kept them moving. To Bessie, it seemed that Frank was always trying to keep ahead of some unknown phantom that might be coming up close behind. She could practically feel it in his sleep, the way he would lie tensed, or would sit bolt upright at the sound of late-night footsteps in the hallway. Soon, Bessie took on Frank's breathing patterns as her own. She began to feel edgy if they stayed in any one place for too long, and would only begin to unwind when they were back in the station wagon, rolling to the next stop, and the next scam.

For all the running and the risks, Bessie would later describe these as the good days of their marriage, when it was just the two of them, drifting around like small-town criminals in the American West. "We got along fine together in those days, before we ever had any kids. Children weren't something I ever really wanted or planned for; they were something Frank wanted. It was funny, he would want them, but then he would turn against them. And I, who had never wanted them, would fight to protect them. If only we had stayed that way forever, without kids."

It was said to hurt us, and it did. We felt we were to blame for the hell of everything. In our own hearts, the childless family became the ideal family.

THE GOOD DAYS DIDN'T LAST THAT LONG. Only a few months, really. In early 1939, Bessie became pregnant. The two of them kept traveling for much of her term, and then when the baby was due they settled into a bungalow in the Glendale section of Los Angeles, where my oldest brother, Frank Harry Gilmore, Jr., was born. Contrary to what Bessie expected from Fay's warnings, Frank appeared eager for fatherhood. He showed up at the hospital nervous and proud and a little drunk, dragging along some old friends of his. He did the whole routine—passed out cigars to everybody in sight, gave the doctor a bottle of whiskey with a ribbon around its neck, sweet-talked every nurse on the floor. First time my mother saw him holding Frank Jr., she thought she had never seen her husband look more pleased with himself, like holding this baby made him feel truly a man. Frank looked down at Frank Jr.'s face and turned to Bessie and said: "Here—I've given you a son to take care of you in your old age."

One thing was for sure: Frank seemed to know exactly how to handle a baby. He had no misgivings about feeding or changing Frank Jr., or staying up with him late at night when he cried or was sick. Bessie later said it was one of her best memories of him, the way he would handle a baby. Frank would sit in a chair with his baby, cooing at it, talking tenderly to it, singing it a lullaby in his broken voice. Before long, the baby would curl up in Frank's lap like a little kitten and fall asleep, safe in its father's presence.

They stayed in Los Angeles for a few weeks, Frank looking after the baby and Bessie, then went up north to see Fay. Something about seeing Frank fuss over his new baby boy got to Robert, and the two began to argue more frequently. The arguments were almost never expressly about the lack of love that Frank had shown Robert. Instead, Robert began to suspect that his father had not been fair and loving enough to Robert's mother, Nan, which brought out a nasty streak in Frank. He would say the worst things about his "ex-whore wife," until Robert would walk out on the discussions, halfway to tears. Then Bessie and Frank would go at it. Bessie felt Frank was in the wrong, the way he demeaned the mother that Robert had never even got to know. Frank would say: "I know you're soft for Robert, but you'd be better off if you learned to keep your mouth shut."

"Well, Frank," Bessie would say, "I'm too old to learn."

Early the following year, Bessie became pregnant again, but this time the development didn't seem to please Frank. In fact, he went on a drinking binge and checked into a hotel for a few days by himself, in nearby Oakland. When he came back, he was restive and irritable. He announced to Bessie that it was time for the two of them to travel again. Bessie wasn't thrilled to hear the news. It was almost summer, she had a seven-month-old baby and was almost three months along with another. She didn't look forward to driving all over the country under those conditions, and when she learned that this time they were heading for Alabama, she liked the idea even less. Didn't see why they needed to go so damn far, just so Frank could run one of his silly scams. Something felt dead wrong about the whole venture—even the route Frank had planned. Instead of taking the more direct route—swinging south and cutting through Texas—Frank wanted to head over through Utah, so Bessie could show the new baby to her parents. After that, they would drive across Colorado, Kansas, and Missouri, down through Arkansas and Mississippi to Alabama. Bessie knew her husband could care less about Will and Melissa seeing Frank Jr. She suspected there was something else at work in Frank's reasoning, but whatever it was, he wouldn't say.

Things didn't improve when they hit Alabama. By then it was summertime, and the sticky, palpable heat felt unlike anything Bessie had ever known. Plus, there was something about the place itself that scared the hell out of her. Maybe it was all the talk she had heard over the years about the South's insularity and violence, but she felt the locals were giving her a hard, assessing stare every time she opened her Yankee mouth. One time, ordering in a roadside diner, she was given a nasty look by the waitress, who said: "Where the hell are y'all *from*?"

Also, Frank didn't help her calmness. They had rented a small motel cabin in a little roadside town south of Selma, in the central part of the state. There wasn't much to do there. A couple of picture shows, a drugstore with a soda fountain, where Bessie could get lunch. Except Frank wanted her to stay inside their room most of the time by herself, and not get too close to any of the neighbors. She especially wasn't supposed to share much information about them or their lives, or to answer the inquiries of any strangers. "These are curious people," Frank had said. "They may seem genteel on the surface, but deep down they hate you because you're different. You're a Yankee, and Yankees are unwelcome intruders. Leave these people alone, Bessie. They may seem all right by the daylight, but by night they'll cut your throat and nobody will ever find what's left of you."

One night, Frank got drunk and told Bessie a bit about his earlier stay in Alabama, a decade before, when he had been married to Barbara Solomon, a Jewish woman. They moved into a town called Greenville, and Frank got work as a newspaper ad salesman. One day some local members of the Ku Klux Klan came around and invited him to a rally. Frank declined and when they wanted to know why, he told them that he was a Catholic and his wife was Jewish and he'd got along fine with black people all his life, so he couldn't really see himself joining the Klan in its various campaigns. A couple of nights later he came home from work and found his wife and baby sitting in the dark. Barbara told Frank that some men had come by, banging on the door and making terrible threats. They told her that Jews and Catholics weren't welcome in these parts, and if they were here come the next sunset, they would cut her husband's balls off in front of her. Frank believed they weren't bluffing. That night, he and his wife left Greenville before dawn and headed to Montgomery. The marriage only lasted another year or two.

Whatever Frank was doing in Alabama this time, it went on too long for Bessie's liking. She kept pressing him to leave—she wanted to have the new baby back home in California, in Los Angeles, or at Fay's, in Sacramento. Frank said: "Soon. We'll leave soon. I have to finish what I came here to do, get paid, and then we'll go."

Thanksgiving Day that year Frank got up before dawn, got dressed and left, and didn't come back until after midnight. Bessie was sitting in the small cabin with her baby in the dark, like Barbara Solomon ten years before. She was wondering what to do if she never saw Frank again, how she would get out of this frightful place. Or maybe they would come for her too, in the night. About 2 A.M., Frank came in and said: "I'm done here. I think we should leave right now. You can sleep in the car while I drive." She was dead tired, but something about the way he said it made her exhaustion beside the point. It was another one of those towns they left without packing their belongings, another moonlight flight. This time, Bessie didn't mind. She was glad to leave that awful land.

Frank again wanted to take the long way back, bypassing Texas altogether. Bessie said: "It makes no sense, when we can drive straight across. I don't want to have this baby along the side of this road, Frank, in the back seat of this car. I *want* to get back to California." For once, Bessie won the fight, and they began making their way across the infinitely wide state of Texas. This time, there was no doubting it: Frank did not want to be in Texas. He seemed nervous every mile of the trip, and since Texas was so damn big, Frank's nervousness lasted. He tried driving all night so he could get through the state faster, but there's no such thing as an unbroken drive across Texas. Bessie would wake up in the morning light, in the backseat with the baby, and find her husband passed out from sleeplessness in the front. It felt so urgent to get through and out of the place, Bessie drove the car herself a few times, eight and a half months pregnant, though she barely knew how to drive.

Then, driving along Route 67, it became evident that they wouldn't make California. The baby was coming and they needed to find a hospital. A man at a gas station directed them down the highway to McCamey; it was an oil worker's town, he said, and it had a good hospital. As the car wheeled into the hospital driveway, and Bessie sat in the backseat clutching the door handle with one hand and her overfull belly with the other, Frank turned to her and said: "Don't tell anybody a damn thing in this place. Let me do all the talking." That was all Bessie could remember. Next thing she knew, she was on a gurney, being wheeled under hallway lights into the delivery room.

A FEW HOURS LATER, SHE AWOKE TO THE SOUND of a Texas nurse's twang. "Mrs. Coffman?" the nurse said. "Are you all right, Mrs. Coffman? Can you hear me?" In her groggy state, Bessie thought: *Why doesn't Mrs. Coffman answer the woman? Is Mrs. Coffman all right?*

Then she felt my father's hand on her shoulder, shaking her lightly. "Bessie, can you hear us? It's okay, it's me, Walter."

Bessie opened her eyes to see her husband, standing on the right side of the bed she was in. On the other side stood the nurse, holding my mother's new baby. Seeing the baby, Bessie came to and reached out to hold her child.

"Here's your baby, Mrs. Coffman. You have a healthy and beautiful son. In fact, I'd say that little Faye here is just about the prettiest baby I've ever seen in these parts."

That finished waking Bessie. "Little *Fay*?" she asked.

"Yes," said Frank. "I already gave them the information for the birth certificate. I told them we had settled on the name Faye Robert Coffman."

"It's a beautiful name," the nurse said. "And you have a truly devoted husband. He insisted on staying here by your bedside. He wanted to be here when you woke up."

All Bessie could do was stare at the new baby and its already vivid blue eyes and think: *Did I wake up a different person? Or have I gone crazy?*

LATER, WHEN THEY WERE ALONE, IT HAD ALL COME BACK to Bessie: the desperate drive across Texas, and the news that they were using yet another name. All that made sense to her—at least as much as anything made sense in their lives at this point—but what she couldn't fathom was the particular name that Frank had come up with for their new son. "How," she asked, "could you give a child a name like that: Fay Robert Coffman?"

"I don't think it's such a bad name. You couldn't do any better. Besides, I spelled it a little differently. I put an *e* at the end of Fay."

"I don't care *how* it's spelled. You've still named your son after your *mother* and another one of your sons—somebody you don't even love. What the hell has gotten into you?"

"Calm down," said Frank. "We're not going to stay in Texas forever. But while we're here, his name is Faye Robert. And my name is Walter. Don't forget it."

A couple of days later they checked into a local hotel, the Doyle, while waiting for Bessie to get her strength back for traveling. The hotel manager, an older woman, came by on their first night to fuss over the baby. When Bessie told her the baby's name, the woman looked quietly dumbstruck. "Yes, his father named him," my mother said, while Frank—that is, Walter—swelled with pride. The next afternoon, while Frank was out getting food, the woman came back. "Too bad about the baby's name," she said, stroking the child's head.

"Yes, I know," said Bessie. "Well, I don't plan on it having that name much longer. Let me know if you have any better ideas."

Every day after that, the woman came by with suggestions for new names. Finally, she decided Bessie should name the child Doyle, in honor of the hotel. After that, the woman called little Faye little Doyle every time she saw him. It drove Frank crazy.

A FEW WEEKS LATER, MY PARENTS and their two sons were driving west, out of Texas. When they passed through El Paso and crossed the New Mexico border, Frank turned to Bessie and said: "Okay, you can rip up the damn birth certificate. We're going to give him a new name."

"Yes," said Bessie, "I know. I've already settled on the name. We're going to call him Gary. Gary Gilmore. I thought I'd name him after Gary Cooper, because he's going to grow up to be handsome, just like the actor."

Frank's response was immediate and forceful. "Like *hell* we're going to call him Gary. No son of mine is ever going to have that name."

"And why not?"

"The name of the man who stole Robert's mother from me was Grady. The name 'Gary' has always reminded me of him. I hated that man, and I hated his name. I'm not about to think of him every time I call my son."

"Frank, it isn't even the same name."

It didn't matter to my father. The two of them argued about the baby's name all the way to Sacramento.

My father's last word on the subject: "I'm not going to keep a son with that name."

My mother's last word: "The name stays."

I NEED TO INTERRUPT HERE FOR A MOMENT. An important thing just happened: The murderer in our story was born. Right now he is a baby with large blue eyes and an inviting face. A little over thirty-six years from this time he will be a man who has killed at least two other men and who sits on death row as the most famous murderer in America, because he is the only murderer in America who demands to be killed. You look into those blue eyes at that point, and what stares back is something that chills you in the deepest part of your instincts. It is a look that is terribly smart and terribly deadly. It is the look of a man who is afraid of everything but death, a man who would kill you if you crossed him, and maybe even if you didn't. The only thing separating the baby's face from the killer's face is a history of destruction.

Or perhaps it was something else that ended up turning this baby into a killer. Many times in the last few years I have found myself dwelling on a simple pair of questions: When and how does murder begin? Or, to put it another way: Could I locate one moment where everything went wrong, one moment—or period of time—that might have made all the difference? And if I could find such a moment, would it be one inside Gary's life? Or would it be one outside him—one, say, in the secret darkness of his own father's history? There are no simple answers to questions like these—there are only endless arguments and speculations. Even so, I can't help searching out our history for those answers, like my mother at the end of her days, examining each terrible link in the fateful chain. Where could we have altered this history? How could we have saved my brother's soul from murder, and spared the lives of innocents as well? You tell yourself you could learn from such a moment, that understanding it would explain all the destruction and free you from its repetition. But when you start looking at all the links in the story closely enough, you discover something worse: *Each* moment made a difference, and there were just too damn many of them that were bad. The only way to solve the deathly construction of this man's history would be to toss out all the moments and build a new chain of better links.

Obviously, this child's life is not off to an auspicious start. He has just been born of two people who carry their own bad legacies and who are presently in flight from certain unknown demons. If a parent's fears can be passed on to a child at its birth, then Gary began life as a bundle of insecurity. On top of that, he has been given two names: one, the name of the woman who could never bring herself to love his father; the other—the name he will be known by, that he will become famous by—is a name that reminds his father of a loss that will always invoke his bitterness. There's a horribly ironic twist that comes from all this name switching: What it means is, Gary Gilmore was never born; he would only die. (Years later, in fact, the federal penitentiary system would refuse me access to my brother's files because I could not prove that any such person by his name had ever been born, or had ever had an official name change.)

I have to marvel at the complexity and stupidity of all these circumstances of birth—particularly the thought of two adults bringing a child into an atmosphere of fear and forcing on him identities that, one way or another, would ensure a loss of love. Do any of these factors matter? Does something as seemingly small as a wrangle over a child's name really play any role in determining the child's bloody fate? I can't say for sure— I'm too mired in the webwork of my family's mythology to sort it all out. It's too easy for me to read significance into every oddity of fate, and I'm afraid I'm close to doing that here. At the same time, I know that all this business about the names would later matter to Gary a great deal, though by then he was already well down his particular road to hell.

SOMETHING IN FRANK STARTED TO GO A LITTLE WILD after Gary's birth and the return from the South. It was like he needed to be somewhere different all the time. In the first few months of 1941, the new family drifted in and out of small towns every couple of weeks. Meantime, the fights between Frank and Bessie were becoming more frequent and rougher. One time in Santa Barbara, Frank went off on a five-day drinking binge. By this time, Bessie was used to these episodes. She knew to stay put with the boys and wait for Frank to return. This time, he came back wearing an exceptionally unpleasant mood. He walked into the hotel where they were staying, moved over to the bed where the new baby was sleeping and pointed down at Gary. "This isn't my son, is it?"

Bessie wasn't prepared for such an out-of-the-blue remark. "What are you talking about? Whose son *could* it be?"

"It's Robert's son, isn't it? You think I don't know about what's gone on between the two of you back in Sacramento when I haven't been around."

Bessie looked at Frank for several long moments. Then she laughed. "You're crazy," she said. "You've been drinking so much it's softened your brain and turned you into an old man."

Frank hit her, hard, in the face. "Don't lie to me, you python-spitting she-devil straight from hell. I've been lied to enough."

He kept hitting her until she lay on the floor, her face bloodied all over, while the children cried. Through the whole ordeal she insisted the child was Frank's. But after that instance, my father spent much less time holding his new baby son.

The two of them fought and shouted their way around America, with two babies in tow. One day in late spring, they were driving through northern Missouri. Frank had been in a miserable mood the entire day, yelling at my mother and driving the car at reckless speed, and the babies were growing restless from being cooped up for so long. This time, Bessie thought something was closing in on Frank. It was the only way to explain his behavior. It was like she could feel the hot breath on both of their collars. Late in the afternoon, Bessie insisted Frank pull into a service station along the highway. She needed to change little Frankie's diaper, and she wanted to move her legs around a bit. She could see Frank wasn't happy with the stop. "Be quick about it," he said, and stayed in the car, watching the baby.

After a few minutes, Bessie and Frankie came back out of the rest room. She looked around. The car was gone, her husband was gone, the baby was gone.

"What happened to the man who was sitting here waiting for me?" she asked the service station attendant.

"He took out of here a few minutes back. He seemed in a hurry."

"Did he say anything before he left? Did he say he'd be back in a little while?"

"No, ma'am," said the attendant. She could tell from the look the young man was giving her he'd never seen anything quite like this. A man driving off with one kid, leaving his wife and the other kid in the middle of nowhere. Great, Bessie thought. Frank's got some wild hair up his ass because I made him stop, and now he's taken off for a while, to teach me a lesson. What a royally spoiled son of a bitch.

She and Frankie sat at the service station for hours, awaiting Frank's return. The sun went down, the moon and stars came up, and the attendant began putting away his signs and equipment. Just before he locked the door and switched on the night light, he said: "Lady, I don't think your husband is coming back, and I can't really leave you sitting here. Let me give you and your boy a lift over to Chillicothe. They have a hotel there, and a bus station."

From the bus station Bessie called her parents and got them to wire her enough money to return to Provo. When she got home, Will Brown wanted her to call the police, but Bessie refused. She told her parents that Frank was deeply worried about something and that she shouldn't have kept fighting with him at such a time. His leaving had been her fault. She was confident that he would be back, and she was sure he wouldn't do anything to harm the baby.

"If he shows up here," said her father, "there will be trouble. No man has a good reason to walk away from his wife and child and leave them stranded."

SEVERAL DAYS LATER, BESSIE GOT A CALL from an orphanage in Des Moines, Iowa. They had Gary; he had been turned over to them by his father, who was now sitting in a neighboring county's jail, doing thirty days on a bad check charge. Did Mrs. Laffo want to come and claim her child, or did she prefer to leave him in their care and surrender him for adoption? My mother later said, "If it all hadn't been so tragic, I could have laughed out loud at the Mrs. Laffo part. That was the first time I'd been called that."

Bessie borrowed more money from her family, gathered Frankie, and went to Iowa. She got Gary out of the orphanage and took a job doing housekeeping in exchange for room and board, while she waited for her husband to finish his jail stretch.

On the morning he got out of jail, she was waiting for him outside with Frankie and Gary. "What the hell," she said, "do you have to say for yourself? What were you thinking, leaving me there and running off with our baby?"

"Somebody got too close that day," he said, looking weary. "I had to leave. That's all there is to say about it."

Bessie began to wonder. Maybe all this business about Frank fleeing from something was just an excuse. Maybe nothing was on his trail, except his own fear of staying with his family and being a committed father. Maybe Fay had been right after all. "Frank," she said, "no matter what it is, you can tell me about it. If it's another woman or another family, let me know. I won't turn it against you. Only tell me the truth."

Frank shook his head. "No," he said. "Anything but that. It's a frightful truth, Bessie. You're better off not knowing."

THAT'S THE WAY IT WENT FOR THE REST OF THE YEAR. Zigzags across the American West, Frank carting the wife and kids from sinkhole to sinkhole, drinking harder and harder along the way. By the start of the holiday season, Bessie and Frank and the boys were living in a wheat and cattle-farming town called Holyoke, in the topmost northeastern corner of Colorado. Frank was running his usual scam of hundred-percenting—he had phony business cards, a telephone listed under an assumed name—this time they were Mr. and Mrs. Harry F. Laffo—and a checking account from a bank in a larger nearby town, Sterling. He was hitting businesses throughout the area, gathering advertising money for a regional travel magazine, like *Arizona Highways*. One day he cashed a check with one of the merchants he was selling advertising to. The merchant got suspicious and called the bank right away. When it turned out the check wasn't good—there was only three dollars in the account, and the check had been for fifty—the man had Frank traced to his hotel and arrested. It was early December 1941. The day the Japanese attacked Pearl Harbor, my father was sitting in a dirt-water jail on a bad check charge.

The police did a little checking around, realized Frank was selling phony advertising all over the place for a nonexistent publication. This was worse than simply passing a bad check; the charge was bumped up to running a confidence game. At the trial—held three days before Christmas—the prosecutor managed to produce a copy of Frank's criminal record, insofar as it was known. Bessie was surprised by what she learned that afternoon, as the district attorney detailed her husband's previous offenses. The record began in May 1914, when Frank had been arrested as Harry Sevilla, in Fresno, California, on charges of contributing to the delinquency of a minor; he had served ninety days in the county jail. The next known crime occurred in August 1919, when, as Frank Gilmore, he had been arrested in Sacramento, on a charge of embezzlement. The judge asked for clarification. "Apparently," said the prosecutor, "the accused managed to steal a truckload of fur coats from a place where he was employed." Frank somehow finagled probation on the embezzlement charges (Fay, Bessie learned later, had hired a well-connected lawyer) and was ordered to remain in the state. But he didn't. Less than two years later he was picked up under the name Walter Saville in Seattle as a fugitive from justice, and returned to Sacramento. Once he was back in California, the sentencing judge revoked his probation and gave him ten years in San Quentin. He was paroled after two years of hard labor.

"We believe," the prosecutor said, "that there may be other records for Mr. Laffo under other names in different jurisdictions. It is also likely that this defendant has committed other confidence game and embezzlement crimes—and perhaps crimes of a more serious nature—elsewhere in this state or country without being detected, or perhaps has fled proper arrest. He is obviously a man adept at wielding numerous aliases. We, in fact, are not certain of his real name, even at this time. We recommend a lengthy sentence. Though this was not a terribly serious crime, Harry Laffo is a man clearly given to criminal behavior, and if nothing else, we would like to hold him long enough for other states to run a record on the names that we have and see if he's wanted under any other charges."

Judge H. E. Munson sentenced Harry F. Laffo to five years in the Colorado State Penitentiary. Seeing the devastated look on her husband's face, Bessie found herself feeling more pity for him than anger. He looked like a crushed man, and for the first time she saw that he was already an old man. "This is outrageous," she thought. "He has already paid for his other crimes, and these small-town nobodies are railroading him to puff up their own measly feathers."

After a few days, Bessie came to the difficult decision that she could not stay in Colorado while Frank served his sentence at the penitentiary at Canon City. She didn't feel equipped to support herself in a strange place and take care of two small children at the same time. She took Frankie and Gary and, right after the New Year, headed back to her parents' farm in Provo to wait for her husband while he did his time in prison.

I HAVE IN MY POSSESSION A COPY OF MY FATHER'S Colorado Department of Corrections records. There isn't much to the file, though the little that is there tells a fair amount, at least as far as my father is concerned. For example, the file contains documented confirmation of his use of several pseudonyms, a criminal record that spanned at least a quarter century, and the implicit suggestion that he may have been involved in other unknown or unsolved mysteries.

Beyond that, the records are of value to me for two other reasons. First, these are not merely the earliest documents I have been able to find regarding Frank Gilmore; they are, in fact—aside from his death certificate and listings in various city and telephone directories—the only hard information I have ever been able to find regarding my father's life on this earth. None of his school records survived, he never served in the military, and his employment history cannot be verified. Not even his tax or Social Security records can be found.

The other value of these prison files for me is that they contain the earliest photo I have ever seen of my father's face. It is not a particularly young face. He was about fifty-one when this mug shot was taken (Colorado State Prison #22470), and with his false teeth missing and his ruffled, prematurely gray hair, he looks much older, more like a man of sixty. I try to read what's in his face. I can't learn much, of course, about his secrets or the source of his dread from this picture, but I can plainly see that deep sorrow and a difficult courage were fighting for possession of him on that day in early 1942. He looks like a guilty man who cannot understand his own crimes and who fears that worse consequences are coming his way.

My brother Frank thinks that I have my father's looks, but I have never seen the resemblance. When I see this photo, though, I am reminded of something I would like to forget: I recall seeing my face in the mirror one evening a few years ago, after several hours of drinking and probably crying. I believed on that night that I had lost my last chance for the sort of happiness that I might gain from having my own family—that I had lost my heart for such a dream and would now have to live without the dream. If I did have kids at this point, I feared I would end up committing the same arrogant error my father had committed: waiting too late in life to have children that I would never live long enough to love and protect properly. I hated realizing that truth about my life and I hated seeing knowledge of it on my face—it made me look empty and old and ugly—and I never wanted anyone in the world to see me with that look.

That is close to the look that the prison photographer caught on Frank Gilmore's broken face the day he was taken away from his family and, for all he knew, cut off from his future as well. He had no idea, of course, that fifty years later one of his sons would see that photograph and discover something of himself and his inheritance in it.

It is funny. For years I think I was as close to my father as anybody has ever been—as my mother said, I was the only one in the family who still loved him at his death. Though I would spend my adolescent years living with my mother, it was my father—more than anybody else—who raised me, and it was my father I felt safe with. But now when I look at this picture of his face, I think of the things he did to my mother and brothers during this time and the time to come. I try to reconcile my sense of him, and the sanctuary I felt in his presence, with his brutality and his abandonments of his other children. I cannot understand how a man who could be so loving could also leave a baby of his on a park bench while he went off to try and pass a bad check—because that is what truly happened on that day in Atlantic, Iowa, when he lost custody of Gary to a state orphanage. I cannot believe that man was my father, that I once loved him more than anybody else in my world. That I still love him, because I don't know how not to.

My father feels so close, and yet so far. He's the biggest enigma in this history, and I'm worried that if I can't solve him—if I can't uncover his secrets and explain his fears—I have no right telling this story. Maybe to know my father, I'm going to have to examine my own heart and face up to the part of him that dwells there. At the same time, *my* greatest fear is that I am too much like the man, that I already own his sins.

BACK IN PROVO, BESSIE'S PARENTS LET HER STAY in the shack out back, while George roomed with Uncle Charley, next door. Will and Melissa weren't thrilled to have their black-sheep daughter back home. They had little money as it was, and they figured they had already finished raising and housing all the children they were going to raise. Even the young twins, Ada and Ida, were now married and living away from home. Bessie had been one of the first to leave the Browns' household, and it seemed to them that she had thumbed her nose when she took her leave. Then, she went on to marry a non-Mormon man she knew too little about—inarguably a criminal, as her father had surmised—and now she was back to make a nest at the home she had once spurned, while she waited for her husband to be released from prison. Plus, she had done all this without regard for the shame that she now brought to their home. The Browns didn't think of themselves as petty-minded, righteous types who would hound a man for small mistakes; they had seen many Mormon boys take missteps over the years, and they had seen how a mix of swift punishment and loving forgiveness had helped redeem these men. But to their way of thinking, there was nothing small about Frank Gilmore's mistakes, and there was likely no redeeming him. He had violated the trust of his wife and endangered the welfare of his children with his repeated crimes, and he apparently had no regard for the basic laws of society. He was a sordid man, they decided—a man whose evil ran much deeper than their gullible daughter suspected. Will and Melissa Brown didn't like anything about Frank Gilmore, and neither did anybody else in their family. "I was afraid of him," Bessie's little sister Ida would say, years later. "I'd hide whenever he was around. I didn't even like to look at him."

Bessie felt the family's damnation enwrap her, almost as if sentence had been passed on her as well. She felt humiliated by her husband's actions, and she hated being relegated by her parents to the backyard, like some bad animal. It wasn't long before all the rancor—the censure she felt from her family and the disappointments of her still-young marriage—began to churn inside her, and her pain and resentment melded into rage. She and her mother would get into fierce shouting matches about the mess of Bessie's life, and Bessie would say nasty reciprocal things about the hypocrisy of her sisters and the meanness of her father. Melissa couldn't stand it. "If you are going to dare talk that way about your own kin," her mother said, "godly people who have prayed for you out of the love and charity of their hearts, then you can go and sit by yourself out back. I will not allow you to speak that way about your family in my home."

Bessie stormed back to the shed where she slept with her children and slammed the door behind her. She looked at the paltry furnishings around her. Broken-down chairs and tables, a dilapidated bed—things she couldn't even call her own. She thought about her sisters in their nice homes with their new furnishings, and she hated everything about her life that had brought her to this disgrace. My brother Frank, nearly three years old at the time, watched his mother's movements with a learned fear. Bessie picked up a bowl from the table and hurled it against the wall. Then she picked up a chair and threw it at the door. The smashing sounds woke Gary, and he began to cry. Bessie yelled at him to stop, which only made him wail louder. She became livid and turned to Frankie. "You make him shut up," she shouted. "Make him shut up!" Frankie went over and tried to hush his baby brother—patting him lightly on the head—but Gary kept crying. Bessie grabbed a pillow off the bed and began to slam Frank across the face with it, accompanying each blow with the same imperative: "YOU-MAKE-HIM-SHUT-UP." She kept hitting Frank with the pillow until he ran outside, his mother on his heels. Frankie fell on the ground and lay there crying, covering his head, while Bessie pounded him, over and over. Later, he told me it wasn't the hitting that bothered him so much; it was Bessie's screaming, her frantic craziness.

She beat him until the noise of his crying brought her half-deaf mother outside, to demand that she stop. "If you don't quit hitting these children," she said, "I'm going to take them away from you." Then Melissa gathered Frankie and Gary and took them into the warmth of her home. She dried Frankie's tears and fed him cookies and rocked Gary at her breast, while Bessie sat in the shack out back, crying alone, without her children or her parents.

These beatings of the babies became common, my brother Frank recalls. One time, when Bessie and her mother were arguing, Frankie interrupted, asking them to stop. "I don't even love you anymore," Bessie told Frankie, and then shoved him. Frankie was off balance and fell and hit his head hard against the wall. Seeing the dazed, scared look on her little boy's face, Bessie knelt and cradled him, petting his blond hair. "Oh, Frank, I really *do* love you," she said, crying. "I'm so sorry, baby. I'm so sorry."

Melissa felt she had seen enough. "That's it, Bessie. We're just going to have to take these kids away from you. We can't stand by and watch this anymore."

Bessie dressed Frankie and Gary and fled the farm that day. Later that night, her baby sister Ida found Bessie wandering the streets of Provo, carrying Gary in one arm and leading Frank by the hand. Ida and her husband Vern loaned Bessie twenty-five dollars and got her a room for a couple of nights at the City Center Motel, not far from where they lived. It was at this same motel, a lifetime later, that Gary would commit his second murder. He walked into City Center's office and shot the motel manager in the back of the head. In the next room, only a few feet away, the man's baby boy lay sleeping. The boy was about the same age Gary had been when he stayed there, in 1942.

BESSIE'S FIGHT WITH HER MOTHER GOT SMOOTHED OVER and she was allowed to return to her shack in the backyard. On July 3, 1943, after eighteen months in prison, my father got time off his sentence for good behavior and was paroled from Canon City, Colorado, to Provo. Bessie felt relieved to see him, but Frank Gilmore came home a harder man than when his family had last seen him. My brother Frank told me: "He had been gone so long that I don't think we remembered him. He was like this new man in our lives, and he was real mean. One time we were eating dinner and I dropped my cake and, man, he just went bananas. Made me get down and pick up every crumb and gave me a few good whacks along the way. He's screaming and yelling at me and hitting me the whole time for dropping a piece of cake on the floor. Maybe he'd had a bad day, but it was an immature way to treat a little kid." After that, the boys found themselves punished for the slightest things, like not eating their food fast enough, or crying too loud, or knocking things over. Apparently, it was not difficult to get my father angry enough to hit.

My father hadn't been back a day when he learned that Bessie's parents had recently been considering proceedings to have Frankie and Gary taken away from Frank and Bessie, and turned over to the custody of the Browns. Frank and Will almost came to blows in the argument that followed, and Will ordered Frank off his property. That night, Frank and Bessie and their sons were on the road, hitchhiking their way back to Sacramento. If Frank hadn't arrived when he did, Bessie realized, they might have lost their sons to her parents and the dull life of their farm. The thought made her feel new hate throughout her veins.

AFTER MY PARENTS GOT BACK TO CALIFORNIA, Frank wanted to join up and fight the Nazis, but he was too old, plus there was the matter of his criminal record. Instead, my father took jobs working as a ship fitter in various ship plants and steel yards. For the rest of the war, that was the family's life: Bessie and Frank would move into some place where there was a war project going on and both would work until the project was finished or until Frank got too restless being in one place. Then, on December 12, 1944, my mother bore her third boy, Gaylen Noel Gilmore, in Los Angeles. Gaylen was born with dark brown, almond-shaped eyes and an unceasing smile, and my father quickly formed a special love for him. It was as if, overnight, the novelty of the other boys wore off for him.

Then came the end of the war. My mother said that when the facts of the Nazis' atrocities against the Jewish people were revealed, my father sat and cried into the night. Even though he was Catholic, he believed himself to be partly Jewish, because of the Houdini rumor. I remember that years later, when Adolf Eichmann was found and arrested for the crime of engineering the S.S.'s death camps, my father was elated. He would sit in his large easy chair and watch the news of Eichmann's trial every night, and he kept me by his side, with his arm draped around me. I remember him saying: "They're going to bury that man in a grave of his own making, six million souls deep."

With the war's end came the end of Frank Gilmore's parole. My father went back to his occasional petty criminal scams, and the family went back to its vagabond life. My parents and brothers would drift from state to state and town to town for almost the duration of the 1940s.

NOT LONG AGO I WAS TALKING WITH somebody about these years when my friend said: "I can't imagine leading that sort of gypsy life for all those years. It's heartbreaking to think of those kids living that way for so long. Also, imagine your mother, living on the road with three kids and a drunk husband, and absolutely no money. What would ten years of that life do to a woman, especially one who was raised in traditional circumstances? She must have felt like the most awful of outcasts."

I have heard other friends say similar things over the years, and yet I have to be honest: I have always felt left out because I was not a part of this time of wandering. It was a vital passage in the family's history. For all the ways it may have been miserable, it united my parents and brothers in a common range of experience, which I never got to share. I was born apart from that time, and in many ways it made me an outsider among my brothers.

Earlier, I asked if my family had ever been a real family. Did they share in recreational activities, did they attend church together? The answer is, no, they did not. Here are some of the types of experience that my family shared instead:

Once, when my parents were working at the shipyards in San Pedro, California, there was a local dining room that provided cheap meals for the poor and government employees. Frank would often take the family there for dinner. One night, the eatery was serving spaghetti and meatballs, and an older man, a vagrant, was making the rounds of the tables, eating the food that others left behind. When the guy got around to my brother Frankie's plate, he snatched a meatball without asking and started to eat it. My father flipped. "You crazy son of a bitch," he yelled. "You *like* spaghetti?" Frank Gilmore took his plate of spaghetti and shoved it in the man's face. Then he grabbed the man and began using his face to mop up spaghetti on all the other nearby plates. The cooks came out from back and pulled Frank off the man, and then told him to get himself and his kids out of there and never come back. When they got home, Frank gave Bessie some money and said: "Here. Go back down there and feed the boys, but watch that Guinea son of a bitch. He loves spaghetti."

Another time, in an Oakland hotel room, my father decided to reenact his famous pyramid of chairs, from his days as an acrobat in the circus. He pulled a dining table over to the center of the room, piled its chairs on top, plus a couple of end tables and upright ashtrays and flower stands, and then proceeded to climb his self-built tower while my brothers watched excitedly. The whole time, Bessie kept saying, "Now, Frank, be careful." Frank managed to make it to the top. He stood up, spread his arms in triumph, and then, of course, the whole construction toppled, furniture and father flying in all directions. Frank landed hard on his back, staring blankly at the ceiling. Bessie and the boys leaned over him. Bessie shook him and said: "Frank, are you okay? Speak to me, Frank." In reply, Frank said: *"Ooooooooh."*

The noise had brought the hotel manager to the door, and she was not happy when she saw the broken chairs and the sprawled man. "I'm sorry," she said, "but you people will have to leave. This is a respectable place. We can't have this kind of commotion."

Bessie pointed at the prone drunk on the floor, who was now moaning louder and had progressed to saying, "I think I'm dying."

"How can we leave," said Bessie, "with my husband in that condition?"

"You might have thought of that," said the manager, "before your husband decided to throw himself around the walls of my hotel room. If you aren't out of here within the half hour, I'll call the police and have you put out."

Somehow, Bessie got her children and drunken husband packed and out on the sidewalk. It took her the better part of an hour to get everybody the four-block distance to the bus depot. She would walk the bags ahead a few feet, go back and get the boys and have them watch the bags and the baby, then go back and gather her husband, who would have fallen asleep on the sidewalk by that point. So it went, until they reached the depot. Bessie had just enough money to get them all to Sacramento and Fay's place.

When it came time to board the bus, Bessie led the boys on and then went back to get Frank, who stumbled and moaned coming up the bus steps.

The bus driver said, *"Hey,* lady, you can't bring that man on here. He's drunk."

Bessie looked at the driver, looked at her husband, who was already falling asleep on the bus steps, then sat down next to Frank and started to bawl her head off, telling the driver her sob story.

Either the driver softened or he got tired of hearing it. "Okay, okay," he said. "You can bring him on as long as you keep him quiet. If he creates any disturbances, he's out on the side of the road."

Bessie agreed, wiped away her tears, and dragged her husband to his seat. He passed out immediately and was quiet the whole trip to his mother's house.

That was one of the better nights. Other evenings the family ended up sleeping in vagrants' missions, flophouses, in depots or Salvation Army shelters. Sometimes they had a car of their own, sometimes they rode buses and trains, often they hitchhiked. My brothers grew up around desperate strangers throughout this time—people who had lost everything, people who were mad or drunk or violent, or all three. They saw people stabbed, and they saw people die of hunger and sickness.

Sometimes my father would say he was going to the store and then not come back for weeks. My mother would go to a local church and beg the bus fare to take her and her sons on to the next town, or back to Provo. It was like that day after day, for the better part of a decade.

You might think all this sounds heartsickening and damaging, and no doubt it was. Just the same, I would have given anything to have been a part of that time.

ALL THROUGH THESE YEARS, the mythical *something* stayed on Frank's tail. My mother recalled one of the times she actually saw the face of one of those who pursued my father.

It was an early summer evening, in 1946, in Sacramento. Frank and Bessie had taken the boys to a diner near downtown, and they were seated in a booth, having dinner. Bessie saw a tall, thin man with slicked-back hair walk in and take a seat at the counter. He ordered a cup of coffee, then swiveled around on his stool and stared at Frank. The man was dressed nicely—he had on a cashmere overcoat and a fresh fedora—but he had a mean countenance, and he was definitely looking at Frank as if he knew him. Bessie nudged Frank's arm. "There's a man at the counter watching you," she said.

Frank glanced up at the stranger, then quickly looked away. "Stop looking at him," he said. "Pretend you don't see him." She could see Frank begin to break out in a sweat. After a few minutes, he got up. "I'm going to the rest room," he said. Bessie and the man in the overcoat watched as Frank walked into the back. After a few moments, the stranger followed him. A minute later, the man came back, hurriedly paid his bill, gave Bessie a glare, then left. The look the man had sent her spooked her for days.

Bessie waited for Frank to return from the rest room, and then waited some more. She thought: Is he lying in there, hurt or dead? She asked the man behind the counter to go and make sure her husband was okay, since he'd been gone so long. The waiter returned to say that nobody was there; that the window had been opened and it looked like somebody might have climbed out of it, and he sure hoped nobody was trying to skip out on their dinner tab.

Bessie paid the bill and took the boys back to the hotel. Frank wasn't there. She waited for a while and then went over to see Fay. Her mother-in-law listened to the story of what had happened and shook her head. "Bessie," she said, "I don't think you should be here right now. I haven't much money but I'll give you what I can, and then I want you to go back to your parents' home in Provo. That's where Frank will look to find you. I don't think he'll be coming back here right away."

"What's going on, Fay? What is this all about?"

"I can't tell you, Bess. I don't know enough for sure to tell you. But I don't think you should stick around here at the moment."

Bessie got the boys ready to travel again. There wasn't enough money to make it all the way to Provo. They took a bus as far as Reno, then started hitchhiking from there to Utah and saved what money they had left for food.

A couple of days later, Bessie and her sons were stuck along the highway in Humboldt County, Nevada, trying to thumb a ride. They were miles past the last place to eat and many miles from the next. They were weary, and the kids were crying from all the walking and from hunger. "Boys," said Bessie, "I want you to kneel down with me and we'll pray. God won't let us down."

The four of them knelt by the roadside, and Bessie asked for God to deliver them from their hunger and their plight. When she opened her eyes, she looked down the road and saw a man a few hundred yards away, walking their way. As he approached, my mother saw that he was about medium height, plain-faced, bald on top. Looked almost like a monk. When he got up to my family, the man held out a small paper bag to my mother. "Here, lady," he said, "would you like some sandwiches and fruit and cupcakes? Some stranger gave them to me on the highway a while back, but I've already eaten and I'm not hungry."

"Oh, thank you, mister," said Bessie, and broke down crying. "We've been so hungry and so alone."

The man placed the bag into her hands. He patted her on the shoulder and said: "Things will be all right, ma'am. You and your boys will be fine." And then he resumed walking down the road.

Bessie took the sandwiches out of the bag and broke them into small parts for her and her sons. She looked down the road, but she could no longer see the man. She looked the other way, but he wasn't there either. Gone.

She decided then that the man must have been one of the Three Nephites. In the Book of Mormon, there was a story about three of Jesus's American disciples, whom he blessed with the gift of eternal life on earth, as he had once blessed John the Beloved. These men would remain on the continent forever, as witnesses to Christ's truth, and as ministers to the needy. According to Mormon folklore, these disciples—who were known as the Three Nephites—had been transformed into human angels and still went about in the land, often appearing themselves as the homeless and hungry, in need of care. These angels blessed those Saints who helped them, admonished or cursed those who did not, and gave aid to the lost and desperate of God's children whenever possible.

She was sure: This righteous man had been one of the Nephite angels. Perhaps he had lifted the curse she had felt fall on her from the devilish man at the restaurant back in Sacramento. Maybe this experience would make true believers out of her boys. Maybe, as the angel said, things would now be all right.

But if the stranger was an angel, the angel lied.

CHAPTER 5
SETTLING
DOWN

TIME FOR ANOTHER GHOST STORY. Then, a little later, another one.

THIS FIRST TALE OF HAUNTING takes place not long after the time the stranger scared my father at the restaurant in Sacramento. Bessie and the boys finally made it back to her parents' farm in Provo. Frank had already sent a letter there, telling her he was all right and that she should wait in Provo for him. She waited three months, and when he came to retrieve her, his behavior was the same as it had been on similar occasions. He would tell her nothing about the man in the restaurant and why he had run or where he had gone. Later, Fay would tell my mother this much: "I believe that man was one of Frank's sons, and I believe they went somewhere together to collect something that was owed them." When Bessie asked Frank about this, he replied: "Don't go sticking your nose where it doesn't belong."

When Frank came and got Bessie and the boys in Provo, it was the middle of 1946. He had some money and a car, and he said he had some jobs to do. He needed to be on the road by himself for a while, and he wanted to take Bessie and the children back to Fay's in Sacramento. Frank was worried about his mother. She was seventy-five years old now, and she had been in and out of the hospital a lot in recent years. "Maybe," said Bessie, "*you* should be the one who stays with her. Maybe she needs you close to her during this time."

"Nah," said Frank. "I wear on her nerves too easily. All she does is bark at me. She likes you and the boys much better."

So back they went to Sacramento, and Bessie, with Frankie, Gary, and Gaylen, moved into Fay's large old house on M Street. Frank stayed for a few days, and Bessie thought she saw a new warmth happen between Fay and Frank. It was the only time she had seen Fay act melancholy when it was time for Frank to leave on business. What a shame, thought Bessie. All those years Frank needed Fay, and she withheld her love. Now, when Fay finally wanted a closeness with her son, he acted aloof. It made her wonder if people's hearts ever truly came together at the same time.

Bessie and the boys took the upstairs in Fay's house, while the old woman kept her bedroom and parlor in the downstairs area. Frank had left a fair amount of money for everybody to live on, but Fay still insisted on holding her séances. Bessie sensed that these events were starting to drain more and more life from the old woman, and yet she also sensed that Fay could not live without them—that at this point she was summoning the dead as much as a way of negotiating the forestalling of her own death as anything else. Bessie still preferred to be out of the house during these sessions. She would take her sons and sit in McKinley Park until the sky grew dark, then sometimes she would give Frankie and Gary the change for a movie, while she sat waiting at the café with Gaylen. Once in a while, though, Bessie would simply keep the boys upstairs at Fay's home while the séances went on below. It gave her the creeps to be there at those times—there were moments when she could feel invisible presences moving through the house around her—but she didn't always like being away from Fay at night, given the old woman's health.

Finally, there came a night when Fay told Bessie that she would be conducting a séance that was a bit unusual. She had a special dispensation, Fay explained, to contact a spirit that had died under the shameful suspicion of murder, and she told Bessie to take the boys to a movie that night and stay out late.

When my mother and brothers came back in the late hours of the night, she found Fay in her wheelchair in the kitchen, looking paler and shakier than Bessie had seen her look before. It seemed to my mother that there was an air of unease about the place that night, that there was, in fact, a smell of something old and wretched in the air. After putting the boys to bed, Bessie slowly got Fay into bed. As she drew the night covers over the old woman, she said, she saw Fay wearing an expression that she had never shown before: a look of utter fear and helplessness.

A few hours later, Bessie Gilmore left that house dragging her three sons behind her, and she never saw Fay alive again. It wasn't until almost two generations later, long after Gary's death, that my mother would tell me the full story of what she claimed had taken place on that ghost night.

Sometime in the hours after midnight, she heard movement in the house. At first it alarmed her, then she remembered that my father had called a day or two earlier to say that he would probably be coming to retrieve her soon, and it was his custom to come in late, drunk and stumbling. She fell back asleep, hoping he would leave her alone when he came to bed. A little while later, she awakened again—this time to an intimate touch. At first, she told me later, it was a gentler touch than usual for my father, and still half-asleep in the darkness, she pressed up against him. And then, this hand that had pleased and hurt her in so many ways over the years touched her in a manner that no man had ever touched her before, and she was outraged. She pushed away and opened her eyes—and what she saw, she said, what had tried to caress her so shockingly, was not my father. It did not even look truly human, though it bore a distinctly hungry leer on its face.

Bessie moved fast—faster than she had ever moved before. She pulled free and ran into the hallway, calling for Frank and Gary. It was there that she met her second shock. Moving slowly toward my mother, her white hair flowing down her shoulders like a wild horse's mane, was Fay, looking entranced and muttering in a low, frightened voice. Fay—who had been an invalid for all the years my mother had known her—had somehow made her way to the upstairs hallway and was walking toward Bessie. At first, my mother was more furious than shocked. Had Fay been faking her debility all this time? But then Fay's words froze my mother's anger. "Bessie," she said, "you must leave here. You must leave this house now. It knows, Bessie—*it knows who you are.*"

Then, my mother told me, Frankie was in the hallway, grabbing my mother's hand, pulling her toward his bedroom. He was crying and pointing toward the door, saying, "Mommy: *Gary*. Mommy: *Gary*." Again, she moved fast. When she entered the bedroom, she saw the same figure that had been in the bed with her, bending over Gary, staring into my brother's eyes. Bessie was terrified but she reached over and swept Gary from the bed, and then she grabbed my other brothers and left the house. My mother and the boys spent the night in a bus depot. She was worried about Fay, but there was no way to get her to leave the house. Besides, she figured, Fay knew how to handle spirits.

Bessie checked herself and the boys into a nearby hotel the next day. She visited and helped Fay in the daytimes but would not stay at the house anymore after dark. A couple of days afterward, my father returned and had a good laugh at the ghost story. A short while later the family moved to San Diego, where my father took a job as a construction worker. On Christmas Eve 1946, my father received a letter: Fay had been returned to the Sacramento County Hospital—which she had been in and out of for the last few years—and died there on December 15. At seven-thirty that evening, her heart just stopped. Shortly after that, Gary started having nightmares. They were always the same dream: He was being beheaded.

THE LETTER INFORMING FRANK OF FAY'S DEATH had been sent to General Delivery in San Diego, so by the time Frank received the news, Fay had already been buried. A brother-in-law, living in New York, paid $256.45 to cover the cost of her funeral and burial, and the attendance of a Roman Catholic priest to say a prayer at her grave. Robert had tried to find Frank to give him the news and inform him of the funeral plans, but he had no address and no phone number for his father.

Fay's death was apparently one of the hardest passages in my father's life. "It took him weeks to adjust to it," my brother Frank recalled. "He immediately went off on a crying and drinking binge, and he quit working. He would sit and drink and tell stories about her and call her name. Then he would sit and drink some more. I think there were a lot of things coming to the surface for him then. He felt he had always been refused by her, and he felt he had even been shut out of her death and funeral."

It was the longest drunk anybody had ever seen my father on. My mother and brothers would find him on the street, sprawled underneath a lamp, a bottle in his hand and other unopened bottles bulging in his coat pockets. They would help him stagger back to the apartment, him drinking the whole way. It went on so long that Frank spent all his money on liquor and the family had to eat each night at the Salvation Army. "He had normally been a tough man," my brother said, "but during that time he just drank and drank, and cried all the time. He had been disappointed in Fay a lot, but he really did care about her. He just couldn't handle losing her for good, is what it came down to."

One night, after coming out of a liquor store, with his wife and kids waiting outside, my father stumbled drunk on the sidewalk and, as he fell, hit his head on a steel pole. The impact cut his face up bad, and Bessie and the boys took him home and put him to bed. Three days later, when he was still lying in bed, Bessie called in a doctor. She was worried that he had hurt himself from the fall, or maybe had poisoned himself from all the alcohol. The doctor took some urine and blood samples and came back with his report: If Frank Gilmore kept drinking at this rate, he would be dead within a year or two. He had destroyed too much of his liver to remain a regular user of alcohol.

The advice managed to take hold on my father. He stopped drinking more or less on that day, and though there were a few lapses in the years that followed, he never returned to the heavy binges that had been a hallmark of his behavior for so long. This should have been good news, but there was a drawback: For all his clumsiness and stupidity as a drunk, Frank had also always been fairly kind-spirited during his binges. Those were the times he would tell stories about people in show business, about making and losing money, about his days with the circus and his feats as an acrobatic clown and lion tamer. He was also ridiculously generous during those bouts. He'd give his sons money for whatever toy they wanted, and he would magnanimously tell them and my mother that he had forgiven them all for whatever had been their most recent offenses against his rules and pride. It was when he was drying up that he could be a real monster. Those were the times he would beat his boys with a belt over any infraction. He was like Jekyll and Hyde, my brother recalled, except it was the drunken Frank Gilmore who seemed more civilized.

Now that my father was sober all the time, he was also meaner and more violent. Bessie had long been the object of his anger, but for the next few years, their bouts became nightmarish and brutal. My brother recalls: "I don't think we ever went two weeks during that time without some sort of wild, fist-banging fights. Many times I saw Mom with black eyes and a horribly swollen face. Man, she looked like she had been in a prizefight sometimes, battered and bruised, her lips all swollen. I saw that so many times. He would just really pound on her.

"I remember once, when I was about nine, stepping in and telling him to stop. I don't know if I must have been crazy or what, but for some reason it startled him. He just looked at me really funny that day. He couldn't believe somebody would say something. And he actually stopped hitting her and turned around and went back to his desk, or whatever he was doing."

Through it all, the children would watch and scream and cry. Frank recalls that Gary, in particular, developed trouble sleeping. My parents' fights got tied in with his other dreams about being executed. He would often wet the bed at night and wake up screaming, sitting in his own sweat and urine.

THERE WAS ANOTHER SIDE EFFECT to my father's newfound sobriety: He became less agitated about traveling all the time. He now started staying put in one place longer than a few weeks. This was fine with Bessie. She had long been weary from all the migrations. She wanted a home and possessions, like the ones her sisters had back in Utah. She also wanted to see what it would be like for the boys to have a stable life—to spend a whole grade year in the same school and be able to develop some uninterrupted friendships. This became a dream for my mother.

In 1948, my family moved to Portland, Oregon, and set up residence at a housing project just north of the city. Frank had come up with an idea for a publishing venture: He would collect all the various statutes and regulations regarding the construction and development of residential and commercial property in the city of Portland and the outlying county of Multnomah, rewrite them into a readable language, and then publish them in a handy guide, full of advertising from contractors, builders, and architects. The publication would be distributed by the advertisers to their clients, and by the city and county's official licensing departments to prospective developers and builders. The idea attracted advertisers quickly, and Frank was raising hundreds of dollars in revenue each week—more steady income than the family had ever seen. After he accumulated several thousand dollars, Frank told Bessie it was time to move on again and try the same idea in another town. They could make a lot of money real fast this way, he said.

It was one of those times that Bessie Gilmore put her foot down.

"No," she said. "You could actually *do* this book. You have everything you need to make it work. You have advertisers who trust you, you have the city's endorsement, and you have the skill. This is your best idea, Frank, and it is your creation. It doesn't have to be something you do just once: You could publish it every year or every other year and make good, regular money with it. We could finally have a home. If you do this book legitimately here, I'll help you with it, and if you want to take it to other places later, I'll support you in that too. But if you hundred-percent on this one and run off with the money so that none of us can ever come back, then I may as well stay here with the boys. I'm tired of all the running."

Frank didn't like ultimatums, but he *did* like Bessie's idea of making the book an annual event. In 1949 Frank Gilmore published his first copy of the *Building Codes Digest* and, with the money he raised, made the down payment on a small house on Crystal Springs Boulevard, in southeast Portland. It wasn't much of a home: two bedrooms, small yard, on the city's industrial fringes—more a wasteland than a neighborhood. Not quite the big, handsome house that Bessie dreamed of, but she realized that Frank was still too skittish for anything that ambitious. Frank and Bessie put a fence around the yard, bought a dog, and bought a brand-new Pontiac. They put the boys in school, and come Christmas time, they put up a tree and bought a Nativity scene. It was my family's first real home, after a decade of marriage and three children, and it was the closest to a conventionally happy time they would ever know.

Frank's son Robert was now an army lieutenant, stationed at Ft. Lewis, one hundred and fifty miles away, near Tacoma, Washington. Robert now had a wife of his own and three children—two girls and a boy. He started bringing his family down every couple of weeks to visit his father's family, and sometimes made the trip alone. Robert liked the changes he saw taking place in his father. The two of them were getting along better these days. They could talk to each other for more than ten minutes without the bitter recriminations and suspicions of a few years before. One day, Robert—who aspired to a career as a professional photographer—gathered my parents and brothers in the backyard of the home on Crystal Springs and took a picture of them all together. It is perhaps my most treasured artifact of my family. Separately, everyone in the picture is in the role that would fit him or her best in life. My father looked no-nonsense, my mother looked like this was not a fun moment, my brother Gaylen wore a darling and irresistible smile, and Gary was already rehearsing his menacing stare. It is my brother Frank, though, who has the most fitting expression of any of them: a goofy, clownish smile that says, *Isn't this ridiculous—all of us posing like a real family?* Nobody in the photo is touching anybody else. And of course, I'm not there, I'm not in this picture yet. In fact, I never would be. This is the closest thing to a family portrait we would ever have. There would never be a photo taken of all of us together.

But not all the family's changes were good. There was, for example, the matter of the new dog. According to my mother, the dog was half Alaskan husky, one quarter chow, and one quarter German shepherd. It had been bought as Gary's dog, and he had named it Queen. The dog ended up like its owner, in more ways than one: She started as something small and harmless and became vicious and deadly. Originally, the dog had been one of those things my father wanted and my mother strongly opposed. After it became a part of the family, my father turned against it and began to punish it, while my mother fought to protect it. My father's favorite disciplinary trick was to roll up a newspaper like a baseball bat and beat the animal with it. "He beat the dog for the same reason he beat anything," my brother Frank said. "What reason did he need?" The dog took it until it got old enough not to take it, then it turned on my father. It was only my mother's ability to command Queen that saved Frank Gilmore from being severely hurt.

Queen kept her distance from my father, but she was devoted to Bessie and my brothers. Frank and Gary used to take the dog for walks all the time in the neighborhood, and if other kids gave them trouble, or any other dogs became threatening, Queen took care of them. By my mother's count, Queen attacked at least fifteen people—biting some of them savagely—and killed at least two other dogs. One time, Gary and Frank had been in mischief down the road and got a neighborhood man angry. He picked up a meat cleaver and began to chase my brothers down Crystal Springs Boulevard. My mother—who had Queen locked up in the house that day—heard her sons' cries, and when she looked out the window, she saw the man chasing them. She said that was the only time she ever purposely unleashed Queen on anybody. She opened the front door, pointed at the man, and Queen moved like a cheetah. She knocked the man down from behind, bit him all over his arms and probably would have ripped the man's throat out if my mother hadn't called her off.

It's a wonder nobody ever shot the damn animal during those days, or the people who owned it. As one of my friends once pointed out to me, the dog wasn't a pet so much as a weapon—a killer beast, to defend the family in its protective posture and keep the outside world at bay, as my father finally ran the risk of settling down.

THE DOG HAD TO MOVE INTO THE BACKYARD after I came along.

A year or two after Gaylen's birth, my mother had another baby boy, which only lived a few days or weeks and then died. I never knew anything about this child until recently, when my brother Frank told me about him. According to Frank, the baby was born, died, and was buried, and nobody ever mentioned him after that. To this day, I do not know this baby's name, or where it might have been born or died. It was one of those things that was never discussed, and had Frank not had some memory of the event, I would never have known it happened.

After that, my mother was told she could have no more children. But as she watched my father take each of her sons into the Catholic faith, she began to feel guilt for letting it happen, and she found herself wishing she had stood up more for her own religion. She wanted a child she could raise as a Mormon; my father, meantime, simply wanted another child. The two struck a deal: If my mother could safely bear one more child, my father would let her raise it as a Mormon.

I was born on February 9, 1951, at Portland's St. Vincent's Hospital. My father was sixty-one, and my mother was thirty-eight. (By the way, I was born as Michael, not Mikal. I changed the spelling in high school, and it became an affectation that stuck. For the sake of consistency, I'll keep the spelling in its current form throughout this story.)

"I remember the day you were born," my brother Frank told me a while back. "Dad came running upstairs in his shorts and said, 'Boys, I don't know how to tell you this, but you got another little brother.' I never saw him that happy, before or after."

The joy was short-lived. One day, during the time I was doing the research for this book and was talking almost daily with my brother about his memories of the past, Frank arrived at my door with a troubled look on his face. "I have something I need to tell you," he said. "I think about telling you every time I come over here. I don't want to hurt your feelings, but I have to find a way to say this."

This is the story that my brother told me:

"When they brought you home from the hospital, at first everybody was real happy, and all that. But a few weeks later, things changed. Mom was always reading these stupid medical books, and she didn't know how to interpret them. This one particular book said that if you take a new-born baby and toss it up playfully in the air, it's supposed to have a certain reaction. Move its arms in a certain way, smile and laugh in a certain way. But of course, what happens is that every baby reacts a little differently. Mom would take you and she'd toss you in the air and you wouldn't react the way that she thought you were supposed to. You were probably already so accustomed to all the hell around there that somebody tossing you in air and saying stuff wasn't likely to faze you. Anyway, Mom began to carry on. 'There's something wrong with this baby. It's not right. It's damaged.' She went on and on about this, until Dad told her to shut up about it.

"Well, one day we found her standing over your crib with a pillow. She was getting ready to put the pillow over the top of you. She was going to smother you. Dad grabbed her. She was all worked up and said something like, 'We can't let this baby live.' And Dad . . . he just knocked the hell out of her. He beat her up real bad and told her never to try it again. We were all there when it happened, me, Gary, and Gaylen.

"I have to admit, from that day on, I never felt quite the same toward her."

When Frank got to the end of his story, I could see that the telling of it had shaken him. It was hard for me, though, to connect to the instance emotionally. It seems almost certain that what was tormenting my mother at the time of this episode was postpartum depression—the chemically-based form of severe depression that can sometimes follow a pregnancy. But given the era, and given my father's inclinations, there wasn't much chance that Bessie would get the proper diagnosis or help. Instead, she got a savage beating.

I realize now that this episode was crucial to much of what would follow and the relations that I would form to my parents. It was a large part of the reason that my father kept me close to him over the years, and it turned me into a central issue in the growing war between my parents. And though I feel nothing specifically about that moment—I do not feel horrified or angry that my mother might have smothered me—I realize that much of the fear I would later feel about her had been created by the possibilities of that moment. I remember that my father often accused my mother of some shameful form of craziness and that these accusations would hurt her so visibly that I felt sorry for her. But the charges would also inflame her so much that the rage she displayed seemed to affirm my father's perceptions, and I became deeply afraid of the madness I thought I saw in her face.

My father later used the incident as an excuse to renege on his promise that my mother could raise me as a Mormon. "The day he's baptized a Mormon, I'll throw you both out on the street."

"And the day you make him into another Catholic," my mother said, "I'll knife your evil heart in your sleep." Between those two arguments, I never saw the inside of a church until well past my father's death.

FRANK'S *BUILDING CODES DIGEST* WAS A SUCCESS in Portland for two years running, and then he published a profitable Seattle edition. But even though he was dividing his time between two cities, the regularity of it all probably felt too much like capitulation to him. Frank wanted to pull up roots one more time and move back to the place where he and Bessie had first started: Salt Lake City. Bessie was furious at the idea. The family was finally settled, the kids were in school and had good friends— why disrupt all that? Besides, she had no desire to return to Utah. She didn't want to live around her snotty sisters and deal with all their talk of one-upmanship regarding their husbands and fine homes, and she had no desire to be subject again to her parents' judgments.

Frank didn't care. He had an old partner back in Salt Lake that he thought could really make Utah sales soar. Also, he thought all the bad blood between him and Bessie's parents would be in the past, now that he had a successful and legitimate business.

Bessie thought the truth was something else: Frank had simply not stopped running from his past yet. Sitting in one spot too long, he got sore from looking over his shoulder to see who might be catching up.

In the spring after my birth, my parents sold the home on Crystal Springs Boulevard and packed the car for the trip to Utah. At Frank's insistence, Bessie placed Queen with some next-door neighbors. She knew that the woman drank heavily and could act mean, so Bessie warned her that she should never whip the dog. Queen gave my mother a rueful look when she walked away, and bayed at her. It tore Bessie's heart. She hated leaving Queen. She had never loved an animal before.

Frank and Bessie fought the entire way to Salt Lake City—so persistently that Frankie, Gary, and Gaylen would sit in the back seat with their fingers in their ears, making mocking faces. Then my father would catch them from the rearview mirror and turn around and slap the laughs off their faces. A thousand miles of arguing and slapping.

My mother, however, did get one advantage out of the trip. On June 7, 1951, my family pulled into Elko, Nevada, and on that day, in a simple ceremony with a township justice of the peace, my parents were finally, lawfully married. They never let on to any of the kids about the belated event until my mother told Frank about it in the last few months of her life. When Frank told me, I was skeptical—I couldn't imagine my mother as somebody who could have so long tolerated an "unlawful" marriage— and then I located a copy of the marriage certificate. "It looks like we were all born bastards," I told Frank, when I showed him the document. We had a good laugh over that one.

"Jesus," said Frank, "what a thing to realize about your life, this far along."

IN SALT LAKE, MY PARENTS SETTLED INTO a small three-bedroom house on the fringe of the city. It lay close to the train tracks, which more or less divided the city. On the north side lived the good people—the Mormons and the acceptable Gentiles. South of the tracks was where the vagrants, immigrants, minorities, and hopelessly poor settled—in those days, a spacious, bleak no-man's-land. My family lived just a few blocks north of the tracks. I think my father liked the idea of living on borders. Maybe it gave him the sense that all he had to do was cross the train tracks and he would be again safely lost in America's hinterlands. The family settled in, and promptly my father hit the road, selling advertising throughout Utah and Idaho for his new book.

It didn't take long for Bessie to figure out that her new home was haunted. She began to feel malevolent presences near her, and she heard noises, both day and night, that made no sense. She wasn't the only one; the boys, too, felt these things breathing in their faces in the dark. After a while, my mother noticed that most of the odd occurrences seemed to take place in the rooms and space surrounding the family's newest and youngest member—me. There were times when I would be alone in the bedroom, I was told later, and my mother and brothers would hear me babbling away, and they could swear they heard somebody talking back to me. But when they came into the room, it was just me, chattering and pointing. This went on for some time, and then one night, when my mother was home by herself with me, she heard the second voice again, this time more distinctly than before. She made her way quietly toward the room, and when she entered, she saw a face much like the one she had seen those years before at Fay's, and she swore it was reaching out to kiss me. She yelled, and then it was gone. When my father came back to town, my mother tried to tell him about these things, but he wouldn't take any of it seriously. He'd been around "hauntings" his whole life, he said, and he had never seen or known of an instance that could be called the real thing.

"Chances are," he said, "all you're hearing in the night is the sound of a mouse. If we got a cat, you'd be rid of your spooks."

"I *saw* the damn thing, Frank," my mother said. "If it was a mouse, then it was a *big* mouse, with a face from hell."

It was also during the Salt Lake stay that, according to my mother, Gary first started to go wrong. He and Frank Jr. missed the friends they had made back in Portland, and the new companions that Gary found were ones that Frank Jr. wanted to have nothing to do with. The new friends were rough boys, who made a point of swearing, smoking, stealing, and talking about guns. But whatever their bad habits, Gary aspired to outdistance them. Frank remembered finding him once with some kids, playing Russian roulette with a pistol. It was one of the few times that Frank told on his brother. Gary insisted the gun wasn't loaded, but he got a whipping anyway. Another time, Gary got into a fracas with one of the men in the neighborhood. The man chased the eleven-year-old boy, and when he caught him, he started to beat Gary's head against the wall of a garage. Frank Jr. ran and got my mother. She leaped a fence, grabbed the man, and began pounding *his* head against the garage, until neighbors had to pull everybody apart. Later, when she told my father, he went and found the man, bent him backward over a sawhorse, and beat the hell out of him. I think we always had a little trouble getting along with our neighbors.

For months during this period, Gary was stealing things and hiding them in the garage. It was mostly little things—packages of cookies, yo-yos, comic books—that he pilfered from the Big C grocery store down the street. He didn't seem to be doing it for any particular reason. He just stole and stockpiled the things and then would show them off to his friends and my brother. Somehow, Frank Sr. found out about it, and the shit hit the fan. He beat the hell out of Gary and made him put all the stolen objects in boxes and furtively return them to where he'd stolen them. Nobody ever found out about it; no charges were pressed. My brother Frank thinks the whole thing may have scared my father more than Gary. Maybe in that moment he saw something of himself coming alive in his child, and he wanted to kill it before it grew.

In the lateness and darkness of night, though, Gary was a smaller child. He would have bad dreams most nights of the week, and he would wake up, calling for my mother, swearing to her that something had been in the room with him, that he had seen it.

One night, following one of these episodes, Bessie studied Gary as he fell back asleep. Maybe he had spent too much time around Fay and her damn spirits, my mother thought. Maybe that awful ghost that night had somehow gotten inside him—or maybe the spirit that dwelled in this very house had found entry into his vulnerable soul. Something about Gary's face, as well as his recent wrongful behavior, Bessie decided, was inexplicably different.

No question about it. There was now a terrible spirit living inside her son.

ON NEW YEAR'S EVE, MY MOTHER'S FAMILY had a party at their home in Provo. My mother had known about it for weeks, but she and my father and the rest of us had not been invited. Finally they got a last-minute call and drove down to the Browns' farm. When they got there, they were treated rudely. Nobody would talk with my father, even though he had taken Bessie's parents the present of a new radio. And while others were allowed to sneak drinks of liquor that night, Frank's bottle of beer was taken away from him.

Both my brothers Frank and Gary didn't like seeing their father treated this way, and they insisted to my mother that everybody go back home. They were gone before the New Year had been rung in.

THE NEXT NIGHT, JANUARY 1, 1952, my family was seated back in the living room in Salt Lake, tired and dispirited from the trip to Provo. There were odd noises around them during the evening, and everybody seemed a bit on edge. Then a sound came from the attic—a moan that was long and mournful, like the noise of a creature caught in the agony of death. Everybody in the family gathered under the ceiling door to the attic and looked upward. Bessie turned to her husband. She said: "How would you like to go up there and have a talk with that big mouse?" Frank said nothing. He stood there with the rest of his family, staring at the place where the noise was coming from. But Bessie could see that the dark presence in the house had finally got to him too. "If we don't leave here, Frank," she said, "we're going to die under the weight of that evil thing."

The following day, my father put the Salt Lake City home up for sale.

A year or so ago, my brother Frank and I went back to the old neighborhood in Salt Lake to see if we could visit the house where we had once lived. Frank looked around the streets and walked up and down the blocks, double-checking the address we had found. He remembered the neighborhood well, he said. All the old homes were still standing, Frank pointed out, except for one. The house where we had once lived was the only one gone. Where it had stood was now flattened, barren land.

I'VE TOLD ENOUGH GHOST STORIES NOW that I should make one thing plain: All these stories came from my mother's memory or from other accounts of family legend. None of them are my own remembered experiences, except in the sense that they are part of the tormented and hyperbolic family mythology that I grew up with. I listened to my mother attentively when she told me these stories, but I think she knew that, for all the love and compassion that passed between us, I did not—in fact, *could* not—believe her ghost tales. She knew that I believed that if anything haunted us and our dreams, it was ourselves—that we did not require evil spirits to bring sins and cruelties and stupidities into our lives. We had our own history, our own dark hearts, to do that work for us.

No, I never believed in the stories of the goddamn ghosts. I did not believe that a spirit had killed my mother's sister or had crouched over Gary on that fevered night or had reached out to kiss me as a baby years later. Nor did I believe, as my mother did, that somehow that ghost had followed Gary, finally catching up with him again when he made the fateful mistake of returning to Utah in April 1976. I knew there are worse things than an inhuman touch in the night. There are memories of rage and loss and longing that are so ruinous and transforming, you can carry them to your grave before they will leave you alone. It is easy to be frightened of the unknown, and it is also easy to give superstition the power to rule you. By contrast, it is much harder to confront the real demons—the faces of all those people, those loved ones and others, who shaped your character or your history. Dealing with the memories and legacies of *those* faces, I figured, could be haunting enough. I did not need any other ghosts. But I allowed my mother her stories. She came from another time and another culture, and maybe those beliefs helped make sense of just how much had been lost or destroyed over the years.

No, I never believed any of it. I'm not even sure I believed it when, many years later, after I had tried to return to my home, I finally came face to face with something terrible in a small, dark room—something that grabbed hold of me in the worst hour of my life and said: "I *know* you: You are the last one left, and now I am coming for you." No, I told myself, this ghost is not real, this haunting is coming from someplace else, some dark place deep inside. Even then, I told myself, there were more horrible things that could be gripping me than a ghost.

But that's another story, and it is not yet time to tell it.

MY FAMILY WENT BACK TO PORTLAND, OREGON. Another miserable trip, Frank and Bessie fighting the whole way about who was to blame for the Salt Lake move in the first place. When they got back into town, Bessie insisted that the first thing they should do was to go and retrieve Gary's dog, Queen.

They pulled up to the house where they had left the dog and knocked. Nobody answered. They went to another neighbor and asked him if he knew where the dog was. "I hate to tell you this," the man said, "but Queen was shot just a couple days ago." It turned out that a few days before, when the woman who now owned Queen was drunk, she beat the dog with a belt and it attacked her in return. Queen put the woman in the hospital, so the woman had the animal shot.

Bessie cried for days over Queen's death. She could not believe that somebody had shot Gary's pet. It was as if the dog had come to embody the family's calamity—the hatred and punishing fate that she saw in store for herself and her sons. Right then, Bessie would later say, she knew what the future held.

PART THREE

BROTHERS

And a man's foes shall be they of his own household.

—ST. MATTHEW 10:36

MY FIRST MEMORY of my brother Gary goes like this:

I must have been about three or four years old. I had been playing in the front yard of our home in Portland on a hot summer day, and I ran inside to get a drink of water. When I came into the kitchen I saw my mother and my brothers Frank and Gaylen sitting at the kitchen table, and seated with them was a stranger. I remember that he had short brownish hair and bright blue eyes and that he gave me a shy smile.

"Who's that?" I asked, pointing at the stranger.

Everybody at the dining table laughed. "That's your brother Gary," my mother said. She must have seen the puzzled look on my face—the look that said, *My brother Gary? Where did he come from?*—because she added: "We've kept him buried out back next to the garage for a while. We finally got around to digging him up." Everybody laughed again.

The truth was, he had been at a reform school for boys for the last year or so, and nobody wanted to explain that to me.

For years afterward, that's how I thought of Gary: as somebody who had been buried in my family's backyard and then uncovered.

IN 1952, MY FAMILY bought another house on the outskirts of Portland, and my father returned to publishing his building codes book. In this case, the term *outskirts* is no exaggeration. The house, which was located at one end of a rural-industrial highway called Johnson Creek Boulevard, literally sat on the line that divided Multnomah County from Clackamas County. In fact, the perimeter line ran right through the bedroom in which my three older brothers slept. When it came time to decide which nearby school the boys would attend, a county official came out to examine the situation. He decided that the side of the county line the boys slept on would determine which school they would be assigned to. Gary and Frank ended up going to junior high in Multnomah County, and Gaylen wound up going to grammar school in Clackamas.

The house itself was one of those weather-wasted dwellings that my father seemed to have a mystifying affection for. It was a two-story, dark-brown-shingled place with an unfriendly-looking face, and it sat with one or two other homes between a pair of large industrial buildings that filled the night with an otherworldly lambent glow. Across the street lay the train tracks that carried the aging trolley between downtown Portland and Clackamas County's Oregon City. Just past the tracks ran Johnson Creek—in those days, a decent place for swimming and catching crawfish—and beyond that there was a large, densely wooded area. It was rumored that teenagers gathered at nights in those woods and drank and had sex in hard-to-find groves. It was also rumored that a gruesome murder had taken place there years before, and that some of the body parts from the crime had never been recovered and still lay buried somewhere among the trees.

On the far side of the woods was a lengthy range of small, cheaply-built houses that made up the poor part of a neighboring town called Milwaukie. Beyond that was an area of rolling hills, full of stately, privileged homes—the better half of Milwaukie. Up the hill behind our house was a neighborhood known locally as Shacktown, where laborers' families dwelled. Drive a few blocks past that and you would hit the old moneyed district of Eastmoreland, where you could find the state's most prestigious school, Reed College. If you were to draw two concentric circles on a map—the outer ring, a loop of wealth; the inner one, a wheel of privation—then our home on Johnson Creek Boulevard would lie at the core point of those circles. A null heart, in the inner ring of the city's worst back country.

This is the home where my first memories come from. This was also the place that we would live the longest as a family, before imprisonment and death and hatred began to sunder us.

ONCE THE FAMILY HAD SETTLED INTO ITS NEW HOME, my father became obsessed with the idea that his sons were in need of strict discipline. Maybe it was an outgrowth of all those years on the road, when the family had been without any sort of firm or dependable structure, but my father began to see the emergence of a willfulness that he did not like in his older sons and had even started to see some signs of that same boldness in Gaylen—now all of seven, and fast losing his standing as favorite son to me. Frank Gilmore could love his sons until they defied or challenged his rule. Once that happened, he treated them as his worst enemies. It was as if my father perceived any act of defiance by his sons as a denial of their love for him, and love's denial had already cost him his heart too much in his life. As a grown and strong man, he did not have to abide such a refusal from children.

The pattern of my father's temper hadn't changed all that much from the previous years when the family was on the road—that is, any infraction or displeasing act was enough to invoke a punishment—but the methods of correction had changed considerably. Instead of spankings, my father now administered fierce beatings, by means of razor straps and belts, and sometimes with his bare, clenched fists. With each blow that was thrown, my father was issuing the command that his children love him. With each blow that landed they learned instead to hate, and to annihilate their own faith in love.

"This is something you never really saw about him," my brother Frank told me one day. "When Dad got angry at somebody he knew no limits. He wouldn't have cared what he did. He would come at you with his razor strap, and he'd really bring that thing down on you. He was merciless at those times. We would end up with cuts and bruises all over us, though he was careful not to leave marks on our faces, or anyplace else where other people might see them."

Apparently the beatings were commonplace affairs—that is, if you can ever call the pounding of a child commonplace. On an at least weekly basis, my father would whip either Frank Jr. or Gary, or more likely both of them at the same time, until my mother would insist that the beating stop. Usually the punishments were the result of small matters—for example, one of the boys forgetting to mow the lawn behind the backyard tree—but just as often they seemed to occur as the result of my father's bad whims. Frank Jr. gave me an example of such an occasion. "One time," he said, "when Gary and I came home from school, Dad was hiding behind the door and we didn't even know it. We got in the door, we heard the door shut, and the next thing we knew we were getting razor-strapped across the back. He really went wild that night, because we were something like five minutes late—and I'm not kidding when I say five minutes. I don't even remember *why* we were late, maybe the schoolteacher stopped us and talked, or maybe we visited with a friend. I can't remember. I just remember he was hiding behind the door with the razor strap. We didn't even get a chance to give an explanation, and we got whacked I don't know how many times."

On another occasion, some money had been stolen off my father's desk. He gathered Frank and Gary before him and asked which of them had taken it. Frank knew Gary had stolen the money, and though he was angry at his brother for doing so, he wasn't about to tell on him. "If that's the way you want it, then you'll both get the whipping," my father said, with the logic of a gym teacher or army sergeant or some similar small-time despot. That night he doubled up the strap—it could do more damage that way—and flailed his sons until they bled through their jeans. With each thrash, he called them thieves. Later, Frank asked my father if he would still have whipped him if he'd said that Gary had stolen the money. "Of course I would have whipped you," my father said. "Nobody likes a damn squealer." That night Frank learned that, one way or another, he was bound to pay for his brother's crimes.

"When Dad would grab the razor strap and go haywire on us," Frank told me, "he wasn't talking to us about anything that we'd done wrong, nor was he telling us how we needed to improve our behavior. It was simply that we had upset him. He was angry with us and this was his way of getting revenge. He wasn't doing it to teach us anything, except possibly to fear him. That was the reason he punished us: not to make us better, but to make us sorry.

"But when you get punished like that," Frank continued, "how are you going to *be* sorry for what you did? If you were to take some guy that shoplifted a loaf of bread, and you took him out and castrated him, is he going to feel sorry about the loaf of bread, for crying out loud? He's not going to care about it. It's not going to impress him at all what he did, because he wasn't punished in a way that would make him stop and realize: Well, hey, I deprived somebody of their loaf of bread. All he's going to think is: For a lousy loaf of bread I was mutilated. He's going to have hatred. And that's what built up in us, resentment, because even as kids you know you are being overpunished for simple things. Like dropping something from the table, cleaning up the yard but not doing the immaculate job you were supposed to, or being a few minutes late from getting home from school."

Frank Jr. now believes that the beatings had as much to do with the relationship between my father and mother as with any desire to discipline rowdy children. Frank Gilmore would beat his sons until his wife intervened. She would come in and let him know that she was angry, that he had gone far enough, and then he'd start a fight with her. Frank Jr. recalls that as he was getting beat, he would pray for his mother to work up her nerve to put a stop to it. "I'd count the lashes. It would be seventeen and eighteen razor straps across the back, which was pretty fucking painful, before she'd finally get her ass up off the chair and come and say something.

"Sometimes," he added, "it felt like all the aggression was really just between the two of them. Gary and me were in the middle, waiting for one of them to pick on us, so the other one could have something to say or do. It was like they were each trying to get the attention of somebody else, and we were merely the scapegoats."

Finally, Frank found a way to endure the punishments. He discovered at a young age that the more he seemed scared or upset by a beating, the harder his father would hit him. "If you cried or screamed," Frank said, "then Dad knew he was hurting you, and it only made him go harder. So I would just cover up and just hold it in. Let him batter on me as much as he wanted. As a result, I got hit less than Gary, because Gary used to really jump and yell and scream. Dad would really go to town on him then. He would go completely off his rocker, and he just wouldn't stop. He'd keep swinging and swinging and swinging, and Gary kept yelling and crying and begging him to stop, which would only make Dad hit him harder and longer."

I suspect that what Frank means is that he simply shut down emotionally, though the psychic costs must have proved enormous. Gary, however, couldn't shut down: The outrage and unfairness of being beat that way became a sticking point in his heart. It was as if, for the rest of his life, he would be reenacting the drama of his father's punishments with every authority figure he encountered. Years later, when Gary was locked up in prison, he would go out of his way to challenge the dominance of the guards around him. Many of these men were cretinous and brutal, and they would hold Gary down and beat and kick him until his mouth was too bruised to talk and his legs were too sore to stand. Still, he would find a way to stand up and spit at them and call them the foulest names he could muster, knowing full well that they would just beat him again. He would not stop fighting the battle that he knew he could never win.

Once, a generation after their childhood, when my brother Frank was visiting Gary at the Oregon State Penitentiary, Gary told him: "The whole reason I hate authority is because it reminds me so much of Dad. Let's face it, all those senseless razor strappings the old man gave me did not keep me out of trouble, now did they?"

THOUGH I WOULD LATER see indelible signs of my father's violence, I never experienced it in the unrestricted way that my brothers did. In fact, I remember being hit by my father on only one occasion. The cause of the spanking is vague—which only goes to support Frank's belief that all you truly carry away from such an incident is the bitterness of the punishment. I think I probably did something like drawing on a wall with a crayon or sassing my mother, and my father deemed that the act called for a whipping. I remember that he undressed me and stood me in front of him as he unbuckled his belt—a wide, black leather belt with a gleaming silver buckle—and pulled it from around his waist. This whole time he was telling me what my whipping was going to be like, how badly it was going to hurt. I remember I felt absolute terror in those moments—nobody had ever hit me before for any reason, and the dread of what was about to happen felt as fearful as the idea of death itself. My father was going to *hit* me, and it was going to hurt. It seemed horribly threatening—like the sort of thing I might not live through—and it also seemed horribly unjust.

My father doubled his belt over and held it in his hand. Then he sat down on his chair, reached out and took me by the arm and laid me across his lap. The next part is the only part I don't recall. I know I got whipped and that I cried out, but I can't remember a thing about the blows or the pain, or whether it was even truly bad. All I remember is that a few moments later I was standing in front of him again, this time held in my mother's embrace. "That's enough, Frank," she said. "You've gone too far. You're not going to do to *this* one what you did to the others." I stood there, looking at my father, rubbing my naked, sore butt, crying. I remember that what had really hurt me was that I felt I had lost my father's love, that the man I trusted most had hurt me in a way I had never expected. My father was smiling back at me—a smile that was meant to let me know that he was proud with what he had just done, that he enjoyed the power and the virtue of this moment. I looked back at him and I said: "I hate you."

I know it is the only time I ever said that to him in my life, and I cannot forget what those words did to his face. His smile fell—indeed, his whole face seemed to fall into a painful fear or sense of loss. He laid his belt on his desk and sat studying the floor, with a weary look of sadness.

My mother led me out of the room and dressed my nakedness.

My father never hit me again. After that, he touched me only in love. I realize now I was the only one in the family that he saved that touch for, and to this day I still feel guilty for that singularity.

That was it—the one and only childhood beating I ever received within my family. It might have proved less memorable had it been a weekly occurrence, as it was for my brothers. At the same time, had I been beaten as much as they were—in particular, as much as Gary, whose pain and fear only seemed to gain him especially savage thrashings—there's a good chance that I also would have ended up as a man who spent his whole life preparing to pull a trigger. When I think of what my brothers went through almost every week of their childhood and young adolescence, the only thing that surprises me is that they didn't kill somebody when they were still children.

THE DIFFICULTY GARY HAD GOTTEN INTO BACK IN SALT LAKE was a fairly unremarkable sort. "He was doing stuff a lot of kids would do," said Frank. "The sort of trouble people would talk about for a couple of hours, then forget. They figured he was just a kid growing up." Chances are, Gary would have found worse trouble in Salt Lake, though he might have had to look a little harder for it. In Portland, trouble was easier to find.

By the early 1950s, Portland had been Oregon's largest and most important city for more than a century, though it was still groping in many ways to define itself. It didn't have the sort of history or ambition of other West Coast cities like Seattle, San Francisco, or Los Angeles—in fact, Portland was a town that pointedly decried ambition. The city's sense of conservatism was a carryover from its earliest days, when its original New England settlers had sought to build a place that would be a refuge of civility and comfort in the midst of the rowdy Northwestern frontier. That attitude of smugness held sway in Portland for several generations, keeping the place hidebound and insular. Consequently, Portland was largely unprepared for the influx of population and the resulting cultural change that followed the end of the Second World War. In the time we settled there, much of Portland still looked and felt like a prewar town that did not want anything to disrupt its heart of fearful pettiness.

Still, a little disruption was inevitable. The postwar sense of release— plus all the new citizenry—had temporarily forced a crack in the city's Victorian veneer. By day, downtown Portland was still a conventional shopping and business district, though like many American urban centers it was starting to lose its prominence to the outlying suburbs. By night, though, downtown Portland changed its character. Along the main drag of Broadway there was a strip of bustling bars and restaurants, and many of them stayed open all night. Inside these spots, you could find an interesting late-night social life: a mix of Portland's rich folks and aspiring bohemians, plus a colorful smattering of its would-be criminal types. In the blocks off Broadway, down toward the Willamette River, there were other all-night emporiums, if you knew where to find them. Places like twenty-four-hour movie houses, where the last thing anybody did was watch the movies. Instead, various hustlers worked the patrons, dispensing oral sex or hand jobs for a few dollars, or selling marijuana or harder drugs to the more daring customers. There were also all-night gambling dens and crowded brothels that weren't shy about servicing teenagers. I wish I could have seen this Portland. It seemed like a somewhat sordid place in those days, instead of the dull and mean town it struggled to become in later years.

The police knew about all these vice dens and tolerated them as long as there was a kickback in it for them. At the same time, they never let major organized crime get a foothold in the area, if only because they didn't want the competition. Eventually, a newspaper-led, politically-motivated morality campaign changed the city's night life forever. The all-night bars were shut down, the whorehouses were moved to the northwest corner of the city and the around-the-clock movie houses simply became cheap sleeping quarters for drunks and transients. Meantime, the city's murder rate began to grow. In short, Portland became a lot like other midsized Western towns: a place hell-bent on believing that the darkness of its nights held nothing more provocative than the protected decency of American family life.

The early 1950s were also, of course, the period that saw the rise of juvenile delinquency—the term that many people used to describe the perceived upswing in dissatisfaction and violence among American adolescents. By the middle of the decade, the adventure called rock & roll would come to signify the growing enterprise of youth rebellion, and it would upend American popular culture in ways that it still has not fully accommodated or recovered from. My older brothers were coming of age in the midst of this time, and Gary and Gaylen in particular did more than merely enjoy or consume rebellion; they brought it home. They wore their hair in greasy pompadours and played Elvis Presley and Fats Domino records. They dressed in scarred motorcycle jackets and brutal boots. They smoked cigarettes, drank booze and cough syrup, skipped—and quit—school, and spent their evenings hanging out with girls in tight sweaters, or racing souped-up cars along county backroads outside Portland, or taking part in half-assed small-town gang rumbles. Mostly, they spent their time looking for an entry into a forbidden life—the life they had seen exemplified in the crime lore of gangsters and killers—and more and more, those pursuits became dangerous and scary.

In time, I wanted to be a part of my brothers' late-night comings and goings, wanted to share in their laughter and friendship. I also remember being frightened of them. They looked deadly—like they were beyond love, like they were bound to hurt the world around them or die trying.

For Gary, none of this would end up as a simple youthful passage. It became instead a sensibility that encased him, like a creature caught in the ice of another age. Gary's ideal of badness was formed in this time, and for him it would always remain a guiding ethos.

As I SAID EARLIER, it is tempting to try to find a moment in this story where everything went wrong—an instance that gave birth to my family's devastation, and especially to Gary's. My mother held to the belief that Gary's ruin was born during the brief move to Salt Lake, and even my brother Frank believes that something crucial changed in Gary during that period. For my part, I believe that the beatings were a decisive turning point, though I also suspect the simple (and more frightening) truth is, Gary's fate was finished at about the instant in which my parents conceived him.

Gary himself, though, had his own view of the moment that made all the difference. It's a strange instance, and it took place during the first year or so that we lived on Johnson Creek. Toward the end of my brother's life, Larry Schiller—through Gary's lawyers—asked him: "Is there any one event in your early life that you remember as fateful, that might have totally changed your life?" Gary replied by telling about a time when he was around twelve or thirteen years old and was heading home from parochial school and decided to take a shortcut. He crossed over from 45th Avenue—the long, winding road that connected Johnson Creek Boulevard to the street where his school was—and made his way to the top of the hill that loomed about a block behind our house. Gary started down the hill and hit a thicket of brier bushes, full of blackberries. From the hill's top, the berry brambles had looked relatively small, but once Gary had entered them he saw they weren't small at all. Some of the briers had apparently been there for years and formed a tangle of thorns that stretched up the hill's incline, as much as thirty feet above his head. The farther down the hill Gary went, the more dense the brush became, and he saw that there was no easy path through all the overgrowth.

At first Gary might have climbed back up the hill, but he decided to push on. An hour and a half later, he was hopelessly mired about halfway through the brier patch. He thought about screaming, but it was unlikely anybody would hear him. He figured he could keep pushing on and work his way through, or he could die in this place. Hours later, Gary came out the other side, torn to pieces and bleeding. "I finally got home about three hours late," he told Schiller, "and my mom said, well, you're late, and I said, yeah, I took a shortcut."

When Schiller later related the story to my mother, she said: "And that changed the course of his life, because he figured he could get into things and get out of them? Is that it? That was a dangerous thing for him to do, and it was a dangerous thing for him to think."

Gary himself told Schiller that the story represented the point at which he became aware that he would never get afraid. "It left me with a distinct feeling," he said, "like a kind of overcoming of myself." Of course, whether he knew it or not, my brother was only telling half the truth. By talking about an overcoming of himself, Gary might have meant an ability to surmount his own fear, but I don't believe that's something he ever truly accomplished. I saw his face every day in the last week of his life. I knew how to look into his eyes, because I'd been looking into those same eyes throughout my own life, in my mirror. Those eyes would never lose their terror, not for a moment, even when they terrified other people.

The truth is, Gary wasn't talking about overcoming himself so much as he was talking about having learned to kill or silence the part of himself that needed to cry out in fear or pain. When Gary overcame himself in that manner, he finally found the power to ruin his own life and to extinguish any other life that it might take to effect that destruction.

I went back to Johnson Creek Boulevard during my recent stay in Oregon and found the area greatly changed. Almost nothing is left of the old neighborhood. The dingy, brown house we lived in is long gone, as are all the other dingy houses in the immediate vicinity. They have been torn down and replaced by sprawling industrial constructions. Maybe it's just as well. Johnson Creek was never much more than a strip of wasteland. Now it's simply another ugly city boundary road that people drive through as impatiently as possible, to get from one barren place to another. About the only thing that still survives from those days is the stretch of bramble bushes, growing down the backside of the hill above Johnson Creek. Those bushes look as primordial and fateful now as they did forty years ago, and somehow it doesn't surprise me that nobody has dared to remove them. They still stand, an ugly relic of the moment a boy realized his life was a thicket, and that no matter how much he screamed, nothing would save him from his fear.

AFTER FINISHING OFF their grammar school years at a local Catholic school, my brothers were transferred to Joseph Lane Grade School, where they attended junior high in Portland. Many of the boys who were in the same classes as my brothers would go on to kill or to be murdered. It was that kind of school, that kind of place.

"Joseph Lane had a large population," said Tom Lyden, one of the men who taught my brothers during that time. Lyden is retired these days, but back in 1952 he was a newly married young man, trying to teach hard boys. "There were nine hundred kids in the school," he told me one morning at a breakfast diner, not far from the old school, "and as far as I recall, there was only one family among those students that could be called professional—that is, where the head of the family was a doctor or lawyer or had a college education. It was largely a working-class population from out of the state, comprised of families who had come to work in the local shipyards. As a result, Joseph Lane was regarded as one of the two most difficult schools in Portland to teach. It was a physical environment. The kids were physical and the teachers were physical. We spanked kids, though I wouldn't say we were violent with them."

Lyden handed me a photograph he had taken of the first class of boys he taught at Joseph Lane. Gary is standing dead center in the group, looking off to one side, his head tilted, and framed with the backlight of the camera's flash as it radiated off the window behind him. "That's him right there, with the halo behind him," Lyden said, laughing lightly. After a moment, he continued: "My first impression of Gary was that he was a quiet boy. He had beautiful handwriting and a clear artistic ability. I think that learning came easy to him. But it wasn't long before he started getting into trouble, and then he became one of the most disruptive students I've ever seen. He had all this innate intelligence and ability, but he refused to develop it. I used to get angrier with him than any other student I had. Whenever I turned around, he was doing something to turn the classroom environment upside down."

My brother Frank remembers well Gary's misbehavior. It was something he lived with daily. "Gary was always in fights," Frank said. "He wouldn't study. He'd come to school dressed in his leather boots and leather jacket, wearing his hair like Marlon Brando. He'd sit down and go to sleep in class. Sometimes, when we were in different classes, I'd hear a disturbance in the hall and I'd know automatically. I'd hear the teacher out there dragging somebody from the room. I'd go out and it was *always* Gary that they were taking out. He was always doing something. Sleeping, showing off, telling the teacher to drop dead or something. He didn't care about anything. He would get the worse grades he could get. He thought it was cute. And there was no need for it, because Gary was a bright guy. He could have been getting the best grades. He humiliated the hell out of me at Joseph Lane. By then I had reached an age where I wasn't really interested in being a complete fool, and he was.

"One day," Frank continued, "Gary and a couple of other school toughs pantsed some guy in the school yard. They held him down and pulled his pants and shorts off him and ran them up the flagpole. I didn't see it happen—if I had, I would have got into a fight with Gary, trying to stop it—but the news of it was all over school. Gary didn't do it for any reason except to be funny. But I could see right then, there was a cruel streak developing in him. Ripping some poor guy's shorts off and running them up the flagpole, leaving the guy standing there in his buff, trying to find something to cover himself with. That wouldn't have been much fun. The guy was a nice guy. He was somebody I got along with.

"I saw this same guy on the street a couple years ago. He asked me if

I remembered that incident. I could see that Gary's little act had left its mark on him, and I still felt embarrassed that my brother had done that."

After one incident too many, Lyden either hit Gary or threatened to hit him. "Gary and I went into it, I know that much," said Lyden. "There just comes a point when you have to say to a kid, 'Okay, that's it—this is the consequence of your behavior.' "

At eleven-thirty that night, Lyden got a call from my father. He was in a rage. "Tomorrow," my father told Lyden, "when you come to school, I'm going to blow your goddamned head off."

"Strangely enough," Lyden told me, "I went to school the next day, and it didn't intimidate or frighten me. I guess I was pretty naive." Frank Gilmore didn't make good on his threat, but he did send along another message to the teacher: "Do not ever touch my youngster again. If there's any touching to be done, I'll do it."

Lyden paused and glanced again at the photo of his old class. "I remember that I always felt sorry for your brother Frank," he said, "but I never felt sorry for Gary. One night after a school dance, my wife and I were driving along and we saw Frank walking home by himself in the dark. I recall thinking that if he and Gary had been close, wouldn't they have walked home together? Frank was walking along alone that night, his head bent down, his shoulders stooped. He looked like he was carrying the weight of the world on his back, and he was just a kid. I remember thinking, 'He's the one who never gets any attention.' Gary always got a lot of attention. Much of it was negative, but negative attention is still attention."

Many years later, when Gary was on Utah's death row and was news all over the nation, Tom Lyden was following the story as closely as anyone. The day Gary was shot, Lyden felt a special pang. No matter what Gary had done, he hated to see him come to this end. That same day, he got a call from Larry Schiller in Provo, Utah. Schiller wanted to talk to somebody who could tell him something about Gary's childhood. At first, Lyden was surprised that Gary had even remembered him, but what Schiller said next devastated the teacher: Gary had told Schiller and his lawyers that Tom Lyden was the teacher he had most valued and respected. In fact, he cited Lyden as one of the few people he had reached out to for help, but my brother realized he had probably been too recalcitrant for the teacher, and he felt bad that he had let Lyden down.

"At that time in 1977," Lyden said, "I was principal at Rose City Park School, in Portland, and we had a kid there who was a real problem to us and to himself and to his school. I had wanted the two teachers involved to reach out more for this boy, but they'd had it up to here and just wanted to get rough with him and turn him over to the authorities. The day after I got the call from Mr. Schiller, we had a staff meeting about this kid and I told those teachers the story. I said, 'Yesterday, I got a telephone call about Gary Gilmore. Gary told somebody that he once had an eighth-grade teacher whom he'd held his hand out to, and that teacher didn't quite reach for it. He said he thought that perhaps that teacher could have made the difference in his life. That teacher was me. Now, what are you going to do about this youngster?' After that, they were falling all over themselves to reach for that kid.

"In all the years since then, I've never forgotten the lesson that Gary taught me," said Lyden. "I have always told teachers, 'Take all the steps that you're capable of, and then take one more. If this were your kid, you would want people to keep reaching for him.' "

I HAVE STUDIED THE picture of Gary that Tom Lyden gave me many times. No other image of my brother has ever torn my heart more or made me feel closer to him. It captures one of those few moments in Gary's life that I can readily identify with, because it's one of the few in which I can easily find myself. The first thing about the photo that strikes me is that I had a face that was almost identical to Gary's at the same age. Gary wasn't smiling in the picture, he didn't look like he belonged with these people in this place, and that was a feeling I carried about my own identity throughout all the years I attended school. Everything about the way he held himself in the picture—the way he pulled his body back from the grouping of the other students, the way he was looking intently at something outside of the photo's frame, some distraction that interested him more than joining the gaze of his friends—all this says that he was a boy who felt different from the people and the values around him. Some of that, no doubt, was a pose. Gary wanted to be respected, but he didn't want to be regarded as square or nice or ordinary. Instead, he wanted to be feared—probably because that was the only thing that could give him a little parity in his life. He had spent so much time feeling fear and being brutalized that he was ready to return those favors to the world around him.

I look at this picture and I feel both sorrow and anger. For the life of me, I cannot understand why somebody didn't value this kid enough to offer him something other than scorn and the rod. Gary was a smart kid in a time and place that did not value his brand of intelligence. He was smart and brave enough to want to rebel—to fuck things up as a way of declaring how things had fucked him up—but the world was not going to accommodate or tolerate that rebellion. It was going to see it as simple disobedience, and it was going to destroy that spirit, or take revenge on it. When I look at this photograph, I see a damaged boy. Or more accurately, I see the face of a broken angel as it looks away from the easy certainty that everyone else is looking toward and contemplates taking on the devil's face for a lifetime fit.

IN SPRING EVENINGS after school, as the daylight hours stretched longer, Gary and his friends began hanging out in the woods behind Johnson Creek. They would take girls into hidden groves and they would sneak along bottles of beer or whiskey. Gary had a little camera he had stolen from my father, and whenever he could, he would talk the teen-aged women into posing for pictures in the nude. Within a few days, Gary would be passing the photos around school. "That was a big thing in those days," says Frank. "Most kids didn't have stuff like that. Gary was living the way that people twenty years old would be living, for example. In that sense, he was real popular with the guys because he was kind of a century ahead of us."

Deeper in the woods there was an old train trestle, crossing the creek's swimming hole. Sometimes, after Gary had a few drinks, he would climb out on the trestle and wait for the train to come along. He would stand in the middle of the span until the moment the train would hit the start of the bridge, then he would race to the opposite end, jumping to one side at the last possible second, as the train reached the other bank. He did this frequently, and he had several close calls as the train's engine bore down on him. Word about Gary's bravado got around Joseph Lane, and kids would come to the trestle in the early evenings to watch him race the train. Nobody else would risk matching the feat. Some of the kids admired Gary for his recklessness, but others began to keep a distance from him after they witnessed him make the run. They realized that a boy who did not seem to fear the momentum of a train might be too dangerous to get close to.

One day Frank went to watch his brother run along the trestle, and when he saw how close Gary let the trains come to hitting him, Frank was terrified. "I tried to talk to him," he told me. "I didn't want to see him get killed. Showing off was one thing, but this was suicidal." Gary kept racing the trains. Finally, Frank went to my mother with his concerns. "We weren't tattletales on each other," he said, "but I was afraid Gary was going to get killed, so I asked her to talk to him. But I told her not to tell Dad, because he would just have got out his razor strap and made a big thing out of it, and what would that have accomplished?" Bessie finally prevailed on Gary that it would be an easy matter for his foot to get caught in the tracks and for him to end up ground under the engine's razorlike wheels. Gary promised my mother and brother he wouldn't outrun the trains anymore. But I'm willing to bet he kept on awaiting engines on the trestle, until something equally nihilistic caught his fancy.

IN PORTLAND IN THOSE days, if you were a teenager interested in proclaiming your lawlessness or toughness, the hippest thing you could do was join the Broadway Gang. A combination street gang and car club, the Broadway Boys—as they were also known—dressed in pachuco-style clothes and hung out late at night on Portland's main avenue, outside a restaurant called Jolly Joan's. Though some of its members occasionally stole cars, sold drugs, and ran prostitutes, the Broadway Gang was perhaps more obnoxious than it was genuinely dangerous. "They were just little street bastards," one of Gary's friends told me. "They used to raise hell downtown, you know, push people around, and they were just bastards. Every once in a while one of them might flash a switchblade. But they were not used except for show. I never heard of any of the Broadway Boys ever using a knife on anybody."

My brother Gary longed to join this gang. Whether he actually knew any of the group's members at the time, nobody seems to know. Still, even to talk about enlisting in such an outfit enhanced his outlaw standing among his peers. After school, when Gary and his friends would meet at the swimming hole and drink beers, my brother boasted that he knew that the Broadway Gang members needed guns. If Gary could supply them with a few pistols, he claimed, then he could join their league.

Gary took on an after-school paper delivery route, for the purpose of finding homes that might have guns he could steal. He learned to watch the houses on his route carefully, to become familiar with the comings and goings of the residents—when they took dinner or left on a vacation. It was at this time, at about age twelve or thirteen, that Gary began to break into houses. He would look for an unlocked or easy-to-jimmy window, then he would pry it open and climb inside. He liked those first few moments, standing in the stillness and darkness of somebody else's home, feeling the power of violation that he brought to their world. He soon learned that breaking into homes was a good way of learning other peoples' secrets—where the residents hid their money or dirty books or photos, what size brassiere the blond girl in his homeroom class wore, whether her parents were heavy drinkers or Bible freaks, or both. He'd feel the intimacy of their underwear, he'd taste their liquor, he'd pocket some of their pornography. To Gary's disappointment, though, he never found any handguns in those homes. It was a time when most Americans hadn't yet armed themselves, in fear of the world outside.

For some reason, Gary became convinced that the house down at the corner of our street, right next to the small grocery store, had a collection of guns stowed away in a trunk in its garage. One night, Gary talked a friend of his named Dan into breaking into the garage with him and cracking the lock on the trunk. They didn't find any guns, but the family that owned the house somehow figured out that it was Gary who violated their place, and they went to the police with their suspicion. The neighbors raised a lot of hell, but since nothing had been stolen and nothing could be proven, the juvenile authorities let Gary off with a warning: He was starting to get a bad reputation for himself, they told him, and from here on out, they would be keeping an eye on him.

ONE NIGHT AROUND Halloween 1954, Gary was waiting for the trolley back home, at the depot in downtown Portland. It was close to Portland's Skidrow, a rough slum area of town. The trolley only came once an hour, so it was a long wait—long enough to look at all the shop windows in the nearby district. Down the block from the station there was a pawn shop, its window full of .22 rifles. Gary saw a Winchester semi-automatic he liked. A beautiful gun, but at a price much higher than he could afford. It was already past midnight. The streets were quiet, deserted. He was the only person within howling distance. He wandered over to a deserted building and sorted through its rubble until he found a brick and then came back and threw the brick through the window. No alarm went off, nobody reacted. He climbed in, grabbed his Winchester, then filled a paper bag with a few boxes of cartridges. He cut his hand in the process of climbing through the window, but he didn't much mind.

Gary found a newspaper in the shop. He dismantled the gun—it broke into two parts—wrapped it in the paper and stuffed it in a large shopping bag. It looked like a paper bag of laundry or groceries. Then he waited for the trolley and rode with his rifle and bullets back to Johnson Creek. When he got off the trolley, Gary walked into the woods and hid his gun and ammunition in a place where he also often hid the items he stole from the neighborhood's homes and grocery stores. He could not chance having the rifle in our house, in case my father might discover it.

The next day Gary told his brother Frank and a few of his friends — Dan and two other pals, Charlie and Jim — about the rifle he had stolen. Frank wanted nothing to do with the matter; he didn't even want to see the gun. But Gary's other friends felt differently. One night, as the Oregon sky was turning from indigo to black, Gary met his friends at Johnson Creek's swimming hole and showed them his gun. The small group made their way through the woods over to the tracks and then up the tracks to the Johnson Creek trolley station, which was located across the road and a few hundred feet down the way from our home. The station was a three-sided timber construction — a weather shelter, with an overhanging light. Gary lay on the tracks, with his friends behind him. He aimed at the station's lamp through a side window in the building. He squeezed the trigger, and the lamp exploded. A woman came running out of the station as fast as she could. Gary kept shooting her way, laughing all the time.

For the next couple of weeks, Gary and his friends would meet at the swimming hole and Gary would fire his rifle at tin cans and paper targets. He got to be a good shot. But he soon tired of having to hide his treasure. One afternoon he sat by the swimming hole with Charlie and Jim, and he stared at his rifle. It felt spoiled to him, and he no longer wanted it. He asked his friends: "Listen, if I throw this gun here in the crick, do you guys have the guts to jump in there and dive for it?"

"You're goddamn right," said Charlie. "As soon as you throw it in."

Gary could tell they thought he was kidding. He took the rifle barrel in his hand and swung the gun in a long arc over the creek. It hit the water about six feet from the bank, right past a big, sharp rock that jutted up out of the swimming hole. His two friends just stood there, staring at the place where the gun had disappeared. They were amazed that Gary had tossed away the rifle he loved so much. "Go on," said Gary. "You can have the gun if you dive for it." Jim jumped for the place where the gun had sunk, but he landed on his knee on the sharp rock. It gashed his leg open, and Charlie had to help him back to the bank. Gary laughed his head off. Thought it was the funniest thing he'd ever seen. Nobody ever retrieved the Winchester. It still lies past the sharp rock, at the bottom of Johnson Creek's swimming hole.

The friendship with Charlie and Jim didn't last much longer. On

Gary's fourteenth birthday several weeks later, my mother and father allowed him a party at our home. The only two guests he invited were Charlie and Jim. For his present, his friends told him they were going to pay his way to a movie. When the three of them were halfway to the movie house, Charlie and Jim told Gary they were just kidding and were going to spend the money on themselves and not on him. They ran off and left him there, at the top of 45th Avenue, overlooking the tangle of brambles that he had climbed his way through a few months before. Gary walked back home. When he came in through the kitchen back door, my mother asked him what had happened. He said, "I don't ever want another fucking birthday party as long as I live," and then went up to his bedroom.

A couple days later, Gary and Charlie and Jim were at Jim's parents' house, playing around. They were out back, in an old trailer that the kids used as a play area, and they were wrestling. Gary had learned a few new moves at school and had a trick he wanted to show. He told Jim, "Get me in a full nelson and I'll show you how quick I can get out of it." As it turned out, the trick didn't work, and Jim didn't break the hold. Gary told him, "Okay, let go," but Jim started to apply more pressure, like he was really going to show Gary. Just like that, Gary went crazy. He got out from under Jim and clambered on top of him. He got a grip around Jim's throat and began to choke him and pound his head against the ground. Jim passed out and Gary continued beating on his face. Charlie stood there watching the violence until he decided it had gone too far, then ran in the house, yelling for help. Jim's father came out, a big man named Buck. He hit Gary. Then he lifted my brother up by the back of the neck and held him in one hand, his other fist doubled. Gary could tell the man wanted to punch him hard. But he didn't. Instead, Buck helped up his son, who was choking and bleeding and gasping for breath. Gary had given him quite a beating. Jim's father asked his son if he wanted to go out in the yard and finish it, but Jim backed down in front of his dad. Gary didn't say anything, but he was ready to fight more. He could see that Buck didn't like the fact that his son wouldn't fight anymore. The father turned on Gary and said: "Leave right now, and don't ever come around here again."

Gary didn't say anything. He got on his bike and left. The incident didn't bother him much, but he remembered thinking that Jim's father had looked at him in a way that a grown-up shouldn't look at a child. Somehow, it made my brother feel good, like he had accomplished something.

The next day at school, Jim didn't show up. Charlie approached Gary between classes and seemed to want to talk about the whole affair but didn't know what to say. He walked up to my brother, looked at him, and then turned around and walked away. Twenty-three years later, after telling Larry Schiller about his friendship with Charlie and Jim, Gary said: "Charlie was a pretty sensitive kid, and it's like he'd seen something he didn't want to see. Something that was more than just a fight, which at first he was enjoying. We'd fought all the time. But this was the most vicious fight I'd ever been in as a kid, and I don't know what would have happened if Charlie hadn't gone in and got Jim's dad. The way Charlie looked at me the next day, it was like he'd seen something he didn't understand."

GARY'S MISADVENTURES CONTINUED.

In early 1954, he ran away from home and was picked up by the police in Burley, Idaho. It is one of the few early incidents in Gary's life that my brother Frank can recall nothing about, and I have no idea what the reason was for Gary's running away. Most likely, he had simply taken one beating too many and decided to find a better reality somewhere else. Maybe he and everybody else would have been better off had he never been caught. Chances are, though, he would simply have come back on his own. The ruin was already in his blood, and he couldn't quit it.

After that, Gary's life was one long unbroken chain of trouble until the day he died.

The following summer, after school had let out for the season, Gary and a couple other friends visited Joseph Lane early one evening and threw rocks at the school windows. "We weren't going to leave any windows unbroken in that place," one of the friends said, many years later. The school pressed charges. Though there was no doubt about Gary's guilt in the affair, my father hired a private investigator to prove that his son had been out of town at the time of the incident. He also went to the extraordinary length of hiring a lawyer to defend Gary on the matter in juvenile court. The court was offended by the extravagance of my father's actions, but just as Fay had once saved her son from jail time many years before, Frank Gilmore got Gary off the hook for his vandalism.

My brother Frank recalls: "All Dad or anybody cared about was Gary not going to jail, as much for what that would do to the family's reputation as for any other reason. I think everybody saw that Gary was going down the road of shortcuts to hell. They just kind of took it for granted, like it was something that was supposed to happen. I don't remember anybody taking him aside and saying, 'Listen, if you keep going this way, you could end up on death row.' I don't remember that anybody was all that concerned about Gary's fate at all. All they cared about was preserving the family's name."

AT SOME POINT during the first year or two that my family was settled into the new house on Johnson Creek, a visitor came around. My mother opened the front door one day to find the same man she had seen six years before, seated at the diner in Sacramento. He was still thin, still well-groomed. Up close, Bessie saw that the man had light blue eyes and an attractive, close-mouthed smile, much like her husband. *Yes,* she thought, looking at this face that both scared and attracted her, *this could indeed be one of Frank Gilmore's missing sons.*

"I'm here to see Frank," the man announced.

Before she could answer, my father was standing by her side. "It's okay, Betty," he said. "This is somebody I've been expecting."

My father took the stranger into his office and shut the door behind them. My mother had learned to accept her husband's secretive ways—or at least she had learned that prying was simply a futile process; if Frank Gilmore didn't want to talk about something, he didn't talk about it. For too many years, though, she had lived with the burden of his secret without knowing the truth behind it, and her curiosity was too strong to resist. Next to my father's office was the staircase that went to the upstairs bedrooms. My mother could sit there and overhear a good part of what was being discussed in the office without being detected.

The man and my father talked for about an hour. The man's name, my mother learned, was Clarence. She couldn't understand everything that was being said, but she heard enough to get a fair idea of what my father's business with this man was, and what had kept him on the run for so long. *I'll never eavesdrop again,* she thought to herself, as she moved from the stairs and went to sit at the kitchen table.

After the man left, my father found my mother sitting at the table, staring into her cold cup of coffee. He poured his own cup and sat down beside her. He looked suddenly ten years younger. "Well, that was some good news," he announced. "That was somebody who came to talk to me about an old debt that I owed. But it's all been settled now. We don't have to move around anymore if we don't want to. I think we can stay here and make Portland our home now."

My mother kept staring at the table. "Frank," she said, after several moments, "you can be as angry as you like, but I listened in on some of your conversation with that man. All I can say is, I wish I hadn't heard what I just heard."

For once, Frank didn't seem angry. In fact, he seemed almost relieved. "It all happened a long time ago, Betty," he said. "I was younger then, drinking more than you've ever seen me drink, and I was foolish. I suppose I was desperate, too. It all seemed so easy at first. By the time I realized what I was truly involved in, I was on the run. Running is all I've ever known since that time. Running, hiding, living under different names, trying to keep in touch with some people while also trying to lose others. All the time, I kept looking to find a way to make up for it."

He sighed and sipped at his coffee. "Anyway, that visit I just had means that I'm finally free of it. We don't have to worry about it ever again. And we don't have to talk about it ever again."

"Don't worry," my mother said. "I won't ever say anything about it to anybody. Nobody would believe me anyway. But the next time you're beating Gary for getting into trouble, you might ask yourself where he got all that from. I think he got the trouble from your blood, Frank. I think he's your walking shadow."

My mother kept her promise. Whatever she had learned that day about Frank Gilmore's secret, she would never fully declare to anybody. One time, though, a few months after my father's death, she had a phone conversation about the matter with my father's attorney. Gary was in the house the night she received the call—it was during the last few days of freedom he would ever enjoy with our family—and something about my mother's hushed tone made him think this was a conversation he should listen in on. While Bessie talked upstairs, Gary picked up the downstairs phone, and learned the same hidden truths my mother had learned years before.

When my mother came downstairs, she saw Gary sitting in the dark, his hand still on the phone. "Were you listening in on my conversation?" she asked.

Gary nodded.

"Damnit, Gary, why are you always where you shouldn't be?"

Gary didn't say anything at first. By this time, he was already a hardened man who had spent many seasons in jail. He was no stranger to theft, drugs, violence, or the criminal rationale. But the conversation he had overheard, my mother could see, had clearly shaken and saddened him. "Man," Gary said, "I knew Dad could be a real bastard. That was bad enough, but it would have been okay remembering him that way—as a bastard who didn't love me. I didn't need to know this about the old man."

"I'm sorry you had to learn this about your father," my mother said, "but you shouldn't judge him too harshly. This is something that he tried to protect us from for many years. I don't think you would be doing your brothers any favors to share it with them. Don't ruin what good memories they have left of their father."

Like my mother, Gary kept the secret. No matter how terrible another man's crimes were, Gary would never divulge somebody else's trespasses. He had learned the code of silence well, both at home and in jail. but I have sometimes thought that what my mother and Gary learned about Frank Gilmore did something to them, haunted them in ways they couldn't erase and couldn't admit. In the last few years of her life, my mother referred over and over to the horrible mystery that surrounded my father, as if it were something she felt could still rise up and hurt us all. And on the last day of his life, Gary's final comment about his father said much regarding the cost he had paid for being Frank Gilmore's son. "My father was the first person I ever wanted to murder," Gary told our Uncle Vern in his last few hours. "If I could have killed him and got away with it, I would have."

CHAPTER 2
THE BOY IN
THE CORNER

MY BROTHER GARY SPENT the first half of 1955 trying to cram as much experience into his life as possible. Looking back, it makes a sort of sad sense. These were among the last free months of his adolescence. For that matter, they were among the last free months he would know for the next twenty years.

In February, Gary quit school and hitchhiked with a friend to Texas, with my parents' permission. Gary's first few months at Franklin High School had been a full-force disaster, and my mother thought that maybe if Gary got away and worked out some of his restlessness, he would soon settle down. By this time, my father simply liked the idea of Gary being gone for a while.

The trip was brief, but it became one of the legends that Gary later told about his youth. His main objective was to see McCamey, the oil workers town he had been born in. Along the way, he later said, he and his friend got picked up by a man who tried to make a sexual move on them. Gary said he beat up the guy, dumped him at the side of the road, and took his car into Odessa. Within a few days, Gary and his friend were running a poker game out of a hotel and making enough money to keep themselves stocked in liquor and hookers. Then the boys got homesick and made their way back to Portland, hitching rides and hopping freights.

Back home, Gary and a couple of other friends started a small car-theft ring. They would steal a car, repaint it, drive it for a few days, then abandon it and steal another. Once, for the hell of it, they stole the same car ten nights in a row, always returning it to the owner's driveway before dawn. In early May, they got caught at their dangerous hobby and were hauled into court. My father was adamant that it was all a big mistake, that Gary had been an unwitting accomplice in the whole affair. The judge was inclined to be lenient and released Gary to my father, with a warning.

Two weeks later, Gary was back in court again on another car-theft charge—stealing a 1948 Chevrolet. Once more, my father insisted that Gary could not be guilty, but this time the judge was not so tolerant. The court ordered that Gary be committed to MacLaren's Reform School for Boys, in Woodburn, Oregon, for an indefinite period, and also ordered my father to pay thirty-five dollars a month to finance Gary's stay at the institution. My father was furious and called the judge a few choice names, and the judge had my father thrown out of court.

After the sentencing, the judge sent MacLaren's supervisor a letter, stating the following:

The boy had come to this court's attention for delinquent behavior on several occasions. Mr. and Mrs. Gilmore consistently refused any counseling from the court and simply refused to believe the clear facts with reference to their son's delinquency on several occasions. The attitude of Mr. Gilmore particularly left no alternative to the court other than commit the boy to MacLaren. He is simply carrying through the same attitude by endorsement on the back of his check, which reads: "Blood money to the State by compulsion, under protest." Thirty-five dollars per month is less than Mr. Gilmore should reasonably be expected to pay for his son at home, and I believe Mr. Gilmore is fortunate not to have to pay more upon his obligation. If he fails to make these payments, as required, I certainly expect that he will be cited into my court to show a reason why he should not be found in contempt.

In other words, Gary was being punished as much to teach my father a lesson as for his own errors. The sins of the fathers, indeed—and the sins of the judges.

FOLLOWING HIS SENTENCING, Gary was manacled to another boy, placed in the back seat of a state police car, and driven the forty miles south to Woodburn. In those days, MacLaren's sat not far off the main highway. It was a sprawling estate, full of green lawn and walnut trees, and hemmed in at the front by an eight-foot-high stone wall. The police car made its way down the school's entry road, past the main administration building and the various cottage dormitories, to a reception cottage on the rear grounds. There, Gary and the other boy were turned over to a burly, balding man whom I'll call Mr. Blue. Standing by Blue's side was a big German shepherd, which immediately jumped up and put its paws on Gary's chest and bared its teeth in his face. Gary tried to raise his manacled hands to ward off the animal, but Mr. Blue delivered a stern warning. "You are not allowed to touch the dog, even if you're trying to defend yourself," Mr. Blue said. "In fact, if you make any sudden or threatening moves, the dog will probably tear you to pieces." The dog sniffed each boy in turn, then went back and sat beside its master. "Mr. Blue had this cockeyed theory," another MacLaren's inmate told me years later. "He believed that if we could relate to a dog we could start to relate to other people. Perhaps it wasn't such a bad idea, though I think it might have worked better if the dog was smaller and less aggressive, and didn't seem like it was just waiting for a chance to bite your nuts off."

Gary and the other boy were then herded into an adjoining room with other staff members. The boys were told to strip off their clothes, and then the supervisors ran their fingers through the boys' hair, checking for lice. "Okay," said Blue, "now bend over and reach back and spread your butt cheeks." Blue walked along behind the boys, carrying a yardstick. He lightly batted the boys' scrotums with the yardstick, then raised the ruler and tapped at each boy's anus. "Looks like we have a bunch of tight asses here," Blue said to the other staff, and all the men laughed.

Next, each boy showered and was issued his uniform—boxer shorts, blue jeans, and a green denim shirt—and then Gary and the others took turns sitting in a chair, while a supervisor wielded an electric razor and burred the boys' hair down to nothing, like a marine-style cut. After that, the boys were led into what was called the squad room. It was about fifty by twenty-five feet and was full of maybe fifty-five other kids, milling around on the floor or sitting on a few tables. On one side of the room was a row of toilets, with no walls separating them from the rest of the room, no barriers that would allow privacy. This was the room where all the incoming boys spent their spare time for their first few weeks at MacLaren's, while the counselors determined which of the school's other cottages each boy would be assigned to. There were a few chessboards and card decks in the room for entertainment, but that was all. No books, no television, no radio.

At the end of the evening, the boys were taken upstairs to the dormitory sleeping quarters, and the newcomers were assigned their beds. Each wall of the room was lined with small individual beds, laid in close formation. In the center of the room stood a guard's booth, protected with bulletproof glass and prison bars. Periodically throughout the night a supervisor would come in and make the rounds of the beds, or sit inside the booth, watching the sleeping kids. Inside the booth was a phone. All the supervisor had to do was lift the phone and he was in immediate touch with the state police station down the road.

At 9 P.M. the boys hung up their uniforms and slipped into dressing gowns. "Stay in your beds," Blue told the new boys. "If you need to use the bathroom, wait and ask a supervisor when he comes around. And *no* talking once the lights go out."

A few minutes later, Gary was lying there in the dark. He was probably already thinking how he could get out of this place. After a few moments, he noticed a curious sound—a noise like something being rubbed vigorously, accompanied by a chorus of rapid breathing and a few odd giggles. Next thing he knew, something hot and viscous hit him across his face. Then another warm, wet stream landed on him, running into his eyes and his nostrils. It was the semen of the boys in the beds that flanked his own.

This was Gary's introduction to MacLaren's "cum fights." Several nights a week, as soon as the lights went out, the boys would pull down their blankets and pull out their penises. They would stroke themselves as fast as they could, trying to pump up to an immediate ejaculation— something like the ultimate boy's race. Whoever came first had an advantage: He would catch his shooting semen on his hand and fling it in a nearby opponent's face, sometimes effectively disarming the other boy's rhythm of masturbation. But the worst targets were newcomers. It was part of their initiation. On a boy's first night, he would likely find his face drenched with semen. If he tried to cover up, a few boys might hold him until the others could finish masturbating, and then wipe their semen all over the boy's face. Sometimes as many as fifteen or twenty boys would douse a rookie. The supervisors were never in the room when the cum fights took place. Maybe they never knew about the activity. In any event, the practice was never acknowledged in MacLaren's records.

A LITTLE AFTER 1 A.M., Gary was awakened by a movement in the dark. He looked up and saw Mr. Blue, walking down the aisle between the beds. He was carrying a small stool with him, like the kind you place alongside a cow when you milk it. He paused alongside Gary's bed, and Gary shut his eyes, feigning deep sleep. Blue moved away, down the row to another boy's bed. In the room's dim light, Gary could see Blue sit down on his stool and whisper something to the boy. Gary rolled back over and shut his eyes again.

According to somebody who had been at MacLaren's at the same time as Gary, Blue's nighttime visits were not uncommon. "My first night there," this person told me, "Mr. Blue came up with his stool and sat down by my bed. He reached out and grabbed me by the thigh, and squeezed me, and then in a very quiet voice said: 'How are you doing?' I took his hand and moved it away. Blue got mad. He grabbed me again, this time harder, and said: 'I'll squeeze your leg if I feel like it.' I said: "No, you won't. I have a family. They won't like it.' Blue glared at me for a moment, then gave me an extra hard squeeze and pulled his hand away.

" 'All right,' Blue told me. 'If that's the way you want it.' Mr. Blue scared the hell out of me that night with this bit. I'm sure that if he were questioned, he would say he was trying to find out whether I was gay, but I don't think you have to do that to find that out. I knew other boys who described similar experiences with him. Of all the counselors and disciplinarians I knew at MacLaren's, the one that I hold the most contempt for in memory is Mr. Blue. He was a cold, sadistic son of a bitch, a very scary person, and last I heard, he was still working within the Oregon corrections system."

That was Gary's first night in incarceration, away from our family.

GARY WENT INTO MACLAREN'S as a smart and talented fifteen-year-old boy, on his way to a life of trouble. He came out a little over a year later fully committed to living a criminal's destiny. "Reform schools disseminate certain esoteric knowledge," he told Larry Schiller years later. "They sophisticate. A kid comes out of reform school and he's learned a few things he would otherwise have missed. And he identifies, usually, with the people who share the same esoteric knowledge, the criminal element, or whatever you want to call it. So going to Woodburn was not a small thing in my life."

This isn't to say that reform school was principally culpable for Gary's degeneration. I have read through MacLaren's file on Gary—a body of documents that became so legendary following Gary's execution that the school kept it intact and occasionally made it available for the perusal of curious law enforcement and corrections officers. Though the school would not let me see my brother's psychological reports (possibly the most important part of his file), I still found the records fascinating—sometimes full of real insights about Gary and about his family. Indeed, if there's any single theme that emerges from these documents, it is this: Gary's troubles were inextricably linked to the influence of his father—a man who seemed altogether reluctant to face the difficult truths necessary to save his son. Following the first intake interview with my parents, one supervisor wrote the following: "The counselor feels that the fact that the father sat outside in the car during the interview with the mother indicates either a lack of interest or shame or the feeling of inability to do anything about the problem. At the same time it should be honestly recorded that the four-year-old Mike was in the car, and that possibly Dad thought it best to sit with this small boy during the time that the mother had the interview." A few paragraphs later, the counselor added: "Mr. Gilmore . . . appears to govern that which is under his authority as [an] . . . absolute monarch . . . Unfortunately, the much younger but completely overshadowed mother would seem to count little in Gary's parole plan if Gary were sent home." And, from another record: "Physical standards of the home are very good, but because of the paranoid attitudes of the father, the boy has been severely damaged."

Throughout Gary's stay at MacLaren's, my father remained hostile to the school's efforts to bring about a better home atmosphere for my brother. The family, my father insisted, was not to blame for Gary's trouble; Gary had been set up by others and was being wrongfully punished. Exonerate Gary and set him free, my father told the school officials, and the problems would be solved. One counselor was smart enough to figure out that my father's unswerving defense of Gary wasn't so much a sign of love for his son, or a desire to protect him, as it was simply an extension of my father's belief that the world was out to ruin Frank Gilmore, even through his family. "Whether [Gary's innocence] is true or not," wrote the counselor, "Gary, at home, could scarcely avoid feeling that the school, the judge, the important community citizens and maybe a few others were conniving to destroy the entire family."

But records don't tell the whole story. I also spoke with (or read the recollections of) several men who had done time at MacLaren's during the same period that Gary was there. Putting together these two perspectives—the accounts of the officials and the remembrances of former inmates—is like viewing two largely disparate versions of the same history. On one hand, it is clear that certain counselors at the school tried their best to understand my brother and to effect a change in his life. In turn, he paid back their efforts with a series of escapes and violent episodes that forced them to impose on him their worst punishments. But it is also plain from the stories I have heard that, despite everybody's best intentions, the reform school experience of the 1950s had many brutalizing aspects about it. Boys were locked up in cold and isolated conditions, beaten at the discretion of their counselors, and subjected to an environment in which astonishing acts of violence and sexual abuse took place. For some kids, being caged up in such a world only deepened their fears and their hatred. "It doesn't make sense to a normal person," one former inmate told me, "but when you're locked up you can become a very hate-filled individual. And if you can't externalize that hate—or if a fantasy about going into a bank with a tommy gun and blowing everybody up isn't enough for you—then you turn that hatred on yourself. You reach a point of self-destructiveness where you're going to have somebody really give you the ultimate. And sometimes the only way to do that is by hurting or enraging other people as much as you can."

THE MOST RELIABLE and articulate observer I found on the subject of MacLaren's was a man named Duane. He was in the reform school for almost exactly the same period as Gary, and he knew my brother well. One morning Duane paid me a visit at my apartment in Portland and shared with me some of his recollections. Duane had been a star student at his school until, at the age of fifteen, his stepfather began beating him viciously. Then he began hanging out with rough boys and stealing cars and other things. One time, they made the mistake of breaking into a cop's home and stealing his revolver. They became the objects of a big chase and were arrested at gunpoint. The incident ended up getting splashed across the front page of *The Oregonian*. As a result, Duane and the friend he was caught with came into MacLaren's with some standing. The other boys saw them as something like full-fledged outlaws. "Actually, we were a couple of dickheads," said Duane, "but the kids didn't know and we sure as hell weren't going to tell them, because ninety percent of what you do in a place like that is bluff. You're in there with some real bad apples. If they find out that you're not a homicidal maniac like they may be, they're going to put you in your place."

Duane had been at MacLaren's about a week when Gary was brought in. Duane's first memories of my brother had to do with the psychological tests that were administered to the boys, to determine school placement and parole prospects. "They had this big fat psychiatrist," said Duane. "This guy probably weighed three hundred pounds if he weighed an ounce. He's a medical doctor, for Christ's sake, and he's talking to reform school kids, so how good can he be? Anyway, you go in there and sit down at a table across from this guy. He sits there and stares at you for twenty or thirty seconds, the sweat just pouring off him, and then the first question he would ask, right out of the chute, was: 'How many girls have you fucked?' Almost everybody I ever knew at MacLaren's had the same experience with him. In my case, I figured if I tell him I screwed a girl, that's another six months to my sentence. On the other hand, if I tell him I'm a cherry, my esteem will be lowered. So you're torn. But I really *was* a virgin when I went up there, so I opted for honesty. Most of the guys would try running a bluff. They'd say, 'Oh, *fifty*.' And then the psychiatrist would want names, and he'd very patiently list all these names. I remember there was this one guy named Raymond, who told him he'd screwed something like two hundred girls or some damn thing, and the doctor had him put two hundred names on a list. Then Raymond signed it and MacLaren's sent the list back to his high school. I imagine the shit hit the fan back there when they started bringing those girls in and asking them if indeed they had been sexually active with Raymond. See, they used to be much more intrusive in teenage lives back in those days than they are now. Back then, if a girl had three guys she was a whore. Five, and she was the arch fiend of all times, could never be married to anybody.

"The next thing the psychiatrist would do," Duane continued, "was give you pencil and paper and say, 'Okay, draw a house for me. Now, draw a picture of your*self* inside the house,' and so forth. Well, I knew right away what he wanted. He wanted to see a house and he wanted to see where I was in this house. He was looking for me to give him clues to myself. I went ahead and played it straight with him, because I had already heard that if the psychiatrist thought you had a lot of problems, he'd assign you to one of the rougher cottages. I wanted to get sent to one of the better cottages, where the kids were likely to get out the soonest, so I wasn't going to fuck up my psychological profile.

"When I got back to the squad room, I was sitting around with my buddies and we're all laughing about this psychiatrist, thinking about ways we could fuck him up. That's when I met Gary. I remember he was a nice kid, a little shy, but he was eager to get along with us and to establish himself as somebody notable. He saw what we were doing, and he was anxious to run a bluff on this psychiatrist and his fucked-up theories. Also, I think he wanted to impress us guys. He was a little younger than us—maybe a year and a half younger."

Duane paused in his story for a moment, then shook his head. "I remember this so well and afterward I felt really bad, especially after I heard what happened to Gary in later years. I mean, it's humorous to tell about, but if I could change anything of what I did back then—and I include my so-called crimes—if I was only allowed to change one thing, I would not have done this to Gary, because I saw him take the bit and run with it. I told him, 'Okay, what you want to do is draw a picture of yourself, and give yourself a little mouth, big eyes, big ears, and no hands. You know what this tells this idiot psychiatrist? You've got no voice and no hands, so you're helpless to change anything. But you *hear* everything and you *see* everything, so you're obviously a paranoid.' Now, Gary wasn't really like that, you know what I mean? But he did what I told him—he went in there and drew the picture of himself that way.

"I shouldn't have been doing that," Duane said. "I thought it was cute as hell that some other dumb-ass kid would follow my instructions, even though I *knew* that fat-ass psychiatrist was a contemptible fucker in many ways, and he had the power to assign Gary to one of the rougher cottages. You've got to realize, when you're a kid and you get locked up, it screws you up. I had the idea that there were only so many people who were going to get released every month. I wanted to be sure I kept myself on the pipeline to get out as quick as I could, and I felt like I was in competition for release with the other kids. That's the way those places can make you think. I was playing a game I shouldn't have been playing."

MacLaren's Reform School for Boys offered its wards both counseling and educational opportunities, or, if a boy preferred, some vocational training—primarily farmwork. Gary, for the most part, chose MacLaren's unlisted fourth option: full-time punishment. In fact, Gary had only been at MacLaren's a matter of days when he began getting into trouble. His first punishments came at the hands of Mr. Blue. "Mr. Blue loved to administer something he called 'spats,' " Duane told me. "I got them a few times. It didn't take much—all you had to do was yell at or push another kid. Any sign of belligerence. I know your brother got spats quite a bit at first. I remember seeing it happen."

And what exactly, I asked Duane, were *spats*?

Duane grimaced. "Mr. Blue had a glassed-in office in the reception cottage. If you violated a rule, or just pissed Blue off, he'd call you into his office alone and he'd close the door. He would tell you to peel your shirt and drop your pants, so you're naked. Then he'd tell you to reach over and grab your ankles. That's when he would take this hard Ping-Pong paddle that had holes drilled in—to lessen the wind resistance—and he would pound your ass with it. You'd get ulcers on your buttocks from these spats. We called them headlights. I don't know why we didn't call them taillights. I guess because they were white and looked just like the headlights on a car. The minimum spats Blue would give you was twenty-five, and if you really pissed him off he'd give you fifty. I know your brother got this punishment several times, because I saw it happen.

"It was really weird, because with Mr. Blue there was no emotion. It was like a force moving against you. When he said he was giving you spats it was with a smile on his face. He'd say, in a monotone voice, 'I'm really sorry I've got to do this, but I have to do it to you, Gary, because you asked for it,' and then *WHAM*. I've never been beaten like that, never in my life. Believe me, it was a frightening experience."

Spats, though, were just the start. MacLaren's had bigger punishments to offer, and Gary found them.

A few weeks after entering MacLaren's, Gary was on a camping expedition with one of the counselors and several other boys, near Seaside, on the Oregon coast. It was something of a test: If the boys could work cooperatively in a setting like this, and proved responsible and trustworthy, they might be likelier to win an early parole. As the boys were heading back from a morning fishing trip, Gary and two others lagged at the rear of the group. Soon as they saw that the counselor was safely out of sight, the three boys ran hard the other way. They cut through the brush and made their way into Seaside, where they hitched a ride into Portland. That night, Gary and the others slept in an empty, trashed bungalow that stood behind our house on Johnson Creek, and the next morning, after my father had left for the day, Gary went inside to inform my mother about his escape. The school had already called and told her the police were looking for Gary, and she tried to talk him into returning to the school. But Gary refused. "I'll go crazy in that place," he said, and then he told her about some of what he had already witnessed and experienced at MacLaren's. My mother gave Gary fifty dollars and a change of clothes. She told him to be careful and to write her from wherever he ended up. She did not call the police or MacLaren's to let them know that her runaway son had come around. She decided right then she would never turn a son of hers over to the law, for any reason.

Gary and the others spent the rest of the day hiding out in movie theaters and sleeping in abandoned cars. The next morning, Gary hot-wired a 1947 Chevrolet coupe that was parked on Division Street and drove over two hundred miles to Pendleton, Oregon, where the car threw a rod. The boys then stole a 1955 Chevy and were close to crossing the Oregon-Idaho border when a state policeman pulled them over. The arresting officer reported that the three escapees seemed excited by the chase and proud of their exploits, and that Gary in particular bragged about his knack for car stealing.

Back at MacLaren's, the escape went over badly. "Every effort had been made to give [Gary] opportunities to improve," wrote his counselor. "The boy has air of instability that does not inspire trust, is resistant to authority and resentful of his commitment. [He will] continue to be a security risk on open campus and would benefit by the program offered by L. E. Darling."

L. E. Darling—also known as L.E.D.—was MacLaren's equivalent of a maximum security unit. It was a large cottage located at the rear of the grounds and separated from the rest of the place by a tall wire fence.

Said Duane: "I think the kids in L.E.D. had a daily routine something like ours, except they didn't get to go outside and the discipline was much more harsh. By harsh I mean, rumor had it that instead of being sent into segregation, L.E.D. allegedly had a room with manacles where you'd actually be chained to the wall, which we didn't have. I never had to endure that, but I heard from other kids who were in L.E.D. that they were manacled to the wall, and that the supervisors beat them. Instead of spats across the butt it was a real whipping, with a belt across the back, like being flayed. And if they put you on bread and water in L.E.D., you were on bread and water—with a cup of milk in the middle of the day—for up to three weeks. I received that treatment for a week a couple of times and didn't suffer any lasting effects. I don't know what would happen if you went for two or three weeks on it. I think it would be pretty bad."

Gary spent the rest of 1955 in L.E.D. Shortly before Christmas, the cottage manager made the following note: "Gary is still our boy in the corner. I still believe Gary will not trust anyone, staff or boy. He tries to be one of the group but seems unable to do so. When I talk to a group he will go into a corner and not take any part in the discussion." The manager also noted that Gary seemed to have bad dreams almost every night and often talked in his sleep.

But while Gary was quiet and aloof, the supervisors in L.E.D. didn't find him particularly troublesome. "Some staff thought Gary was the best boy they had ever had and did not belong in L.E.D.," one counselor wrote. "Different ideas were expressed that perhaps the boy was caught in a web of circumstances not his fault, and therefore may have minimal if any delinquency."

On January 1, 1956, MacLaren's released Gary from L.E.D. to the custody of Cottage 3—considered by many to be the school's best cottage. Two days later Gary went to the cottage's manager and told him that if he was not put back in L.E.D., he was going to run away again. He didn't like the fact that he couldn't smoke in the regular cottages, plus he found life outside L.E.D. too crowded and loud. The manager put him back in L.E.D. for the night, then decided that Gary had been bluffing and returned him to Cottage 3. The next day he ran away, and within a week he was back in custody and assigned again to L.E.D.

This penchant for hard-time punishment became a pattern that would hold true for my brother for the rest of his prison career. He would invariably commit flagrant violations that had the effect of earning him sustained bouts of severe punishments—usually in isolated circumstances. Indeed, by the time of his death, Gary had spent roughly half of his jail time in isolation, segregation, or some other form of maximum incarceration. MacLaren's was where he established the pattern: For the next several months he would behave admirably inside L.E.D., and as soon as he was released into the school's general population, he would run away or commit some infraction that would land him back in maximum security.

"One of the last times I saw Gary," Duane told me, "we were having lunch together in one of the cafeterias, and he was trying to talk me into joining him in L.E.D. He was telling me how much he liked it there, and I knew that was bullshit. Who could like being locked up twenty-four hours a day? Also, everybody knew that if we had any cases of serious perversion going on, it was in L.E.D. But Gary insisted it was a great life. He said, 'Man, Duane, we get to smoke and swear as much as we want there. We don't have to live by the same rules. We don't even have to go to school or work.' What he didn't seem to understand was, those weren't privileges. That treatment was the school's way of saying that the boys in L.E.D. were beyond saving. They could smoke and they could swear, but those kids were locked up, and they would stay there until the authorities were ready to let them go."

ONE OF THE INCIDENTS associated with Gary's stay at L.E.D., Duane said, involved a fight. "If you got into a fight at MacLaren's, the supervisors would never step in. I remember watching twenty minutes of amazingly brutal combat between two rough Medford logger kids, with everybody cheering and the supervisor standing back, sucking on a cigarette, getting his jollies watching these two kids beating each other half to death. I think the supervisors handled it that way because they saw it as a pressure release. If they stifled these things the tension would build up and sides would be formed, and they might end up with a first-class riot or gang fight on their hands. All I know is, the fights that I was in and the fights I witnessed at MacLaren's were savage. They were fights to the finish, because you knew there'd be nobody there to protect you. Nobody was going to jump in and say, 'Okay, you guys, break it up.' Consequently, you were ready to fight at the drop of a hat. You're tough, you told yourself—you're a killer.

"Anyway, there was this one guy named Skip, and he was in the same cottage as your brother. I can't remember Skip's last name, but he had murdered both of his parents—it was a notorious case in Oregon at the time. He was a twelve-year-old boy, and his parents were a couple of drunks who used to beat him regularly. One night they beat the hell out of him and then they passed out in bed. The only thing Skip loved in the world was his puppy dog. That night Skip killed his parents and his dog. The police found him lying alongside the puppy crying, and the court put him up at MacLaren's. Skip was dangerous; he really should have been in the insane asylum."

One day, according to Duane, Skip and Gary found themselves working together in the cottage's food preparation area. "Whatever cottage Skip was in," Duane said, "the number one rule was to keep him away from knives because he was psycho. If he got a knife, chances are he's going to use it. This one morning Skip and Gary got into an argument and Skip got hold of a knife. Gary went straight up against Skip and got the knife away from him, and then Gary beat the shit out of him. Gary left Skip on the floor, crying. After that, Gary was seen as nobody to fuck with. He got to be regarded as one of the tougher guys at MacLaren's, and his closest buddies were not very nice guys. I would not have dreamed of trying to start a fight with Gary or push him around. First off, we got along fine—it never would have happened anyway. But I guarantee you that I would not want to have gone down with him, because he was *tough*. If you messed with him, he would be looking for revenge."

Duane told me another tale about Gary's time in L.E.D.

"There was a kid at MacLaren's named Fritz, and he was a real sociopath sadist. He'd been sent there when he was about eleven. He used to catch cats, bind their tails together with a rawhide thong, and then throw them over a clothesline tied together and watch them fight to get free. Of course, the cats would kill each other. That's what he was up there for, animal cruelty. He was a monster, especially for his age. At MacLaren's, Fritz used to like to sharpen pencils and get them to that point where they were just like a needle and then stick them into people.

"One night," Duane continued, "I'm in the bridal suite, which was the nickname for unit number one in segregation, right alongside L.E.D. There were no toilet facilities or anything—you'd just sit on the floor and that's all there was to do. I'm sitting in there late at night and I hear voices coming from the shower area. I recognize one of the voices immediately. It's Fritz. He's being held down and he's begging for mercy. And then I heard the voices of the boys who were holding him down. It was Gary, with a couple of his friends. Do you know what they did to Fritz? They took pencils and shoved them up his ass. I could hear them talking about it as they were doing it. I never forgot this kid screaming, and hearing Gary say, 'Don't move, you'll break the fucking pencil, you son of a bitch.' And then I'd hear them laughing, and I could hear Fritz screaming. I don't know what Fritz did to deserve that. He was clearly nobody's sweetheart, but you can imagine what a pencil could do if it broke off in your rectum. It could be fatal. That's the kind of thing that went on in L.E.D., the ugly side of it.

"After that, Gary's reputation—at least among the kids—got worse.

He became seen as somebody who was frightening, and other boys kept their distance."

IN CONTRAST TO THESE HORROR TALES, the following story is almost tender, though in its own way it is also worse.

I remember once finding a letter that Gary had written my mother, that she kept hidden in the back of her desk. The letter had been written several years after his time at MacLaren's—probably when Gary was about twenty, and was serving a sentence in the Portland City Jail, on one charge or another. Gary wrote it from a hospital, shortly after he first started making suicide attempts in jail. He would break the lightbulbs in his cell then slash his wrists. When the bleeding got bad enough, he would kick his sleeping cell mate in the head. The poor guy would wake up to find Gary's hand spurting blood in his face, and then he'd yell for a guard to come and save my brother's life. It got to be something of a regular routine, and my mother had written Gary, asking him why he seemed bent on playing such a deadly game.

Gary wrote back that he had been haunted by something that had happened years before at MacLaren's—an incident that he had never told anybody about. Gary wrote that he had befriended a young boy, about fourteen, who had a pretty and a fragile manner—a bad combination inside a jail. The boy was sent to MacLaren's because his foster parents could no longer handle him, and he had no living relatives who would claim him. In other words, he was alone—an orphan. No family, no visitors, no friends. He was one of those kids, Gary wrote, that both the counselors and the inmates felt they could treat any way they wanted, because nobody would speak for him. Gary said he watched one time while ten other boys held the kid down and took turns raping him. Gary said that when his turn came, he refused to take it, and that his refusal seemed to win the boy's trust.

The longer the mistreatment of the boy went on, the more fragile he became. One day the boy got sick. The supervisors took him to the infirmary a few times, but he never seemed to get better. Finally they decided he was faking his illness, in order to pull off an escape. Gary was bunking with the boy at this time, he told my mother, and he thought of him as somebody innocent who deserved love and protection. One cold night, the boy had called to a night watchman and asked to be taken to the infirmary, but the guard refused. The boy made his way into Gary's bunk and asked my brother: "Can I stay here with you tonight? I'm scared and I need somebody to hold me." Gary lay in bed with the boy most of the night, holding him, running his hand over the boy's fevered brow, talking gently to him. "I just want to disappear," the boy told Gary, and then he tried to curl up into a ball in my brother's arms. "I want to disappear into the nothingness inside myself, where nobody can hurt me ever again." Finally, the boy fell asleep, and so did Gary, holding him. When Gary awoke, he was still holding the boy, who was now curled up into himself, cold and dead. Gary said he stayed there and kept holding the boy, caressing his face. "This is what will happen to me if somebody doesn't get me out of jail," Gary wrote. "I'm too healthy to die the way that boy died, so I tried to escape the only way I knew how. I'm sorry, Mom."

This story is, I believe, another one of those necessary lies that the members of my family learned to tell about themselves in order to tell far worse truths. MacLaren's has no record of any such death from around that time, and there's no reference to anything remotely similar in Gary's files. I don't believe the incident happened in any literal sense, though in a figurative and perhaps more important sense, the story is almost certainly true. I think the boy Gary was writing about—the boy who tried to disappear into the nothingness within himself—was Gary. I think Gary was writing about his last night on earth, before he became as cruel as he needed to be to survive the rest of his life.

THEN, SOMETHING SEEMED to change in Gary. His cottage and school reports improved steadily, and he seemed more receptive to counseling efforts. In June 1956, Gary's therapist wrote: "Counselor has seen Gary regularly and he has used the time well to discuss his problems in relationship to his own feelings of fear and anger. He expresses a great deal of fear about any personal relationships and seems to be afraid both of what he might do and is afraid of what might be done to him. He still seems to have a compulsive personality makeup in that he feels compelled to behave as he does. He has expressed a feeling of rejection from the family, particularly the father, has been hurt by the father both physically and mentally. Gary has talked of his early life of moving around and has reported a great number of fights and aggressive activity."

In general, the school's officials felt Gary had turned an important corner, and that it was now time for him to apply his new perspective to the real-life demands of living and working with society and his family. In the summer, Gary's counselor initiated a parole program which Gary helped shape. He would return to live at our home, and he would enroll as a sophomore at Portland's Franklin High School. He would also agree to seek part-time work, to avoid contact with anybody with a delinquent record, and to refrain from any illegal activities. In addition, Gary agreed to see a therapist on a weekly basis at the University of Portland Psychological Service Clinic. "Gary appeared to be very anxious to continue such a plan," Gary's counselor wrote, "and he expressed an interest in paying for the services himself, as he did not want to burden his father with any more expenses. It was felt he would continue with his therapy . . . and benefit greatly thereby."

On September 1, Gary was paroled from MacLaren's Reform School for Boys and returned to our home.

"I never saw Gary again after that," Duane said. "I got paroled myself and went into the service. A short time later, I got my girlfriend pregnant and I decided I had to tell all my old friends good-bye. I knew if I continued to hang around them, the marriage had no chance. I grew up real fast at that point. I would read in the paper about a lot of the guys I knew up there. A lot of them went on to prison for one reason or another, and a lot of them died hard deaths. Then, *bang,* one day there's poor Gary on the front page, asking Utah to kill him. I was living in California, working in the Bay area representing a paper mill, on the morning that they executed him. I just didn't think that they would ever do it, that somehow or another somebody would intercede. What Gary did was wrong, there's no question about it, but my God, we keep Mansonites alive, and that type. There are so many that are worse that had nowhere near the redeeming value that Gary had, the potential.

"I wished many times, when I was watching Gary in the news, going through his pathetic Don Quixote routine, that I could just go up there and put my arm around him and say, 'Goddamnit, Gary, *cool* it—quit humiliating these sons of bitches, they'll kill you if you don't. For once in your life bow to it. If you just give them what they want, tell them you're sorry and beg for forgiveness, you'll live.' I am firmly convinced that if Gary had admitted he was up against a higher power that he could not beat, they would have found it in their hearts to spare him somehow. He just challenged the wrong people. I remember telling my wife, 'Those goddamn Mormons have God on their side and they don't question their right to carry out God's edicts as they see it.' That kind of religious fervor is scary."

Before he left my place that day, Duane had a final thought he wanted to share. "It must be painful for you to hear some of these things. It sure would be for me if my brother had gone through something like this. Gary was one of the guys. He is an old friend to me in my heart and I'm loyal to my old friends. He wasn't a simple, mindless monster, in the way that the newspapers often portray somebody who has committed a violent act. He was a good guy that got fucked over. A lot of it, I admit, he did himself. But not all of it. Not all of it by a long shot."

CHAPTER 3
RUNNING
WILD

IN GARY'S ABSENCE, the family seemed to enjoy an unusual period of quiet. My father's publishing business was now thriving, and he had expanded it to include a yearly summary of traffic laws in the states of Oregon and Washington. He was now making enough money to run offices in Portland, Seattle, and Tacoma, and he stayed on the road much of the time, supervising the itinerant men he had hired to work as his salesmen. My brother Frank, now a seventeen-year-old junior at Franklin High School, had developed a strong interest in the craft and vocation of magic. His passion had been inspired, in part, by the ongoing family legend that Houdini was our grandfather, but no matter: Frank had a flair all his own. Meantime, Gaylen—now a ten-year-old, in parochial school—seemed to have the makings of a child prodigy. He had already read much of Shakespeare and he could quote Poe's gloomiest verses at length. He appeared to love poetry more than anything, except for girls, whom he loved even as a child. In the end, he would die in the middle of an unfinished poem, and in the midst of a love affair that had already effectively cost him his life years before.

Only my mother was counting the days until Gary's release. The more she had watched my father beat him and treat him as if he weren't his own son, and the more Gary was punished by school and law officials, the more my mother came to feel that Gary was her special son, the one she had to love the most. It wasn't merely that he was now living the role that she had once held in her own family, as the black sheep. There was something more to it. Like my father, Bessie Gilmore had her dark secrets, and she watched over them with a vigilance all her own.

WHEN GARY CAME HOME, the peace broke. He hadn't been back a few days before he and my father were engaged in war again, day and night. Every time Gary violated some house rule or showed any insolence, my father threatened him with a swift return to MacLaren's, and once or twice called in the parole officer to enforce the threat. "It appears that these two people, Gary and his father, can not establish a working basis . . ." the officer wrote after one of these visits. "[The] two personalities are so suspicious of each other, that a good healthy father and son relationship appears to be beyond their reach. Both the boy and his father wish to be friends, but apparently both have decided that a good offense is the best defense so there is apparently little give and take. It is not an impossible situation, however, and perhaps with Gary seeing [a psychiatrist] regularly, we may bring about an understanding between these two quite hostile people."

Unfortunately, after one of the many quarrels, my father refused to pay for any more of Gary's psychological counseling. He couldn't see where it was benefiting anybody. After that, Gary's parole officer effectively threw his hands in the air. "Mr. Gilmore appears to be incapable of establishing even a marginal constructive emotional relationship with Gary . . ." he wrote. "The only hope is that Gary can acquire the necessary maturity through his school relationships that will enable him to continue on parole in spite of these negative factors existing at home. However, the writer realizes this is wishful thinking in a sense, due to Gary's ambivalence in regard to academic school."

The renewed enmity had a way of spilling over to the whole household. One time, my mother found Gaylen sitting on the back steps, screaming and crying. Gary had just had a row with my father and had stomped out the back. Gaylen was sitting on the back steps and was in Gary's way. Gary picked him up and threw him off the back porch. The brother that just a year or so before Gary had still played with was now fair game for his rage. "He's changed, Mother," Gaylen said, sobbing. "He doesn't like us anymore."

"Yes," my mother said, holding Gaylen, "I know, he's different now. But sometimes it is too late to change people. Sometimes, you just have to love them anyway."

It was about this time that the dinnertime fights at our house became fierce and constant. Dinner had never been the easiest hour in our home—in large part because it was the only hour of the day when the whole family was certain to come together. Indeed, to miss dinner, or even to show up late for it, was to violate one of my father's most inviolable rules. But after his return from MacLaren's, Gary began missing the dinner hour more and more, lingering after school with his friends, or coming in after dark and making his own meal from what was left over. This offense was enough to result in horrible fights between him and my father, or to induce my father to banish him from any meals in the house until he learned to live by the rules.

My brother Frank remembered these dinnertime bouts vividly. The kitchen was a smallish room at the rear of the house. That's where we dined. My mother sat at one end of the table and Gaylen sat at the other. Frank and Gary were seated on one side, and my father kept me next to him on the other side. "We'd sit down at that table," Frank said, "and we'd have fantastic food. Breaded veal cutlets stacked up, baked or boiled potatoes, all kinds of vegetables, dessert, and whatever you wanted to drink. Sometimes fresh homemade bread. I mean, you're talking eating like a king. Yet there would be no way you could enjoy that meal. We would be sitting down, just starting to eat, and invariably Mom would say something like, 'Well, I wonder where Gary's at.' And that would set Dad off. He'd say, 'I don't care where he's at, I'm glad he's not here.' Or Gary would come in, and Dad would say, 'What the hell are *you* doing here? We're not running a café. Get out.' Then Mom would come to Gary's defense and say, 'Well, *I* fix these meals and he's welcome to eat. I have some say in this.'

"That's all it would take. Just like that, she and Dad would be yelling and screaming. And if one of us tried to get them to calm down or save it until after dinner, that just made things worse. Before long, Mom would have picked up some part of the dinner—usually the choicest part, like the roast or a pie, or maybe a plate or kettle—and she'd heave it on the floor or at Dad. Then *he'd* stomp out, calling her a crazy crack-brained bitch, and the rest of us would be sitting there, with her at the table crying, and the food ruined, and no recourse. I'll tell you, it could really get to you. It became so damn common that for years I dreaded eating; it would ruin my digestion just to think about it."

Even on the nights when Gary wasn't the issue, fights were still the rule. "I got so fearful of those dinners," said Frank, "that I used to pull my plate up close to me at the edge of the table, and I'd eat nervous and fast. Dad didn't like it when I did that, and this one time—"

I jumped in, because suddenly I remembered the incident. It was one of the few incidents from around that time that, for one reason or another, I *could* recall. "Father took your face," I said, "and shoved it into your plate."

"You remember that?" Frank said. "You couldn't have been more than five. But, yeah, that's exactly what he did. He reached over, grabbed the back of my head and pushed it right down into the beef stew. That's what we were eating." Frank paused for a moment, then laughed. "I came up with beef stew, carrots, and potatoes mashed all over my face. I've got to laugh now, but at the time I wasn't laughing. It was humiliating and disrespectful and disastrous. I didn't finish my meal. I got up and left the table, went and washed up and sat outside. I remember Gaylen coming out afterward, sitting down beside me. 'Man,' he said, 'I wish we could eat a meal once in a while without all this trouble. But they'll never let us. They'll always find a way to turn it into a fight, or as an excuse to beat up on us.' I remember he had tears rolling down his face as he said it.

"I knew what he meant. Jesus, it's *not* the way to eat. I mean, there are people out there starving to death, begging to have a meal like this. We're fortunate enough to have the food and we can't sit down and eat it because we have two fools that can't keep their mouths off each other long enough for us to do that. I was bitter as hell about it."

Frank sighed, and stayed silent for a few moments, looking into the memory of that time. "Dad just had too damn many rules," he said after a bit. "He'd make ten thousand rules, knowing that nobody could obey them all. That way there was always something he could punch you for. And after MacLaren's, Gary really loved to trespass on Dad's authority."

Gary began missing more and more meals. In many ways, he had already quit our home, and his father's rules were now something to be refused at any cost.

GARY HAD FOUND HIMSELF quite a life outside the house. As the counselor at MacLaren's had surmised, Gary's school relationships didn't figure much into it. Gary's new friends were boys whom he had met during his time in reform school, or older and more experienced associates of these friends.

In particular, Gary started keeping company with those who lived by night. In those days, in the lower part of downtown Portland, there was a bar that catered primarily to a homosexual clientele. Because the police didn't see the customers as a violent or criminally inclined group—and because most vice cops felt stigmatized by having to make gay arrests—it was also rumored as a safe place for teenagers to frequent, as long as their fake ID was credible and they didn't make trouble. This bar became one of Gary's favorite hangouts. Though he would later proclaim loud and hard that he had never been involved in the homosexual activities that are common to prison life, I've found men who would swear otherwise. I've also talked to people who went to this bar with him, who saw him sitting in corner booths, stealing kisses with other young men, or letting the older ones rest a hand on his tight jeans. A man named John used to hang out at the bar, and he took a special interest in Gary and his crowd. John would let the boys bring their girlfriends to his downtown apartment and hold all-night parties, and later, when Gary and some of the others began stealing regularly and needed to hide their goods, John sometimes let them use his place for that too. In exchange for these favors, Gary and the other boys would flip coins, and the loser of the toss would have to suck off John, and sometimes a friend or two of his as well.

Despite his gay flirtations, Gary began to get something of a name for his prowess with young women. Reportedly, they liked the cool way he looked and dressed, and some of them appreciated the ease with which he could come up with not only booze, but also marijuana, cough medicine, and speed tablets. In any case, if a girl went out with Gary, according to some of my brother's friends, they knew it was a fuck date. That was his reputation. Either they would put out, or they would get stuck out on some far distant road, walking the long and scary walk back to their homes alone. Sometimes, Gary and another friend would make a date with a couple of girls, then they would go steal a car, pick up their dates, and take them out on a rural road. Gary would take one in the front seat while his friend would do the other in the back. Then the girls would climb over the seats and repeat the rite with the other guy. Gary was known as being pretty direct, his friends said. "He didn't like to waste much time," according to one crony. "Gary would say something like, 'Okay, how about letting me fuck that pussy of yours now?' Most of the girls didn't mind him talking like that. That's what they hung out with him for."

THE NIGHT ACTION started getting heavier. Gary began breaking into pharmacies or other closed stores, looking for drugs, money, and the odd gun. He liked to build up around a thousand dollars or more, buy some new clothes, some drugs and liquor, and then throw parties until dawn. It was the same thing, night after night. Smoking weed, taking girls up to John's or taking them for a ride, then drinking until everybody passed out. On the nights Gary and his friends couldn't get women, or when the money ran out, they would burglarize another home or store. In the homes they would look for rings and watches. They always liked seeing how other people lived.

On those evenings when Gary still came home, he had to walk past a large supermarket located up the road from Reed College, on Woodstock Boulevard, about a mile from our house. It was one of my family's favorite shopping places, and my father had long been regarded as one of the market's best customers. Once, a few years before, Gary had been caught shoplifting there, and the store manager dragged him by the arm through the store in front of everybody and called my father. My father remained welcome at the market, but Gary was permanently banned. The episode must still have rankled him. Coming home one night, Gary found himself outside the store at closing time. He put a woman's nylon stocking over his head, walked into the store's office, and stuck a gun in the manager's side—the same man who had dragged him by the arm years before. "Unless you want me to put this barrel up your ass," Gary told the manager, "and then squeeze the trigger, you'll give me all the money you have in that safe."

Gary walked out of the store with $18,000 in a grocery bag that night. It held him over for a while. He was never arrested for the robbery. He was never even suspected of it.

ANOTHER NIGHT, GARY was out with a friend named Clyde. They took some pills and went to a Little Richard show. They were celebrating. In an effort to get Gary to straighten up, my father had bought him a used

Oldsmobile. This was Gary's first night with the car. It was a beauty and he was proud as hell of it. Around two in the morning, Gary and Clyde were driving down 82nd Avenue—the main drag on Portland's east side, and a haven for car lots. Gary's Olds ran out of gas.

"Shit," Clyde said, "what do we do now?"

Gary shrugged. "I don't know." He looked out the window and saw a used car lot. "I guess we steal another car."

A few minutes later Gary and Clyde were speeding down 82nd in a 1956 Chevrolet, Gary behind the wheel. They ran a red light, and a moment later a cop car was on their tail, its red lights flashing.

Gary and Clyde looked at each other. "What do you want to do?" Clyde asked. Gary smiled and said: "Fuck 'em." Then he hit the gas.

In those days, 82nd Avenue led quickly and easily to the rural roads around Portland—a no-man's-land then, a no-man's-land now. Gary headed for one of the country roads, roared onto it, and had the Chevy up to 110 miles per hour. There were three police cars coming up fast behind them. Up ahead, Gary saw a blockade of trucks. He swung wildly around the blockade at the last moment, cleared it, and kept on going. Behind him, two of the cop cars wrecked.

"Hoo, boy!" shouted Clyde. "We're *gangsters.*"

A few minutes later Gary heard a sputter. The car was running out of gas. He pulled into a farmhouse driveway, and he and Clyde jumped out. Within moments, fifteen cops were swarming the place, firing warning shots in the air. They grabbed Clyde before he could run or hide, but Gary got away. The next day, trying to save her brother's ass, Clyde's sister told the police: "You can find Gary Gilmore staying at a fruiter's place in downtown Portland." She gave them John's address.

Gary and Clyde stayed in the county jail for a few weeks and were remanded to adult court. Clyde was scared as hell, but Gary seemed to be taking it in stride. His confidence paid off. My father hired a good lawyer—one of Portland's best political attorneys—who somehow got Gary off with one-year probation. Even got the other kid off too. It was back to the good times.

SOONER OR LATER, something had to give.

It happened on a hot summer night, in the middle of July 1957. Gary and Clyde had been out late, looking for the usual fun, the usual trouble. They were coming from a party on the east side, where they had been smoking weed all night, and were walking along 52nd Avenue, near Division. At about 2:30 A.M., they passed an office building. Gary looked around the streets. They were empty and silent in all directions. "Let's hit this building," Gary said. They found a loose window, jimmied it, climbed in. Moments later Gary was going through a desk when he came across a .32 automatic. The gun was loaded and already cocked, but Gary didn't know.

There was a big drugstore down the street. Gary and Clyde decided to go rob it. Walking down Division, Clyde said to Gary: "C'mon, Gary, you've never robbed anybody with a gun before."

"I have too," said Gary. "I robbed a grocery store over by Mom and Dad's house."

"Oh, bullshit. *Show* me how you'd rob somebody."

"Like this," said Gary. He turned around, aimed the gun at Clyde's midsection, pulled the trigger.

Clyde saw blue flame come from the end of the gun, and felt a burning sensation in his stomach. "Aw, man, you shot me," Clyde said, and fell down.

Gary looked at Clyde a moment, then ran down the street.

A little while later, Clyde heard two more shots. "Jesus Christ," he thought. "what'd Gary do—kill somebody, or shoot himself?"

Clyde managed to get up, make it to the street corner and flag down a passing taxi. Told the driver he'd been shot, and to take him to a hospital. When they got to the emergency room, Clyde told the driver: "I'm broke."

"You fucking punk," the driver said, and took off.

An hour later, Clyde's mother was at the hospital and so were the cops. Clyde wouldn't say how he'd got shot or who had done it. His mother turned to an officer and said: "Why don't you check out Gary Gilmore? This looks like something he would do."

NO MATTER HOW MUCH Clyde's family insisted, he would not press charges against Gary for shooting him. "I would have done the same thing," he said later. "I would've thought, 'Hell, I killed the guy. Better take off.' "

It pissed off the police, but they could still hold both of the kids on burglary charges. Once again, they remanded Gary to adult court. This time, a good lawyer couldn't help. He was sentenced to one year in Rocky Butte, the Multnomah County Jail. It was his first real jail time. He was sixteen years old.

———

AGAIN, I HAVE BEEN TELLING you stories that do not come from my own memory. They have been passed on to me either by the oral tradition of my family, or by witnesses, or by interviews or documents of one sort or another. Gary isn't somebody who comes back to me that much through my own memory—or at least not through the memories of my childhood. To be truthful, I don't remember Gary as somebody I saw around our house on a daily basis, like my parents or other brothers. I remember him more as somebody who was talked about—a sort of distant force, whose activities outside the home had a tremendous impact on our peace of mind, like a storm, always looming outside the door.

My mother told me Gary used to hold me on his lap when I was a toddler, that he loved playing with me. She also told me that he used to enjoy taking me downtown with him when he went shopping for school supplies or clothes, that he would usually bring me back loaded down with new loot he had bought for me with his own allowance. When my mother pointed out to him that he had just spent all his money on an already over-indulged child, Gary would laugh. It seemed he got a kick out of the idea that a small kid had actually conned him. I have to take my mother's word for these stories. I simply have no memory of any of these occasions.

I clearly remember only a handful of incidents involving Gary from my early childhood. Here are a couple of them:

One morning—probably during Gary's stretch of freedom between MacLaren's and the county jail—my mother told me to go wake him up. He was going to be late for school. I ran up the stairs and opened the door to my brothers' bedroom. Gary was sitting up in bed. On his right side was a girl with black hair, naked. She was bent over him, her head over his lap, bobbing up and down. On his left was another girl, with long brown hair. She was on her knees and she had one of her breasts in his mouth. Gary looked up and saw me, then tapped the girl with black hair on her head. She stopped sucking my brother and then settled down on the pillow next to him. "This is my little brother Mike," Gary said. The girls giggled, and the one with the black hair made a beckoning gesture. "Hi, Mike," she said. "Want to join us?" Then she shimmied her large breasts for me. I still remember the oval shape of her dark brown nipples.

"Do me a favor, partner," Gary said. "Don't tell Mom and Dad about this. Tell them I wasn't here."

I nodded, then ran down and found my mother. I told her Gary had two girls in bed with him. I don't know why I did it. I always wanted my brothers to like me. Looking back, I figure I just had to tell *some*body, and she was the first person I came across. It's the only time I remember my mother ever being truly mad at Gary. She went into the kitchen and told my father. I remember that my father laughed. "Aw, hell," he said. "He's just being a boy." He went up and talked to the girls in soothing tones. Got everybody dressed, put them in the car, and drove them away.

The other incident I remember vividly took place on a Christmas night—maybe the Christmas after MacLaren's, but more likely a year or two later. This holiday night I was sitting in my room, playing with the day's trove of presents, when Gary wandered in. "Hey, Mike, how you doing?" he asked, taking a seat on my bed. "Think I'll just join you while I have a little Christmas cheer." He had a six-pack of beer with him, and he was speaking in a bleary drawl. "Look, partner," he continued, "I want to have a talk with you." It was probably the first companionable statement I remember him making to me. But what followed was an intimacy I had never expected and could not really fathom at such a young age. Sitting on the end of my bed, sipping at his Christmas beer, Gary stared off into some harsh, private place and told me horrible, transfixing stories. Stories about the boys he knew in the detention halls and reform schools where he now spent much of his time—stories about the hard boys who had taught him the merciless codes of his new life, and about the soft boys who did not have what it took to survive that life.

And then Gary imparted to me one of the few lessons I remember ever hearing from him. "You have to learn to be hard," he said. "You have to learn to take things and feel nothing about them. No pain, no anger, nothing. And you have to realize, if anybody wants to beat you up, even if they want to hold you down and kick you, you have to let them. You can't fight back. You *shouldn't* fight back. Just lie down in front of them and let them beat you, let them kick you. Lay there and let them do it. It is the only way you will survive. If you don't give in to them, they will kill you."

He set aside his beer and reached out and cupped my face in his hands. "You have to remember this, Mike," he said. "Promise me. Promise me you'll be a man. Promise me you'll let them beat you." We sat there that winter night, staring at each other, my face in his hands, and as Gary asked me to promise to take my beatings, his bloodshot eyes began to cry. It was the first of only two times I would ever see him shed tears. And then I promised him: Yes, I'll let them kick me. But I was afraid even as I said it—afraid of actually taking a beating from anyone, and afraid of betraying Gary's plea.

I thought he was telling me how to survive in jail. I realize now he was telling me how to survive in our family.

CHAPTER 4
LIFE WITH
FATHER

IN THE YEARS AFTER I WAS BORN, my father kept his own photo albums, and in those books he had almost exclusively photos of me. I suppose that about sums up the reality of my early years: My father kept me. For many years—in fact, until the day he died—my father and I were our own family.

Nowhere else in life have I known such safekeeping and such love. He would bounce me on his knee and sing "This Old Man" to me ("With a knick-knack paddywack, give the dog a bone/This old man came rolling home"). He would hold me in his arms, tickling me, calling me Tamarac. I have no idea where the name came from or what it meant, I only know it was my father's name for me when I was a child.

As I say, nowhere else did I know such love. And nowhere else have I known such loneliness and fear and guilt.

———

WHEREAS MY BROTHERS lived through vicious physical fights between my parents—all those occasions when my father battered my mother, and my brothers were made to watch—I remember a different experience of argument. I never once saw one of my parents strike the other—or if I saw it, I simply don't remember it. I don't doubt that it happened in the earlier years, but perhaps by the time I was born my father either had learned a certain belated restraint, or was simply too old to whale the shit out of everybody *all* the time. Maybe beating my brothers was now enough to satisfy his rage.

To be sure, my parents fought, and fought frequently. Frightful, mean-spirited yelling matches that would approach the brink of violence but never quite cross over. Instead, my mother and father would hurl terrible invectives at each other. My father would call my mother a "python-spitting she-devil straight from hell" and "a crazy, crack-brained bitch." Even as a small boy—and even as somebody who often took my father's side in the end—I knew these were exceptionally awful things to call anyone, especially the person you loved. In turn, my mother would lash into my father for all the women he had loved, married, and left, or at other times she would call him a "cat-licker"—a Mormon epithet for *Catholic*. Compared to the names my father had thrown at my mother, her insults were mild, but they seemed to goad my father even more. After she made fun of his religion, he would go on a tirade about Mormons—about the evil Danites and how they did Joseph Smith's work of murder, and how Brigham Young, who was once married to twenty-seven women at the same time, had been nicknamed "Bring 'em Young." At the end of these rants, he would turn to me or my brothers and say: "The next time you're in Salt Lake City, boys, I want you to take a look at that pompous statue they have of Brigham Young in Temple Square. I want you to look real good. If you look, you'll see that he's got his hand to the bank and his ass to the church." It was a dumb-enough joke (though as it turns out, an apt description of how the statue actually stands), but it would hurt my mother deeply. She probably felt in those moments that my father was denigrating her entire past, reducing it to a petty joke. What maybe hurt more was that, to some degree, she had herself repudiated that past—her history and legacy as a Mormon, her hope of being a good church member and enjoying access to God's care and truth—so that she could be with the man who now took such delight in belittling her.

One way or another, these arguments always seemed to mount to the crescendo of a threat. My father would threaten to leave my mother and my brothers and withdraw his support, leaving them to their own inept resources, or he would threaten to throw my mother out of the house and make her live on the street, without money or forgiveness. I can still recall the hubristic, brutish tone with which he would taunt her, and I can still recall how her face became contorted in a pain-filled fury as my father's warnings wore on. Then he would start in on her sanity. This was probably the most malicious behavior I ever saw from him—even uglier in a way than when he hit my brothers—and it had a wicked, surefire effect. By calling her crazy, Frank Gilmore could provoke Bessie Gilmore to a state where she acted crazy. Her eyes would turn sharp with anger, and her face would become a strange mask that would seem in one moment both frozen and wild—as if she were containing the worst impulses a heart and mind could bear. And then she would say: "You're right—I *am* crazy. I am crazy enough to kill. Go ahead, accuse me some more, try to walk out on me. See what I'll do. I'm crazy enough that some night, when you're in your sleep, I'm going to take a sharp knife and cut your throat, and I'll laugh while your blood runs out and you gasp for the last breath of your rotten, cruel life."

Whether my mother ever meant her promises of harm or not, she was convincing in her delivery. In those instances, she was the scariest thing I have ever seen. Her eyes fixed on my father with the sort of deadliness that can only come from having been deeply wronged by the person you love most. It was in those moments, when I saw that look of menace on my mother's face, that I learned to fear anger. In particular, I learned to fear the anger of a hurt woman. Unfortunately, I also learned how to make some of that anger.

When my mother finally became the crazed creature my father accused her of being, it would break the momentum of the battle. It was as if my father felt he had won his point, but also feared what might come of his victory. He would quiet down and withdraw into his office, and my mother would be left standing there with her anger and her humiliation, in an empty room.

What made these scenes especially indelible for me was that the fights were often about the same subject: They were about me. They were about which of my parents would enjoy the custody and company of me, from day to day and place to place.

Maybe my father never fully trusted my mother with my welfare after the incident in my infancy that Frank had told me about. Maybe he felt he had to keep me close to him to assure that no sudden harm would come to me. Or maybe he simply realized he was getting older—he was nearing his late sixties during the period that I am describing here—and perhaps he simply wanted a faithful presence close to him. I suspect I might have been my father's last chance for love—a love that wouldn't refuse or betray him, or question his hard ways too much. "That man loved Mike," my mother told Larry Schiller, years later. "Really loved him. It might be the only person in the world he ever loved, but he loved that kid." And Gary himself said: "I think Mike was the only one of us that Dad ever really loved."

Whatever his reason, my father wanted me with him wherever he went. Since he traveled often for his publishing business, this meant he and I would spend a season or two in Portland, then a few months in Seattle or Tacoma, and then back and forth between these various stations. After I turned six, this meant that I would also have to go back and forth between schools, sometimes attending as many as three or four different schools in a single grade year. (With the possible exception of the first grade, I never attended any school for the entire duration of a single year until the sixth grade, the year after my father's death.)

Neither the local grammar school in Portland nor my mother thought that all this moving was such a good idea, and this is part of what became the core of contention between my parents. My father wanted me to go with him when he would travel, and my mother wanted me to stay on Johnson Creek and remain in our neighborhood school. But the argument went further. My mother also viewed my father's possessiveness of me as an attempt to keep my love to himself and to turn me against the rest of the family. "He's my baby boy," my mother would say. "He needs to be with his mother, he needs to be close to his brothers. You're doing a horrible thing: You're turning him against me, you're making him spurn us."

I hated these fights. I remember I used to stand among my parents, spreading my arms between them, trying to keep them from hurting each other. I would beg them to stop fighting. It was like I was at the center of two monstrous, clashing forces, and if I could just make plain that I loved and wanted them both, then maybe I could stop their quarrels. Maybe then we could be a family together. Sometimes, when the bickering reached a fever pitch, my mother would say: "Let Mike choose for himself." My father would agree to this plea, but it was apparent from the way he looked at me or instructed me that I really had no choice. "Go ahead," he would say. "Choose which of us you want to be with.

Stay with your mother if you like. I'll just go away by myself, and maybe I won't come back. If you don't want me, nobody wants me." Also, by this time the arguments would invariably have reached a point where my mother had been called crazy and was hurt enough to appear that way, and the prospect of staying alone in that house with her terrified me.

I would be standing there, looking back and forth between my father and my mother, and I would almost always choose my father in these moments.

I remember well—indeed, will never be able to forget—the impact this decision would have on my mother. Her face would lose its frantic aspect and would fall into undisguised heartbreak and I would feel a horrible guilt, as if I had just hit her myself. I remember one time watching her crumble into a heap on the sofa, crying into her hands. I immediately regretted my choice, and I wanted to comfort her. I went to my mother and reached out to hold her. She flung me back, anger reddening her face, and cried: "Stay away from me. You don't love me." I ran to my father's side for protection. My mother said: "Oh, Mike, I would never hurt you. I *do* love you. Come to me." But by that time I was too wary, and I would stand next to my father, my arms wrapped around his strong legs, fearing her, pitying her, and wanting to be as far away from her as possible.

"That was your cross," my brother Frank told me, many years later. "I used to see you carrying that around inside you when you were little, the way you stayed away from everybody else. Many years later I used to think about that—you, stuck between them, having to choose which of them to be with. I felt for you at those times, but there wasn't anything I could say or do. There wasn't anything any of us could say or do."

This is the way I learned how to love: choosing between two loves that I could not live without and that I could never hope to reconcile. I learned that, in some ways, loving could be like killing—or that at least a certain kind of choosing was like murdering. I knew I had to hurt my parents by choosing to abandon one or the other, by being forced to declare which one I preferred over the other, which one I loved more than the other. In effect, I would kill the heart of one of them by revealing this truth, and for the most part, it was my mother's heart I had to kill. (No wonder I feared her.)

Years later, all this would feed into not only my own betrayals in love, but my misgivings about the hopefulness of the whole enterprise. Because I knew how awful it was to withhold or withdraw love, I came to fear somebody doing the same to me. I knew that to be left was to be rejected, condemned, declared unworthy. I feared, above all, somebody telling me that they didn't love me or want me or need me or want to share a life with me. In other words, I became afraid of ending up as the victim of the same sort of choices I'd had to make virtually every season of my early childhood. So sometimes I would withhold love or hedge its bets, sometimes with one too many lovers at the same time. Just as often, I would end up on the receiving end—as the one not chosen, the one left behind.

It's possible, of course, that I'm leaning too much on these childhood dramas. Maybe my failures in love are simply mistakes that I alone hold the deed for. I botched the chances God gave me for love, on my own. I made for myself the unworthiness that lives in my life.

But still I have to wonder: I never thought of my parents when I kissed a woman. So why did I think of them every time I lost or failed a woman?

A FEW TIMES, WHEN MY mother would threaten my father with murder in his sleep, he took her warnings seriously—or else decided to dramatize her craziness further—and folded out the couch in the living room, to make his bed for the night there. On these occasions, he kept me next to him. The idea was either to keep me under his protection or to ensure his own safety by having me near. Before he would turn out the lights, he would take the chairs from the dining table and line them up in front of the sofa, and then he would take a heavy cord and loop it through the backs of the chairs, stringing them into a barricade. On the cord, he would hang a pair of large, rotund Chinese bells that he usually kept on his desk. That way, if my mother tried to sneak across the barrier, we would hear the bells clang. Sort of a makeshift alarm against familial murder in the dark.

Then my father would lie down, with him on the side closer to the chairs and me on the wall side, and he would fall asleep. I, however, would lie awake. I could never sleep through these nights.

I would lie there in the dark, waiting for the sound of my mother's footsteps, prepared to see the glint of a blade. I heard sounds—maybe my brothers moving around upstairs or stealing off into the night—and I'd wonder: Was it the sound of somebody coming down to kill us?

I sat up in the bed and studied the shadows of the forms about me. I could see the outline of the chairs. I could see the bells hanging on the string. But in the far reaches of the room's darkness—in the corner by the staircase, in the doorways leading to and from other rooms—I thought I could see other things. I could imagine what might be moving in that darkness. Anger and hatred and the spirit of murder moved there, in my mind's view. My mother's madness moved there. My brothers' pain. They were crouched in the shadows: forces ready to sweep down on us and stab out our lives.

Next to me my father kept sleeping, one arm sprawled out toward me, his mouth open, declaring his age: the pink, vulnerable gums that showed when he removed his dentures. In that dim light, in that insensible pose, he already looked like a dead man.

I lay back and kept listening for a movement. For a creak from the floorboards. For the rattle of the knife drawer. There are so many sounds that make so little sense in the silences of a deep night. So many that could be everything you fear the most. I would shut tight my eyes and try to force sleep to come, but it never would. Then I'd try studying the patterns on the stained wallpaper, the configurations in the lacy curtains. I think sometimes during these all-night vigils, something in me went a little mad. The forms in the wallpaper, the web in the curtains, looked like little silhouettes of demons, vignettes of hell. I was afraid I'd caught some of my mother's madness. Maybe it had found its way to me, through the straits of darkness that moved in that house and in our lives. Or maybe it was merely the sleeplessness of an anxious child. I've never been a very good sleeper. Sometimes, even now, I wake up sudden. I know that something has just moved in the dark room that I am in. I feel somebody standing by my bed, and I have just heard the quick sucking sound they made, as they abruptly hold their breath. Of course, nothing is ever really there. It's just something that comes up out of my sleep, up out of me and my memory.

I would lie awake for hours on those nights, expecting my mother to come and keep her promise. When the sky began to lighten, and the room's blackness turned to the horrible dull gray of morning, I would finally feel safe enough to roll over on my side, press my feet up against my father's legs, and fade into sleep.

THAT'S WHEN THE DREAMS STARTED. *When I was around five or six years old, the dreams took basically two forms. The first set of dreams had to do with things dwelling in the darkness. My father and brothers had built a wooden porch on the back of our house, and at ground level the porch had a door which led to a storage shed for garden tools. It was a dark, dank place, with a dirt floor, and I hated it. I would never go into it. In the dreams, I would be standing in the night in front of the porch's door and it would open. I would see things spinning in the dark inside. They had fierce red eyes and sharp teeth, and they ran fast in circles, in coiling motions. I decided they were rats, and I was afraid of being devoured by them. Other times, I dreamed that something lived in our basement. In the dreams, the basement was like a dungeon—like what you might imagine from Edgar Allan Poe's descriptions of the labyrinths that ran under houses rotting from their own secrets, though I didn't associate Poe with the dreams until many years later, after reading him and taking him for my first muse. What moved in that basement in my dreams had no form. It was like a vapor, and stepping halfway down the stairs, I saw it swirl at my feet. I ran upstairs and tried to wake my family and tell them there was something coming for us from the depths of our home, something that would enter our breath in our sleep and kill us. But I could never succeed in waking them.*

My other childhood dreams were more disturbing, and I have never disclosed them until now. The most common scenario of these dreams ran like this: I was a policeman or a detective—a little blond boy in a detective's suit, with a snap-brim hat and a pistol—and I was investigating a killing. I always had a partner in the dreams, and the partner was always a little girl, also with blond hair—somebody I knew I was in love with. But as the dream went along, I would realize it was I who was the killer I was seeking, and the only way to protect myself and my guilt was to kill the little girl who was my partner, whom I loved. I would kiss her, hold her close, then shoot her. I remember also—in one particularly horrible variant of this dream pattern—that sometimes I would kill any other child or baby that I came across in the story.

I had no idea what these dreams were about when I was a child—naturally, I had no idea that dreams could be about anything—and even at this date I wouldn't profess to understand or explain them. I know that I would wake up from the dreams feeling terribly guilty, and I never told anybody about them. Sometimes, I'd go to sleep at night praying to God: "Please don't let me dream the killing dreams."

But prayers never stopped the bad dreams. Never once.

AND SO I BECAME MY father's constant companion. Every several weeks, we would pack up and make the two-hundred-mile drive to Seattle or Tacoma. We would sing songs the whole way—silly, spirited stuff, like "Giddyup, Napoleon, It Looks Like Rain" or "Oh, Susannah" or songs from *Oklahoma!* We even sang "This Land Is My Land" and "Blue Suede Shoes." And when my father felt like taking the solo spot, he'd try his hand at a Verdi or Puccini aria. We were both god-awful singers, but I don't think we knew and I'm certain we didn't mind. On the occasions when somebody else came along for the ride, they could barely withstand the musical part of the trip.

When we would arrive in the town where we were going to stay, my father would rent an apartment or small house. These accommodations were always in an aging, somewhat forlorn part of town. In Seattle, we lived in neighborhoods like Queen Anne Hill and Ravenna. Today, Queen Anne has been refurbished and looks like it could have been transplanted from San Francisco's Nob Hill. In the 1950s, though, it was a tired part of town—a bargain district for affordable housing—and parts of it were creeping up on dilapidation. We usually rented rooms or suites in old post-Victorian-era houses that were clearly on their last legs. Sometimes we were the only tenants who would occupy rooms in these places. To me, they resembled the moody, ramshackle, haunted houses you saw in a black-and-white ghost thriller, and maybe that's how I got my abiding attachment to horror stories.

I suppose these places we rented reminded my father of the older world he had grown up in, or maybe the disappearing world where he had hidden for so long and where he still found a certain comfort. These were the years before fast-moving urban renewal projects had razed cities of many of their antiquated structures of desolation and replaced them with cleaner, ready-made structures of desolation. There were people living in these old houses who had grown up and lived in such rooms and buildings their whole lives, and they wanted to die in those rooms before the world built its new rooms. I can't say for sure that my father was somebody enamored of an old world—actually, he was somebody who always loved buying the newest camera and recording technology and who was excited when Americans began to explore space—but there was a certain milieu that was his realm, that he felt fully confident within, and nothing could budge him from it.

I remember one place in particular where we lived in Seattle. It was set back off the sidewalk about two hundred feet—a dark old house poised on top of a large, trestle-style wooden framework. To get from the sidewalk to the front door, you had to cross a half-rotten wooden bridge that had a few planks missing. Beneath the bridge was nothing but a jungle of briers and weeds, so overgrown and vast that you couldn't see down to the ground where the tangle began. There were steps off the side of the building going down into that snarl, but nobody in their right mind would have walked those stairs. According to my father, in the early twentieth century there had been a massive fire that had half-leveled many of Seattle's homes. When the area was rebuilt, he said, a false ground was raised over several of the collapsed homes. In other words, there was a dead city buried under the part of town we lived in. Some people even thought that some of the old houses still stood under the ground, or at least, the husks that were left of their burned remains still survived there. Down in that web of thorns and bushes beneath our house, my father told me, were the remnants of another house. Sometimes I'd stand on the bridge and look down into that moat of undergrowth, and I'd imagine the skeleton of the other house down there. I would wonder if it was still full of the skeletons of the people who had once lived in it. Every time I saw a rustle in that underbrush, it gave me a chill. I didn't dream well in that house, but that was nothing new.

JUST AS MY FATHER LIKED old houses, when he went out on a shopping spree he preferred to make the rounds of secondhand and rummage outlets, like the Salvation Army, Goodwill, or St. Vincent de Paul stores, or Seattle's Farmers' Market complex (these days a refurbished mall of hip stores and cafés sprawling along the city's downtown pier, but in the late 1950s a maze of rummages and old bookstores, and coffee shops full of vagrants). These were my father's favorite places to find old clothes to dress us both in, and to find antediluvian furniture for our antediluvian dwellings.

Naturally, I accompanied my father on these outings. I was his appointed shadow. He dressed me in fashions that matched his own. He'd slick my hair back with a thick pomade—the same pomade he used on his own thinning gray hair. He'd outfit me in slacks and sport coats and pastel or woolen dress shirts like his own, and then he would put a string tie on me and a fedora on my head. I know we were a striking and strange pair—an old man with a nearly identical little boy. Because of his age, many people assumed that my father was in fact my grandfather. I would reply that, no, he was my father, and people seemed surprised, even disbelieving. I couldn't understand this, and it bothered me. Later, when I began to make a few friends in grade school and would go over to visit at their homes, it was my turn to be shocked when I saw that they had parents who seemed so unaccountably young—parents who, no doubt, were in their late twenties or mid thirties. I had never been around people of such age or manners. I couldn't understand them, couldn't relate to them and, to tell you the truth, couldn't really relate all that well to their children, who were supposed to be my friends. They seemed like aberrations to me, though of course it was me and my father who were the aberrations. Maybe that's why I never formed any lasting friendships with other kids until after my father died.

I was supposed to be in school during these moves, but my father was not overly concerned with such niceties. Sometimes, after we first moved into a new area, he would keep me at home for several weeks before enrolling me in the local school. If it was spring, he'd figure it wasn't worth enrolling me at all and would keep me home until fall. There were numerous ways in which these prolonged absences from school weren't all that good for me, but the one area I felt it most immediately in was math studies. In the late 1950s, second or third grade math levels might vary considerably between two school districts, especially school districts in different states. I would move into a school in Seattle, and they would be teaching the basics of division, when I barely knew how to carry my ones when adding multiple numbers. In theory, teachers should be helpful or patient with a confused student, though I don't remember many who were, or who were inclined to make exceptions. Most just figured I was dumb or lazy about math. Or perhaps they knew that my father was something of a perennial floater, and that made me the roving son of a roving man, which made me hardly worth their trouble. In any event, I never became too adept at math, never developed much affection for its intricacies. Its laws and mysteries intimidated me, and I felt like I *must* be stupid after all, because I couldn't figure out the arithmetical rules and regulations that other kids seemed so quick to understand.

However, when it came to reading, it was a different matter. My father had taught me to read long before the first grade. He would sit me on his knee at his desk, pointing at words in picture books, teaching me to recognize them and how to master the logic of their shapes and the pronunciation of their letters. It's true, he wouldn't read to me at night— maybe because he wanted me to read to myself. And read I did. Reading became one of the activities I loved most in life. It was something I could do alone, and of course it was a great method of escaping the reality of the life around me. The first stories I remember falling in love with were EC crime and horror comics, and comic book adventures by Carl Barks—the man who wrote the great 1940s and '50s Donald Duck and Uncle Scrooge tales for Walt Disney's comics. Barks was a smart man—

he knew the scope and meanings of the ancient mythological tales inside and out, and he transformed them to the world of talking ducks with a wit and moral integrity that cost the original stories none of their depth or wonder. After Barks, it was an easier step to appreciate not just the adventurism of Jack London, Jules Verne, or Alexander Dumas, but also the full-breadth drama and incredible longing that one found in ancient epics like the *Iliad* or the *Odyssey,* or some of the other Roman and Greek legends. A few year later, I would form a deep passion for horror writers, like Poe and Bram Stoker, and the ghost stories of Henry James and Émile Zola and Ambrose Bierce. I didn't always understand the language of what I read—and I certainly didn't get some of the more subtle themes of the stories—but the world these people described was a world I felt at home in.

In the evenings, I would sit on a sofa in the living room, near where my father worked, and I would read my comic books, or the Scribner hardbacks of books like *Treasure Island, Kidnapped!* or *20,000 Leagues Under the Sea,* with their lusty N. C. Wyeth illustrations. Then my father would turn out his desk lamp and join me on the sofa, and he would turn on the television. He had a regular slew of shows he liked to watch—mostly crime fare, like *The Untouchables, Richard Diamond, Highway Patrol*, and *The Defenders,* or Westerns, like *Gunsmoke, Wagon Train, Maverick*, and *Have Gun, Will Travel.* Unlike my mother, my father would never try to stop me from watching the horror films I loved, and he always seemed to know fascinating anecdotes about Bela Lugosi and Boris Karloff that had the effect of humanizing the men behind the monsters. (Which was hardly necessary, since I almost always took the side of the monsters anyway. To me, the human characters were boring and expendable time-wasters; they existed so the misunderstood monsters could kill them and pay back humanity's unkindnesses.)

I remember that whenever *Les Misérables* would come on—the 1935 version, with Fredric March and Charles Laughton—my father would make me sit and watch it with him. "Remember this story," he told me once, after we had witnessed the merciless police inspector Javert hound Jean Valjean for his petty criminal past. "Remember how the world can persecute a man for his simple mistakes, and remember what a horrible thing a pious judge is."

He would put his arm around me and draw me close to him. In those hours, I felt safe against the world, but I knew from my father's words that there were hard punishments yet to come.

SOMETIMES WHEN WE WENT out dressed alike, my father would visit what were known as the skid-row parts of town, where transients and heavy drinkers hung out. Today some of these people would be called homeless, but in those days were called bums. In Seattle, which had once been something of a rowdy pioneer and gold rush town, and which still had some fairly hard types working on its docks, the skid-row parts of town were considered rough quarters. My father would visit the area's missions and its taverns. He would order a short beer and talk to bartenders about their customers. My father knew that broken men could be found in these places, and for one reason or another, these were the men he wanted to have work for him. In part because they would work cheap and were easy to domineer. Also, they probably reminded my father of his own down-and-out times. Often, he would bring these whiskered men to live in the same house with us. He'd buy them clothes—used clothes, of course—and he'd put them to work as telephone salesmen. If they kept their drinking out of our home and never let it affect their work, and if they did not steal from him or become temperamental, he treated them well. But if they abused his trust or became drunk and rowdy, he fired them on the spot. I remember well the two or three times he punched out men who were probably half his age and twice his strength. My father would make a fist and throw it at their stomach. That always disabled them. Then he hit them in the face until they begged him to stop. Then he would throw them and their belongings out the door, give them a few dollars, and warn them: "Never come around us again."

In those times, when my father visited the bars or taverns, he expected me to take care of myself. He would give me a few dollars and tell me to find a store to shop in or to go catch the bus and find a movie to see. Looking back, I realize I was allowed an amazing amount of movement for a kid. I was free to ride buses to downtown Seattle or the city zoo by age eight, and I was free to stay out until past the hour of darkness. I don't remember anybody ever threatening or scaring me during these times, and I don't remember any adult asking me what I was doing out on my own, without a parent or guardian. When I couldn't find a good bookstore or movie house, I'd spend hours exploring abandoned old houses in the Queen Anne district. It was rumored that if you dug around in the basements of the older dwellings in the area, you would sometimes find passages into an antique underworld—the world left by the awful fire from generations before. All I ever found, though, were dirty ruins and an occasional discarded keepsake.

THE TRUTH IS, I WAS a young boy living with an old man in what was left of an old world. We shopped in old stores, we ate in old diners, we dressed in old suits. It's as if I were a child dressed up for the 1940s, living on the verge of the 1960s.

All this seemed normal to me—it was the only world I knew. But perhaps on some level I recognized that it wasn't normal, and maybe this recognition took its toll. Looking back, I now believe I probably experienced some periodic childhood depression—which shouldn't seem surprising. Once in a while, during these periods of living with my father, I would catch an illness that was like an odd, prolonged spell. These bouts would usually last for a whole day and night, during which I would lie in bed or wrapped up on the sofa, and I'd imagine that other people— usually members of my family—would come in and out of the room and talk to me. For some reason, when I was lying in the darkness, I'd concentrate on my hands. It felt like there was a great weight at the center of my palms and that if I could just close my fist around that feeling—if I could just capture it and hold it—I'd be okay. I'd squeeze hard enough to cut my nails into my palms.

Once or twice I hallucinated something else: my father sitting on the edge of my bed with a strange woman. He'd pull the top of her dress down until her breasts fell out, and she would look at me and giggle. "Leave the boy alone," my father said, and I'd fall back into my fitful half sleep. Some might say that what I've just described is an example of recovered memory—in other words, that a scene like this may actually have happened, but I probably suppressed conscious memory of it. I don't believe that's true. I don't think for a moment that my father brought other women into the houses where I lived with him, and I have no evidence that he had any affairs during his marriage to my mother. I'm not sure where a child gets a vision like the one I had. Maybe from a part of my unconscious that I somehow shared with my father, or maybe from some presentiment of my own future erotic fever.

Still, my fever dream reminds me of something I saw a few years later, when I was poking through my father's desk drawers. It was a photo-graph of a nude man standing by a swimming pool, between two nude, large-breasted women. With each hand, he is reaching out and petting the women's pubic bushes. Meantime, the woman on his left has her hand wrapped around his erect penis, while the other, smiling widely, has reached over and is cupping his balls. I remember it vividly for two reasons: One, it was the first explicitly sexual picture I'd ever seen, so of course it inflamed my mind. The other reason: I am fairly certain that the man in the picture was a younger version of my father. Either that, or perhaps he was one of my father's other sons—somebody who carried the stamp of Frank Gilmore's face—but then, that would be a bit *too* weird, wouldn't it? All I know is that later, when my father died and we were dividing up his stuff, I went into his desk to find that photo. It was gone, and I never saw or heard anything about it again.

ONE YEAR, WHEN IT WAS clear that my father and I would be spending much of the Christmas season in Seattle, my mother boxed up some of our old, no-longer-used holiday decorations for me. These ornaments were as old as everything else in our life—a chipped Santa Claus figurine, an incomplete Nativity set (missing the head of the baby Jesus), and a plastic chime box in the shape of a cathedral. When you wound a key on the back of the box, a hymn would play and the painted plastic golden doors would slowly crank open, revealing a backlit Renaissance painting of the Ascension. (I realize now it was actually an Easter relic, though that wouldn't have made much difference to my childhood comprehension of the holiday's religious importance.)

When Christmas came around that year, I fell sick again with one of my spells, and my father and I were unable to make the drive to Portland to spend the holiday with the family. My mother was bitterly disappointed, and she accused my father of lying to her, or me of faking the sickness so that we could spend the holiday alone. I spent that actual Christmas day in bed with the plastic cathedral next to me, endlessly winding its key and watching its doors open to the painting of the flock of angels surrounding the rising Lord, while my father sat in the apartment's front room, arguing heatedly on the phone for hours with my mother. The longer I stared at the old Christmas decorations and at the old walls of the apartment and its old doorframes, the sicker and more depressed I became. I felt like I wanted those angels to take me away from all this, into their bright, promising realm of love. I prayed for them to let me die and to lift me into heaven. Of course, they didn't.

By the middle of the night, still in a delirium, I'd come to curse the angels and the damn chime box. I threw it against the wall, breaking its cheap doors. I hated the angels, I told myself, because they wouldn't let me die.

A day or two later I was better, and my father drove us under the winter sky back to our home in Portland. We sang our silly songs in our awful voices the whole way, right until we turned into the driveway.

DESPITE HIS VIOLENCE, my father was not much of a fan of guns. My brothers were allowed BB or pellet rifles, but the rules on how they handled these weapons were strict. Handguns were out of the question— though I now recall that after my father died and we were sorting through his possessions, we came across what I believe was a Luger, in a shoulder holster. Some of us thought we should keep the gun, along with his rare East Indian jade and ruby rings, but my mother said no. There were bad memories tied to these things, she claimed, and she would not let anybody in the family keep them. She had a friend of hers take the gun and sell it at a pawnshop.

At one point, though, my father decided it was okay for the family to own a rifle. (This was probably after Gary's adventure with the stolen Winchester.) My brothers were reaching the age where boys went hunting, and my father thought they should learn how to handle a gun safely.

In the abandoned yard behind our house there was a thicket in which lived a couple of pheasants. In the early evenings, we would watch as one of the pheasants—the male, I think—would rise into the sky and fly off. A half hour or so later, he would return to his mate. We loved these birds and admired their beauty and their freedom of movement—and so, of course, my brothers decided to kill them, and my father agreed to supervise the shooting. He figured it would be a good test of their hunting skills to try to hit a moving target.

I remember these sessions pretty well. It was late spring, in the hours after school was out and before dinner. It was one of those few occasions all the males in my family, including Gary, gathered together for a common pleasure. My brothers would take turns shooting at the male pheasant as it made its flight upward and then back. Because the bird usually made this flight only once each evening, the shooting sprees were fairly limited ventures. Each brother—except for me, who was too young to handle a gun—only got to squeeze off a few shots each night.

During these times, my father sat on the back porch, watching his sons shooting, saying little, except to offer an occasional instruction or caution. The shooting sessions went on for a few days, without anybody scoring a hit on any of those poor dumb, lovely birds. Finally, my father lost his patience. "Jesus Christ, some shooters you guys are. You couldn't even hit the broad side of a barn."

Gary turned to my father and said: "I don't see you doing any better. It's pretty easy just to sit there and criticize, oh, great white hunter."

My father got up off the porch and walked over to where we were standing. He took the rifle out of Gary's hand. "Watch," he said. A few minutes later, the pheasant was making his return sweep. In one move, my father lifted the rifle's butt to his right shoulder, took a quick sight on the bird, and squeezed the trigger. The pheasant seemed to explode in a circular spray of red and dropped to the ground. My father lowered the rifle, turned, and walked off. He went inside the house and shut himself into his office.

Gaylen ran to the thicket to find the pheasant. It took a few minutes to locate it amid all the brush. After a bit, he came running back, holding the bird by the neck. He laid it on the ground before us. What had a few minutes before been the bird's head was now an ugly mess of bloody pulp.

"Son of a bitch," said Gary. "He nailed the fucker right through the head."

Looking at the bird, I felt sick and awful. I had wanted to see this creature shot dead as much as my brothers had wanted to shoot it, but now that I was looking at its sprawled, lifeless form, I realized I would never see the pheasant fly again or hear its call. It felt like we had just committed an unforgivable sin.

I went off and sat a few feet away while my brothers plucked the bird's feathers. I told myself that I would never pick up a gun, never fire one, never shoot anything.

And to this day, I never have.

PART FOUR

THE WAY

SOME

PEOPLE DIE

The graves grow deeper.
The dead are more dead each night.

Under the elms and the rain of leaves,
The graves grow deeper.

The dark folds of the wind
Cover the ground. The night is cold.

The leaves are swept against the stones.
The dead are more dead each night.

A starless dark embraces them.
Their faces dim.

We cannot remember them
Clearly enough. We never will.

"THE DEAD,"
by Mark Strand

CHAPTER 1
BROTHERS:
PART TWO

I HAVE SAID VERY LITTLE so far about my other brothers, Frank Jr. and Gaylen. In part, that's because the marriage of my parents and the troubles with Gary occupied so much space in our family drama. But by concentrating on those stories—particularly Gary's—I run the risk of saying that those are the family's only stories that truly mattered. Also, by reporting that Frank Jr. and Gaylen were physically and emotionally mistreated just as much as Gary was, and yet neither of them went on to match Gary's criminal life or to kill anybody or to die at the executioner's hands, is to invite some people to say: "Look, these boys had it bad too, yet they did not kill. Therefore, Gary's evil must have been his own doing—it had to arise out of his own will and his own peculiar meanness." Even my mother had to face this possibility. "I raised both Frank

Jr. and Gary side by side," she told Larry Schiller in 1977. "One son picked up the gun. The other did not pick up the gun. Why?"

That one child killed and the other did not is, obviously, an important matter. But the fact that my brother Frank wasn't a killer does not mean he did not also suffer a damage worthy of killing. There are all kinds of ways to die in this world. Some die without taking others with them. It's a victory, no doubt, but that doesn't make it the same as redemption.

I HAVE ALREADY MENTIONED that Frank was a magician. As a child, I spent many hours watching him pull silk scarves out of thin air or make a bouquet of flowers materialize and then disappear with a wave of his hand. I begged him to show me how to perform the same wonders, but Frank took pride in what he had learned and would not easily give up his secrets. He showed me how to accomplish a few tricks, but when he tried to show me the intricacies of his legerdemain—for example, how to manipulate or hide coins or playing cards with a subtle movement of your fingers—I couldn't match his skills. Frank Jr. simply had remarkably deft hands and a keen patience. A few times over the years, when he would perform at local schools, he let me work as his assistant on a handful of tricks. Those were some of the proudest moments I ever had with any of my brothers.

I never really understood why Frank Jr. didn't stay with his avocation. Obviously, magic or any other performance skill can be difficult to parlay into a successful career, but Frank probably had the talent to make such an ambition work. For that matter, he is still an accomplished sleight-of-hand artist. One day, a year or so ago, Frank came over to my apartment in Portland and showed me a few card tricks he had been working on. He would tell me to draw any card from the deck, memorize it, and put it back in the deck. He'd ruffle the cards, pass his hand over them, and the card I had chosen would rise mysteriously upward from the pack as he held it upright in his hands. He could even make my chosen card pop up in the deck backward. I was just as impressed that day by Frank's artistry as I had been as a child, and so I asked him: Why had he never gone on to become a professional magician? Frank smiled that shy, broken smile of his, folded his deck and put it back in his pocket.

His interest in magic, he told me, stemmed from a time when he was nine years old and had seen a magician perform a few feats at a Portland school assembly—standard stuff, like pulling rabbits from a hat, producing doves from a silk handkerchief, drawing half-dollar coins from an unsuspecting schoolboy's mouth. Frank Jr. went back home and told our parents what he had seen. It was all he talked about for a week or two. When Frank Sr. saw that his son was interested in magic, he told him he knew a thing or two about the craft himself. Said he had been around it a lot during his circus career and in the years with Fay, and had learned how to perform many of the stock tricks when he worked as a clown with Barnum & Bailey. My father offered to introduce Frank to some local magicians and to supply him with some texts about the secrets of magic.

Frank Jr. started learning a few tricks, and he would take them to my father and practice them for him. My brother had a trick where he would break an egg in a pan and then make a little chick appear. My father showed him ways to improve on the effect. "I never showed Dad a trick that fooled him," Frank Jr. told me. "He never watched one on television that he couldn't tell me how it was done. I don't care if they were sawing a lady in half, making her float, making somebody disappear, he would tell me how it was done. Dad knew all about it. He was way ahead of me."

When he was about fourteen, Frank Jr. was preparing for a show at the Portland Magicians' Society. "It was my initiation show," Frank said, "and I was real nervous about it." Frank proceeded to rehearse his routine in front of our family, but at one point, when he faltered a little in a particular trick, my father stepped in and finished the effect for him, showing him how a polished magician would present it. Frank Jr. was astonished at how good Frank Sr. was. "He was totally confident and smooth," he said. "In fact, I had never seen anything at the Magic Society to match it. He was good, Mikal, very good. But he also embarrassed me that day. He said, 'What you have, Frank, is a love for magic. You don't really have the talent.' He told me that. It's pretty obvious he was right. I *do* have a love for it. I did a lot of it at one time. I actually did it for months and months. But I was never as good as I wanted to be. Certainly not. I was never as good as Dad, to be honest with you."

I was discussing this episode with a friend one day—a woman whose heart and mind have taught me much—and she commented: "What a dirty, rotten trick. To intimidate a fourteen-year-old kid like that, and to make him feel shitty about the one positive thing in his life." She was right, of course. My father's criticisms of Frank's vulnerable pride effectively ended my brother's magic career, just as he was starting it. He went on to give his show at the Magicians' Society, and it went well. But in his heart, Frank Jr. believed he could never match his father's talents in this area. My friend said: "It's as if your father took any accomplishment on his sons' parts as a diminishment of himself. In fact, he made damn sure that they didn't dare do anything he could do. I feel so sorry for fourteen-year-old Frank. And he just accepts this as fact—'I'm not as talented as my father.' Poor guy. He was just a kid."

FRANK NEVER HAD THE appetite for trouble that Gary developed, though when the two of them were young they shared a flair for mischief. Kid stuff, like squirting strangers with squirt guns, tossing eggs and water balloons at passing cars, getting in slug-outs with neighborhood kids.

One night recently, Frank and I were having dinner at a wonderful low-end Chinese restaurant in Portland, memorably named Hung Far Low—a place we had been eating in since we were kids with our family. Over a bowl of soupy Chinese noodles, I asked Frank if he had ever been tempted to try his hand at criminal acts, as Gary had. Frank laughed hard enough that he had to stop eating his soup.

"The beginning and the end of my life in crime," he told me, after a few moments, "involved a Milky Way candy bar. When I was a youngster—in fact, when I was in Catholic school and before the time, I'm sure, that Gary started stealing things—I went into a grocery store and stole myself this Milky Way candy bar. Grabbed it, put it in my pocket, took off. That is, I *almost* took off. The guy working there, he had been watching me. He stopped me and took the Milky Way candy bar from me and said: 'Where do you come from?' Wanted my name and everything. I was real scared, and I told him: 'Well, I go to this Catholic school up the street.' So he called them up and one of the nuns came down and said: 'Yes, that's Frank. What did he do? He stole a *candy bar*? Well, we have got to do something about this. You can't let this go.' And the man said, 'I'm not going to let it go.' He had me dump all these garbage cans, then he had me take the dust mop and dust all the aisles, up and down all of them. Had me go out front and sweep the sidewalk. Man, for a little kid it seemed like a mountain of work. I took all the stuff back in and I said: 'Well, I think I got everything done, and I'm sorry about what I did.' And the man said: 'Okay. By the way, here's your candy bar. You finally earned it.'

"I said, 'Thanks,' and I took my candy bar. I went back home, ate the candy bar, and I wasn't going to say anything. When I went to school the next day, the sister made me go to confession and tell what I did, and when I came back I had to write 'I will never steal again' on the board two or three hundred times. I said to myself, 'Now I *know* I've earned the candy bar—I've done all this.' When I got home that night one of the school's priests had called Dad and told him. On top of everything else I got the razor strap for stealing that candy bar. So, you want to know why I never became a thief? *That* was the reason. At the time it really bothered me, but to this day, when I think about it, I wonder: What if I got by with that candy bar? I think I would have kept stealing candy bars. And who knows—it might have wound up being a lot worse for me."

If punishment deterred Frank, I asked my brother, then why had it never deterred Gary?

Frank thought about the question for a long time. After a bit, he said: "In a way, I would have liked to have seen Gary get that just to see what it would have done. At the same time, he *did* get punished all the time. Not only did all that punishment fail to deter him, it actually seemed to make him act worse. In fact, I think something in Gary *wanted* all that punishment. Something in me, though, definitely did not. I don't know why. I sometimes think that Gary and Gaylen got the crazy side of Mom and Dad, and you and I did not."

Frank looked at me, smiled, shrugged, and went back to eating his soup.

As Gary pursued trouble more, and got into worse fights with my father, Frank Jr. found himself trying to hold the peace at home whenever possible. But it wasn't easy. My father would go to Frank Jr. and Gary and tell them: "I want the garbage out and the lawn mowed tomorrow." The next day, Frank would take the garbage out and mow the lawn, but Gary wouldn't. To save hell for everybody, Frank Jr. would do Gary's share of the work. But none of that seemed to count for much with my father. Apparently he only reacted if you defied him or somehow failed his instructions. If he figured out that Frank had done the work and Gary hadn't, he'd punish them both anyway—forbid them their allowance or their weekend movie or some other promised privilege or reward.

"One time," Frank said, "Dad wanted the basement cleaned up. At that time I had some allergies and I didn't want to go down and clean it up—there was too much dust and dirt down there. I knew I'd get rashes all over me, and when you're a teenager, it's important to look your best. But I didn't know how to tell him. I just said something like, 'Couldn't Gary do it this one time?' Dad said, 'No, I told *you* to do it, and I want it done.' So the next day when he came in, it wasn't done. I wasn't trying to break his rules. But he wasn't the kind of man you could explain things to. I couldn't be honest and say, 'Well, Dad, I'm worried about these allergies I have.' He would have found a way to make sure that I did that particular chore all the time. It was safer to keep it to myself and to take the punishment that I took, which was to be kicked out. He came up to me; his fists were up. He told me to get out, and he wasn't messing around. Said, 'This is my house. You're under my roof. You didn't do what I told you. Get out!' Hell, I'm not going to fight with him, so I got out. Went downtown and lived in a cheap hotel for three or four days, and then I came back. There were plenty of times when he hated me just as much as he hated Gary. And I would go for long periods when I wouldn't even talk to him. We would be at the dinner table, and I wouldn't even talk to him."

My father's minefield of rules became so treacherous that Frank grew tired of trying to traverse it. Toward the end of high school, Frank Jr. decided he wanted to learn the craft of carpentry. He found a good local carpenter's school, enrolled in it, and took a part-time job to help cover the cost. My father agreed to pay the remaining tuition. But during the first week of the course, on four different occasions, Frank Jr. happened to run afoul of various house rules, and on each occasion, my father threatened to cancel the course.

My brother looked at the prospect of a year of school along these lines and decided it wasn't worth all the pain. Frank Jr. went to my father and told him he was quitting carpentry school. He did not want my father holding that power over his future. "The idea that he could build you up to something like that," Frank said, "and then four times in one week take it away from you . . . I thought, man, I'm not going to study all these months just to have him wait until the last moment and say, 'Well, now I see you have something you really want. You've studied for nine months, you're ready to graduate next week, but you're *not going to* because *I'm* not sending the check; you displeased me or violated my rules in some way or another.' Dad would always say, 'My word's my bond,' but that only held true if he promised he'd punish you. If he promised something else, his word was not always his bond. That sort of thing . . . it takes something out of you. I felt like I was being half-killed sometimes."

I hate to say it, but hearing Frank's stories, I became grateful my father died when I was still young, before my own hopes got in his way. I say it in part because I'm glad I never had to fight with him, never got stepped on in the way my brothers did. I also say it because I know the range of my own anger and determination, and my own awful, unswerving stubbornness. If my father had held out the world to me and then taken it from my grasp, I know I would have hated him for it. I may even have killed him for it. Or worse, I might have killed the next person who did such a thing to me. I am glad that my hope and ambition weren't murdered in this way, but more than anything, I'm glad I never killed anybody as revenge for my dispossession.

LIKE GARY, FRANK JR. WAS starting to find his own life outside the family. He was a little embarrassed to tell me about it, though he shouldn't have been.

"I had a friend," Frank Jr. told me during one of our evening visits. "His name was Ron. We were buddies for a long time, quite a few years, and we ran around here in Portland. We would just . . . Well, I'm going to try to put this so you don't look down on me too much, but in those days there used to be a fair amount of prostitution to be found in Portland. Ron and me, we would save our money and go down to this one particular place, and we would mess around. At that time, it was a lot safer and we both ran kind of wild for a while. But then Ron, through his mother, got involved in the study of religion—in particular, a study of the Jehovah's Witnesses. He would talk to me about it all the time, but I wasn't interested. In fact, I had spent several years of my life telling myself I was an atheist. I had big doubts that there even *was* a God. So when Ron got into this religious thing, I didn't want to hear it, because we were into these other things I was telling you about. At the time and because of my age, I was far more interested in *that* than religion.

"One day," Frank continued, "Ron came to me and said: 'I've decided that this religion is right, and I'm going to dedicate my life to it.' He said, 'You and me got one more month of going down the street to where the prostitutes live. At the end of that time, I'm straightening my life out.' So Ron and me went down there and we'd have our fun. We drank and did things. And at the end of the month, Ron lived up to his word. He became a Jehovah's Witness and he stopped. He'd still come over and visit with me, because we remained good friends, and he really wanted me to come into the organization with him. I wouldn't do it. But he did talk Mom into having a six-month study with him. She loved to argue over religion. I would sit in the next room and listen to them, because I didn't want anything to do with it. And Mom, of course, would not accept any of it. She'd say, 'That guy, he's getting worse every week.' But at the end of the time, I was convinced from sitting in the other room and listening to what he said, that Ron was right. And I told Mom. I said, 'I like this; I'm going to take it up.' Mom got really mad at Ron at this point. She went to the Mormon church and had the local bishop come over and talk to me. He told me that what the Jehovah's Witnesses taught was wrong. He said it was better for me to remain a Catholic than become a Witness, because Mormons and Catholics both believed Christ died for your sins, so that when you die you can go to heaven, and the Jehovah's Witnesses don't believe that. I was polite to Mom and the bishop, but I told them: 'This is what I believe.' And I stayed with it. I started subscribing to the Witnesses' magazine, started going to their meetings. I was nineteen years old when I finally accepted it."

There are a lot of things about Frank's story that I like. In particular, I like the idea of these two kids who were thoughtful and conscientious enough to care about salvation, but who were also smart and lustful enough to make sure they squeezed in a few good sins before it was too late.

What I like better, though, is that the story also says that Frank knew there were limits worth knowing. There were limits to how much he should risk his soul for indulgence, and there were also limits to how much he owed his family. By choosing a religion that neither my mother nor father could adhere to, Frank Jr. was making plain that he didn't want to live according to their construction of the world and its worth—that he wanted to find his own path. It was his way of saying he was no longer duty-bound to the family. He had now envisioned a better home, a better life, and he was waiting for the day he could make it his own.

GAYLEN'S STORY IS ANOTHER matter, and trying to tell it raises some peculiar problems for me. Aside from my father, Gaylen—who was born as Gaylen Noel Gilmore—was the only member of my family who was never interviewed at one time or another about his life. In addition, I could find few witnesses or sources willing or able to fill in the missing chunks and secrets. Consequently I have little testimony from which to reconstruct him, except for the narrative of my own memory and the memories of my brother Frank and my cousin Brenda. What's troubling about all this isn't that I don't have interviews or sources about my brother's life, but rather that I should feel I even need such a thing so that I *can* tell his story. After all, I did grow up with Gaylen—I fought with him, laughed with him, resented him, and mourned him. I should know him—and if you had asked me at the outset of this project, I would have said that I thought I knew Gaylen better than I knew almost anybody else in my family.

But it wasn't long before I realized that I didn't know any of these people as well as I should and that I might never know them well enough. There were simply too many spaces between me and my brothers, and Gaylen, like Gary, was somebody who was gone from our home a lot—either in jail or halfway across the country or carousing in the night, looking for the same forbidden rapture that we all ended up looking for. There is only so much I know about what went on during Gaylen and Gary's absences from our home—and, of course, it is in the space of those absences that the two of them tried to make or remake their lives. In other words, it was in their private lives away from the scrutiny of my family that they pursued their biggest desires, committed their worst sins, and felt their worst fears, and whatever those experiences were, their memory and meaning died along with my brothers. Maybe that's for the better. Maybe I should know only so much about those secrets.

Still, I'll never stop wondering. I look at what happened to Gaylen's life and I know that I am looking at another mystery—one that I feel especially disturbed by. If it is true that the way a person dies can sometimes tell us truths about the way the person lived, then I know this much: Gaylen lived with horrible wounds that could not be healed, but they weren't what killed him. What killed him were the things he could not stop doing to himself.

I have never missed anybody in the world as much as I miss Gaylen. Not my parents. Not Gary. Not even the woman I thought could take the place of them all. If I could choose one lost person to spend one more hour with in my life, Gaylen would be that person. I would ask him to solve the mystery, and tell what it was that made him obliterate himself.

GAYLEN WAS PROBABLY THE brother I had the most combustible relationship with. I know that we played together as children. I can see that from some of my father's photos, and I can even recall it, in a fuzzy way. But even in the best of families, the fraternity between us could not have been that easy, given the gap in our ages. By the time I was six, Gaylen was twelve. He was already discovering the wonderful passions and anxieties that come with adolescence, and a kid who reads J. D. Salinger and Jack Kerouac, and who is on the brink of sex and rock & roll, does not want to be caught lingering in the world of Disney. When I would beg Gaylen to take me downtown to see a film like *Darby O'Gill and the Little People,* he would instead take me to see something like *Suddenly Last Summer,* a Tennessee Williams story about a cruel family, cursed by

God and its own demons. When the movie would get too talky for me and I started to complain, Gaylen would say: "Be quiet and sit still or you'll miss the leprechaun scene that's coming up."

By the time my memory really takes hold, I remember Gaylen as somebody who not only pulled tricks on me, but also was one of the more hostile forces in my childhood. Some of the strain between us had to do with the relationship we each had with my father. For years, Gaylen had been my father's favorite son. He was a good-looking, exceptionally bright and charming boy—the one, before me, that my father kept closest to him. But as Gaylen grew older, he began to grow strong in his own ideas, and he also began to develop a quick and nasty temper. My father saw these developments as signs of willfulness and insubordination, and he started beating Gaylen in the same way he beat Frank Jr. and Gary. Also, around age thirteen, Gaylen began putting on a little weight—a brief period of fattening out, before he turned rail-thin for the rest of his life—and my father would make fun of this gain, blaming it on an uncurbed appetite. If Gaylen had a second helping of food at the dinner table, my father ridiculed his request. "Where are you going to fit that?" my father asked. "In your leg? I think your gut's too fat to take much more."

The rupture that developed between Gaylen and my father was exactly that: a rupture. My father's relationship with Gary had always been bad, but Gaylen had once known my father's love. Now, as his position of favor was displaced by me, Gaylen came to know rejection and mockery, and he could not hide the hurt and fury he felt over this. As a result, I sometimes became the target of his anger—like the time he pushed me down a flight of stairs in our home, the same way that Gary had once thrown him off our back porch, or the many occasions he twisted my arm behind my back, to secure my promise to keep one of his increasingly illicit secrets. I remember my father punishing Gaylen once by taking something from Gaylen that Gaylen wanted very much—I think it was one of his pearl-handled, nickel-plated toy six-shooters—and giving it to me. A day or two later, after my father left town on work, Gaylen dragged all my toy guns out in the side yard and locked me in the house. I watched out the dining-room window as my brother smashed toy after toy with an ax. He tossed the shattered heap of plastic in the trash can, and when he came back in, he was crying. "Someday," he said in a voice thick with pain, "he'll hate you too. Just wait."

My worst memory of any of the incidents during this time involved both Gaylen and Gary, and it took place on a Christmas Day. I don't remember where the fight started, but at some point my father and Gary were embroiled in an ugly confrontation. They were each daring the other's toughness, and then they started threatening to kill each other. My mother was pleading with them to stop, but the moment was too tense to get between them. Finally, Gaylen stepped in and asked my father to leave Gary alone. My father—who was already an old man but still amazingly strong—doubled his fist and punched Gaylen in the stomach. I have never forgotten that moment—the sheer awfulness of that blow. Gaylen doubled over in pain and hurt shock, and Gary went over to help him. My father grabbed me and said that we were leaving—that we would spend Christmas in a hotel. This time, though, I did not want to go, and I said so. "Don't *you* turn against me too," he said, and the look of rage on his face was enough to make me go with him. I was afraid of what he might do to us all if I stayed.

My mother begged my father to remain, to apologize to Gaylen and Gary and try to repair the Christmas, or at least to let me spend the holiday with my brothers. My father would hear none of it. As he and I were in the car, pulling out of the driveway, I looked up at my mother and brothers gathered on the porch, watching us leave. I could tell from the way my brothers were looking at me that they would never forgive me this moment, that they would never let me into their fraternity after this.

Pulling out of that driveway, I felt like a traitor. I wanted to join my brothers—to be standing with them on that porch, watching as the source of their hurt left them.

One afternoon a few months later, Gaylen led me out on the back porch and told me he had a present for me. He handed me a small package wrapped in white tissue, with a red ribbon around it. I was thrilled. I loved presents. I undid the ribbon and pulled off the outer wrapping. Inside was a small, odd-shaped object—about the size of one of those prizes that were common at the time in cereal boxes—and this item was also wrapped. I unfolded the inner package, and inside was my present: a hardened clump of dog shit. Gaylen laughed when he saw the stricken look on my face and said: "Don't be such a crybaby. And don't tell Mom and Dad. If you do, I'll pound the living hell out of you." I sat on the porch, looking at my present, feeling like my brothers must hate me. After a while, I threw the gift away and went and sat under the backyard tree for hours. That was the first time I remember thinking that someday I would leave them all behind.

WHEN MY FATHER WOULD QUARREL with Gaylen, he would accuse my brother of following Gary's course. "You're turning into a cheap, no-good crook, just like your brother."

It is true that as Gaylen became disinherited of my father's love, he tried to become possessed of crime. Whereas Gary acted on almost every criminal impulse he had, Gaylen got stuck in contemplating the idea of the criminal life. He lived the ideal enough to impress a few friends and women—and enough to get thrown in jail several times—but he didn't live it in the constantly threatening, deadly way that Gary did. Gary committed the deed; Gaylen loved the thought. In the end, violence took them both: the murderer and the murdered.

In part, Gaylen's fascination with criminals was simply the pose of a smart, rebellious youth, adopting decided antiheroes as a way of setting himself apart from the easy values of the culture around him—a common-enough stance among certain young people in the 1950s and '60s. In particular, Gaylen liked to talk about the idea of the perfect crime, much the same way that another kid might talk about setting a new sports record, or another might dream about writing a great book or great music. Gaylen kept reading his books of poetry, but he also started bringing home books about famous crimes—such as the 1932 kidnapping of Charles Lindbergh's infant son. Gaylen was thrilled by the case, and he talked about it often. At the peak of Colonel Lindbergh's fame, somebody sneaked into his Hopewell, New Jersey, mansion and stole his twenty-month-old son, Charles Lindbergh, Jr. The kidnapper left behind a note, demanding fifty thousand dollars in exchange for the boy's return. Lindbergh paid the ransom, but the child was not returned. A few weeks later, the baby's body was found in a grove of woods not far from the Lindbergh home. He had been dead since the night of the kidnapping. There was a famous trial—of Bruno Hauptmann, a German immigrant caught in possession of some of the ransom money—and there was also a famous execution. Four years after the kidnapping, Hauptmann was electrocuted in the electric chair at New Jersey State Prison, while souvenir hawkers sold models of the chair and replicas of the kidnap ladder to cheering mobs outside. But the mystery and appeal of the case did not die with Hauptmann, and to many observers, something felt unfinished or unsolved about the whole affair. After studying the case, Gaylen became convinced that Bruno Hauptmann died an innocent man—that some other party had committed the kidnapping and murder and had gotten away with it. Gaylen studied the details of the case for weeks and weeks, like an aspiring artist studying a masterpiece, trying to understand or assimilate the genius in the pattern of the work.

Gaylen was also intrigued by the infamous Leopold and Loeb case. Nathan Leopold and Richard Loeb were two brilliant University of Chicago students who had come from families of great wealth and status. Both were fascinated with Friedrich Nietzsche's doctrine of the superman, and both had been subjected to intense acts of sexual abuse at early ages. In 1924, Leopold and Loeb talked a fourteen-year-old boy named Bobby Franks into entering their car. Loeb stabbed the boy to death in the back seat with a chisel. The two college students then had dinner, and later that night they stripped the dead boy of his clothes, poured acid on his face to prevent his identification, and buried him in a drainpipe, near a Chicago swamp. They went on to demand a ransom from the boy's worried parents. The idea had been to commit a perfect crime, an outrageously offensive act that could not be solved, though they ended up leaving several telltale clues. The idea also was not to feel anything about the deed—to murder the child without compunction or guilt. It was this last aspect of the Leopold-Loeb story that intrigued Gaylen the most. "They didn't want to feel a thing about what they did," he told me once. "They thought they were superior men, and that superior men had a right to kill weaker people for the pleasure or experience of killing."

When I was younger and Gaylen used to talk to me about these infamous crimes—or when he disclosed that the first girl he ever fell in love with was actress Patty McCormack, because of her performance as little Rhoda, the child who blithely killed anybody who got in her way in *The Bad Seed*—I would tell myself that Gaylen was not as bad as the people he pondered. I told myself he was studying evil so he would not commit it himself—that if he allowed himself to entertain horrible crimes in his mind, then he would not have to perform them in his life. Maybe I was right, because Gaylen's reported crimes never amounted to very much—petty thievery and bad checks were about as bad as he got. That, plus a bad habit of fucking his best friends' wives. I'd like to think Gaylen was too moral or concerned ever to murder somebody, or commit the sort of act of ruin that forever costs another person his or her hope or happiness. And, since he apparently never did commit such acts, I'd like to think it's because the better part of him won out. Or, if Gaylen did ever pull off the perfect crime, then he also found a way to keep quiet about it—though I think he was probably too much of a drunk to stay quiet about any such thing for long.

I guess I'm not making him seem too appealing here. In truth, Gaylen was a charming, funny, incredibly bright and talented person—easily the best writer the family produced. But Gaylen also had a mean and fairly ruthless side to him, and as far as I can tell, both his good and ugly parts emerged from the same place in his heart. Gaylen wanted the importance and sanction he had once known in childhood, when my father had treated him with love and favor. When the love between them became contorted into hatred, all of Gaylen's internal reality got upended. The person he had loved most now regularly hurt him in shameless and cruel ways. Such a twist in the world might not only cause you to hate the person you once loved—it might even be enough to make you want to hate and mock the signs and values of love itself.

In any event, crime and darkness weren't Gaylen's only obsessions. True, he dreamed of monsters, but he also dreamed of a love that might help him rise above himself. I know, because I saw both the monsters and the hope in the poems that he eventually wrote. Gaylen's poetry was really something—it spoke about devastation as both choice and fate, about being on life's outside, headed for a self-willed, expiatory inferno, and it was full of passionate rhythms and startling turns of phrase. Gaylen was proud of the two hundred or so poems he had written, but then one night, when a bitter fight with the woman he loved had resulted in her walking out on him, he opened up a bottle of peppermint schnapps and sat up into the dark hours of morning reading his poems, one after the other. When he was done, he poured the remainder of the schnapps on his sheaf of poems and set them on fire, swearing he would never write another poem until the woman loved him again and he could write something worthy of her. Later, as Gaylen died his painful death, the woman sat beside him in the hospital. When the nurse cleaned out my brother's nightstand, she found a scribbled poem that Gaylen had been working on, about the difficulties of an impossible love—the last thing he ever wrote. Its opening lines were: "A story can't be told/Until a story's done."

BUT I'M GETTING TOO FAR ahead of things here. Gaylen's troubles seemed to begin when he was about twelve or thirteen and he started cutting school, sneaking off to hang out in Johnson Creek's woods with other truant kids. Like Gary, he took to dressing in motorcycle jackets and tried adopting the looks of James Dean and Elvis Presley. (Later, when Gaylen lost his weight, he sometimes looked a good deal like a younger Elvis.) He also took to smoking and drinking. More upsetting to my father, though, was when Gaylen began stealing. Stealing, like drinking, became one of Gaylen's constants. If my father left any money on his desk or in his pants, Gaylen would take it and then lie about the theft. If he saw something he wanted in a store—a sharp-looking model car, say, or a stylish sport shirt—he would look for a way to lift the item without being caught. If that wasn't possible, he'd take something from around our home and sell it to a pawnshop. My mother lost many of her nice clocks and prize keepsakes that way. Looking back, I see now that Gaylen *was* hungry all the time. He wanted everything and he wanted it in a hurry, without working for it. Like somebody who didn't have much time.

The drinking, though, was the worst part of it. My brother Frank thinks Gaylen started drinking when he was about twelve and never gave it up after that.

One time, my mother and I took the bus home to Portland from Seattle, and when Gaylen opened the door to help my mother with her luggage, he was completely bald. My mother just about fainted. She stood staring at his gleaming, round dome, as Gaylen tried to act nonchalant, and her mouth made several motions before she could form words. "What the *hell* have you done to your hair?" she finally blurted. Gaylen explained that he'd wanted a fashionable Mohawk cut, like many of the tougher kids were starting to wear. A day or two before, he and a friend had several beers and began shaving and trimming each other's hair. His friend, it seemed, couldn't quite get the lines straight, as he tried to shave my brother's hair into a hedgerow, and after a few passes, Gaylen finally got pissed and flat-out drunk and ended up shaving everything off. "You are *not* going to be seen in public with me looking like that," my mother announced. "You better get used to wearing a baseball hat or stocking cap or some damn thing until your hair grows out, because what you've done looks hideous." I don't remember her saying a word to him about his drinking.

Not long after that, I was sitting in the living room watching television, when Gaylen walked through the front door. He was still baldheaded. On this day, he was also bare-chested, and from his head to his waist he was covered in jots and rivulets of blood. He had wanted to join a local gang, and for the initiation the ganglord had my brother stripped and tied up, then shot repeatedly with a pellet rifle—or at least that's the story I remember hearing. Gaylen sat in a chair at the kitchen table as my mother washed the blood from him and picked the pellets from his arms and chest. She was crying and talking about calling the police, but Gaylen made her promise she wouldn't. He said he would take care of it on his own. He didn't look scared, simply coldly determined. Some time later, we heard that the teenage ganglord had been assaulted in an alley and badly injured by a BB shot to his eye. It all made a certain kind of sense.

But that's not what I remember most about the affair. What I remember most is this: When I saw my brother walk through the door, blood running in thin stripes down his almost naked body, I knew I was seeing something both frightening and thrilling. In a way, I wanted to be him— to be able to walk with that kind of poise and determination, as the blood ran off my skin. To bleed, and be able to act as if it didn't hurt a bit.

EVENTUALLY, GAYLEN'S DEFIANCE became as full-blown as Gary's. "As you know," Frank said, "Dad always had a thousand rules, and one of them was that you had to be in at a certain time at night or he locked the door and you stayed out. Ten o'clock, I think it was. Gaylen, though, would make it a point to come in about 10:30 or 11 P.M., and of course the door was locked by that time. He would stand out there drunk, screaming and pounding on the door, yelling to Mom and Dad to open up. And Dad *would* open the door—usually with his foot flying or his fists swinging, and there would be a big hell-raising. The neighbors used to say you could hear it all the way down the street.

"I remember thinking, 'Things are bad enough with Gary. Now we have two trouble-raisers around the house, and Mom and Dad to boot.' After that, between Gary and Gaylen, there was never a moment's peace in our home."

DURING THE SAME PERIOD that I am writing about here, Gary was serving his year at Rocky Butte Jail for burglarizing the office where he stole the pistol. He was discharged in May 1958 and somehow managed to get his job back at Bresse Appliances. Throughout this time there was the usual flurry of nocturnal misadventure—a car theft or two, probably more burglaries—but for a while, my father's money managed to keep Gary from a quick return to jail.

Then, there was the incident with the underage woman. Let's call her Anita.

I got this story from a couple of different sources. On the interview tapes that Larry Schiller loaned me, during the last forty-eight hours of Gary's life, one of his attorneys asked him, "Are you sure you don't have any kids?" Gary responded: "I don't think so. I had one kid, but he died . . . That was a long time ago, in Portland . . . He died when he was born." I was jolted when I heard this—it was complete news to me—but the subject was finished as soon as it had come up. Gary had nothing more to say on the matter.

A few months later, I was poring over Gary's arrest and trial records from Multnomah County, when I came across an indictment for contributing to the delinquency of a minor, as well as rape. From what I could tell, it looked like Gary and another young man probably got an underage woman or two drunk and then seduced them, but I couldn't be sure it was that cut-and-dried. Later, I got in touch with the man who had been Gary's codefendant in the matter—a man I'll call Richard—and he consented to meet with me and tell me the circumstances of the event.

One morning, as heavy rain fell on Portland, Richard showed up at my door. He was a handsome, gray-bearded man, about fifty-two, and in contrast to many of Gary's friends I would meet, there was nothing about him that seemed hardened or weary. Instead, he seemed like a friendly and decent family man. As it happened, his experience with Gary had proved a turning point in his life. Richard first met Gary, he told me, when they were both working at Bresse Appliances. "There was a kind of aloofness to your brother," Richard said, as we sat and talked over coffee. "It was as if he were partly shy and partly scared—like everything was just too new for him. I felt a kind of kinship for that. I was sort of lonely in those days, and I'd always had a bit of a hearing problem. It had made it difficult for me to make new friends easily, because I was self-conscious about it. Anyway, I decided to befriend your brother. I'd try to help him along—show him where things were and how they worked—and we'd go out for a drink now and then.

"I had an apartment on 23rd and Weidler, in northeast Portland. I met a couple of girls who lived about three or four blocks from my apartment. They had a habit of coming over on weekends. Sometimes, one of them would stay late. We'd have a few drinks and I would proceed to do what young guys do.

"This one Tuesday morning," Richard continued, "Gary and I had both been on swing shift at Bresse, and Gary had sacked out at my place. Early in the morning, the girls knocked on the front door and got us both up. They had their younger sister with them. She was about fourteen years old. She was on her way to grade school and the other two girls were on their way to high school, and they had to catch a bus over on Broadway someplace. The two older girls figured they could still get to school on time, but the young girl—Anita—didn't want to leave. So the older girls left, and Anita and Gary and I sat around and talked and played cards. I kept telling her she better be going home because we had to go to work at about three-thirty. After a while, the day wore on and Gary says, 'Well, maybe I won't go to work today.' I said, 'Okay,' but I remember thinking, 'Hell, this isn't right.' But there's no arguing with Gary, so I jumped in the car and went to work.

"When I came home, Anita was passed out drunk in the middle of the bed. All she had on was a thin slip, and Gary was nowhere around. I let her sleep because it was one o'clock in the morning and she was out of it—she couldn't wake up. I just sat in my chair and dozed a little bit. I woke her the next morning and told her to get dressed and go home. Naturally, I knew there was going to be something bad coming down about this, so I just waited for it to happen. The following morning, *bangity-bang-bang* on the front door. It was the police, and they had a warrant for my arrest.

"They threw me against the wall and handcuffed me, then threw me in the car and took me downtown and put me in jail. My brother read about my arrest in the paper and made bail, and I told him what the story was. Then I got in touch with the girls to find out what had happened. I learned that the mother wanted to press charges. She said her daughter had been raped, or some doggone thing. Actually, I think Gary had seduced her, but given her age, it was the same as rape. And because it had happened at my place, it left me holding the bag. Finally, the girls came forward and testified that I had nothing to do with it and, of course, I had to give up Gary's name in order to save my own skin."

A few days later, the police arrested Gary at our home on Johnson Creek. They took him to the city jail in downtown Portland and began interrogating him and Richard in adjoining rooms, trying to get their accounts straight. Once, for a few moments, the officers left Gary alone so they could go check out one of his statements with Richard. Gary moved a stool over beneath a half-open overhead window, jumped and grabbed the window frame and hauled himself up and out. He dropped twenty feet out the window to the ground below and took off running. The police didn't catch him.

Eventually, Gary got revenge on Richard for turning him in. Richard came home one night to find that a guitar and radio had been stolen, as well as a rare railroad pocket watch—Richard's only memento of his deceased father. Later, he heard that Gary had stolen the things. Richard got the guitar back—warped beyond repair—but despite searching all the city's pawnshops, he never found the watch. When he came to see me that winter morning, he was hoping I might somehow have it for him. Unfortunately, I did not.

"I guess I'd been gullible about Gary," Richard said, before saying good-bye. "Looking for friends, I was a pretty easy touch, and I figured that Gary needed friendliness as much as I did. But Gary didn't keep our friendship. I would never have violated a friend's home and trust the way Gary violated mine."

GARY HEADED OUT FOR CALIFORNIA and made it all the way to San Diego. There, he stayed with an old girlfriend and changed his name. He was now John Rohr. His life in San Diego wasn't much different than it had been in Portland. In a single month in San Diego and Los Angeles, he managed to get arrested on five different occasions—everything from driving without a license to stealing liquor. Gary headed on to Texas, where he was picked up for vagrancy. The El Paso Police figured out that John Rohr was really Gary Gilmore, wanted back in Oregon for rape. They shipped him home.

Gary was initially charged with rape, but there had been a complication: The young woman had ended up pregnant. According to what my mother told others, my father offered to pay the hospital costs and a few years of child support in exchange for the dropping of the rape charge. The family and prosecutors agreed, as long as Gary never contacted the woman again or attempted to see her child. In mid 1960, the woman delivered a baby boy. (I do not know his name, nor have I tried to learn it.) My mother later told somebody she had once visited the family and held the baby on her lap. Soon, the girl and her family left Oregon, though my mother stayed in periodic contact with her. The baby boy, contrary to what Gary believed, had not died. "I don't think Gary loved the woman," my mother said, "but he probably would have loved the child. It was better for him to think he was dead and not ever try to see him."

Gary still ended up getting a year for larceny, on an old car-theft charge, and in September 1960 he was remanded to the Oregon State Correctional Institution in Salem—also known as OSCI: the midway step between county jail and adult state prison. In his intake interview, Gary said of his father: "I don't really know him too good. He treats me like I ask to be treated." And of his mother: "A pretty fine woman, lets me have my own way. She thinks I'm old enough to make up my own mind and never interferes. She respects my judgment." At the same time, he said he had never confided in either parent, nor in anyone else for that matter. "It would embarrass me to do so." In the accompanying psychological profile, the interviewer noted: "Gilmore operates on the pleasure-pain principle and his personality structuring remains predicated to the infantile concept of self-gratification. Underlying this is a destructive interfamilial history where the mother was ineffectual and the father domineering and openly hostile toward authority . . . Dynamically, then, this is an inmate who had developed under the tutelage of a father who was himself unable to accept the authoritarian role. Gilmore had undoubtedly identified closely with these trends and it is noticed that his arrest record is elaborate . . . Gilmore may be seen as a character disorder." The writer also made note of Gary's clear artistic skills and his high scores in scholastic tests. It added up to a troubling profile: an extremely bright kid, hell-bent on doing dumb and self-destructive things.

Following Gary's intake, OSCI's superintendent wrote to Texas seeking my brother's birth records. What he got back was a letter stating that they had no birth record for a Gary Gilmore; however, on the same date, a Faye Robert Coffman had been born in McCamey to a Frank Walter Coffman and Dessie Brown—names that were apparently aliases for my parents. The superintendent wrote my parents, asking them to clarify the matter, but my parents refused to reply. My father was never going to reveal to anybody the truth behind either his use of the name Coffman or the circumstances of that Southern trip, and my mother acted as if the whole thing had never happened. Despite repeated requests from OSCI, my parents offered no explanations.

The superintendent had a resident sociologist ask Gary about the matter. Gary told the sociologist he had no idea what he was talking about and asked to be taken back to his cell. Over the next few nights, Gary began to have severe headaches. It was the beginning of his lifelong bout with migraines—a problem that also afflicted Frank Jr., Gaylen, and myself. Over the years, Gary's migraines became so chronic and disabling that prison authorities sent him to hospitals on several occasions to try to determine the cause of the headaches. Nobody ever found the cause, and nobody ever found the cure. Thirty years later, Gary's girlfriend Nicole told me she remembered my brother walking out into their backyard in Spanish Fork, Utah, and pounding his head against a tree to try to mask the pain.

The question about his birth name began to bother Gary more and more. He visited the sociologist on several occasions to discuss the matter. At first, Gary denied the documentation could be correct, until he saw a copy of the certificate. Gary, however, refused to discuss the question with my parents. Neither he nor my father ever let on to the other that either one knew about the false name, and it would be several years before Gary discussed the subject with my mother, during the last day of his freedom that the two of them would ever spend together.

THESE WERE THE PATTERNS OF LIFE on Johnson Creek as I remember them: my parents fighting relentlessly, my father dragging me all around the Pacific Northwest. My brothers coming and going, living lives outside the home that I could not figure out and could not take part in.

In all this time, there was only one common pleasure that my father and Gary and Gaylen and myself all shared. On Tuesday and Friday nights, my father would take the entire family to the professional wrestling matches, held in Portland's Armory Stadium and Civic Auditorium. Professional wrestling was as phony and flamboyant then as it is now—all ludicrous ballet, no real risk—but we loved it. We'd sit ringside, and my father and brothers would cheer the heroes and hiss the villains, and I would cheer and hiss along with them. Meantime, my mother and Frank Jr. would sit many rows behind us, trying to look demure and unrelated, as the rest of us did our best to outgeek what was almost certainly the Northwest's geekiest sports audience.

There was one villain in particular we all hated, a chubby but muscular guy who wore a fierce, skull-like mask over his head. My father and Gary would grow apoplectic over this nasty brawler and the obvious ways he cheated. One time, the man in the skull mask got thrown out of the ring and landed at our feet. My father and brothers proceeded to call him terrible names, and he looked up at them and shook his head. "Get back in there and fight like a *man*, you cowardly slob," my father bellowed. The wrestler took a seat next to my father, leaned over to him and said: "Jesus, Mac, give me a fucking break. I'm just trying to make a living, like everybody else."

After that, my father and brothers liked the guy. Took him out one night for beers. Later, Gary started to run around with the wrestler and they would drink booze and cough syrup together. I later heard rumors that the two of them might have pulled a few jobs together. These days, the wrestler is a local conservative radio talk-show hero.

———

IN THE FIRST WEEK OF NOVEMBER 1960, we moved to a nice, fancy new home and started life over as a family. The same day we began the move, John F. Kennedy—the only man either of my parents ever voted for—was elected President of the United States. The world was changing. It felt different—more promising.

None of that would matter. By the time we got to the new home, the ghosts were waiting for us, prowling the hallways and crawl spaces.

A DREAM: I AM DRIVING PAST *the house where we once lived on the hill—the house we moved to after we left Johnson Creek. In the car with me are two people: one, a famous newsman and interviewer; the other, Nicole, Gary's last girlfriend. It is late afternoon as we make the drive, and I can see that my old home has changed dramatically. An extension has been built on to its main structure; a tower reaches up into the air for seven or eight stories. At the top, there is a Victorian-style turret. House of Usher, I think to myself.*

For years now I have been wanting to revisit this old home. I have wanted to find a way back into it, so I could once more walk through its insides. I feel like I've lost or left something there, and that if I could just explore the rooms once more, I'd find what I've been missing. Also, I'm convinced there are secrets I need to know, and the only way to learn them is to reenter the house where I grew up, the house I once fled.

Now, I see a way back in. There is a sign out front: ROOMS FOR RENT— UPPER LEVELS. *The reporter agrees to pose as my brother, and Nicole as our sister. We are a family, looking for a new home. We enter through the front door into what was once the living room. Now it's a central office of some sort, though it's outfitted remarkably like the foyer in the funeral parlor where ceremonies were held for my father and mother and my brother Gaylen after their deaths. There's a desk in the middle of the room, with a nice older woman seated at it. I think: So much once happened in this room; now I barely recognize it. Nevertheless, I can tell that something is still dwelling inside this house. I can feel it in the air around me. It feels thick and malicious.*

The woman arranges for us to have a tour. She tells us that we shouldn't take too long, because after dark all the employees leave. Then, the buses will stop running and we would have a hard time getting back to the city.

We climb narrow, turning stairs and enter many rooms. Some of the rooms have unfinished plank floors, and in the middle of those rooms are trapdoors leading down into nothing. Other rooms are windowless, like cold offices.

In room after room I come across people who want to tell me their stories. The stories go on forever and ever. I don't remember much about them, except most are sad, as are the people who are telling the stories. A young black woman tells me that when she goes out to walk around the neighborhood, the other people in the area act as if they don't know her or see her. "They treat me like a zombie," she says. "Maybe I am a zombie."

As I get closer to the top of the house, I find that the rooms are empty. I notice that I have lost track of my friend the reporter and Nicole. I start back down the stairs to find them, but I find nobody there. I go outside to the front yard. I see that it is now getting dark. I also see that the terrain surrounding the house has changed. A crosswork of train tracks now encloses the place, stretching into an empty distance, filled only with the blink of an occasional signal light.

I go back into the house to seek a ride out of here, but all the rooms are either empty or locked. I realize that I am left alone here, and that my only company is the presence of evil that I had felt earlier, upon entering the house. I am alone in the house with its evil, and I must stay there.

I wake up in a panic, certain that somebody has just walked into the room where I am sleeping.

———

OUR NEW HOME WAS ON THE SOUTHERN BORDER of Milwaukie, the town that lay just across the tracks from our old house on Johnson Creek Boulevard. Milwaukie was one of the larger cities of Clackamas County—an area considerably more rural than Portland's Multnomah County. Clackamas didn't have the sort of diversions that Multnomah offered—the variety of nightclubs, whorehouses, gay bars, and twenty-four-hour movie theaters that made Portland a tempting place to seek vice in the late-night hours. Just the same, there was something dark at the heart of the place: In Clackamas, it was possible for people and their families to live their lives in utter isolation and disinterest. Anything could come from such conditions—transcendence or destruction—but often what came was not for the better. Multnomah may have had a higher crime rate—robberies, drugs, and such—but there was a deeper natural meanness to be found in the outlands around Milwaukie. Many of Oregon's deadliest men—killers and country-bred gangsters—came from homes in Clackamas County. My brother Gary was one of them.

We knew none of this, of course, when we bought our new home. My father was now making decent money, and as the family became wealthier, my mother renewed her fight for a better house. In part, I think she simply wanted the sort of nice surroundings that her sisters had long enjoyed with their families back in Utah. But she also wanted to give her sons a new start. She thought that if Gary was released from OSCI to return to the world of Johnson Creek, he would simply drift back into old ways and bad company. But if he could come home to a better neighborhood, a higher standard, maybe that would be enough to turn him around. Something about this argument finally convinced my father that it was time to move his family up in the world. It was a fine idea, as far as it went. But what my parents didn't understand was, it was what went on inside a house, rather than what street the home was on, that made all the difference. Perhaps it was too late to understand that.

In any event, we got our new home, and a nice new address as well. To get to the new place, you had to drive across the train tracks into Milwaukie, along the winding stretch of 45th Avenue. That would take you through the poorer section of town—an area where some people still lived in hapless shacks and tar-paper lean-tos—until you came to another set of train tracks. Take a right, follow those tracks west toward the Willamette River, and you would come to Milwaukie's city center, such as it was. Milwaukie was (and remains) essentially a one-street downtown—a five- or six-block stretch called Main Street, with a couple of pharmacies, grocery stores, and cafés. You drove along Main Street until it ran out onto a highway called Lake Road. It was a long, spacious stretch of road that carried you past several solidly built farm-style houses, set back off the street, overlooking large yards filled with chestnut trees. At the top of Lake Road, you took a right onto a street called Oatfield Road. Suddenly, the whole world looked different. Oatfield coasted down a lovely, wooded hill lined with oaks and pines, until it hit a stone bridge, spanning a creek lined with château-style nice houses. Then the road began to climb left, around a large hill. As you ascended that hill, each house you passed was an unmistakable statement: old money, old ways, no disorder or disruption.

You followed that road up the hill in a long, semicircular loop, and just before it crested out, it turned sharply left. You made that swing and you were at the top of the hill. There, on the left, at the highest point of Milwaukie's nicest hill, was our new home. In those days it was a two-story gray structure, set back off the highway, high upon an embanked yard. Several wide steps took you up to a large front porch, with squared pillars and a hanging bench swing. On the left of the house was a large side yard, and to the left of that was a long driveway loop that circled around a teardrop-shaped garden island. In back there was another acre of yard, with a big cherry tree at its center.

Walk through the front door of the house and you entered the living room, with a red brick fireplace along the main wall. To its right there was a double-width sliding door that took you into the dining room, and alongside that was the kitchen. At the rear of the house was a glassed-in sunporch. The upstairs held four bedrooms, plus the main bathroom and another sunporch. From the upstairs windows you could see the church steeples and rooftops of Milwaukie, and beyond that, you could see the skyline and night lights of downtown Portland, eight miles away. It was a mesmerizing view.

I loved that house on the hill, and I also grew to fear it. It is, beyond question, the central house of my mind, my life, my memory. Not a week goes by that I don't dream of it.

I know that if I could return there, I would. When I was living back in Portland a couple of years ago, I wrote the people who were the current residents of our old home. I told them I was working on a book about my family's life, and I asked if I could pay the house a brief revisit. I never heard from them. I can't say that I blame them. I'm not sure I'd want somebody connected with such a bad past walking through my front door.

As I SAY, MY MOTHER SAW THIS RELOCATION as a new start for the family. This was the home she had always wanted, and she set about landscaping the yard with elaborately-patterned flower gardens, while filling the house with fine furniture imported from Europe and Japan. I think she hoped that a new, better home would rehabilitate the family—that it would give my wayward brothers some new pride and, in turn, win back my father's faith and support for his sons. She wanted us to be the family on the hill, not the family near the tracks.

But something that none of us had counted on was about to happen. We began to die.

There's an episode I've always thought of as the harbinger to this development, though I can't say exactly why the particular memory works this way in my mind.

I had just started school at Milwaukie Grammar School—the middle part of the third grade. It was my father's custom to drive me there and pick me up afterward; he did not like me riding the bus with other children. This one afternoon in early December a heavy snow had started to fall on the Willamette Valley. As school let out, our teachers advised us to check the radio listings early the next day, since they expected the school would be closed due to weather conditions. That afternoon, at four-fifteen, I waited in front of the school for my father's 1960 green Pontiac station wagon to pull up. He was late this day—something I had never known him to be before—and it gave me a bad feeling.

When he finally pulled up, long after all the other kids and school buses had departed, he had a worried look on his face. "Whatever you do," he instructed me after I got in the car, "don't say anything to your mother that might upset her. We've had painters and decorators at the house all day, and she hates the colors and patterns of everything, especially the kitchen floor tiles. She wants to redo the whole goddamn place, and right now she's having a royal shit-fit." These remarks, which might have inspired humor or disgust or exhaustion in others, froze me and inspired in me real terror—in part, because it announced to me we would be dealing with my mother's formidable madness and unpredictability. But there was more to it than that. As we climbed the snow-covered hill of Oatfield Road, I saw something in my father's manner—an exhaustion in his face, a resignation in his voice—that seemed to signal something new: a weariness and sadness that I had not heard from him before, and this frightened me even more than what I had seen of his strength and his rage. It's possible my father had put more hope in the regenerative ability of this new house than the rest of us. Maybe he thought that buying a new home would finally buy not only respectability for his family, but also a lasting peace with my mother. However, we all knew it wasn't panning out that way. My mother wanted our new home to be perfect in every detail, and when something failed her standards, she would rage at my father, and he would simply give in to her demands and then walk out of the room. From this time on, I would see him more and more as a tired and helpless man—somebody who just wanted a little concord and who looked increasingly drained by all the troubles.

Of course, the other thing my father's statement about my mother announced to me was a rotten home life for the next few days. Since my mother was having the entire place re-wallpapered and repainted, the rest of us had been told where we could and could not move in the new house. There was a narrow pathway we were allowed to navigate between the downstairs kitchen and bathroom and two of the upstairs bedrooms. We also weren't allowed to touch the walls outside of the light-switch panels. If we did, there was real hell to pay. The practical result of all of this was that, for the next few days, anybody who wanted to live in that house (and since it looked like it was going to be frozen over outside, that meant all of us) would have to live in the dining room, which was already filled with a TV, unpacked boxes, and extra furniture. Now, during the family's nonsleeping moments, it would include two adults and three restless boys. I had already made a corner in the room where I could sit and read my favorite stories: tales of Jesus and monsters and Odysseus and Captain Ahab.

That late afternoon, when my father and I entered the house through the back door into the kitchen area—the present object of my mother's obsessiveness—I saw my brothers Frank and Gaylen sitting around the dining booth. They were looking unmistakably like men who had been trapped in a room with my angry mother for a few hours too long. I saw my mother sitting on a steel chair in a corner of the room, her arms folded over her chest, studying the linoleum patterns on the floor tile that had just been laid that morning. A few days before, when she had picked this tile, she declared it one of the most handsome domestic designs she had ever seen. But now, viewing the new floor under her feet, she decided the pattern was actually a product of somebody's hellish vision, and she was brooding about it. I saw her sitting there, and I instantaneously felt a great compassion for her. I not only recognized her familiar wrath, but I think I also saw the private tickings of a mind that knew such vast and deep grief and anger that what it wanted and feared most were one and the same thing: the space to live inside its own private madness, unhindered. I remember that in this moment, I simply wanted to go up to her and hug her, comfort her, say to her that I understood, that she should get what she wanted—she *should* get a floor pattern that truly fitted into her own inexplicable sense of order.

I don't remember what happened next exactly, but I know that in some way I acted on that impulse. I went up to my mother. I hugged her, kissed her cheek—things we were all forbidden to do, and had always been forbidden to do. Next thing I knew, I was shoved across the room. "Keep away from me, you little bastard," she yelled. Immediately, my father was between her and me, shaking his fist; my brothers were between him and my mother, trying to calm the two of them down; and I was holding on to my father and reaching out for my mother, trying to make it all okay. I remember my father pulling me out the door and my mother regretting what she had done, crying, reaching out, saying, "No, Frank, bring him back! I'm sorry. You know how much I love him!" And I remember Gaylen saying, "Jesus Christ, I'm getting the hell out of here, I can't take any more of this shit," and Frank following us all out to the car. From there, my father and brothers and I went to a Chinese restaurant, and it was dark before we got back home. My mother had baked some chocolate chip cookies while we were gone and had them waiting for me. It was my favorite thing that she made, and she was the best cook I've ever known. She had also decided by then that she didn't really mind the floor pattern all that much, and she'd be happy to live with it—provided, that is, they could just redo the entire wall patterns throughout the downstairs in a different color. "That's fine," my father said. "Whatever you want."

I felt horribly sorry for both my parents at that moment—for my father because, I guess, I recognized then that he was a broken, finished, doomed man; for my mother because I knew that none of this was what she really wanted, and that she would have to live with this disappointment for the rest of her life. The funny part is, it was a fairly common floor pattern of various-sized squares, one you still see in many kitchens and bathrooms. I never see it without memories of that day and without memories of what was about to happen in that haunted palace of ours.

———

LATE ONE WINTER AFTERNOON, MY MOTHER was home alone at our new place, working in the kitchen. She heard an odd noise in the adjoining dining room and looked around the corner just in time to see the figure of a man disappearing through the glass doors of the back-room sunporch. She thought it must have been Frank Jr. or Gaylen, home early. She went and opened the door to the room, but nobody was there.

This could have been discounted as merely another example of my mother's hyperactive imagination, but the incidents kept happening. One evening a week or two later, Gaylen was seated in the back sunporch, watching one of our four televisions. The door opened, and a man in white clothes with gray hair, he said, stood staring at him for a moment, then moved back through the doors. Gaylen went and found my mother and asked her who the stranger was. She said: "What stranger?"

Before we moved into the house on Oatfield, it had belonged to a well-known local doctor. According to one report we heard, the doctor had died in the house, lying on a sofa in the back sunporch. The stuff of a typical haunting, except there was no emotional resonance to the story. Did this doctor die an unhappy or bedeviled man? Not as far as I know. So what would keep him bound to the house he died in? Why would he bother to spook the place?

These questions hardly mattered. Once my mother heard this story, she was convinced we had another haunted house on our hands. For a while, she even thought we should give up the place, but my father was not moved by this suggestion.

Still, odd things kept happening. They never stopped happening. Let me repeat what I said before: I do not believe in ghosts. But like everybody else in my family, I heard and felt strange things in that house that I could not account for. There was an unusually large gap space between two of the upstairs bedrooms, and we could not figure why that space existed, or what it might hold. There was an attic structure built onto the house, but there was no entrance available to the attic—no trapdoor, no ladder or staircase. Maybe the gap space had once held a narrow staircase, but like the stairwell in Robert Frost's poem "The Witch of Coös," maybe it had been sealed over once the house's evil had been trapped up the stairs. Anyway, we all heard inexplicable noises in that area—the sounds of a heavy breath or painful moan, the sound of 3 A.M. voices holding muffled conversations. For a time, Gaylen actually theorized that another family might be living above us in our inaccessible attic. You should have seen the look on my mother's face when Gaylen voiced this idea.

When I recently asked Frank Jr. if he remembered the sounds in that hallway, he said: "Yes, I remember them well. I've given those noises a lot of thought over the years. I finally realized there was probably some sort of crawl space between the walls that an animal of some sort—maybe a bird or a rodent, maybe even a cat—had managed to enter and couldn't escape, probably by crawling through a hole somewhere in the eaves of the house. I think what we were hearing was the sound of that poor trapped creature as it was trying to escape and was slowly dying."

Frank's explanation sounds reasonable, except that if something was dying in those walls, then it took several years for it to finish the task. That, or there were a lot of dumb animals that wandered into our walls over the years. No, I don't believe in ghosts, but I know this: There were rooms in that house—like that downstairs sunporch, which always felt horribly chilly and uncomfortable to me—that I did not like entering, and whenever I walked through the upstairs hallway, I walked as quickly as possible. It always felt like something was at the back of my neck when I was moving through that space.

MY FATHER KEPT TRAVELING TO SEATTLE for business, and I kept going with him. By this time, my leaving no longer resulted in fights between my parents. I think my mother had grown to accept the condition. Also, she had her new home to keep her increasingly busy. She worked constantly on furnishing its central rooms with fine Victorian-era furniture—marble-topped tables, velvet-covered easy chairs, coffee tables with Moroccan leather inlays imprinted with gold leaf. She also spent countless hours landscaping the yard, planting rare Japanese trees out front, and cultivating a lovely flower garden in the driveway's island bed. I guess all this work must have given her pleasure, but it never quite felt that way. A slight imperfection or blemish in a new item of furniture was enough to send my mother into one of her enraged depressions, and if a flower pattern in the garden didn't turn out the way she planned, she would rip up the offending plants and trounce them, then stomp inside the house. She would slam a few doors and then sit at her table in the kitchen, crying. Anybody who was smart learned to stay away from her when she was gardening.

In Seattle, my father and I settled into an older district, not far from Queen Anne Hill. Down on the corner was a general store with a good diner attached, and next door was a well-stocked bookstore that also carried all the newest comics. We lived only a mile or two from downtown, and as usual, I was free to come and go as I liked. This was during the time when Seattle hosted the World's Fair, and I visited the grounds several times a week. One day, astronaut John Glenn was touring the site, and I got to shake hands with him. I hurried home and told my father. He was proud of me. We both had watched TV the whole day when Glenn made his historic orbits of the earth.

In an apartment building next to ours lived a middle-aged couple with a teenage son. My father took a special liking to this family, and we would visit with them several evenings a week. My father was always taking them presents. Sometimes he would sit around with Walt—the husband—and have a beer or two and play draw poker. The son's name was Larry, and he took a kind interest in me. In fact, he treated me as I had always wanted my brothers to treat me. Whenever a classic old movie was on television—like *The Sea Wolf*, or *The Last of the Mohicans*, or *The Heiress*—Larry would have me over and make popcorn for us, and then he would try to explain to me some of the movie's finer meanings. Larry also took me to theaters and museums, and bought me several books. He gave me an illustrated, hardcover copy of *Moby Dick* and tried to help me grasp the idea that the story's whale was something more than a whale.

I did not know it then, but I now believe that Walt was one of my father's hidden sons, which would have made Larry my nephew. It was years before this would become apparent to me. I have tried to find that family in recent seasons, but like so many other people we once loved or hated or were related to, they have disappeared.

BACK AT HOME IN MILWAUKIE, life was heating up. My brother Gaylen had dropped out of high school—he felt there was nothing the teachers could really teach him—and the school officials were happy to see him go. He joined the U.S. Navy, but the adventure lasted less than a month. After he had gone AWOL five times and had turned up drunk even more times, the base's commanders surmised that Gaylen did not have much of a military career in store, and shipped him back home, with an honorable discharge.

Then, in the fall of 1961, Gary came home from Oregon State Correctional Institution. His stay at the facility had proved rough. He got into constant fights with the authorities, and the guards noted on several occasions that Gary was particularly vicious toward older men—sometimes threatening their lives. The anger in Gary became so strong that he repeatedly blew whatever good time he had accrued and ended up adding time to his sentence.

The counselor who wrote my brother's post-OSCI evaluation noted that Gary had experienced a poor custodial adjustment during his imprisonment. "He received a total of 23 disciplinary reports, most of major proportion," the counselor wrote. "Fighting, refusing to work, disobedience, disrespect were characteristic of the inmate's reaction toward authority and toward incarceration . . . At no time did Gilmore show any interest in vocational goals or vocational planning . . . The inmate did not participate in any educational programs, although his intellectual capacity indicated he was capable of functioning at a higher level than at which he was presently operating . . . Gilmore indicated that he had no interest in leisure time activities, seeing no need to alter his past behavior in this area. As his disciplinary record indicates, the subject was unable to relate to any staff members or any authoritarian figures. Outside relationships and contact were solely limited to subject's mother and father who continued to excuse, condone, and indulge their son without end. Gilmore had no release plans at the time of his discharge, and from statements of the inmate's, it was assumed he was not planning on working when he was released but [would] just live off his parents." Another counselor noted: "Gilmore . . . substitutes his own pleasure principles for a moral code of any adequacy and is used to gratifying his desires immediately. Has great fund of hostility toward other individuals which has led him to [a] somewhat paranoid isolated approach [to] life . . . and he has a good deal of difficulty controlling his temper."

Indeed, the Gary who came out of OSCI was a changed person—a boy only in his infantile needs, a deadly man in every other respect. "He was brutal in those days," my brother Frank remembered. "He got mad at you, and his terms were that he could kill you or hurt you or injure and ruin you. You could not reason with him and he could not punish you enough. It was like being around Mussolini. Sometimes, I felt like he was just looking for reasons to hurt somebody."

This is the Gary I remember best from my childhood. He was twenty-one years old, but he dressed like a man at the end of middle age, in a shabby black raincoat and curl-brim porkpie hat—junkie wear. He eyed all persons around him with an appraising and wary leer, like a man who knew that everything on the outside of his skin amounted to a threat. Interestingly, Gary also came out of OSCI with his artistic talents blooming like mad. When I say that Gary was an artist, I don't mean simply that he could draw well, or that he had pretensions. The truth is, he could draw and paint with remarkable clarity and empathy; the best of his work had the high-lonesome, evocative power of Andrew Wyeth or Edward Hopper, though in Gary's case, the themes tended to drift toward two concerns: death and childhood. Perhaps the most haunting thing he ever drew—a piece that many of his prison friends later commented on—was a sketch of the faces of children as they watch a scene of horror in a movie. You never see the horror they are viewing, but you see what is on their faces—the fear and fascination that comes from learning that there are monsters in the world that will rip you apart and that there is nothing you can do to prevent it.

Yet Gary's artistic gift never really seemed to mean that much to him. Why did he prefer a life in crime over a life in art? I can't say, but I've wondered about it more times than I care to remember.

One afternoon, when it was just Gary and me sitting around the house, I tried to get him to show me some basics about drawing. He was drinking cough syrup that day, and he laughed in a polite but firm way that announced: *No dice.* I tried cracking Gary's indifference, telling him I thought he could be a notable and successful artist if he wanted to. He chased his cough syrup with a swig of beer, then looked at me and smiled. "You want to learn how to be an artist?" he said. "Then learn how to eat pussy. That's the only art you'll ever need to learn."

SOMEHOW, DESPITE ALL THESE SIGNS, we managed to have a nice Christmas at the end of 1961. My father went all out that year, outfitting the house and yard in beautiful lights from top to bottom, and my mother decorated the prettiest tree I had ever seen. Blue ornaments and blue bulbs.

My parents bought everybody nice presents—both Gary and Gaylen, I believe, received cars—and for once, we had a peaceful holiday dinner. My father and Gary were good to each other this day. I remember Gary telling my father: "I appreciate the things you've done for me. It's nice to be back home." My father said: "You know I love you, son. I want good things for you, and I'm here to help you." The day ended with my mother playing her new upright piano, which she had pushed up against a wall in the dining room. The whole family sat around her as her talented fingers played carol after carol, all of us singing along. Six horrible voices, filling the year's most holy night with our discordant harmonies. It was the first time we had ever done anything like that.

It was also the last. Neither my father nor Gary would ever spend Christmas with the family again.

CHAPTER 3

DEATH OF A

SALESMAN

MY MOTHER USED TO COME VISIT my father and me during our stay in Seattle, and she began staying for longer periods of time. In the first few months of 1962, that was the only way she would get to see us.

That's because, during this time, my father began to feel unusually tired and sick. One day he found a lump on his neck, the size of a half dollar. He took me with him when he went to the doctor's office. The doctor told my father that he couldn't make an immediate diagnosis of the problem and that my father would have to enter the hospital to have the lump removed and tested. My mother came up to be with my father for this process, and to look after me while he was laid up in the hospital.

The day after the surgery, my mother and I took the bus to Seattle's Swedish Hospital. It was an overcast spring day on Puget Sound—one of those days when an ocean breeze covers the city, like the smell of an oldness that can't be lost. When we entered my father's room, he was sitting up in bed. He was dressed in a bluish-white smock, and he was looking frailer than I had ever seen him, but he seemed happy to see us. He told my mother that he thought the surgery had been a success, that he was already feeling better. He expected to be back to work in a matter of days. The doctor—a tall, husky German man—came in to see how my father was doing and then asked if he could see my mother in his office.

He took my mother across the hall, then told her that my father had cancer of the colon and had no chance of living. The doctor thought it would be best for my father to hear this news from her, rather than from a medical person. My mother said no, she would not tell him. She also insisted that the doctor not tell my father about his condition. "He has no way of surviving that knowledge," she said.

Meantime, I stayed seated next to my father's bed. He tried carrying on a conversation, but I could tell he was distracted. He kept studying the door, waiting for my mother to come back.

After a few minutes, my mother returned.

"What did the doctor say to you, Bessie?" my father asked.

"Oh, not much, Frank. He just told me that he thought I should stay around for a few days, to give you a hand when you got back to your place. He's afraid you might try to push yourself a little too hard after the surgery."

My father seemed relieved by my mother's words, and we talked for a while longer. My father told us a few of his corny jokes and we laughed at all of them. Then my mother said it was time for her and me to start back home. "You know I don't like to be out too late," she said, and leaned over to kiss my father on the forehead. It was then, in the awful, dark look that briefly crossed her face, that I saw what was coming.

As soon as my mother and I hit the lobby of the hospital, she sank into a chair. She covered her face with her hands and burst into tears.

"What's wrong?" I asked.

"Your father's going to die. He has a form of cancer, and the doctors can't cure it. We'll only have him for a few more months."

I try to remember, as honestly or vividly as I can, how I felt in the moments after I heard this. I know that I remained calm. I did not feel scared, I did not feel panic, I did not cry. I did, however, feel terribly sorry for what my mother was going through. For a few moments, it seemed as if she might not be able to survive this knowledge herself. Beyond that, I think my first thought was that I would be more alone now, but that would be okay. I had already learned how to live with a certain detachment from much of the world around me, and I had already come to accept my distance from my brothers. But about the actual knowledge that my father was now dying—I don't remember feeling grief or anguish. In fact, I think I felt a certain relief for him. Over the years, in the times when he and I lived together, I had sometimes found him sitting alone, his head lowered to his desk as he pounded his fist on the tabletop and said, over and over: "I wish I was dead." I think, in truth, he feared death, but I also think that life was a constant trial for him. Soon, all those trials would be over.

In any event, I knew that my life was now changing. I would be on my own. I felt ready for it, for some reason. If my father taught me anything, that was probably his greatest lesson: how to live alone in this world.

That night, I went next door to visit our friends. My mother had already called them and given them the news. Walt, the man who was probably my half brother, was sitting at the dining table with a glass of whiskey in his hands. I could tell from his reddened eyes that he had been crying for a long time.

THAT SAME NIGHT MY MOTHER called our home back in Milwaukie. Gary was the only one there when she called. She gave him the news. She told him that under no circumstances was anybody to let on to my father that he was dying. She thought he had the right to die without fear and worry. This didn't seem right to me; I thought my father had the right to know that he was dying. I thought nobody should have to enter death without the chance to make peace for his soul. My brother Frank agreed with me on this issue, but it didn't matter. My mother was firm: My father would not know he was going to die.

My brother Frank had not been there when my mother called because he had taken a job down the street at a nearby car wash. That night, when he came home, the house was dark. He went up to his room, lay down on his bed, and turned on his small black-and-white television. A few minutes later, there was a knock at the door. It was Gary. "He had tears in his eyes," Frank told me later. "He said, 'I don't like to tell you this, but, you know, Dad's got cancer and he's going to die.' He was real broke up about it. He sat there and cried for a long time."

SEVERAL DAYS AFTER HIS SURGERY, my father was released from the hospital. My mother and I went to help him make the trip back to the apartment. He was still too weak to drive, so we took a taxi back to our apartment. The taxi pulled up across the street from our home, and my mother gave me the keys so I could run ahead and open the doors for my father. As I started up the steps to the building, I heard a raw growl. I turned around to find a large dog—a German shepherd, I believe— facing me from about six feet away. He had followed me up the stairs without my seeing him, and for some reason, this dog did not like me. He was baring his teeth, growling louder and moving steadily toward me. In a moment, he had me backed into a corner. My father, climbing out of the taxi and leaning on my mother for support, saw the dog closing in. Quick as an acrobat, he bounded across the street and up the stairs, then grabbed the startled animal by the neck and hurled it down to the sidewalk. It ran off, yelping. My mother came rushing up to my father. "Frank," she said, "you shouldn't be exerting yourself like this. You could have yelled at the damn thing or thrown something at it."

"That dog," said my father, almost windless, "was going to hurt my son. As long as I have a breath of life in me, nothing will ever hurt him."

A WEEK OR SO LATER, MY FATHER was strong enough to drive the three of us back to Milwaukie. At home, my mother rearranged their bedroom so that my father would have easy access to his medicine and a television. Their bedroom was right next to the room I shared with Gaylen, upstairs, at the front of the house. Down the upstairs hallway, at the back of the house, was a second sunporch, which my father had turned into his home office. Next to that was the bathroom and, just a few feet in front of that, the staircase. At the bottom of the staircase was a pair of French doors that opened into the downstairs sunporch—the room, we understood, where the doctor had died.

One night, about 3 A.M., we were all settled in bed, asleep. My father woke up, feeling the need to use the bathroom, and began making his way down the hall. The noise that awakened us a few moments later was horrible. It was the sound of my father screaming my mother's name in absolute fear, followed by a terrible crashing. Next, I heard my mother running down the hallway, pounding on all our doors. "Get up, boys," she yelled. "Your father's fallen down the stairs." We rushed to the top of stairs and looked down. My father was sprawled on the downstairs floor, lying halfway through the entrance to the sunporch, as if he had crawled or been dragged there. There was blood on the wallpaper above him, from where his head had hit the wall during his fall. Gary and Frank Jr. were the first down the stairs to get to him, and they carried him around to the green leather sofa in the front room. My mother wanted to call a doctor, but my father said he'd had enough of doctors.

"What happened, Frank?" my mother asked. "Did you fall over the banister?"

"No," my father said. He had a dazed look on his face. "I heard somebody whisper something to me, and then it felt like something grabbed me by the throat and threw me down the stairs. I think somebody might be in the house with us."

My brothers searched the place, but they found nobody, and there was no sign that anyone had entered or left. My father wanted to remain on the sofa, and he asked me to stay in the room with him and keep him company. I lay on top of a sleeping bag on the floor the rest of the night, listening to my father's troubled breathing.

For the remainder of the time that he stayed in our house on Oatfield, my father would never again venture upstairs. He moved his office into the living room, and confined all his movements in the house to the downstairs.

KNOWING THAT MY FATHER WAS DYING had some unpredictable effects on the family. My mother was truly grief-stricken and tried to show him tenderness and care, but sometimes all the years of his abuses and her hatred took their toll. I remember one afternoon, as my father slept in the nearby living room, my mother sat in the kitchen and talked about the many ways he had hurt her and betrayed her, and all the ways she had come to hate him—and how she hated him more now that he was going to leave her alone with this family, with no easy way to support us all. They were the most bitter and pain-filled words I had ever heard from her. After listening for a long time, I left the room to use the bathroom, and as I walked past the place where my father was presumably sleeping, I looked in on him. He was sitting on the side of his bed, holding his head in his hands, and when he looked up at me, I saw a look of agony on his face. I went back to my mother and told her that I was afraid he had overheard what she had said. "Good," she replied. "I wanted him to hear."

I was stunned. I couldn't imagine wanting to hurt somebody that bad.

Also, I was afraid he may have heard too much; this was not the way my father should discover he was going to die.

I was too angry to say another word to my mother. I turned around and walked out on her. I stayed away for a long time.

Later that night, I found my parents sitting at the kitchen table, holding hands, talking softly. My father was crying, and my mother was petting his hand. I had never seen my parents hold each other's hands before.

"How would you feel," he asked her, "if you just couldn't get better if you just kept feeling worse no matter how hard you tried? What would you think? Nothing has ever hit me like this before."

"I know, Frank, I know," she said, petting his hand.

FOR A TIME, THERE WAS AN AWKWARD TRUCE between my father and Gary, but sooner or later it had to crack. My brother was using drugs a lot in these days—uppers, grass, cough syrup, some heroin, plus plenty of alcohol—and he was coming and going at odd hours, bringing strangers around, who sat waiting in his car outside. I never liked the faces I saw on those men. I felt as if they were a danger, just waiting for entrance to our home.

One afternoon, when we are all at home, Gary asked my father for some money. My father was in a bad mood—the cancer was making him nauseous—and he told Gary: "Why the hell can't you get a job and make your own money, like other adult men? Why can't you stay the hell out of trouble for five minutes, you goddamn son of a bitch?"

That was all it took. Immediately, Gary and my father were embroiled in one of their terrifying shouting matches, and as had now become our custom, the rest of us removed ourselves to an upstairs room to wait for the storm to blow over.

Only this time, I could tell, it might not end easy. I heard a mean edge and slur in Gary's voice that frightened me, and I heard a helplessness in my father. I think Gary must have sensed that as well, because he was making threats about tearing the house apart if he didn't get what he wanted. I turned to my mother and Frank and Gaylen and asked them if somebody would please go down and stop the fight. They looked at me and quietly shook their heads. They had seen plenty of these fights, and they knew better than to try to get in the middle of them. I went down to the kitchen myself. My father was seated at the kitchen table, dressed in his bathrobe, and he looked gray-faced and exhausted. Gary was wearing his black raincoat and straw porkpie and was standing across the room, leaning against the kitchen counter.

"I *want* the goddamn money," said Gary.

"And I want *you* to get the hell out of my house and never come back," my father said, as forcibly as he could muster the words.

Gary picked a glass up off the counter and hurled it at my father. If my father had not moved his head quickly, the glass would have hit him in the face. Instead, it smashed against the wall behind him and shattered all over his head and shoulders. My father looked up and saw me watching all this and said: "Get out of here."

I ran back upstairs to my mother and brothers. "You *have* to do something," I said. "Gary is going to kill him."

Frank got up and went down and stood between Gary and my father. "Leave him alone, Gary," he said. "Can't you see he's too weak to fight?" Gary shoved at Frank. Frank shoved back. Gary hit Frank in the face. Frank returned the blow. Then the two of them were brawling, furniture and dishes flying all over the place. "I'm not a great fighter," Frank told me later. "I'm not tough. But Gary knew almost nothing about fighting. He was strong but he was also awkward. If he got hold of you he could hurt you, but I made sure that he didn't, and I was coming out ahead."

Then my mother entered the fray. She came into the room with a broom and started to hit Frank Jr. over the head with it, saying: "Stop this, you've gone far enough. I've called the police on you, Frank—I want you out of here." Both Frank and Gary stopped fighting and looked up, startled, at my mother. "Leave Gary alone," she told Frank once more. Frank looked deeply wounded, got up off the floor and walked out of the house, slamming the front door behind him. My mother sat Gary in a chair, dabbed the blood off his face, and handed him a wad of twenty-dollar bills. "Now please leave before the police get here," she said. "I'll take care of everything."

Frank Jr. came back after midnight. My mother had gone to bed, but my father was sitting up at the kitchen table, still in pain. When my father saw Frank walk in, he said: "I want to thank you, son, for what you did today."

Frank Jr. was a little drunk by this time and was still stinging about the way his mother had thrown him out of the house. "Man," he said, "I didn't think Mom would ever call the cops on me. I was trying to help."

My father said: "She didn't call them on anybody. She just said that to stop the fight. She couldn't very well say she had called them on Gary, because who knows what he would have done? He would take that real serious, because she's the person he feels he can always trust. He might have killed one of us at that point. So she said she called them on you, just to get things straightened out." Frank thought about it and decided it all made sense. Nobody could confront Gary. They had to protect him and themselves at the same time. He finally decided it was one of the smarter things his mother had ever done.

FRANK WAS IN DOWNTOWN PORTLAND a few evenings later when he ran into Gary on the street. They hadn't seen each other since the fight. Gary came up to Frank and extended his hand. "Hey, man, I'm sorry about what happened," Gary said. "I shouldn't have acted that way."

"Yeah, you're right," Frank said. "It shouldn't have happened, and I'm sorry that I hit you, but I got all upset when I thought you were going to hurt Dad."

"Well, you were doing the right thing," Gary said. Frank accepted Gary's apology. He didn't want any bad blood to stay between them.

"Hey, you hungry?" asked Gary. "Let's go over to George's Coney Island, get a couple of chili dogs, then get a beer afterward. It'll be my treat."

Frank agreed.

George's Coney Island was a hot dog diner in the lower part of Portland. It served one thing: hot dogs, but they were the best dogs in town. The place was run by an old Greek man named George. The myth about George, according to my father, was that he was a millionaire who lived in a mansion in Portland's West Hills. But he loved making and serving hot dogs, so he ran the diner as a way of keeping busy and staying in touch with people. My father had known George for many years, and whenever we were downtown, he'd take us to George's Coney Island for a meal. He and George got along famously. "Ah, my favorite customer," the burly George would say in his Greek accent when my father walked through the door.

Gary and Frank took a seat at the counter, and George greeted them warmly. "How's your father? Any better? No? Don't worry, your father's a strong man. He'll kick this. He'll be back on his feet in no time."

As George was cooking the hot dogs, Gary talked to Frank. He said: "I think I'm going to have to go back to jail soon, Frank. Let's face it, I'm institutionalized, plus I miss my friends. That's where all my real friends are: in jail. Also, if I don't go back soon I'm going to wind up hurting somebody. Hell, I'm going to *have* to hurt somebody. I miss my friends."

Frank said: "Don't you think it's time, Gary, for you to start thinking about a career?"

Gary replied: "I already have a career. I'm a professional criminal."

Frank was trying to take all this in when a man seated on a stool a few feet away—a biker—turned to Gary and asked him to pass the ketchup. "Get the goddamn ketchup yourself," Gary snapped back. "You've got two arms. I'm not your fucking waiter." The man stood up, hefting his muscles, and Frank tried to step between the two of them. Punches flew and Frank got knocked down. He woke up a minute or so later with George pouring cold water in his face and talking furiously. "What the hell happened here? Your brother and this guy get in a fight, tear the place apart, and run out. Who's going to pay for all this? What am I going to do, call the police?" Frank got up and felt his lip. It was split open. He dug into his pockets and gave George some money. "You a good boy," said George. "You welcome here. Tell your brother never to come back. I don't like him anymore."

Frank stumbled out to the street, still reeling from the hard blow he had taken. He felt as if he needed a drink. He made his way to the bar on the corner. When he looked inside, he saw Gary and the biker seated at the bar, drinking beers and laughing together. Later, Frank learned, Gary and the biker visited the biker's girlfriend, and they ended up having a three-way. "I looked at the two of them in there drinking beer," Frank said, "and I just turned around and walked away. I was fed up. When I got back home, I talked to Mom about it. I told her, 'I'm really finished with him now, this is it. I'm finished.' As it turned out, that was the last thing I ever did with Gary in public."

MY FATHER, MY MOTHER, AND I went back to Seattle in early June 1962. My father felt the need to catch up with his business. His illness had been holding up the book's production schedule and was now jeopardizing the family's income.

One morning two weeks later, Gary showed up at the front door. He said he had come to help my father with his work. It was obvious from his slurry speech and blazing eyes that he was on one drug or another. My father had not forgotten their last fight, and he wasn't welcoming Gary's offer. My mother could tell that Gary was seeking some sort of last-chance reconciliation, but because he was loaded, she was afraid he might blurt out something about my father's fatal condition. She took my brother aside, told him she thought he should return to Portland, and gave him a hundred dollars.

I remember the look on Gary's face as he walked out the door. I could tell he wanted to embrace my father one last time, to give him a kiss good-bye. But neither man could easily cross the lifetime barrier of damage that separated them. They could not move toward each other. Gary walked out of the apartment with a look of loss that I would not see again on his face until the last few days of his life, when he knew he would die without getting to say good-bye to the woman he loved.

That night, we got a call from Frank Jr. Gary had been arrested in Vancouver, Washington, for driving without a license. Also, there was the matter of an open bottle of liquor in the car. My father put his head down on his desk and cried, long and hard. "Why," he said between sobs, "are they always picking on my son?"

After that, my father began to deteriorate rapidly. He took to his bed one night, and never got up again. He lay there, coughing sputum into a nearby bowl. I can still remember the smell of it: sickly-sweet, like a spoiled flower. That surprised me, that death would end up smelling fragrant.

TOWARD THE END OF THE MONTH, my mother had Gaylen come up to Seattle to stay with my father and help him with his work. She and I went back to our home in Milwaukie. I don't remember what my father said to me or how he looked the last time I saw him alive. I wish I could, but I can't.

A few days later, Gaylen called us early one morning. Our father's condition had grown much worse during the night and he had taken him back to the hospital. Gaylen had stayed with him all night, but his condition continued to deteriorate, and at about 5 A.M. he slipped into a coma. Gaylen had just returned to the apartment to get some sleep.

Maybe an hour later, the phone rang again. I answered. "Give me Mom," said Gaylen.

"Is it Father?" I asked.

"Give me Mom."

My mother took the phone. When she heard the news, she cried out: "Frank, my God, where are you? Where have you gone to?"

THE NEXT FEW DAYS WERE SPENT with the business of making funeral arrangements, getting my father's body back from Seattle, picking out a cemetery plot. My mother tried to find Robert Ingram to give him the news, but she did not have a current address for him. We had lost him, and we would never find him again.

The day before the funeral, we went to view my father's body as it lay in state at the funeral parlor. My father was in an elegant bronze casket, surrounded with bouquets of flowers. He was dressed in a handsome brown suit and his head was propped up on a cream-satin pillow. His arms were folded across his chest. His eyes were closed. Striations of decay were already starting to line the lower part of his face. My mother broke down and cried, and Gaylen sagged against a wall, looking like he was in pain. My brother Frank put his arm around me and held me close. "Are you all right?" he asked. I nodded. I couldn't take my eyes off my dead father's face. I thought he no longer looked much like the man I had known—the man who had once held me on his lap, or saved me from the dog, or yelled at my mother and brothers. I thought: There's nothing there. When you die, you leave your body, and it no longer holds any memory of you. In death, your face could not show any of the love or anger it had known in life. I did not think this was a good thing.

As we left the funeral home, Gaylen said: "Man, seeing something like that takes a lot out of you. I need a drink." He left us, and the rest of us went back home.

GARY WAS IN ROCKY BUTTE JAIL at the time of his father's death. He later told us that a guard had awakened him and said: "Your son-of-a-bitching father just died. That should make you happy." Gary went berserk. He tore his cell apart; he smashed a lightbulb and slashed his wrist.

My mother begged the jail officials and a county judge to let Gary attend the funeral. She offered to pay double-time for guards to accompany him, as a guarantee that he would not attempt an escape. But the officials and judge refused. Gary was placed in "the hole"—solitary confinement—on the day of his father's funeral.

I don't remember much about the funeral itself. We sat a few yards to the side of the bier, behind a veil. Afterward, as I rode to the cemetery with Gaylen in his car, a rock & roll song played on the radio. It was "Point of No Return," by Gene McDaniels. The disc jockey announced that it was a new song, just released that day. "I'm at the point of no return," sang McDaniels, "and for me there'll be no turning back." I was spellbound. In the months that followed, every time the song came on the air, I'd rush to the radio and turn it up.

That July afternoon, we stood beside the casket at the graveyard, while a Catholic priest said a prayer. I was surprised that we would not be there as my father's coffin was lowered into its grave. My mother said, "No, that's not the way these things are done. The families can't stand those last moments." Somehow, it didn't seem right to me, him having to go down into the ground alone.

I remember I was surprised at how hard my mother and brothers took my father's death. I was surprised they still loved him enough to cry over him. Or maybe they were crying for the love he had so long withheld, and the reconciliation that would now be forever denied them.

Looking back, I think I was the only one who didn't cry. I don't know why, but I never cried once over my father's death.

IT HAS BEEN OVER THIRTY YEARS NOW *since my father died and I still haven't cried, though in my dreams it is different.*

Not long ago I dreamed that my mother came to me. She said: "I have a surprise for you. We've found your father. He never really died—he ran away from us—but we didn't know how to tell you.

"He came back the other day, and he wants to see you. But I have to warn you: He is very old now, and now he is truly sick. Be kind to him because he will not live much longer."

She takes me into a room, and there is my father, seated on a chair. He is dressed in a plaid shirt with a string tie, and he is wearing baggy slacks with suspenders. He has his glasses on his face and his fedora on his head. As my mother warned, he looks terribly old and fragile. And yet when he sees me, he smiles and stands up and takes me in his arms.

"Oh, my son," he says, "I am so happy to see you. How did I ever lose you?" Then, he begins to cry.

I hold him and I say: "It's okay, Father. I've missed you too. I'm glad to have you back. We'll be all right."

It occurs to me that now I can learn the answers to so many bothersome questions. I can ask my father who he was and what he did, and he will tell me.

But as I think this, I feel him collapse in my arms, and I feel the life leave him. I am standing there holding my dead father, and finally I can't help it: I cry.

CHAPTER 4

REQUIEM

MY FATHER WAS DEAD. He had been an often unreasonable and violent man—more so for my brothers than for me—and he had managed to sire and sustain a family at the same time he helped damage the souls and hopes of the people within that family.

My brother Frank and I have spent many hours in the last few years talking about the complexities of this man. We both suspect that so much of what was awful and strong in his sons came from someplace inside him. We also suspect that there were ways in which we lived out his legacy for him—ways that we carried on his fear and his damnation. But what has stymied us, as we have talked about him, is that we do not know what the sources are for all that ruin. We do not know the secrets that he kept, the secrets that he took with him. Without that knowledge, it's as if there's a part of ourselves we can never unlock. And it isn't a small part. As I said before, it may be the deepest, most essential part: the part of us that has always turned love into ruin.

"I have never known what Dad's big secrets were," Frank told me one evening. "Whenever I would ask him about those things, he would just say: 'It's better to keep your nose out of other people's business.'

"But even without those secrets, I think Dad would have lived the same life. I think being a drifter was important to him. He was basically in many ways a lonely man, but he also *enjoyed* being a lonely man at times. He really was a kind of a . . . I don't know if you would call it a Jekyll and Hyde, because neither one of his natures were, in my opinion, bad. But he *was* a dual personality; there were two of him. One was a family man—he didn't want to be without a family. But after a few weeks of that, the novelty would wear off and he had to go back to being a drifter. And after he was a drifter a while, he would get tired of that and want to come back to the family. So he was grabbing both sides of life, the two things he wanted: a family and independence. That was a large source of the trouble between him and Mom. She would fight with him about having to live that way, and he'd retaliate by hitting the bottle and splitting. There really wasn't any pretense or mystery about it. He was tired of Mom and tired of the family, and he just had to go. In a way, he did that up until the end of his life. And he left behind him a family of drifters.

"The funny thing is, the more I've thought about him recently, the more I have come to respect him. He made some remarkable changes toward the end of his life. The way he stopped drinking and built a successful business. The way he decided he was going to love and protect you, his last son. I think in time, Mikal, you would have had the same troubles with him the rest of us had. You would have started thinking for yourself or shown a little defiance, and he wouldn't have liked that. He would have tried to break you. His dying spared you that. As a result, you got to know—and keep—the best part of him that anybody got to know. He was good with you, and I respect him for that.

"For the rest of us . . ." Frank paused, and looked back into his past. For a moment, I saw years of agony ripple through his facial muscles. "Well," he continued, "let's put it this way: Dad was a bitter man to have to be raised by. He could be hard. He could hurt you when you weren't prepared for it. He could walk out on you and forget about how you were doing until the next time he saw you or needed you. It wasn't fun. I remember kids that we grew up with used to tell us they felt sorry for us. I heard that several times. That kind of speaks for itself. He was a bitter man to be raised by.

"I would *not* want to go through childhood again. Not for anything. Once was enough."

MY FATHER, OF COURSE, WASN'T THE ONLY FORCE for good or bad in my family. My mother was part of what kept the structure intact. On those many occasions when my father walked out on her, leaving her in some bus depot or flophouse in Bumfuck, U.S.A., she would take her boys by the hand and find them a safe place to sleep, or a way to get them all back to the hated refuge of Utah. She protected her children scrupulously at those times, and she did her best to carry them through a world that she could never have expected to find herself in.

It all had to be a terrible disappointment. There must have been a great gulf between what my mother counted on from tying her fate to my father and what she got. I imagine she had been attracted to Frank Gilmore because he seemed somewhat glamorous, particularly in comparison to the Mormon rubes she had grown up around. She was romantic and young and unrealistic enough to think he was going to take her to a new, exciting, better world. As a friend of mine noted: "Your mother sounds like she was prone to delusions of grandeur, and your father sounds like just the guy to feed those delusions. He probably looked like a pretty slick package, and I'm sure he was the most charming person she'd ever seen outside of a movie."

So my mother married him, and entered his vagabond life, traipsing around the country with a bunch of kids and a man who would periodically dump her. I think it's fair to say that her dreams didn't work out, yet, in a way that was both heartening and foolhardy, she never lost sight of one or two of those hopes. She kept longing for a grand home to put us all in, and it was her hunger and anger alone that finally got us that home, for whatever it was worth.

Of course, like my father, my mother failed to do many things she probably should have done. Most important, she failed to leave my father, despite all the beatings, abandonments, and cruelties that he heaped on both her and her sons. I remember Larry Schiller asking my mother, during one of their conversations: Why did she stay with my father? My mother's reply was matter-of-fact and heartbreaking. "Where would I have gone?" she said. "Who else would have had me? I stayed because that was all I could do. I decided early on, you take the good and the bad with somebody—you can't change them. Anyway, Frank didn't have to keep coming back to me. I asked him once why he did, and he said: 'Ah, hell, I'm too old to find anybody else. Besides, I guess I like your cooking.' "

My mother's failure to leave my father was not a unique thing. People stay in bad relationships all the time in the world around us. Women stay with men who hurt them emotionally and physically, and men stay with women who berate them or shut them out. Sometimes you stay because you love the person, and you can't imagine life without looking into that lover's face. Maybe you hope things will improve. Maybe the love blinds you—maybe you don't know you're being abused. My brother Frank asked my mother once why she put up with all the beatings from my father—especially the ones that left her face knotted with ugly, black lumps and bruises. "Hell," she said, "I asked for all that. I'd mouth off too much and your father would put me in my place. I deserved it. It's as simple as that." Her answer—the idea that she believed she had earned the horrible beatings—makes me angry and sad, but it also makes plain that sometimes we accept the misery of a relationship, and we can't imagine ourselves outside of that misery. It becomes part of our identity. The idea of leaving the misery becomes more fearful than the prospect of staying with it. You might not know who you were if you left that dynamic—you might have to make yourself all over again. Or, at least, you might have to find somebody else you could make the same mistakes with all over again.

I think my mother truly loved my father, and I think my father truly loved my mother. Once, during one of their interviews, Schiller remarked to my mother: "It sometimes sounds like you were awestruck by your husband." She replied: "Well, I could see him as a person with many flaws and everything else. But I still, you know, even to the last day of his life, I would still feel that little click, that beat of my heart, when he'd drive his car up into the driveway. The way he would be seated behind the wheel, all smiles and confidence, or the way he'd be sitting at his desk. That would really win you over."

"How would he sit at his desk?" asked Schiller.

"Oh, like he just would have to do everything so well, and was so unconcerned that you were even in the same room. Then he would get up and walk across the room for something and he'd reach over and pat you under the chin or something. So you would know he was aware of you, even though he'd acted like he was too busy to notice."

I had never known my mother to talk this way about my father. I had never before heard such a tenderness in her voice. Beneath those words, I could tell that her heart was cracking as she spoke.

I remember the look on my father's face as he sat and held my mother's hand that night I found them in the kitchen. I remember my mother hearing the news of his death, and crying out from such an astonishing place of loss and loneliness. Yes, those two people loved each other. It is plainer now in retrospect than it ever was when they were alive. Or maybe I can just see it a little better now, having learned for myself what a bittersweet thing love can be. From my vantage, love—no matter how deep or desperate it may be—is not reason enough to stay in a bad relationship, especially when the badness of it all is damaging or malforming other people. But I didn't get to make that choice for my parents, any more than I get to make it for you.

Of course, there were other reasons my mother stayed. For one, she was a woman in a world that did not encourage women to leave their husbands or find their own way. There were few job options, few support systems available for an untrained woman with several children. She was trapped, whether she knew it or not, in a way that many women before and since have been trapped.

But perhaps the single greatest reason my mother stayed was for the children. Certainly, this is one of the foremost arguments that some people will raise against divorce: the disorienting impact that the separation might have on the children, and how hard it will be for them to find healthy nurturance and a moral paradigm in a single-parent structure. As I think about myself and my brothers, I have to wonder if a divorce would have produced worse results than what the marriage produced: four deeply troubled boys, two of whom helped bring on their own terrible deaths. I hear people argue against separation, and I'm afraid that what is really being said is: Stay together for the sake of the family. Do *anything* for the sanctity and unity of the family. This is the message that we have heard from history time and time again: There is nothing worse than sundering your family's integrity. The family—and the privacies of its authority—must be preserved.

God, I hate families. I see them walking in their clean clusters in a shopping mall, or I hear friends talking about family get-togethers and family problems, or I visit families in their homes, and I inevitably resent them. I resent them for whatever real happiness they may have achieved, and because I didn't have such a family in my life. And I despise them for the ways in which the notion of the family good is still used to shame or subjugate the children within the family, long past the time when they've become adults.

But perhaps I'm protesting too much here. The truth is, I do not judge my parents harshly at all. I do not feel an ounce of hatred or bitterness toward either of them, though maybe I should. I love my parents. These days, I miss them both terribly. But there is something ironic that I have had to recognize about my act of contemplating my own family: In a better world, I would not be telling this story because this story would never have happened. In a better world, my parents would not have met—or at least they would not have married and had a family. In a better world, I would never have been born.

What sad and wretched people Frank Gilmore and Bessie Brown were. I love them, but I have to say: It is heartrending they ever had children at all.

CHAPTER 5
ASSAULT AND
ROBBERY

IN HIS LIFE, MY FATHER WAS A SOURCE OF MUCH OF THE HEARTBREAK and violence in the family, but also an able and resourceful provider. We were hardly rich or socially prominent but we lived well. Now, with him dead, we would have to find a way to take care of ourselves.

My father's business—his annual compendiums of state and county building codes—was still viable. My mother, as well as all my brothers, had worked with him on the enterprise at one time or another. They all knew how the ads were sold and how copy was gathered and laid out, and they knew how to do billing. They also had two or three salesmen who had remained loyal to my father and were willing to help the family keep the business afloat.

But things went bad from the start. Frank Jr. had been hoping to leave our house soon—get his own place, maybe start his own family. Now, he thought he should forestall those plans for a year or two and help my mother make the transition to a self-sufficient life. Frank went to Seattle to finish the work on the current edition of *Building Codes Digest*, and he took Gaylen with him. But as fast as Frank would collect the advertisers' payments, Gaylen would turn around and draw the cash from the bank. Then he would stay out late, getting drunk, chasing women, and winding up too hungover to do his share of the work. Frank and Gaylen had a couple of fights about this state of affairs, and Frank could see all the good work was going nowhere. He sent Gaylen back home and stayed on in Seattle. In a few weeks, he had collected all the payments, sent the money to my mother, got the book to publication on time, and closed out the Seattle apartment. He didn't want to continue supervising the business, but he thought he could do a fair job of helping my mother find a good partner to manage the concern. But when Frank arrived back in Milwaukie, he had a grim surprise waiting for him: Gaylen had wrecked the family car and had been arrested for drunk driving. He had also cashed a number of checks on the family's bank account. All the money Frank had made in Seattle had been eaten up by Gaylen's fines and legal fees, and repair costs for the car.

Meantime, a rival salesman in the Portland area began a competitive publication, and several of my father's older clients had gone his way. The salesman offered to buy out our business and the rights to the name, but my mother refused, and threatened to sue. I don't remember exactly how it happened, but within a year or so of my father's death, my family lost all control and interest in the *Building Codes Digest*, and competitors had the field to themselves.

Still, the family wasn't without options. Though my father had not carried life insurance, he had left a fair amount of money in the bank. Frank estimates it may have been as much as $30,000 or more—enough to live on for a while in the early 1960s. Frank thought the family should give up the large home on the hill and move to a more moderate and affordable place. After all, he pointed out, Gary was hardly ever around these days, Gaylen couldn't be counted on, and Frank himself planned on moving out in a couple of years. There was no reason to keep such a big and costly house. If my mother sold it now, he told her, she could profit nicely and put that money into a smaller but still comfortable home and have plenty left to live on.

Frank's proposal became the beginning of an ongoing argument between him and my mother that would last for the remainder of their life together. It would also, in an odd way, end up keeping Frank tied to my mother's fate, when all he wanted was to escape her world. The first time Frank suggested moving into a smaller place, after having gone through all the family's financial records, my mother exploded bitterly. She did *not* want a smaller house. "You want me to give up my home and go live in a trailer, like a tramp," she screamed, and then picked up a plate of food and threw it on the floor. No doubt the thought of giving up our nice new home was hard for her, especially after waiting so many years to have it. Also, I think she held out hope that the beautiful house was the one thing that might still bind us together. She wanted to keep it as a safe harbor for her sons to come home to, and since it was such a big, demanding place, we would all have to remain there to maintain its up-keep and grandeur. In other words, the house was what could save us— or at least keep us all under the same roof.

My mother defied Frank's counsel in a way that she could never have defied my father. When the issue hit a boiling point between them, she finally agreed: She would go find a new house for us to live in. After a few days of searching she had found the place and was having a contract prepared. She wanted us to go see it. It turned out to be an even larger house, on an even grander, more expensive hill. She had made her point. Frank gave in. We would stay in the house on Oatfield.

After winning the showdown, my mother went out and bought a nice new piano, new furniture, new appliances, and a new television. Within six months of my father's death, Frank figures she had gone through at least $10,000. But that wasn't what ended up breaking the family. What broke us was the trouble that was about to happen with Gary and Gaylen.

IN THE MONTHS FOLLOWING OUR FATHER'S DEATH, Gaylen's life started to grow wilder. He was now drinking more frequently and more openly, and while he was generally a funny or harmless drunk, he would sometimes sit in the dark and glare at the rest of us in ways that frightened me. I could never understand why my mother let my brothers bring li-quor into the home and drink while they were still minors. I guess in part it was her belief that you couldn't force somebody to change their behavior—that you had to allow them to make their own mistakes. Or maybe it was just a practical resignation. They were going to drink any-way, she figured, so why not let them do it in a friendly and safe environ-ment, where they wouldn't get in trouble or get arrested? I also suspect it may have been plain fear. I think that in some ways, despite all her love and support of Gary and Gaylen, my mother was also afraid of them—she knew that anything that smacked of a mandate or a regulation might produce an ugly reaction on their part. Yet I remember that when I would watch my brothers sit and drink, I sometimes sensed the threat of uncontrollable actions on their part—in particular, the chance of violence. I saw something that was dangerous and mean in Gary and Gaylen's red, bleary eyes. They may have smiled a lot when they were drunk, but I thought I saw mean thoughts going on behind those smiles—like the idea of stealing something the family could not live without simply because they wanted the money, or maybe just wiping us all out for the hell of it.

But this darker side of Gaylen hadn't fully emerged yet. For now he was simply drinking much more than a seventeen-year-old boy should ever drink, and he had taken to hanging out with a tougher group of friends, from Milwaukie's poor part of town. He was smarter than these kids, but that didn't seem to bother him. They were willing to do things that the better-heeled kids weren't willing to do.

Gaylen was also starting to hit his stride with the local women. He drove a beautiful, blue Jeepster convertible and he wore fine silk shirts and, for a time, he sported a sharp, hip goatee. He looked like a young Robert Mitchum—dangerous and vulnerable at the same time.

The stance worked like magic. He was always pulling into the driveway with one alluring young woman or another. The one I remember best was Eve. She had curly black, shoulder-length hair, and she would wear her blouse open down the middle and knotted around her waist. She was sweet and she was lovely, and best of all, she was nice to me. She would give me kisses on the cheek that awoke something in me that had not stirred before.

Gaylen and Eve would pull up into the driveway and Eve would wave at me. Gaylen would take the car into the open-sided carport, and the two of them would sit and kiss and pet for hours. From the viewpoint of the kitchen—my mother's constant perch—you couldn't see much more than the rear end of the Jeepster. From *my* viewpoint upstairs, though, you could see a lot more. Gaylen would open Eve's blouse and pull on her nipples, and he would run his fingers down into her tight cutoffs. That always made her squirm memorably. Except for my brief encounter with Gary's adolescent threesome a few years before, this was the first time I'd known the presence of sex around our home. Through all this, my mother was keeping her eye on the car in the carport, and she was quietly fuming.

———

SIX MONTHS AFTER MY FATHER'S DEATH, GARY FINISHED serving his sentence for driving without a license and was released from Rocky Butte Jail. He came back to live with us, and for a while he and Gaylen began running around together. It would seem like a natural enough pairing—two look-alike brothers, partners in crime—but there were ways in which the two of them were fundamentally different. Gary was dealing in a lot of extremes by this point, and he always had a test or code or some damn thing you had to pass to meet his standards. Gaylen, meantime, simply wanted the adventure and experience. He liked dangerous ideas much more than he liked dangerous acts. With Gary, he got a bit of both. Gary got him into drinking cough syrup and running around with some truly mean-spirited thugs, pulling bullshit robberies and attending all-night sex parties.

One night Gary and Gaylen got into a fight. It had to do with a woman. No doubt Gaylen had made a move on somebody that Gary considered off limits. Gary attacked Gaylen and Gaylen ended up decking him, then taking off. Gary sat and nursed his jaw between shots of whiskey and cough syrup. Then he opened his car trunk, pulled out a tire iron, and told a friend he was going to go find Gaylen. He was going to kill him. The way he said it, the friend could tell he wasn't kidding. Somehow, word got back to Frank and Frank got word to Gary. "If you kill our brother," Frank said, "then it's between you and me." Gary got the message. He put the tire iron away and sent back his own message: "Tell Gaylen to stay away from me."

Gaylen and Gary kept a distance from each other for years after that.

THESE WERE AMONG GARY'S DARKER DAYS. He had made friends with people who were running prostitution and dealing drugs. Some of these people did hard things in hard ways, and Gary helped out when he could. I had lunch one day with a man who had known Gary a bit during this period and had also known Gary's friends. "Portland's heavy criminals," he said, "may seem banal compared to the more sophisticated criminal syndicates you find in other places—they might even seem like a bunch of bush-league hicks—but that doesn't make them any less deadly. It might even make them deadlier, since they feel they have to prove their toughness a little more.

"Your brother," he went on, "was somebody who was known as a good, steady backup guy. He was somebody you might take along for a second hand when you had to do a certain bad job, and you wanted somebody who could back your action plus keep their mouth shut afterward. Gary worked that way for some of these folks. He was the guy you might have on the lookout when you went inside a place to do something, or the guy you would have waiting with the getaway car. He was somebody you would use, but only so much. You included him because you were afraid of how he might take it if you left him out. There were harder guys in Gary's circle than Gary, but I don't think there was anybody who wasn't a little afraid of him. They knew he would do anything to make his point, and that he would never be intimidated by a threat or challenge."

Every now and then, one of Gary's crimes would land him in jail, though never for more than a couple of weeks during this particular period. The jailers found Gary's behavior becoming more and more peculiar and disturbing. One time, when he was at Rocky Butte on a hit-and-run charge, the jail had him committed to Dammasch Hospital, which was the state mental facility. Gary had been insisting to the jailers that he knew there was some sort of conspiracy at work against him, and the jail's officers were a part of it. He threw a bowl of hot soup into the face of another inmate, who was working in the kitchen. Gary swore there was poison in the soup. Then he set fire to the mattress in his cell. At the hospital, he told the attending doctor that a radar set had been installed on the roof of the jail and set to his frequency. He also said that he heard voices coming through the jail vents, talking about him late at night. Plus, he was having more savage headaches. One of the hospital's psychiatrists decided this was all a ruse: Gary probably figured jail time was easier to serve in a hospital than in a cell, or maybe he thought the hospital would offer easier escape opportunities. Gary was returned to the jail. That's when he started slitting his wrists. He went back to the hospital and finished out most of his sentence there.

THIS IS ONE OF THOSE STORIES THAT NORMAN MAILER originally related in *The Executioner's Song*, and that I somehow managed to shut out of my memory, even after reading the book two or three times:

My mother came home one afternoon to find Gary sitting in her green leather armchair, holding a document in his hand. He was glaring angrily at my mother, something she had never seen him do before. "I want to show you something," he said, and handed her the piece of paper. It was his original birth certificate—the one from McCamey, Texas—with the name Faye Robert Coffman. "Maybe you would like to tell me about this."

My mother had kept the certificate in her desk all these years. Apparently, Gary had picked the lock and found it. She was taken aback, and she was livid. "What do you think you're doing?" she said.

Gary shook his head. "Hell, Mom, no wonder the old man never liked me. I was never really his son, was I?"

"How dare you make such an accusation. Of *course* you were his son. That was just a name we were using when we were traveling through Texas."

"Don't give me that fucking bullshit."

"And don't *you* dare talk to me like that. You're the one who should apologize. You could have asked me about this. Instead, you were in my desk without permission."

"I never would have gotten this news with permission, would I?" said Gary. He got up out of the chair, grabbed his jacket, and handed the certificate to my mother.

"You can keep it," she said to him, trying to force a smile.

"*No-thank-you,*" he said, biting off each word. It was the iciest way he had ever spoken to her.

"Gary, there are some things you don't know, but this isn't what you think it is."

He said nothing. He walked out of the house, slamming the front door behind him. It was the last time my mother ever saw Gary as a free man.

ONE OF GARY'S FRIENDS DURING THIS TIME was a young black man named Cleophis. Once in a while Gary would bring Cleophis around the house. Mostly, they would sit in a car out in the driveway, drinking beer, talking, laughing. Cleophis was a friendly guy—he seemed nicer than most of Gary's friends—but, like Gary, he had a taste for intoxicating narcotics.

A day or two after his confrontation with my mother, Gary was hanging out at Fred Meyer, a local variety store, with Cleophis. They went into the drug department, where Gary had the pharmacist fill a prescription for a narcotic-based cough syrup. As the clerk was checking the known-addicts list, Gary spotted a man at a nearby register cashing a check. Gary couldn't tell how much money the man had, but he saw him put a wad of green bills in his pocket. "We'll be back for that prescription in a little bit," Gary told the clerk, and then signaled Cleophis to accompany him. They followed the man out to the parking lot, and then got in their car and followed him as he drove along. "What are we doing, Gary?" Cleophis asked.

"We're going to rob this fucker," Gary said. "I've got a lead pipe in the back seat we can use on him."

"Oh, man," said Cleophis, "I don't want to do that kind of shit."

Gary gave Cleophis a hard look—a warning look. "Don't chicken out on me," he said. "Back my play."

The man pulled into his driveway and Gary pulled in after him. He and Cleophis got out of the car and somebody—it isn't clear to me which of the two—brandished the lead pipe. Gary grabbed the man, took his money, threw him to the ground, then he and Cleophis took off. They had come away with eleven dollars for their trouble.

As they pulled away, somebody took note of their license plate, the model of the car, and the direction they were headed.

BACK AT THE HOUSE ON OATFIELD, Frank was sitting in the living room watching TV. He was the only one home. He heard a car pull in and he got up and looked out. It was Gary and Cleophis. He didn't think much about it. They were always coming and going.

A few minutes later, he heard a good deal more noise—like a legion of movement in the driveway. Frank looked out again and this time he saw the yard was full of city and county police cars, their red lights spinning and blazing. There were maybe twenty or more cops standing alongside their cars, all with their rifles and pistols aimed at Gary and Cleophis, who were standing in the side yard. Cleophis had his hands up and was standing still, but Gary was weaving around, like he didn't know what was happening.

Frank went tearing out the back door and put himself between the cops and Gary. "Please don't shoot my brother," he said.

"If you don't want to get shot yourself," one policeman said, "get out of here."

Then, all the cops were yelling at Frank: "Get the hell out of the way!" As they said it, other police cars were flooding up the hill and closing off the street.

Something about the exchange between Frank and the cops pulled Gary back to earth, out of his narcotic haze. He raised his hands, looked at the policemen, and said: "Don't shoot him. He doesn't have anything to do with this." To Frank he said: "Frank, get out of the way. I know what all this is about."

The police closed in, handcuffed Gary and Cleophis, and took them to the Clackamas County Jail, in Oregon City.

GARY WAS IN SERIOUS TROUBLE THIS TIME, AND WE ALL KNEW IT. He was facing assault and robbery charges, plus he already had a long record of offenses behind him. Though none of his previous crimes had been too serious—and none had involved violence—the accumulation was enough to convince the prosecutor that Gary was already a habitual criminal and a danger to society. The D.A. elected to take the case to trial and seek a long sentence.

In the months following the arrest, while preparations were being made for the trial, Gary had started assaulting other inmates in jail—particularly older men—so the judge ordered a psychiatric evaluation. At the hospital, Gary continued to threaten everybody around him and kept cutting himself up. He insisted to one psychiatrist that the suicide attempts were genuine. In his notes for the judge, the doctor wrote that Gary stated "he wanted to bleed to death, wanted to die, but more than that he wants to bleed to death." Looking at those words now, it all seems so apparent: This was Gary's first stab at Blood Atonement.

It is possible, as his jailers and one or two doctors assumed, that Gary was faking his mental episodes. Of course, just because somebody is faking craziness doesn't mean they aren't crazy. In any event, Gary was judged competent and able to stand trial. The state doctor's final diagnosis was: "Sociopathic personality, antisocial type with intermittent psychotic decompensation."

Gary's trial took place at the Oregon City Court House, in the middle of March 1964, and lasted for three days. Cleophis, Gary's partner, had turned witness against him, though it would have been an open-and-shut case even without that testimony.

On the last day of the trial, I was at home when the phone rang. My mother was keeping a doctor's appointment but had left a number for me to call in case I learned that a verdict was going to be announced. I answered the phone. It was Gary. At first I thought he must have been found not guilty. How else could he be calling me?

"How you doing, partner?" he asked. "Look," he said after a moment, "I just wanted to let you and Mom know: I got sentenced to fifteen years."

I was stunned. I didn't really know what to say. "Gary, what can I do for you?" I asked. I think it came out wrong, like I was saying: I'm busy; what do you *want*?

"I . . . I didn't really want anything," Gary said, his voice sounding broken. "I just wanted to hear your voice. I just wanted to say good-bye. You know, I won't be seeing you for a few years. Take care of yourself."

It was a wrenching moment. Gary and I hadn't shared anything so intimate since that Christmas night, many years before, when he told me about his life in reform school. I felt I had somehow messed up something important—that I had failed him at a crucial moment. That feeling stayed with me for years. In fact, it's still with me.

When my mother got home, I gave her the news. She sat down in her kitchen chair and cried long and hard—even harder than she cried at the time of my father's death. I had never witnessed that much grief in a person.

CHAPTER 6
COMING
APART

IN NOVEMBER 1963, WHILE GARY WAS AWAITING TRIAL, President John F. Kennedy was shot in the head, during a visit to Dallas, Texas. Like any other American family, we were stunned by this event. The violence that happened that day seemed much bigger than anything we had ever known before: It was violence that changed the possibilities of the nation and its future and also spoiled a good part of its past, and I think we all understood that, even then. We talked and cried and grieved over that killing for days, but none of us ever said anything about the violence in our own lives. I don't think I even understood there *was* violence in our hearts. The funny thing is, when that darkness later erupted in its ugliest form, it too would become a historical episode of American bloodshed.

In any event, Christmas that year was dismal. Both Gary and Gaylen were in jail. The family was running out of money. The nation was still in mourning. All the winter nights felt black. It was the first time my mother had not put up a Christmas tree, or even a wreath.

SOMEWHERE AROUND THIS PERIOD, MY MOTHER DECIDED it was finally time for me to become a Mormon. She invited some of the church's young adult missionaries to pay us regular visits and to explain the fundamentals of the Latter-Day Saints religion to me. Every few days I would sit in the living room with these young men, and they would tell me the story of Joseph Smith's ordeal—the agony he had known as a young man, trying to find the true church, and the wonder of God revealing himself and the secrets of heaven to this young son of a farmer. I was captivated by this tale—especially by the part about the finding of the golden plates and the coming forth of the Book of Mormon, and the uplifting of the Smith family itself from poverty to fame to tragedy. Something in this story felt familiar—my mother had spoken mysteriously many times about a treasure my father had once had and lost and that might still be uncovered. As a result, I felt that by accepting the Mormons I was, somehow, regaining my father, even though I knew he had hated these people. Also, I could tell that my joining the Mormon church would mean a great deal to my mother. It would be a kind of vindication of her past, maybe even a way of making up for her own apostasy. And so I was baptized a Mormon and began attending various church services several times a week. I would remain active and committed to the church and its beliefs until the middle of my adolescence.

Then, a short time later—during the time that Gary was awaiting trial—something else happened that would end up making a difference in my life. On February 9, 1964 (which was also my thirteenth birthday, and the day I joined the Mormon priesthood), the Beatles made their first appearance on *The Ed Sullivan Show*. I was no stranger to rock & roll. My brothers had loved the music of Elvis Presley, Chuck Berry, Johnny Cash, Jerry Lee Lewis, Little Richard, and Fats Domino, and they played that music around our home constantly. Interestingly, my father—who, obviously, was no fan of youthful rebellion—also liked rhythm & blues and early rock & roll. It was one of the few pleasures he had never forbidden his sons. Looking back, I now see how the music of Presley and the others had helped represent and speak for my brothers' insurgence: It was a hard-tempered rebellion, without an immediately apparent ideology. It was wonderful stuff, but by the time I was an adolescent, the spirit of that music had largely been spent, and rock & roll had lost much of its gift for galvanizing or symbolizing youthful upheaval.

The Beatles, of course, effectively changed all that. I didn't know, of course, as I watched them on *Sullivan* that night, shaking their hair and singing "I Saw Her Standing There" and "She Loves You," that what they were doing would open up for me a relation to the world and a doorway to the future that my family was helpless to match. All I knew right then was that I liked them, and like millions of other kids, I felt they belonged to me and my time. Later, I would like the Beatles even more because they seemed such a departure from the world of my brothers, and because my brothers could not abide them.

Looking back, I realize now how incongruous these two associations were. Like many things teenage, and most things rock & roll, the Beatles were about sex and pushing or raising limits; you might even say they were about disruption and revolution. The Mormons were about freedom and salvation through order and authority; they did not abide nonmarital sexuality, nor progressive culture or politics. In time, the contradictions between these two devotions would become apparent and I would have to make a choice. But in those days I was hungry for anything that resembled a direction, a way out of the curse that I already saw as my family's lot. Rock & roll and the Mormons—each in important ways—helped give me that direction. In fact, I think the confluence of the two probably saved my life. In religion and rock & roll I would find a sense of community, where before I'd known none. I also found a sense of cause, of moral purpose. Interestingly, it was rock & roll that would end up serving me better over the years, and that would do a better job of illuminating the modern landscape of paradise lost and found. But it was still a few years before I would choose a life with the sinners over one with the saints. For the time being, I was happy to mingle with both.

GAYLEN HAD BEEN IN AND OUT OF JAIL HIMSELF throughout this time. It was generally for rather petty stuff—usually public drunkenness or bad checks. Petty or not, the local cops were starting to take a special dislike to him. It didn't help that he was Gary's brother. He was one more item of bad news with the last name of Gilmore. There was also that nasty temper and pride of his. Whenever a policeman stopped him, Gaylen had some lip to give. If a cop insulted or hit him, Gaylen insulted and hit back. Usually, he got the worst end of the deal. I know, because I remember seeing the bruises from his police beatings.

Soon, the police were coming over to our house at all hours. There would be a pounding at the door at three in the morning and I would look out and see a police car parked in front of the house. They were always looking for Gaylen for one thing or another. Often, he was there when they would come in and search the place. He had a special dark hole, behind a false wall in the basement, under the porch, where he liked to hide, and where they never found him. A few times, when the police would be walking up to the front, with their stiff boots clumping on the steps, Gaylen would take off out the back, slide into the front seat of his car, then wheel out onto Oatfield, honking and waving at the cops as he sped away. The police would take pursuit, but they rarely caught him. He was like the ill-fated hot-rod moonshiner in his favorite movie, Robert Mitchum's *Thunder Road*.

Sooner or later, of course, Gaylen would get arrested, and my mother would have to bail him out. This was a common ritual of our family life in these years. I got to know the face of every policeman and bail bondsman in the district, and I grew accustomed to accompanying my mother, in the post-midnight hours, during her numerous trips to the local police station, on Milwaukie's Main Street, while she went about the business of bailing out her troubled, drunken son.

It was inevitable, I suppose, that in time I would be seen as an extension of my brothers' reputation. I can remember, while still in grammar school, being called into the principal's office and receiving a warning that the school would never tolerate me acting as my brothers acted; I was told to watch myself, that my brothers had already used up years of that district's good faith and leniency, and if I was going to be like them, there were other schools I could be sent to. At various times and in various forms, I received admonitions like this throughout the remaining years that I attended junior high and high school in Milwaukie. Once, I was waiting for a bus in the center of the small town when a town cop pulled over. "You're one of the Gilmore boys, aren't you? Goddamn, I hope you don't end up like those two. I've seen enough shitheads from your family." Another time, I was walking down the local main highway when a car of older teenage boys pulled over and piled out, surrounding me. "Are you Gaylen Gilmore's brother?" one of them asked. They shoved me into the car, drove me a few blocks to a deserted lot, and took turns punching me in the face. I remembered Gary's advice from that Christmas years before—"You can't fight back; you *shouldn't* fight back"—and so I let them beat me until they were tired, and then they spit on me and got back in their car and left.

I cried every foot of the way back home, and I hated the world around me. I hated the small town I lived in, with its ugly, mean people, and for the first time, I hated my brothers. I felt as if I would never have a future because of them, that I would be destined to follow their lives whether I wanted to or not, that I would never know any relief from shame and pain and disappointment. I felt a deep rage of violence: I wanted to rip the faces off the boys who had beat me up. "I want to kill them," I told myself, "I want to *kill* them"—and as soon as I realized what I was saying, and why I was feeling that way, I only hated my world and my brothers more.

EVENTUALLY, THINGS STARTED TO CATCH UP WITH GAYLEN. The affair with Eve had not gone well. Or maybe it had gone too well. Eve was now pregnant. She loved Gaylen and wanted to marry him, and I think he felt the same, but neither her father nor my mother would tolerate the idea. One night, Gaylen got drunk and went over to visit Eve at the trailer court where she lived, down the road in Oak Grove. Gaylen got into a fight with her father, an unpleasant German named Adolf, and it ended with Gaylen on the floor under Adolf's foot and a shotgun to his head. The police came and dragged my brother away.

A day or two later, Gaylen and my mother had a horrible argument over the situation with Eve. They were both sitting in the kitchen, yelling at each other, and Frank was with them, trying to mediate. Things got out of hand. "I do *not* want you to see that girl again," my mother shouted. Gaylen shouted back: "To hell with you. You can't tell me what to do about this. Quit trying to fucking boss me."

My mother got up quickly, reached over to the kitchen counter and grabbed a long butcher's knife, and before anybody could react, she had pushed Gaylen back against the wall in his chair, and was pressing the point of the knife up against his Adam's apple. There was fire in her eyes, and her voice was slow and shaky. "You will not *ever* see that damn whore slut girl again. Do you understand me? If you do, I'll kill you."

Everybody stayed still for a long moment, not talking or moving. My mother screamed at Gaylen a few more times, then backed away and went over and put down the knife. She sat down and started to cry. Gaylen got up, tears in his eyes, and walked out the back door. He kicked the screen so hard on his way out, it sailed into the backyard. He spent the rest of the day throwing his bowie knife at the cherry tree out back, until sap streamed like blood out of the knife wounds. The cherry tree never bloomed much after that.

That was more or less the last that Gaylen got to see Eve. From what I hear, she went on to have a beautiful daughter, but Gaylen never got to see her or know her.

GAYLEN'S LIFE OUTSIDE THE HOME GOT STRANGE and mysterious after that—much like the life Gary had been living a few years before.

One night my mother and I were sitting in the kitchen, talking. A car pulled into our driveway with its lights off. It was an older sedan, and it was full of men. Something about the car's approach triggered my mother's fears. "Turn off the lights," she commanded me. The men poured out of the car, rushed up on our front porch, and began pounding on the door. My mother took me upstairs and locked us into my father's old office. From there, we could hear the men outside. "Open the goddamn *door,* Gaylen," they were shouting. "We know you're in there. Don't make us come in." My mother called the police. Soon, the sound of sirens came climbing up the hill. The men rushed back to their car and took off.

My mother and I went to some neighbors up the street and stayed until Frank came home from his job, at about one in the morning. When we reentered our house, we found that a back window had been broken. Gaylen's bedroom had been ransacked.

A night or two later, Gaylen showed up, looking bedraggled. My mother told him about what had happened. Gaylen took it all in and didn't say a word. After a few moments of sitting there, he went out and got in his car and left. It was the last we would see of him for two years. The next we heard, he was in New York, reading his poems at a club somewhere in Greenwich Village, and drinking himself unconscious whenever possible.

IN LATE AUGUST 1965, FRANK JR. WAS DRAFTED INTO THE ARMY. This was during the period when America's involvement in Vietnam was heating up, and my mother and I worried about the prospect of my brother being sent off to fight, and perhaps die, for such a confusing and wasteful cause. Frank, though, had more metaphysical concerns. It was the belief of the Jehovah's Witnesses that if a person served in the armed services and died on the battlefield, then it was the same as dying in a state of violence or sin. In such a case, one would forfeit his right to enter God's kingdom. Frank had applied for the status of a conscientious objector, but his draft board had refused him. He had little choice but to face the army or a federal prison. For the present, he accepted his draft call, though he could not see himself as serving in an armed capacity.

That was it. One night, Frank was there. The next morning he was gone. I felt worse about his leaving than anybody's else's. This was a kind and good man. I knew that the army would try to change him. They would try to make him as violent as his brothers.

GARY WAS IN OREGON STATE PENITENTIARY, GAYLEN WAS IN NEW YORK, Frank was stationed at California's Fort Ord. That left just me and my mother in that big house that we could no longer afford or fill.

This was a lonely and destitute time. We had run out of money, and we were now subsisting on what came in monthly from my father's Social Security payments.

This was also the period when I began to grow closer to my mother. There was little choice—it was just her and me now—but also I suppose I was ready to learn to see the world through her eyes, to hear it described in her voice. What a painful, persecuting world it was. It was in this time that I came to understand just how much my mother, like my father or Gary or Gaylen, identified with the life and causes of an outsider. She had, in effect, been one all her life—first, as a young girl who wanted to break rules, then, as a young woman who *did* break them, and finally, as a woman who had to pay and pay for having broken those rules. I learned that the world would not forgive those who flaunted its rules—that it would destroy you for doing so. My mother was an outcast. My brothers were outcasts. My mother promised that I would be one too. I would have to be strong, she told me; I would have to learn to live with the world's condemnation, and with its punishments. I thought she was probably right, but what I didn't tell her was I thought that the fearful world she talked about included my family. I dreamed of keeping not only the world on the outside, but also of keeping my family on the outside.

One day, I suddenly found myself living that way. In the early winter of 1965, my mother fell gravely sick and had to enter the hospital to have her gall bladder removed, or something similar. I would go visit her every day, then I would go home to the big house. I was just starting high school, and I was living by myself—at least for a few weeks. It was the first time in my life, since the years alone with my father, that I felt happy and safe.

OF COURSE, IT COULDN'T LAST. A FEW WEEKS LATER my mother came home from the hospital. But things were never quite the same. The surgery had taken something out of her. After this, she would start to live a more limited life. The first sign of this came within moments of her arriving back home. She refused to venture to her bedroom upstairs. She said she no longer had the strength to climb those steps. Instead, she moved her sleeping quarters downstairs, to the same sofa and living room that my father had made his own, during his last few weeks in our big lost house. My mother never again went upstairs. Also, after that, my mother rarely let strangers, or even friends, come into our house.

In the months that followed, the house and yard began to fall into disrepair. My mother could no longer take care of her gardens, and I found the place too big to handle. In time, the grass out front grew knee-high. The property looked awful, and forbidding. Eventually, some folks at the Mormon church started coming over regularly to help keep the yard in shape. By now, they more or less thought of us as a welfare family.

WITH MY MOTHER NOW LIVING DOWNSTAIRS, I had the entire run of the upstairs. Some weeks, I would sleep in a different room every night. Then I started hearing the voices.

I would awaken about three in the morning, and I would hear voices outside my bedroom door, maybe five or six feet away, at about the place where the mysterious gap space existed in our hallway. I'd lie there and hear those voices for an hour or two—sometimes until the sky started to lighten outside. They were audible but not distinct, like a mumbling from behind closed doors.

One day, after losing a night's sleep to these sounds, I asked my mother: "Do you ever hear anything odd during the night?"

"Almost every night," she replied, "I hear voices. Sometimes, they sound like they are upstairs, in one of our bedrooms. Sometimes, they're in other rooms, or just somewhere in the air. They speak low, but I think I know what they are saying. They are talking about our future and how they plan on taking the life out of each of us."

I thought to myself: Great—I'm becoming as crazy as everybody else in this damn family. After that, I started sleeping with a pillow over my head. It kept out the voices of the ghosts.

CHAPTER 7
COMING
HOME

FRANK'S TERM IN THE ARMY PROVED ROUGH FROM THE START. His commanders knew he was a Jehovah's Witness and opposed to armed service. They didn't have much sympathy for such a stance. They would dress him down in front of the other men, calling him names, telling him they were going to break him.

For a while, Frank tried to become a medic. But that wasn't good enough for his superiors. They wanted Frank to learn to load, carry, and fire a rifle, and to learn how to wield a bayonet. His commander told him: "You will have to do things according to the military, or you will be subject to court-martial."

Frank replied: "I *can't* do things according to the military. It goes against my religious beliefs."

The officer ordered Frank to pack his duffel bag and march over to the Fort Ord stockade, two miles away. He would have to stay there until he could be court-martialed. "They had no guard on me during my march over there," Frank said. "I mean, I could have easily taken off. The bus station was over there. I could have gone there, bought a ticket, and been gone. I could have been in Canada in two days. But I knew if I did that, this thing would have been dragging on for the rest of my life. I thought I may as well get it over with. Still, all the way over there, I kept thinking: 'I wish they would accept me as a medic.' I *wanted* to go in and do my duty and come out with a good name. But I didn't want to violate my beliefs, and I didn't want to take off running and be AWOL."

While the enlisted men and draftees were in the stockade, awaiting courts-martial, the military guards put them on endless work details. "It would be pointless stuff," said Frank, "like picking crabgrass out of the sand. It was just a nonsense thing, to make you sore and tired—a form of harassment. You would do it for hours and hours.

"We were out on detail one time, and this young kid standing by me just kind of snapped. He turned to me and said: 'I'm going to try to escape. You better hit the ground.' He started running and the guard fired and hit the kid. Later, I heard the guard got another stripe on his shoulder for shooting the guy. That bothered me, to shoot a kid and cripple him. He wasn't a bad kid at all. Why couldn't the guard have shot in the air and warned him? But they had this strict thing: Don't let anybody escape. And while I was there, nobody did escape. After I saw that, I got badly depressed. That's when I knew I was in for hell."

FRANK WAS IN THE STOCKADE FOR THREE MONTHS before his court-martial. The charge was: disobeying a direct order from a commanding officer. It was a one-day trial—another open-and-shut affair. The military prosecutor charged that my brother was as bad as the enemy. In fact, he claimed, Frank was worse than a communist: He was a coward. "I knew better," Frank said: "I was no more of a coward than any of them.

"I told them that. I told them I was happy to work as a medic. But I wasn't going to line up and go out and kill somebody or be killed on the front. I was afraid that if I killed somebody, I would probably have become ruthless. I probably would have become a maniac on the battlefield, to be honest. I thought about that many times. And I knew if that happened, in my mind and heart, I would have been lost. I would have been one of the worst. And then I wouldn't be able to live with myself. I would have gone out and got myself killed. I decided that a federal prison was better than that."

The military court sentenced Frank to three years of hard time at Fort Leavenworth. "If I'd had a civilian lawyer," he told me years later, "I could have gotten thirty days and a dishonorable discharge. I saw it happen to a lot of the white guys who had fancy lawyers. But Mom had no money left for me. By then, she had spent it all on Gary and Gaylen.

"In those days, I was into praying a lot. I thought, 'I'm just going to hang by God and see what happens.' "

GAYLEN GREW TIRED OF NEW YORK. It was a long way from home.

During the time Frank was in Fort Leavenworth, Gaylen turned up in Provo, Utah. Like Frank and Gary, he had fond memories of my grandparents' farm, and he wanted to see his cousins and aunts and uncles. He also had an old friend, named Kerry, who now lived in Salt Lake with his new wife.

Gaylen stayed at Brenda's during his visit. She had recently been divorced, so she was grateful to have the companionship, plus, Gaylen was gracious about helping with house and yard work. He was captivating, cute, and bright, and she liked him as much as everybody liked him when Gaylen wanted to be likable. She could see, though, that he had a thing for women. She could hardly take him anywhere without Gaylen eyeing the good-looking locals or trying to sweet-talk somebody into a date. The Provo girls found him attractive—"He was just about the handsomest, most different kind of boy they had ever met," said Brenda—but Mormon women weren't too liberal about kissing or petting, and they were death on premarital sex, so Gaylen's desires were repeatedly frustrated.

Gaylen had a hard time going without a woman's intimacy. One day, he went up to Salt Lake to pay his friend Kerry a visit. Kerry wasn't there, but his wife was. Gaylen tried his moves on her, and she liked them. Gaylen and his friend's wife started having an affair. They were fucking a couple of times a week and they were liking it—until Kerry came home from work early one afternoon and saw his good friend Gaylen going at his wife from behind. Kerry was a big man, and he decided his friendship with Gaylen was over. He picked Gaylen up and heaved him through the window, then went after him. He kicked Gaylen in the stomach and face for several minutes before his wife could pull him off.

Gaylen spent several weeks in a Salt Lake hospital. His jaw had been broken in five places. He had to eat through a straw, and he couldn't talk too well. Uncle Vern ended up paying all his medical expenses. He also visited Gaylen a couple of times. "You stupid son of a bitch," said Vern. Gaylen couldn't say much in return.

Vern bought Gaylen a bus ticket back to Portland. He showed up at our door late one afternoon, his mouth still wired shut, trying to smile sheepishly. My mother just shook her head and asked him what kind of soup he felt like eating.

GAYLEN'S TROUBLE IN SALT LAKE SLOWED HIM for a while. He started thinking about finding one woman and settling down. He also started attending the Mormon church with me and my mother, and to her great surprise and pleasure, he ended up joining the church within a few weeks.

My mother was glad to have him back. She had recently regained some of her strength and had taken a job working as a bus-woman at a restaurant called Speed's, on Milwaukie's Main Street. Now, with Gaylen back, and apparently rehabilitated, she renewed her hope that our large house might be the thing that would hold us all together.

This was the calmest I saw Gaylen, and it was also the closest the two of us ever became. Our new friendship had little to do with Gaylen now being a Mormon. Something about his conversion never seemed quite solid to me; it was more like a desperate longing for love and community than a declaration of belief. Also, Gaylen was hardly pious about sex. Every once in a while I'd come home from school to find him running around naked upstairs with one neighborhood girl or another. "Don't you dare tell Mom about this," he would say to me, and of course I never did tell her.

In a way, our new closeness had something to do with our respective ages—the same thing that had once helped keep us apart. When Gaylen was twelve and I was six, we just didn't have much to talk about. Now that I was sixteen and he was twenty-two, we had much more in common. By this time, we had read many of the same books, watched the same movies, heard the same music. We talked and argued constantly—he hated Bob Dylan and the Beatles; I loved both—but it was friendly arguing, even respectful. We became companions during this time—something I had never known before with one of my brothers. It helped, I'm sure, that we no longer had to fight over my father's love. For a while, Gaylen was my best friend.

But a peaceful life didn't come easily to Gaylen. He had trouble fitting in with the other young people at the church. Most young men his age were on a mission or enrolled at Brigham Young University, and those were the men that the young Mormon women wanted. Also, Gaylen had seen too much of the world, knew too much about different ways of thinking and living, and the Mormons weren't always comfortable with their knowledge of his history. They often would not invite him to social functions or young people's parties.

Soon, Gaylen was drinking again and seeing his old friends. Soon, he was writing bad checks again, and soon the police were coming to the door again. I was surprised at how quickly and deeply he got himself in trouble. Within a few months, there were warrants out for his arrest in Clackamas County, and there were friends who were angry about things they thought he may have stolen from them. Now when Gaylen got drunk, he was often mean-tempered, and he was almost always looking for new ways to fuck up his life even more.

One night, when he was feeling the pressure of it all, Gaylen sat in the green leather armchair in our front room and drank a bottle of vodka. My mother sat there and watched him. I went upstairs and did my homework. I heard yelling and went back downstairs. Gaylen and my mother were arguing about money. He wanted her to give him two hundred dollars so that he could leave the state, but she told him she couldn't— that was all the money she had. I told Gaylen: "Why don't you lay off her? She can't afford to give you that kind of money. Don't you think she's given you enough as it is?"

"Keep the fuck out of this," he told me. "You're not the big man you think you are." He turned to my mother and said: "I want the money. I'm not leaving here until I have it." There was a palpable menace in the way he said it.

My mother was trembling. She opened her purse and handed him one hundred dollars. "That's *all* I can give you, and now I don't even know how I'm going to feed us for the next month. You can never ask me for anything again," she said, and then she started to cry.

Gaylen stood up, took the money, put on his jacket.

"If you leave here this way, with that money," I said, "you aren't my brother anymore."

He walked past me without a word and slammed the door on his way out. We learned later that he had gone straight to the restaurant where my mother worked and cashed another bad check. She had the employer take the money out of her wages, so he wouldn't press charges against Gaylen.

Gaylen ended up moving to Chicago and living under a different name. This time, we would not see him for five years.

AT FORT LEVENWORTH, FRANK SAW MUCH OF THE SAME HORRIBLE STUFF that went on in all prisons: homosexual rapes and guard brutality. He knew he was in a dangerous place, and so he asked for—and received—a cell to himself.

But staying to himself offended some of the other prisoners. They figured he was either independent or snobbish, and a few times, various prisoners tried to take him down a notch or two. There were some fights, plus an incident where an inmate tried to drop a heavy weight on his head. Frank knew that men got killed in these places. He saw one inmate attacked by others and slashed with a razor blade—so quickly, so many times, the guy was bloodied meat by the time he hit the ground.

It was during this time that I convinced my mother we should start a letter-writing campaign to Oregon Senator Wayne Morse. The senator was known for being tempermental, but he was also a conscientious man—he was one of the U.S. Congress's few early voices to speak out against the war in Vietnam. Eventually, that opposition cost him his Senate seat, during a bitter campaign in which Oregonians decided that Bob Packwood was a better representative of their concerns and beliefs.

My mother and I wrote Morse letters and he wrote back, promising he would look into the matter. He contacted somebody who had influence in this area, and he asked: "Why is this man serving such a long sentence in a dangerous place for a nonviolent crime?"

On March 1, 1967—nineteen months after my brother had been drafted—a Leavenworth official met with Frank and told him they were going to cut his sentence and the army was going to discharge him for "good cause"—which was the same as saying they recognized he had been fucked over. They gave him a little bit of money and a ride to the town of Leavenworth, Kansas. From there, Frank caught a bus back to Portland.

A FEW DAYS LATER, I WAS SITTING IN THE KITCHEN READING, when the front door opened and Frank walked in. Neither my mother nor I knew he had been released. It was a wonderful pleasure to see him, but I could tell that his time at Leavenworth had been hard on him. He seemed a much less happy person, and a more timid one.

I was home alone at the time, and I wanted to call my mother and tell her that Frank was back. Frank said: "No. I'll go down later and visit her where she works. I'll surprise her."

Frank went upstairs to unpack. He came down a few minutes later and gently rested his hand on my shoulder. "Mikal, I have something I want to ask you." There were tears in his eyes. "Have you or anybody else been in my bedroom or taken anything out of it?" I told him I'd gone in a few times to watch his TV or sleep in his bed, but that was about it. "Why?" I asked.

"There's something missing," he said. "I had $219 hidden in my bedroom. It was all the money I have in the world. I was counting on having it when I got out. Do you know *anything* about it?"

I shook my head. I had never known anything about Frank saving any money.

Frank bit his lip and thought for a second, and then he said one word: "Gaylen." It was all he had to say.

He went back upstairs for a few minutes. When he came back down, he was wearing his coat and carrying his duffel bag. "Look," he said, "I don't want you to say a word about me being here to Mom, and don't say anything about the missing money either. I think it's best if I go away and never come back, and it's also best if nobody knows where I am. That money was all I had in the world while I was in prison—it was all I could count on. To come home and find it gone . . . That means I don't have a home here anymore. It means I don't belong here."

I tried arguing with him, reasoning with him, telling him that running away would do no good. Finally, I tried begging him, and I said that if he left and Mother never knew what happened to him, it would be horrible for her—it could even kill her.

Frank shook his head. "Nah. She doesn't care about me. You're the only one who's cared about me. I want to thank you for writing those letters. I'm glad to see you've turned out to be okay. Take care of yourself."

And then he walked out.

I was in a panic. I think it was one of the most painful moments I have ever known in my life. I felt terrible that Frank had gone through all that he had gone through with the army, just to come home to an even greater disappointment. And I felt horrible for my mother. I didn't know how to face her without telling her. Soon, one way or another, she would know Frank had been released from prison, and she would wonder what had happened to him. I knew she would fear the worst.

I sat in the dark on that winter night, crying for hours. I knew then what hell was: Hell was my family. It was having to live with people who did the worst things to people they should love the most.

Later, shortly before the time my mother would arrive home from work, the door opened again, and it was Frank. He said he had gone for a long walk. He walked past the restaurant where our mother was working, and he saw her in there, busing dishes, looking half-crippled, and he knew he couldn't leave her behind. He went in and said hello to her, told her he was back. She was happy and she cried, he said.

Frank had a bag of groceries with him. He was going to fix us dinner.

"Let me help you," I said. "It's good to have you home."

A WHILE BACK, FRANK AND I TALKED ABOUT THAT NIGHT. Frank, I could see, still hurt over what had happened. "It bothered me because a brother would do that," he said. "Here I am, back after having that fucked-up two years of my life and I don't even have any money to go out and get drunk.

"I already felt like such a loser, coming home. And then, discovering that betrayal—I was pretty sour on life for a long time after that."

Did he ever ask Gaylen about it?

"Oh yeah, a few years later. He admitted to doing it. Said he had no idea if I'd ever be coming back home. Couldn't see letting the money sit there, going to waste."

I asked: Did Gaylen ever pay him back?

Frank laughed a pleasureless laugh. "Are you kidding? We're talking about Gaylen and Gary. They never paid anything back to anybody. Well, I guess Gary did, at the very end. I think then he was trying to pay everything back."

FRANK GOT A JOB DOING CUSTODIAL WORK AND BEGAN HELPING my mother pay the bills and keep the mortgage current. He also devoted himself to keeping the yard in shape. He still had dreams of getting his own apartment and having his own family, but he resigned himself to putting that off for a while, until my mother felt secure with her home.

One day Frank met a young Chinese woman at his church. They started dating, and she invited him over to meet her parents. He went over a few times and had dinner. He liked the woman a lot, he realized. He was feeling serious about her.

Frank thought he should return the young woman's courtesy and bring her over to meet his family. I wasn't there the day he brought his girlfriend to the house, but my mother was. Frank opened the front door and escorted the woman into our home. My mother was sitting in her customary spot in the kitchen.

"Mom," Frank said, "I have somebody here I'd like you to meet."

My mother turned around, saw the young Chinese woman standing in her kitchen, and her face turned red. "Get that whore out of my house!" my mother yelled at Frank.

Frank stood there, staring at my mother. He was shocked beyond words. After an awkward, silent moment, he said: "But, Mom . . ."

"You heard me. *Get* her out of here, and don't ever bring her back."

By the time Frank and the woman got outside, the woman was crying. "I'm sorry," Frank said. "I don't know what to say. She can be a little crazy at times. She's been worried about a lot of stuff recently."

The woman wiped her tears and said it was okay, she understood.

That night, Frank went back home and said to my mother: "That's it. I've tried to help you, but you can't be helped. I can't *believe* you would do something like that."

"I'm sorry," my mother said. "She's probably a very nice woman, but at the same time, I know the kind of woman you tend to like—you know, sluts. When I saw her standing there, I thought she was probably just somebody you'd found on the street."

Frank told my mother he was moving out. She begged him to stay. "I'll be lost without you. I can't run this place without you."

Frank said he would stay for a month or two and help her make the financial transition. As it worked out, he ended up staying forever.

I knew nothing about this incident until a couple of years ago, when Frank told me. I asked him what had happened with him and the woman. "She was polite about it," he said. "She was real nice. But what Mom did created an awful memory between us. In effect, it really killed the relationship.

"I think Mom accomplished exactly what she wanted that day. I think she disabled my chance at love, my chance at family. I never came as close to any of it again after that."

CHAPTER 8

REBELLION

AND WHAT ABOUT ME? Well, I was a kid in the 1960s.

I was sixteen. I was a sophomore in high school. Though I liked books and was still moved by religion, I mainly had one thing on my mind—the same thing most kids I knew had on their mind, one way or another: sex.

I didn't really know all that sex was about. Nobody in my family had ever taken me aside and told me the first thing about it. I learned what I could by stealing a look at the occasional *Playboy* and by reading Henry Miller's novels and John Cleland's and Frank Harris's pornographic classics. I hid these things in the closet of my bedroom and brought them out late at night, when I was done with Franz Kafka and Herman Hesse. The truth is, I read Miller and Harris more attentively than I ever read

Hesse or even Melville. Sex seemed like it must be the most exciting and desirable thing in the world. I already looked forward to it more than anything else.

At the same time, I knew that it was not a good idea. My church absolutely forbade any form of premarital or nonmarital sex. Sex was a holy gift for procreation, we were told, and misusing that gift in any form was a sin so severe, it was second only to murder. At our Sunday priesthood meetings, our counselors were always warning us against this temptation. God found it an abhorrence for a man to spill his seed in any manner other than marital intercourse, and even then, seed should be spilled only for the purpose of procreation. An act like oral sex was an outrage. So was jacking off. Although these teachings weren't exactly enough to stop you from having an erection, they could make you ponder what to do when you *did* have one. Somehow, praying for a hard-on to go away never worked.

So, like most teenage males, and like probably every young Mormon man I knew, I masturbated—sometimes to my own passions or imagination, sometimes to the books and magazines I mentioned above, sometimes to the women's underwear section of the Montgomery Ward catalog. And, like the other Mormon boys I knew, I was feeling guilty about what I did. Always resolving never to do it again. One time, I even made that resolution last for a while. Two weeks, I think.

ON WEEKENDS, I WAS GOING TO THE TEEN DANCE CLUBS in downtown Portland. One of them, the Headless Horseman, was located in the space of an old gangster's nightclub, where Gary used to hang out. Now, it was full of teenagers, all decked out in the semi-mod fashion that preceded the soon-to-come hippie era. We would go there in our wide-wale corduroys and polka-dot or flower-print shirts with white collars and cuffs, and our knee-high boots. My mother didn't have much money, but she did her best to make sure I always had modern and fashionable clothes, bless her.

Inside the clubs, we would ask teenage women in short skirts and hoop earrings to dance to the club's regular bands—local groups like the Kingsmen (of "Louie, Louie" fame), the Wailers and, once in a blue moon, Paul Revere and the Raiders. Sometimes we would talk the girls into leaving the club and going to hang out in the stairwell of a large parking structure a few blocks away. We would kiss for hours—we called it making out, of course—and we would try to run our hands over the young women's breasts or between their legs. I remember one girl telling me: "You sure have busy hands for a boy your age." I guess she was right.

The next morning I would be in church along with everybody else, worrying about salvation.

THIS COULD GO ON ONLY SO LONG. It went on until the summer of 1967—the summer that became known in pop history as the Summer of Love. Hippiedom and psychedelia were in full bloom. The Beatles had gone from their pop-informed style of rock & roll to the avant-garde-inspired terrain of *Sergeant Pepper's Lonely Hearts Club Band*. Young people were growing their hair long, dressing fancifully, trying to break themselves off from the conventions of their parents and the surrounding culture and make their own rules. It would all get ruined soon enough—we would pay some hard prices for our generational revolt—but for that one season, it was a wonderful time to be alive. Everything around us—the music, the politics, the nation's emotional stakes—made plain that we were entering a different age, that young people were free to redefine themselves in completely new terms. Everything was worth risking—or at least we thought so at the time.

I spent afternoons during that summer hanging out at Portland's Psychedelic Shop and Lair Hill park—places where the longhairs and bikers congregated. In the evenings, I and my friends would go around the corner from the Psychedelic Shop to the Crystal Ballroom, an old upstairs dance hall that had been a popular place for big bands during the Swing Era. The Crystal's main dance floor was built over ball bearings, and during that summer, when bands like the Grateful Dead and Quicksilver Messenger Service played there, the hippies would dance and skip in circles on the floor, making the whole room bounce and shimmy, like the deck of a drunken ship.

I met a young blond woman named Pamela at one of these shows. Every day for weeks afterward, Pamela and I would meet at the Psychedelic Shop and sit on the floor, talking, holding hands, kissing. Sometimes, after midnight, when our parents were asleep, we would have long, feverish phone conversations, talking about how much we loved each other, and whether we should have sex. We finally decided we should.

One day in late August we met at the Psychedelic Shop. Peter, Paul and Mary had released a new album, *Album 1700*, and we pooled our money and bought it. We took a bus to my home on Oatfield. My mother and Frank were both at work. Pamela and I made a quick bed on the floor of my mother's old bedroom, and we put our new record on my portable stereo. "Leaving on a Jet Plane" was just starting to play when Pamela laid down, opened her legs, and guided me inside her. When I climaxed, "Leaving on a Jet Plane" was still playing. I was lying on top of Pamela, looking at her wide-open, pale blue eyes, stunned by the immense pleasure of still feeling myself inside her, when I heard the downstairs front door close. Somebody—my mother or Frank—was home early from work. Pamela got up hurriedly, grabbed her clothes, and hid in my mother's closet. I got dressed and went downstairs, my heart pounding wildly. It was Frank, home early. Thank God.

I didn't tell him I had a naked young woman in the closet upstairs, though I suppose I could have. Instead, through a convoluted set of movements, I managed to sneak Pamela out of the house without Frank ever knowing she was there, and then I met her later at Lair Hill Park.

I felt some guilt about the sex—after all, I had just committed a sin next to murder. It wasn't small guilt, but it also wasn't enough to prevent me from repeating the sin. One day, Pamela's father figured out what his daughter and I were doing, and he confronted us as we were walking into Lair Hill Park, holding hands. He took Pamela by the arm and led her away, telling me I would never get to see her again. He answered the phone every time I called after that, and he always hung up on me. Pamela never called me back, and I never saw her again.

A LOT OF PEOPLE I KNEW WERE STARTING TO SMOKE MARIJUANA and take psychedelics. I thought about this particular temptation longer and harder than I had thought about having sex, but not that much longer. The first time I smoked enough marijuana to get high I was with two young men who, like myself, were members of the Mormon priesthood. We stayed up all night, talking about rock and & roll and girls and God.

A month or so later, it was Christmas. I and the same two Mormon boys decided we wanted some new records, but we didn't have the money to buy them. We came up with an elaborate, foolproof scheme about how we could shoplift the albums from a big department store in downtown Portland without getting caught. We got caught immediately and were taken to a hidden office on the store's top floor, where we were surrounded by numerous store detectives. They drove us over to the Portland Police Station—the same place where Gary and Gaylen had been held many times before. For some reason, the police detective at the station thought the store should not file charges. "I don't want to see these boys spending Christmas in jail," he said. The head store detective agreed, as long as we would promise never to come back. We promised. As we were leaving, the police detective took me aside. "You have an older brother named Gary, don't you?" he asked. "Don't you think it's hard enough on your mother, having one son in jail? Don't go the way of your brother. If you do, you're only throwing your life away."

I THOUGHT ABOUT THE POLICEMAN'S WARNING A LOT. At times I had feared that crime might be a familial disease: Would I wake up one day and want to rob? Was it inevitable that I would make the same choices as Gaylen and Gary—that I would end up hurting people or plundering their lives and possessions? Was I bound to end up on the inside of a jail cell, thinking about the world outside?

In truth, I not only didn't have much talent for crime (though, come to think of it, neither did my brothers), I also didn't have much appetite for it. For one thing, I had seen up close what my brothers' lives had brought them. In addition, I had my mother's urgings to consider: For years, she had told me repeatedly that I was the family's last hope for redemption. "I want *one* son to turn out right, one son I don't have to end up visiting in jail, one son I don't have to watch in court as his life is sentenced away, piece by piece," she said. After the policeman's warning, her words reverberated even more in my head.

As a result, I felt I now had the job of signifying all the goodness that would make up for all my brothers' failures and misdeeds. I was not allowed, it seemed, to enact my own darkness, my own violence, my own hatred. All such license had been taken up by my brothers, with disastrous results. The only role left in the script for me was to atone for their losses, to set the historical balance right.

Still, I was doing my best to be bad—at least within certain limitations. I was now smoking dope regularly, and I had just started taking psychedelics on weekends. I was also skipping school much of the time—writing my own excuse slips and forging my mother's signature, so I could take the afternoon off and go meet girlfriends at various places, for the purposes of getting stoned and having sex. I told myself I had to become familiar with sin and rebellion—that there were truths within those realms of experience that I had to learn about. They felt like natural truths—like something I had been gravitating toward my whole life.

My drift was not going unnoticed by people at the church. One Sunday, a member of the local bishopric—a man I admired much and had once regarded as something of a father figure—drove over to our house on Oatfield Road and asked me to step outside for a talk. He told me that he and other church leaders had grown concerned about my changing appearance—the new length of my hair and my style of dressing—and they were also bothered by some of the political views they had heard me voice. They found all these changes on my part an unwelcome influence on other young Mormons. Unless I was willing to forswear this new spirit of rebellion, he said, then perhaps I should think about no longer attending the church.

On that day, I realized a line had been drawn in my life, and I knew which side of that line I had to stand on. These new things that had become my passions—rock & roll, politics, art, literature, and sex—had provided me with a new creed and a new sense of courage. Looking back, I now believe that these choices allowed me—and many others in my generation—to act out a kind of formalized, largely permitted brand of "criminality": We could use drugs or defy authority or flout the law or even contemplate violent or destructive acts of revolt, we told ourselves, *because we had a reason to*. Also, through the bravest music of the era, we could believe we were taking part in a form of rebellion that truly mattered—or at least, I told myself, that counted for more than my brothers' brand of rebellion. And in the darkest music of the time—the music of the Rolling Stones or Doors or Velvet Underground—I could participate in darkness without submitting to it, which is something Gary and Gaylen had been unable to do.

LIKE MOST EVERYONE ELSE IN MY FAMILY, I had now adopted some executed men as personal heroes. My picks were Boston's Nicola Sacco and Bartolomeo Vanzetti, and Salt Lake's Joe Hill. All these men were executed—at least officially—for the crime of murder. But they were also killed because they had challenged the nation's conventions of power and authority.

Sacco and Vanzetti were Italian immigrants who were also anarchists, and who advocated the overthrow of the U.S. Government. The Boston Police hated them, and in 1920, they charged the two with a pair of robbery-murders. The trial was blatantly partisan, and numerous authors, poets, and journalists around the world protested the conviction of Sacco and Vanzetti. It was to no avail. On August 22, 1927, Massachusetts electrocuted the two men, despite substantial doubts about their guilt—doubts that have only grown over the decades.

Joe Hill was an American songwriter and poet. In 1913—the year my mother was born—Hill moved to Salt Lake from Los Angeles, where he worked with the radical and controversial Industrial Workers of the World to organize the state's laborers. Utahans did not care for the union movement, and they treated its advocates roughly. The unionists struck back—sometimes violently. In early 1914, Joe Hill was arrested for the murder of a storekeeper and his son. The storekeeper, John Morrison, was a former policeman who had been a strikebreaker, and who had reportedly killed several members of the IWW in gun battles. Hill was convicted, and despite pleas from numerous prominent Americans—including President Woodrow Wilson—Utah was determined to put the poet to death. It would be the most famous execution in Utah's history until that of my brother, sixty-two years later. Like my brother, Hill chose a firing squad as the mode of his execution, saying: "I'll take shooting. I'm used to that. I have been shot a few times in the past, and I guess I can stand it again." When the time for his death came, Hill himself gave the riflemen the command to fire.

Learning the stories of these men forever changed something in me. It made me hate the people and the structures that used their power to keep others under their control. It also made me understand that any state that had the power and the will to put a man to death was indeed a malevolent place.

But my radicalized sympathy for the downtrodden only went so far. I may have been reading Frantz Fanon, Upton Sinclair, and Eldridge Cleaver and writing school papers about the Miranda ruling, but I almost never bothered to visit my brother Gary, who had now been in prison for five years. This is not an easy admission to make. It is, in fact, probably the one misdeed in my life that I feel the most regret and guilt over. It didn't help matters that in Oregon at that time inmates weren't allowed visitors under age eighteen. Gary and I exchanged a few letters over the years, but I always felt a bit bad writing him about what I was doing in school or about friends and pastimes, because to Gary those were things and events that existed on the "outside." Later, during our few visits, we both struggled to find some common base. But I was young and outside; he was growing old, inside. And the distance hurt.

I had no idea what his life was like. Also, the few things I heard didn't make me want to know more. In the fall of 1968, there had been a serious riot at Oregon State Penitentiary, and Gary had taken part in it. I heard a story about how he had taken a ball peen hammer and thrown it at the head of an old enemy in the prison yard, and then beat the fallen man in the head with it. The man went on to live the rest of his life as a vegetable. I also heard that Gary had stabbed a black man many times because the man had in some way hurt or threatened a friend of Gary's.

I must have realized, on some level, that Gary was living in a world of horror, but I never admitted it to myself. I simply wasn't there for my brother during this time. I should have been, but I wasn't. I was too busy planning my own escape.

DURING MY LAST YEAR IN HIGH SCHOOL, I BECAME GOOD friends with my Creative Writing teacher, a woman named Grace Mc-Ginnis. Grace had befriended me and had become my champion—and in the obtuse political climate that prevailed at Milwaukie High School in the late 1960s, this wasn't exactly a riskless effort. Milwaukie was a conservative town—in 1968, we had seen a lot of GEORGE WALLACE FOR PRESIDENT bumper stickers around our parts—and as youth culture grew more radical and daring, and more outlandish, the community and the school reacted with anger and fear. The school passed dress codes—dictating how long we could wear our hair, and prohibiting short skirts and flamboyant dress of any sort—and I and a handful of other students defied these regulations. As our punishment, the school's officials decided we could not take part in extracurricular activities, like sports or drama or band. I was a member of a high school discussion group that debated national and international affairs on local television, and Milwaukie's vice-principal thought I should quit the team unless I cut my hair. Otherwise, I was dishonoring the school and our town with such an unsavory appearance. Grace went to bat for me with the faculty. She made an impassioned speech to them about what she saw as their bigotry, and she lashed out at those teachers who called the longhaired students sissies and who basically treated us as the enemy. As a result of Grace's efforts, I was able to continue with the debate group.

I later learned that Grace's interest in me had in part been stirred by something we shared in common: her maiden name had been Gilmore—her father, in fact, had been a man named Frank Gilmore. As far as I can tell, we were never really any relation, but we used to make a lot of jokes about somehow sharing the same father.

In the winter of my senior year, my mother's financial condition became precarious. She had been keeping up the house's mortgage payments, but she had been unable to keep the property taxes current, and the state was making noises about seizing the property. The total debt came to around $1200, which seemed like a fortune in those days. Frank—who still lived with us—renewed his campaign for the family to move into a smaller place, and my mother resumed her resistance. We sold the piano and much of the fine furniture, but that wasn't enough. I wanted to take a job so that I could help, but my mother refused. She thought it was important that I should keep investing my time and efforts in my education; she had dreams that I might win a scholarship to college, since she could not afford to send me. She had never had a son who completed high school and went on to college, and she wanted me to be that son.

After school one day, I visited Grace in her classroom to talk about my mother's dilemma. Grace was a compassionate and smart person, and I wanted her advice. She asked if she could come over to the house and talk with my mother, so she could make a better assessment of the situation. My mother was reluctant to have visitors, but I talked her into a meeting. Grace and my mother talked for hours and they became good friends. Grace started coming over regularly, and also visited my mother at the restaurant where she worked.

In addition to everything else, Grace was an adept psychic—probably more the real article than Fay ever was. "I don't mean to alarm you," she told me one day, "but I get a bad feeling when I am in your house. I think the place may be haunted, and I'm not sure anything good can come for your mother and your family while she continues to live there." I appreciated Grace's concern, but I told her she wasn't saying anything I didn't already know. I even knew something more. It didn't matter where we lived. We would be cursed wherever we went.

It wasn't long before Grace was driving my mother down to the Oregon State Penitentiary in Salem, so she could visit Gary on Sundays. A short time later, Grace started sitting in on my mother's visits with Gary. Grace and my brother got into long and lively conversations about literature and art, and she was struck by his fine mind and his impressive vocabulary. She liked him very much.

I was invited to join these trips, but I always declined. I told Grace I had seen enough of the insides of jails and courthouses by the age of twelve to last me a lifetime.

———

MY MOTHER FINALLY DECIDED SHE SHOULD GO TO THE MORMON church and ask them for help with her problem. She said that if the church would help her with the property taxes, she would deed the place over to them upon her death. But the church was reluctant to take this offer. After all, she had two sons who had repeatedly got themselves in trouble and had been no help to her. Plus, she had a son who had been imprisoned for his refusal to serve in the army. Such a defiance of convention was unimaginable to the church leaders. And then there was me: The church had once taken me in, befriended me, given me the priesthood, and in turn I had become a rebel who, as far as they could see, now believed in ungodly values and was living a less than exemplary life.

The local bishop decided against giving my mother the help she requested. "It wasn't wise for her to keep the house," he later told Larry Schiller. "It was too large, she only lived in a room or two, and she couldn't maintain it. She wanted to keep it because it reminded her of happier years, but it didn't seem sensible. It seemed wiser to get her into a small apartment. But she refused that idea. I think it was an emotional thing with her. She didn't like people telling her what to do, plus, she had an emotional tie to that house."

The bishop was right: It was an emotional thing. I sat in on a couple of the meetings that he had with her and Grace. My mother got so livid in the discussions that she got up and walked out. She later said: "Who were *they* to think I didn't need that house?"

Grace went with my mother when she visited Gary and told him that the church had refused her plea and that she would now almost definitely lose the house. Grace later said that visit was the only time she ever saw Gary get angry. He couldn't stand the thought that my mother's church had turned her down, and now she would forfeit her beautiful home. Grace said that was the day she first saw a look of murder cross Gary's face.

IN MY LAST FEW WEEKS OF HIGH SHOOL, I WON A TUITION scholarship to Portland State University. Within a week or two of my graduation—in the late spring of 1969—I was looking for my own apartment in downtown Portland. It seemed a reasonable thing to do: I would be attending school in downtown Portland, and I should live close to the campus. But there was another, truer reason for why I was leaving home: I wanted to. I had always wanted to.

I could tell as I moved my last belongings out of the house on Oatfield that my mother was hurting deeply someplace inside, but she was smiling bravely, and she was saying encouraging things. Looking back now, it tears my heart to think about that parting. But at the time, my heart did not feel such pain.

A week later, I went back to the house to visit my mother. I walked up on the front porch, opened the door, and stepped into an empty front room. Where before there had been furniture and a television and people, there was now only vacancy. I walked through the entire place. My mother and brother were gone. There wasn't a trace of them or anything they owned. Being in that empty old house scared the hell out of me. I felt a chill spot as I walked through the upstairs hallway. I feared that at any moment a set of black claws might appear out of nowhere and swipe me into the darkness. I got out as quickly as I could.

I called Grace. She explained to me that my mother had lost the house a few days after I left and was forced to give it back to the mortgage holders. She had been fighting to hold on as long as possible, so that I could finish high school without the disruption or shame of losing my home.

"I didn't know that things were this imminent," I told Grace.

She said: "Your mother didn't want you to know. She wanted to protect you."

My mother and brother had made the down payment on a small trailer and were now living in a courtyard park, down the main highway, in the semi-rural outpost of Oak Grove. They did not yet have a phone.

I went to see them. The trailer was aqua green and white, and had two small bedrooms, a bathroom, and a living room-kitchen area. There was no air-conditioning, and it was hot and sticky in there. I could tell that my mother felt crushed. As she later told me and many other people: "I died the day I moved into this place."

I was officially parted from my family. My brother Frank would stay with my mother until the day she died, but I would never go back home, and the three of us would never sleep under the same roof again.

FOR A LONG TIME, I DID NOT LOOK BACK. I tried college for a while, but after a bad love affair, I lost the footing of my educational career and never regained it. I went on to have many other girlfriends; I went on to participate in radical politics; I went on to use numerous drugs, without ever developing any drug problems—at least not for a time. And when I tired of what I saw drugs doing to my generation, I went on to become a drug counselor—a vocation I worked at for several years.

Only one time during this period did I visit my brother Gary. It was in the aftermath of the love affair I just mentioned. The woman and I had been boyfriend and girlfriend for our last year or two of high school, and we were talking about getting married. Then one day she met a man she really liked—a born-again Christian—and within a few weeks, they were married and she was pregnant. I felt shattered. I felt that a dream—the possibility for a family of my own—had been taken away from me. I started staying up all night drinking, sleeping all day. I quit college, lost my tuition, and ran out of money. I was a mess. It was a classic case of romantic depression, and I was milking it for everything I could.

Then one Sunday, my mother and Grace talked me into accompanying them to Salem to visit Gary. I guess they thought it would do me some good. Gary and I were nervous and tentative with each other at first—we had not seen each other for years, and I was now a young long-haired man, sitting in a room with a lot of shorthaired men, some of whom weren't looking too kindly at me. But after a few minutes of talking with my brother, I realized how much I still loved him, and how much I had missed having him around. When he asked me how I had been, I told him. I told him everything—the whole story about the bad romance and the ensuing despair. I thought he would understand. I thought, if anybody would give me sympathy, it would be him.

Instead, he sat silently for several long moments, regarding me. Finally, he smiled his crooked smile, and said: "Well, partner, that sounds rough. But anytime you want to trade your troubles for mine, let me know. I mean, hell, at least nobody has taken your youth from you. You're still free."

At the time, I thought: He doesn't understand. I realize now he understood far more than I ever could. Once again, Gary was telling me the truth about our lives. Maybe if I'd understood that, things might have ended up different.

ONE DAY IN EARLY 1971, MY MOTHER CALLED ME IN A PANIC. She had a horror story to tell.

She and Grace had gone to see Gary at Oregon State Penitentiary the day before. When Gary entered the visiting room, my mother said, he was a different man than she had ever seen before. His face and hands were bloated—like the flesh of a drowning victim—and he was taking heavy steps, like a stuporous Frankenstein monster. He could barely talk; he slurred his sentences, and a stream of drool ran out of his mouth, between the words. When he tried taking sips from a cup of coffee, he couldn't hold his hands steady, and the drink kept sloshing over the cup's rim. He couldn't even feel the burn of the hot liquid as it poured onto his lap.

My mother put her arms around him. "What is *wrong* with you?" she asked.

"I've been Prolixed," Gary said thick-tongued. "The psychiatrist and warden here have put me on a heavy medicine, Prolixin. They use it to control the prisoners they don't like. They're punishing me because I've been angry with them about my teeth."

Gary tried to explain more, but putting the words together was a terrible effort. He ended up just sitting there, his mouth hanging open. "I'm sorry, Mom," he finally said. "I can't stay any longer. I've got to go back to my cell and lie down."

As he stumbled from the visiting room, all eyes were on him. A few of the other inmates offered words of encouragement as he walked by: "Steady as you go. Hang in there."

When Gary had left, my mother stayed in her chair, sobbing uncontrollably, as Grace tried to comfort her.

My mother and Grace went to find the warden. They ended up talking with the assistant warden. My mother demanded to know why Gary was being given this medicine. She was livid. The assistant warden was unmoved. He told her that Prolixin was the best drug they had available to help them deal with violent prisoners. Gary's behavior, he indicated, warranted the drug.

My mother walked out of the prison, full of fury and hatred, and feeling helpless.

"They've turned your brother into a zombie," she told me that day on the phone, crying. "He was like a walking dead man. We have to do something about this."

THE CIRCUMSTANCES LEADING UP TO GARY'S PROLIXIN EPISODE had been building for years. It all stemmed from two problems: Gary could be a difficult man to handle in incarceration, plus, he was a man badly in need of a set of functional false teeth. The combination of these two conditions created the setting for a terrible conflict that would know few bounds.

Shortly after his arrival at OSP in the spring of 1964, the prison dentist examined Gary's teeth and decided they should all be extracted and replaced with upper and lower dentures. The dentist made Gary the dentures, but they did not fit well. They rubbed against his gums and scraped them raw. Talking or eating had become a painful ordeal. Gary requested new dentures, but when he received them, he had the same problem, so he destroyed them. The prison decided he was being difficult and they weren't going to jump to meet his demands. Gary decided that the officials were refusing to issue him workable dentures as a way of punishing him further.

This battle went on for years. In fact, it would not be until 1975, following Gary's transfer to a federal penitentiary in Marion, Illinois, that he would finally receive a set of comfortable false teeth that he could live with. In the meantime, he raised constant and momentous hell, and the dentures issue became a contest of wills between him and the Oregon prison authorities. He wrote numerous letters to the Oregon State Corrections Board and to two consecutive state governors, complaining about the situation. All these officials wrote the prison, seeking explanations and solutions. Gary got in frequent fights and arguments with the guards and other prisoners, which resulted in his being beaten and then isolated in a bare-bones segregation cell, sometimes for several months at a time. He set fire to his mattress, flooded his cell, and got sent to the psychiatric security unit. He attacked one dentist and threatened to kill another. He had my mother place an ad in Oregon's largest newspaper, urging the public to take up his cause with a letter-writing campaign. For a while, the warden received a steady flow of letters from around the state, all demanding "equal justice for Gary Gilmore."

I have a large file box, full of hundreds of documents related to this affair. You could write a book alone based on the drama of those correspondences and prison reports, and it would be a remarkable tale of outrage and devastation.

In 1970 and '71, the trouble came to full boil. A couple of days after Christmas in 1970, Gary was admitted to the prison's psychiatric unit. The resident psychiatrist, Dr. Wesley Weissert, noted: "Gilmore was, in general, very antagonistic, belligerent, uncooperative, with specific incidents being urinating on the floor, throwing his food against rail, spitting at various aides (including the undersigned), and in general being 'obnoxious.'" Gary told the doctor that his anger stemmed from his problems with the dental department. The doctor thought that perhaps Gary was being manipulative about the whole matter. Gary became angry and spit in Weissert's face several times. Weissert noted: "[An] attempt was made to try and convince him that we cannot fortify bad behavior such as he has been exhibiting. If the acting out continues for the next 24 to 48 hours, he will be given an intramuscular Prolixin to help control his verbal and physical aggressive assaults."

Gary calmed down for a few weeks, but soon his rages resumed. He was threatening suicide, but Weissert thought that Gary wasn't genuinely depressed enough to kill himself. In the first week of February, Gary talked several other inmates in the segregation unit into joining his protest. All of them—Gary included—slashed their wrists. Two of them almost died.

About a month later, Dr. Weissert prescribed Prolixin for Gary. Prolixin is a medication that can provide some true psychotics relief from the nightmares of imagined voices and other delusions. It has also occasionally been used in prisons and jails to calm down troubled or hostile men. Many doctors, though, believe that this is not an advisable use, since the drug can also make some people intensely restless or nervous. An average recommended dose of Prolixin might be in the range of 2 cc. to 4 cc. a month. Gary claimed that he was given 16 cc. a month for three months, which, if true, could be considered a large dose; however, I have not been able to obtain any records that may confirm or refute this claim.

According to some men I've talked with who also experienced the drug, it can sometimes make your body so anxious that you feel a need to stretch or bend as much as possible—a side effect basically known as akathesia. One man told me he had even seen other men try to bend over backward and snap their spines, so that they could end the miserable irritation. In Gary's case—at least according to Gary, though other prisoners from the period corroborated his account—the guards would keep him tied to his cot for hours on end, just to watch him writhe in misery. Gary, however, stayed defiant. One time, when a guard got close enough to him, Gary covered him in spit. The guard, Gary later said, began choking him and then put a pillow over his head. "I was about to go out," Gary said, when another guard thought it had gone far enough. The guards punched my brother in the face a few times while he was strapped down, then wheeled him under a bright overhead light and left him there all night. On Prolixin, my brother said, the brightness of the light was unbearable, and sleep was impossible.

One of Gary's friends from the prison during these days, a man named Steve Bekins, told me: "Gary was never the same man after Prolixin. He was full of hatred, and he simply knew no boundaries. He would go as far as he could to make the prison authorities angry, even if it meant hurting himself. Some guys became more distant from Gary after all that. You could tell he was now a man full of murder."

DURING THE TIME ALL THIS WAS HAPPENING, I got another call from my mother. "Your brother Gaylen has come home," she told me. "He got tired of life in Chicago, and he decided he missed us. He's come back to face his bad check charges, and he wants to make a new life."

I was glad to hear the news. Whatever bad feelings I had once had about my last encounter with Gaylen had long been forgotten. If my mother could forgive him, then I should too. Besides, I missed his wit and his smarts.

"I have to warn you about something," my mother continued. "Gaylen is not the same as the last time you saw him."

"What do you mean?"

"Well . . . for one thing, he's much thinner now. Something happened to him in Chicago. He got sick—something to do with his stomach. I know he had to have surgery, and it's left him a little frail. Also, there was a bad romance. He had to leave behind the girl he loved. He's pretty brokenhearted. I think he needs some friends. I think he needs his family."

Indeed, something *had* happened to Gaylen in Chicago, and indeed, he was no longer the same man. When he showed up at my door later that night, I did not recognize him. He was so skeletal, so dark-eyed, he looked like a walking cadaver. Just as troubling, much of his sharpness was gone. His speech was slurred, and his mind seemed slower. I had seen him drunk many times before—and would again—but this was not drunkenness. I realize now that it was probably an effect of pain medication, or just the accumulated result of all his years of alcohol and drug abuse. But whatever medicine Gaylen may have been taking at this time, it didn't help much. As we sat and talked, it was plain that he was in acute pain and that his grip on his health was not strong.

Yet despite his pain, when Gaylen heard about what was happening to Gary as OSP, he paid his brother an immediate visit. He and Gary had a good, reconciliatory meeting. What a scene it must have been: two dead men, sitting, talking to each other, renewing their bonds as brothers. I wish I had been with them.

Like my mother, Gaylen was outraged and horrified by the impact that the Prolixin was having on Gary. Gaylen stormed into the warden's office, demanding an end to the treatment. An assistant to the warden assured him that the matter was under review.

A few days after Gaylen's visit, the prison psychiatrist made the following notation about Gary: "This patient sustained a quite severe Prolixin reaction and was returned to [the psychiatric unit] on April 5, 1971.

His Prolixin was stopped, and he made a gradual improvement of his symptomatology. He is scheduled for a Parole Board hearing in May 1971. It is hoped that he will have a complete subsidence of his symptoms by that time. His Prolixin will be stopped as of this date, and appropriate medication will be restarted as his condition warrants in the future. He has no hostile or aggressive thoughts with being on Prolixin, and were he not suffering from the Prolixin reaction, I would recommend his permanent continuance on his medication. He, unfortunately, sustained a moderate severe reaction which is predictable in a certain few patients. The good effects from the Prolixin I feel have outweighed the bad side effects."

IT WOULD BE YEARS BEFORE I LEARNED WHAT HAD HAPPENED TO Gaylen in Chicago—in fact, it was another one of those hidden family secrets I learned from reading *The Executioner's Song*. But Mailer didn't tell the full story. That's because the only person who knew the full story was my mother, and she wouldn't divulge all of it to anybody. To this day, despite my best efforts, I have never been able to learn the whole truth of the matter.

This much, though, I do know: Gaylen got stabbed in Chicago. Horribly, viciously, repeatedly. I have heard different accounts of how this happened. One story has it that Gaylen was drunk and was robbed in an alley late one winter night. One man held him while the other stole his money and jewelry and then rammed an ice pick into his abdomen, over and over. The other story I've heard fits in a little better with what I know about my brother. Gaylen had fallen deeply in love with a married woman. He should have learned his lesson from what happened to him in Salt Lake, but of course he didn't. One day the woman's husband discovered the affair, tracked down my brother, stabbed him in the lower gut, and left him for dead. It took several quarts of blood and two or three operations to save Gaylen's life—and the doctors advised him that it was unlikely that he would ever again be able to use his stomach or bowels properly without pain.

Both of these stories, though, aren't much more than grim rumors—all that my brother Frank and I have been able to piece together from what we remember of hushed whispers. I have never been able to find the Chicago Police reports or Illinois hospital records about Gaylen's stabbing. It is likely that Gaylen was living under another name while in Chicago, and nobody seems to know what that name was.

I was, however, able to obtain Gaylen's Clackamas County hospital records. Though I did not know it at the time, he was in and out of the Oregon City Hospital often during the spring through autumn of 1971. Every time it was for the same thing—intense stomach pain—and every time there wasn't much that could be done. Twenty-three years later, as I was reading through those hospital records, I came across a technical medical description of the depth and severity and number of his wounds, and it all finally caught up with me. I cried over the horror of his pain and the loss of his life in a way that I had never cried for him before.

My mother, as I said earlier, knew all along about the severity of Gaylen's wounds and how he had received them. It was simply another one of those ugly truths that she thought I should be protected from. It would not be until almost a decade after his death that I would come to understand that Gaylen had in effect been murdered while he was in Chicago, and that it had taken him longer to die than it did most people.

In the summer, Gaylen's girlfriend, Janet, followed him from Chicago to Oregon. She had missed him as much as he had missed her, and so she left the violence of the world she had known for an unknown small town in the American West. Janet and Gaylen got a motel apartment down the boulevard from where my mother and Frank lived. Janet was a kind, caring person, and one of the few young women my mother would let enter her home. Janet also seemed to love Gaylen very much.

But it was a tempestuous love. The two of them would drink too much and then yell and throw things, until one or the other would stomp out of the motel to go and drink alone. Invariably, Gaylen would find a bottle of liquor and drink it to its bitter end. In contrast to the beer and red wine he had favored years before, he was now drinking stomach-churning rot like peppermint schnapps. I would take one sip of the sickly-sweet stuff and want to vomit. Gaylen, though, could drink it all night long.

On several occasions, at about three in the morning, I would hear a banging at my front door. I would go downstairs and it would be Gaylen, standing in my doorway, swaying in the summer night air, weeping like a baby. He would come in and we would sit and talk, and he would continue to nurse off his schnapps until he passed out on my sofa. I'd put a pillow under his head and a blanket over him, and then I would sit and watch him as he slept his fitful sleep. The next morning, when I'd wake up, he would always be gone.

———

Gaylen turned himself into the court and the court dismissed the charges pending against him. The judge and prosecutors could probably see he was in no condition to be put inside a jail. Also, he had lost all his appetite for crime. He had no more interest in writing bad checks, or stealing, or dreaming about the perfect crime. Instead, he wanted to marry Janet and have a family of his own. He wanted, he told me, to start life over.

One night, around one in the morning, Janet called Grace. Gaylen, Janet said, was in intense pain and needed to get to the hospital right away. He wasn't able to drive, and they didn't have the money for a taxi. Therefore, Janet was asking Grace to help them.

Grace drove Gaylen and Janet to a hospital in Milwaukee, but the emergency room would not accept Gaylen because he did not have insurance or a welfare card. Grace then took them to the Oregon City Hospital. Again, the hospital didn't know what to do with Gaylen—he'd already been there so many times. When it was past five in the morning, and no doctor had yet seen him, Gaylen asked Grace to drive him and Janet home. "What's the fucking use," he said. Somewhere, during that night, in a moment of intense pain, Gaylen had pulled up his shirt and rubbed at his stomach. It was then that Grace saw the massive hole in my brother's abdomen. Gaylen's wounds had never healed. They were open, and they were bleeding.

The day after this incident, Grace received a letter from Gary. He was paying back some money she had loaned him for a new set of dentures, but he also sent along a letter that was full of hatred and venom for the world around him. Grace almost felt the violence jumping off the page. That's when the accumulation of all the bad news caught up with her and made her see how she was spending more and more time surrounded by lives of disaster. Also, there was her spiritualism: Grace looked down the long psychic highway of our future, and she saw something monumental and deadly bearing down on us. She could tell it might take a few other people along with it. So she did the only thing a smart person could do. She called my mother and said: "I do not mean this to offend you—I love you—but I cannot go any further with your family. I have only so much time and energy, and I should be giving it to my own family." When my mother told me the news, I understood. In fact, I was surprised that Grace could have hung in there so long.

―――――

ON OCTOBER 8, 1971, GAYLEN AND JANET WERE MARRIED in a simple civil ceremony, across the Columbia River from Portland, in Vancouver, Washington. My mother and my brother Frank and I attended the wedding, and then we all went out to a restaurant and had dinner. My mother was happy to make it her treat. She had never had a son get married before.

Gaylen looked happier that evening than I had ever seen him. I had known nothing about the night that Grace drove him all over town, seeking medical care, nor did I know about any of his other hospital visits. For the first time since he had returned home, I thought Gaylen might have a second chance after all.

A few nights later, Janet showed up at my door. She was drunk, and she was crying. "I'm through with that lousy bastard," she said. "He's yelled at me for the last time. I'm going back to my friends in Chicago as soon as I can raise the money. Until then, can I stay here with you for a day or two?"

I knew exactly what Janet was asking, and the thought scared the hell out of me. Just then the phone rang. It was Gaylen. "Have you seen Janet?" he asked. "Yes," I said. "She's here right now. I think the two of you should have a talk."

Gaylen showed up a short time later, and he and Janet were in each other's arms right away, crying, promising to be better to one another. Soon, the three of us were laughing and playing Johnny Cash records. As they were leaving, Gaylen paused at the door and turned to me. "I want to thank you for helping us tonight," he said. "I also want to thank you for coming to my wedding. It meant a lot to me."

I was unprepared for this moment of sincerity, so I made a dumb joke: "Oh, you're welcome. Hell, I'll even go to your funeral if you like."

It was one of those things you say that you can't retract—that you later never forget and never forgive yourself for. Still, we both laughed. Brothers could laugh about anything.

Gaylen leaned over and gave me a kiss on the cheek. "Good-bye," he said, and turned and walked down the stairs.

You could already feel winter emerging from the fall. The air was turning cold.

―――――

A COUPLE OF WEEKS LATER, ANOTHER CALL FROM MY MOTHER: "I thought you should know. Gaylen went into the hospital today. It looks like he's going to need a little surgery."

"What's wrong?" I asked.

"It's his stomach. He's been having some more trouble lately, and the doctor thought he should go in and have the problem taken care of."

"Well, what sort of trouble is it? An ulcer?"

"It's some kind of perforation. That's all I really know."

I asked for the name of the hospital.

"He's at Oregon City Hospital, but I think you should wait for a few days before going to see him. It might be a little while before he's ready for visitors."

This didn't sound good to me, but my mother insisted. I hate to admit it, but it wasn't that hard to convince me. I despised going to hospitals even more than I despised visiting prisons. Both places scared and depressed me.

Next I heard, the surgery was delayed for a few days. Gaylen was improving, and the doctor didn't want to operate unless it was necessary. It all seemed less urgent, and I let that suffice as my excuse for not going to see him.

A week after he went into the hospital, my mother called again, at night. "Gaylen had his surgery late this afternoon," she told me. "He's still unconscious, but the doctor thinks he'll be fine."

I told her to keep me informed.

For the next few days, the reports were good. Gaylen was doing a little better each day. Meantime, I always found some reason not to visit him. He would be out soon, I told myself. I would see him then.

FRANK WAS BEHAVING MUCH MORE RESPONSIBLY THAN I WAS. He visited Gaylen several times during his hospital stay. Over twenty years later, he told me about those visits. I would like to think that if I had known how things really were, I would have gone to see Gaylen every day. I would *like* to think that, but what I imagine doesn't matter. The truth is, I never went to see Gaylen once. It would have been like visiting Gary: I could not go see people in places that were built to carry them to death.

This is what Frank told me about seeing our brother:

"One of the times I visited Gaylen, he had several tubes running in and out of him, to feed him food and medicine, and carry his waste out.

The next time I saw him, he had pulled the tubes out that were in his stomach because they were bothering him. I don't know if that effected his death or not. I *do* know that he was very nervous. He felt people were mistreating him, and he was yelling at everybody around him. One time when I was up there, a nurse came in and just slammed his food at him. I guess he had been giving them a lot of trouble. I spoke up to the nurses and said something about it. I don't know if that was wise or not.

"In any event, I never once thought Gaylen would die. The last time I saw him, he was sitting up and talking. Said he was eating Jell-O, and he was starting to feel good. I told him: 'You be sure and eat everything they give you, then I'll come up and visit you tomorrow.' We had been talking all afternoon about Evel Knievel, the daredevil, who was getting ready to make some big jump. Gaylen said: 'Yes, come back tomorrow and let's talk some more about Evel.' He was in fairly good spirits. But he also kept telling me that he was getting a lot of severe cramps in his hands. That worried me. I know that when you get cramps in your hands it can be a serious matter. But I thought, 'Well, he's in the hospital. They know how to take care of him.' That was my last thought, as I shook hands with him and then walked out of the hospital."

Two o'clock in the morning, one of my roommates knocked on my bedroom door. I was sitting up in bed, reading, listening to the radio. "There's a woman on the phone for you," he said. "She says it's important."

I was used to friends and girlfriends calling me at odd hours. I lived during odd hours.

I picked up the phone.

"Mikal, it's Janet. Gaylen's dead."

"What? Are you sure?"

"He just died on the operating table. He had to go back into emergency surgery."

I was stunned. There was no reprieve for news like this. When you heard such a thing, you would have to find a way to accept it and still be able to breathe in the next moment. Otherwise, you might fall into a pit of such deep fear and pain, you could never climb out.

"Janet," I said, "stay where you are. I'm going to call a cab and come out to get you."

"No," Janet said, "I don't want to stay here. One of Gaylen's friends,

John, is here. He'll bring me over to get you. We have to go tell your mother."

I hung up the phone and went back to my bedroom. A song by folk and country singer Mickey Newbury was playing on the radio. It was called "An American Trilogy."

"Hush little baby, don't you cry," sang Newbury, in his mournful, brandytone voice. "You know daddy's bound to die/And all my trials, Lord, will soon be over."

Years later, Elvis Presley would adopt this tune as one of his signature songs. Elvis was the American artist that Gaylen loved above all other singers or poets, and a half decade later, when Elvis died—only a few months after Gary was executed—I never heard that song but what I thought of my brothers, leaving behind so many fragmented, incomplete hearts to ache over them and all their terrible deeds.

I put on my coat and went out on the front porch to wait for Janet. I sat there in the night and began to shake. Death had come very close. It had swooped in, with its unerring scythe, and taken my brother. It could have taken me—it was just a matter of death making the choice. I wondered what it was like to pass into whatever realm or place of nonbeing that Gaylen had passed into, only minutes before. I looked around at the silent streets and then above, at the darkness and its few stars. I thought I saw something moving up there. I thought it was death. I felt it hover, and I felt it regard me. If I tell it to take *me* instead, I thought, and return Gaylen to Janet and my family, death will do that. But I could not bring myself to make this offer, and then death moved on.

I am glad it was not me who died, I thought, and a chilly wind kicked up, around me, as if in reprimand to my ugly and selfish thought.

GAYLEN'S FRIEND JOHN DROPPED ME AND JANET at my mother's trailer in Oak Grove at about four in the morning.

I knocked on the door. In a few moments, a light went on and I heard my mother fumbling at the latch. "Who is it?" she asked.

"It's Mikal, Mother. Mikal and Janet."

My mother flung the door open. Her eyes were wide. "It's Gaylen, isn't it?" she said. "He's dead, isn't he?" And then she and Janet wrapped their arms around each other, crying for everything that was now lost and would be forever dead.

My mother woke up Frank and gave him the news. "Don't say that," I heard Frank yelling from the other room. "You *have* to be lying."

————

AS THE SUN WAS RISING, WE WERE ALL STILL SITTING around the trailer's small living room. My mother gave Frank and me a necessary assignment: We should go to Oregon State Penitentiary and give Gary the news. He should not hear it the same way he learned of his father's death—from cruel guards.

As Gary entered the visitors' room that morning, he looked unusually old, unusually tired for a man of thirty. He also looked frightened. He knew, by the earliness of the hour that something was wrong.

"We have some bad news for you, Gary," Frank began.

"It's not Mom, is it?" Gary asked, his face sharpening in pain.

No, it wasn't our mother, but as we told him of Gaylen's death, Gary doubled over in tears. It was only the second time I had ever seen him cry.

GAYLEN'S FUNERAL WAS A FEW DAYS LATER, at the same parlor where my father's funeral took place. My mother paid the prison overtime fees, so a pair of guards could escort Gary to his brother's funeral. The guards sat behind us, in the family's private pews. They wore pistols under their suit jackets.

I spoke a few words at one point from the chapel's altar. For the life of me, I can't remember what I said: something about how we would always love and never forget our lost brother.

When I sat down, Gary was watching me. He leaned over and kissed me on the cheek. Then he put his arm around our mother and held her close to him for the rest of the service. She kept her head on his shoulder the whole time, crying softly.

LAST NIGHT, I HAD A DREAM ABOUT ONE OF MY BROTHERS *being executed. I have these dreams often.*

This time, it is Gaylen who has been sentenced to die, and it is for a crime that should not have earned him the death penalty—something like being simply an irretrievable, small-time sinner. My family and I are waiting for a reprieve to be granted him. It doesn't come, however, and the time for his death draws near. Finally, it is somehow decided that I should be the one to do the killing—the one who would do it with the most expediency, the most kindness.

We go out to a field. It is sunrise. I am handed a rifle, and a target is pinned above Gaylen's heart. He is watching me, his dark brown eyes wide open. They seem to be pleading for me to get this over with, to do it fast and clean.

I don't think I can do this, I say to myself, and yet I know I have to—that whatever other way Gaylen would have to die would be so much worse. I take a careful bead on my brother's heart, and I hold my aim steady. For a moment I think I'll just hold the aim, then close my eyes and pull the trigger. But I know that would run the risk of a missed or botched shot, which would only make his suffering worse. This is why they have firing squads, I tell myself: in case somebody loses his nerve or misses his aim. It is a great responsibility, I realize, to put a man to death.

And so I aim at Gaylen's heart—a careful, steady aim. I tell myself that after I've done my duty, the moment I have pulled the trigger, I can wake up from this awful dream. So I pull the trigger. I see the bullet enter Gaylen's chest. But before I can awaken, I see his heart burst out from him and fall to the dry dirt, pulsing blood onto the dust. It is then that I remember my mother's often-repeated admonition to my brother Frank about Gary's death in Utah: "They shot your brother's heart out, onto the ground."

PART FIVE

BLOOD

HISTORY

Blood is our only permanent history, and blood history does not admit of revision.

— HARRY CREWS,
Fathers, Sons, Blood

There is no crime of which I cannot conceive myself guilty.

— GOETHE

I dreamed that love was a crime.

— O. V. WRIGHT,
Eight Men and Four Women

CHAPTER 1
TURNING
POINTS

AFTER GAYLEN'S DEATH, GARY SEEMED TO CHANGE. He had lost two members of his family without the opportunity for some final reconciliation, and he wanted desperately to be free. He and I started writing each other more frequently. In his letters, Gary began to express more concern for me, more curiosity about what I was doing, who my friends were. He was trying to be my brother.

The supervisors at the prison were also taking note of this change in Gary. One day a few months after Gaylen's death, the warden allowed Gary a supervised home visit with my family. An armed guard drove him in a car from the prison in Salem to my mother's trailer in Oak Grove. Gary, my mother, my brother Frank, and I sat around the whole afternoon, eating snacks, talking about old memories and future hopes. I brought along my guitar and Gary and I played and sang some Johnny Cash songs together. It would be hard to say who had the worse voice, but it hardly mattered. Gary and I then got into a discussion about music. We shared a lot of the same favorites: Duke Ellington, Hank Williams, Charlie Parker, Miles Davis, Little Richard, Chuck Berry. It was nice to realize we had a few things in common. As we talked, the armed guard sat in an easy chair close by, reading magazines, keeping a quiet eye on Gary.

We later heard from the prison that the warden and others had been heartened by Gary's behavior on this day. They thought he might be hungry enough for freedom to try calming down and living a more sensible and productive life. Gary had recently started working in the prison art shop, and the warden and a few of the guards had liked his work so much, they bought some of it for themselves. The warden also encouraged Gary to enter some art contests, and in the fall of 1972, after he had won first place in several, the prison supervisors granted Gary a school release to attend a community college in Eugene and study art. All in all, it was a great opportunity: If Gary did well under the terms of the program—if he attended his classes, got fair grades, followed the rules of the campus and the halfway house where he would live during weekdays, and if he would never leave the Eugene area without the consent of his counselors—then the chances were good that at school's end he might receive an early release from prison and would probably also receive a job placement at a Portland-area art or advertising firm. In other words, if Gary handled this right, he would come out of jail with a start on a good career and a new life. We all saw it as a turning point.

MEANTIME, GARY HAD HIS OWN HOPES.

Among his friends at Oregon State Penitentiary was a young man I'll call Barry Black. Some of Gary's other inmate friends would later express their belief that Barry might have been Gary's secret prison lover, but Gary steadfastly denied that he ever had homosexual affairs or partners in his prison years. Still, there is little doubt that, in some form or another, Gary loved Barry Black. Barry was the friend that Gary turned to first when he needed help—Barry was the man who had comforted my brother after Frank and I had given him the news of Gaylen's death—and apparently Gary thought that the two of them might have a successful friendship outside of prison as well. When Gary learned Barry was going to be taken for some dental surgery to the University of Oregon Dental School, up in the West Hills of Portland, he talked Barry into arranging for the trip to coincide with Gary's own school release schedule. Gary told his friend he would meet him in Portland at the dental school. He had a plan for the two of them.

ON AN EARLY MORNING IN LATE FALL, A PRISON GUARD drove Gary to the halfway house dormitory in Eugene, where he would spend his evenings, and released him. He gave Gary a new set of clothes and his first week's school allowance. He told Gary that he had a day or two to get registered at school and become familiar with the campus, and to buy his books and art supplies. He also told Gary that he had to be back at the dormitory by early evening. He could leave the dorm in the evenings only for the purpose of approved night classes.

"You're on your own now, Gary," the guard said. "Don't fuck up. We're counting on you."

Gary told the guard not to worry and shook his hand.

Gary walked over to the campus and found the gymnasium, where school registration was taking place. He picked up his packet and began to fill out his forms, but he got intimidated, he later said, by all the confusing lines of people around him. The students all looked so young and confident, so attractive, so nicely dressed. It made him feel nervous and out of place. He went for a walk and found a bar. He had a few drinks. He thought to himself that he could still register for school the next day, but that he needed to use this day to relax. He found his way over to the freeway and hitched a ride to my mother's place, almost a hundred miles away in Oak Grove. He knew he was violating his release agreement, but he was sure he could be back to the dorm by early evening.

Gary visited with my mother for an hour or two, until it was time for her to go to work. She had been overjoyed to see him. Around noon that same day, he showed up at the door of my small house, near Portland State University. I was taking my own second stab at college, and I was close to being late for class. But when I saw Gary at my door, smiling and looking nervous, I felt like I had to take the time for him. He came in and we talked for a while. I asked him if he had started his classes yet. He told me about going over to the campus and being flustered by all the young people around him. He said he just wanted to see his mother and me and a couple of his friends, and then he would be all right. "I'll go back before the night," he said. "I can still register tomorrow without getting in any trouble."

But the next afternoon Gary showed up again, wearing the same clothes. He had a red glare about his eyes. He obviously had not returned to Eugene and, for his failure to do so, would not only lose his scholarship but could be sentenced to additional jail time.

"Gary, what in the hell are you doing here?"

He skirted the question. "Let's go get some lunch someplace. Know any good places?" I was pissed. Gary was blowing something important, plus, he was being pushy. But I didn't know how far I could push back with him. I went to get my jacket. When I returned, he was on the phone. He asked me what my address was.

"Why?"

"I'm calling a taxi." I explained that there was a restaurant within walking distance. He said he didn't want to be seen on the streets. I didn't like the sound of that. We ended up at a topless bar—the only place Gary felt comfortable. He seemed in a trance as he studied the girl onstage.

"I want you to tell me what's happened," I said, trying to break his spell. "It's obvious you're not going to school."

He was silent for a long time, staring at the table between us. When he spoke, it was with his slow, countrified drawl. "I'm not cut out for school. Man, they can't teach me anything about art that I don't already know. Besides, there are more important things." He leaned toward me and locked his stare into mine. "A friend of mine from the joint is being brought up to the dental school here next week. A couple of guards are bringing him up and I want to go see him. Uh, I need a gun. Can you help me?"

I felt horrified. I was being pressed into a place where I never wanted to be—a place with guns. I didn't know anything about that world. I didn't know anything about buying guns or using them, and I didn't want to know. Instead of saying that, though, I gave Gary some sort of warning about his getting shot or shooting someone and getting more time in prison.

"Hey," he interrupted, "if you're worried about being an accomplice or something, then forget it. I'm no snitch."

"It's not that. I just don't want to have anything to do with anything like that. No matter what happens, Gary, you're throwing away your life."

He narrowed his eyes. "It's a matter of dignity," he said. I looked away, shaking my head. Gary stared without expression at me for a long time, fidgeting with a book of matches. "I'd do it for *my* brother," he said, and motioned for us to leave. Once more, he insisted on taking a taxi, back to my place, but he didn't get out with me. He smiled and ruffled my hair as I got out of the cab. I started to say something but he stopped me. "It's okay," he said, but there was a terrible hurt in his eyes. I got out of the taxi feeling ashamed—feeling that I had let down somebody whose love and approval I had always wanted—and also feeling scared. I could tell that Gary was determined to get his gun and set his friend free, even if it meant a shoot-out. I didn't see how my brother could come out of such a scenario alive. Even if he did, I didn't want to be the person who had put a gun in his hands. I would feel guilty for whatever that gun did.

This was the first time that Gary put me in the place of making a horrible choice. I knew what his plans were. He had told me the day and the hour he planned on springing his friend from the guards at the dental school. I knew that when that happened, there was a good chance somebody would get killed. I thought about whether I should turn my brother in, and then I thought how I would feel if it was Gary who got shot dead on that day. I decided I could not turn him in. I did not want him dead. But as soon as I decided that, I felt as if I was already morally implicated in whatever killing he might do. He was a dangerous man. He should not be on the streets.

I hated knowing what I knew, I hated having to live with my choice. I hated the idea that I loved him more than the people he might kill.

I ONLY SAW GARY TWICE MORE during that escape period of less than a month. He stopped by for a couple of hours one night while I had a girlfriend over and asked me to play Johnny Cash records for him. He was charming and sober. He kidded the young woman. "You being nice to my brother? He's my little brother you know, and I feel like I have to look out for him."

Privately, I tried to prod him out of his plans. "Let's just say they've changed," he said. "Don't you worry about it. The less you know, the better off you are."

Another day I came out of class at Portland State and Gary was waiting for me outside. He had borrowed a car and said he wanted me to meet some friends. We drove out, Gary drinking beer all the way, but he was in a friendly, conversational mood. His friends lived in a mansion high on a hill on the east side of Portland. These were the people, it turned out, who were running Portland's largest pornography and massage parlor business. They were dressed nicely and were polite, and they lived in a beautiful home. They were sitting at their dining table, looking at large black-and-white stills of blow jobs. They were trying to figure the best sequence for arranging the photos. Gary and I sat in another part of the room. He showed me his prize cache of drawings and paintings, a voluminous folder of poignant studies of everything from ballet dancers to bruised boxers, and an occasional depiction of violent death. Mostly, though, they were drawings of children, round faces with a bewildered, inviolable innocence. "Here," he said, "take whatever you want." To him, pictures were just something one drew and gave to somebody.

He wanted to take me on a tour of his friends' premises, to show off the luxury that wasn't his. While showing me around the indoor swimming pool, Gary, without warning, opened his jacket, took out a pistol and handed it to me, butt first. "Think you could ever use one of these?" he asked, head cocked in his best Gary Cooper fashion.

I felt as though I were being tested, and I didn't like the method. I also felt awkward and vulnerable, holding a gun for the first time. I kept the barrel pointed toward the pool water and my finger away from the trigger. "I suppose I could if I had to, Gary, but I hope you're talking about a situation where it's a matter of survival, not choice." He took the gun and put it in his jacket pocket. "C'mon," he said. "I'll drive you home."

We drove in silence back to my apartment. I felt he was angry, but I wasn't sure why. Gary started to honk at a car in front of us that was going too slow for him. The driver decelerated. "Son of a bitch," Gary muttered, and swerved violently into the left-hand lane, right into the path of an oncoming car. The car honked and braked and at the last possible second Gary yanked our car off the road onto a sidewalk.

We stared at each other, twin mirrors of wide-eyed, openmouthed fear. "You almost got us killed!" I shouted. He rested his forehead on the driving wheel, breathing deeply. "Sometimes," he said, "you just have to be willing to face that possibility."

A FEW NIGHTS LATER, WHILE WATCHING THE NEWS, I learned of Gary's arrest for armed robbery. He had walked into a service station in southeast Portland, high on whiskey and some opiate. He put a pistol to the attendant's head and said: "Give me everything you have in your register or I'll blow your fucking head off." He was pulled over just a few blocks from the gas station and taken into custody without incident.

I felt relieved: Nobody had been killed. I also felt angry and saddened. Once more, Gary had thrown away his life. I tried to visit him at Multnomah County Jail, where he was being held, but this time he wasn't allowed visitors. A couple of days later, my mother called me. Gary had been found lying on his blood-soaked mattress in his cell. He had cut himself on his right arm and he had also lacerated his abdomen. He was at the emergency clinic of the same hospital he had planned on springing his friend from.

Jesus Christ, I thought. There's no fucking end to this.

GARY'S TRIAL FOR THE ROBBERY ATTEMPT was held in Multnomah County on February 12, 1973. My mother and I attended.

Gary entered the room in handcuffs. He asked to address the court, and the judge granted him the permission.

"I hope you don't mind if I refer to my notes," Gary said. "I'm not much of a public speaker."

"Not at all, Mr. Gilmore," the judge said.

Gary went on. "You have read the pre-sentence report and have decided probably what you are going to give me, but I would like to make a special appeal for leniency. I have done a lot of time, and I don't think it would do me any good to do any more. What I mean is, I have been locked up for the last nine and a half calendar years consecutively and I have had about two and a half years' freedom since I was fourteen years old. I have always gotten time and always done it, never been paroled, only had one probation, that was when I was a juvenile. I have never had a break from the law and I have come to feel that justice is kind of harsh and I have never asked for a break until now. I still have time to do at the penitentiary . . .

"Your honor, you can keep a person locked up too long, the same way that you can keep them locked up long enough. What I am saying is, there is an appropriate time to release somebody or to give them a break. Of course, who's to say when this is? Only the individual himself really knows and it's more a matter of just convincing somebody. There have been times when I felt if I had a break right then I would probably never have been in trouble again, but like I said, I don't feel that I have ever had a break from the law. Last September, I was released from the penitentiary to go to school in Eugene at Lane Community College and study art, and I had every intention of doing it. One day I'm in the pen for nine years and the next day I'm free, and I was kind of shook. Things have changed and it was different, man, and nothing prepared me for this. While I was waiting to register at the college, I got drunk. Well, I didn't get drunk, I had a couple of drinks. I realize this was a pretty stupid thing to do, and I was afraid to go back to the halfway house with booze on my breath. I thought I would be taken back to the pen immediately, and to be honest, I guess I kind of wanted to continue drinking. It tasted kind of good.

"Anyway, I split and went to Portland, out of fear of going right back to the penitentiary. I honestly intended to do good down at Lane, like I said. I wanted to study art and that is what I was there for. After I left it occurred to me to go back, but I didn't. Freedom tasted pretty good and I hadn't been out for a long time. It's a pretty nice world out there. It wasn't long before I was broke and I spent a couple of days looking for a job but couldn't find one. I didn't have any work background. When you are free you can afford to be broke for a few days and it doesn't matter, but if you are a fugitive you can't afford to be broke at all. I needed some money and I wanted to leave, I wanted to go far away, I wanted to change my name, I wanted to get a job, and I wanted to just live, and I needed some money, and I committed a robbery. When I committed this robbery I had no intentions of hurting anybody, and that's the truth.

"I stagnated in prison a long time and I have wasted most of my life—at least half of it. Probably the best years of my life. I have had a brief taste of freedom and to tell you the truth I had almost forgotten what I am missing. I am not a stupid person although I have done a lot of stupid and foolish things, but I want freedom and I realize full well that the only way I can have it and maintain it is to quit breaking the law. I never realized that more than I do now. If you were to grant me probation on this sentence you won't be turning me loose right now. I still have time to do. On the other hand, you can sentence me to additional time, but like I said, I have had about two years of freedom since I was fourteen and I have got problems, and if you give me more time I am going to compound them. That is all I have to say."

The judge sat quietly for several moments before giving his reply. He told Gary that he thought he had stated his history and his case effectively, and he had been moved by his plea. But the crime that Gary was appearing for—armed robbery—was a serious one, and he had already been convicted once for this same crime. Given the severity of the offense—given that another man's rights had been violated at the end of a gun—the judge felt he had no option but to impose an additional sentence. All together, for the escape and the robbery, Gary would be sentenced to another nine years. The judge promised, however, that if Gary's performance at the prison was satisfactory in the time ahead, then the court would not oppose a possible parole at an earlier date.

"Your honor," my brother said, "my next parole appearance is this month. Do you think the Parole Board might parole me right away?"

The judge smiled grimly. He recognized there was a little humor in the remark. "I would doubt it, Mr. Gilmore, but I think if you were sitting on the Parole Board you wouldn't consider yourself for a parole right now either, in the light of this past experience.

"All right. That will be the sentence."

After the proceedings, Gary asked for a moment to speak to my mother and me. My mother was shaking, she was crying so hard. Gary leaned over and kissed her on the cheek. "Look, don't worry," he told her. "They can't hurt me any more than I've already hurt myself."

He turned to me. We shook hands through his handcuffs, then he ruffled my hair. "You did right. Now do me a favor. Put on some weight, okay? You're too goddamned skinny."

The next time I saw him was six days before his execution.

WHAT NONE OF US KNEW, THROUGHOUT ANY OF THIS, was that Gary had been betrayed by his best friend, Barry Black. Barry had known that Gary planned on meeting him and the guards at the dental school with a gun, but he grew afraid that he might get killed himself, or that he might end up drawing additional time for attempting such an escape. Barry went to the warden and made a deal. He told the warden what Gary's plans were, and who he might be staying with in the Portland area. In exchange, the warden gave Barry protection, and an assurance that all this would be taken into consideration during his next review before the Parole Board.

When Gary arrived back at the prison, he made it known that he was hurt and angry. Barry was kept in a separate part of the prison yard, away from Gary. Gary would stand outside and yell, "Barry Black is a fink!" so loud and so long, the guards would drag him off the field and into his cell. Barry went into isolation for protection. Gary got into a fight with somebody so he could also be placed in isolation. When the warden caught wind of this, he had Barry Black transferred to another prison. There was little question in anybody's mind that Gary would have killed his old friend the first chance he got.

———

YEARS PASSED. I wrote Gary a couple of letters during this time and he wrote back, but there was a coldness and bitterness in what he wrote. I figured he had never forgiven me for my resistance that day in the topless bar. In turn, I had my own anger: Gary's request had been unfair, and he had been a fool to destroy the best chance he'd ever had at a second start. But it was more than anger: I was also afraid of my brother. I saw him as a walking deadly force.

I returned to my habit of not going to see him, and we both drifted into a long silence. We were each too proud to give the other person's viewpoint much thought. In time, Gary had me taken off his visitors list. I didn't feel insulted, I didn't feel ashamed. Instead, I felt relieved.

Meantime, Frank continued to see Gary. Not long ago, he wrote me a letter, telling me about those visits:

> I started these visits because of a letter I received from Gary. He was filled with pain and hatred because he had been forgotten by his family. He sounded like a man who was ready to jump off an eleven-story building.
>
> On my first visit, I was really surprised at how much he had changed. He was much meaner-looking than I had remembered him being before. I remember one of the first things that we talked about was the guards. Gary was of the opinion that all guards were pussies, and that they were trying to make him and his friends look bad all the time.
>
> I asked, "Well, Gary, are they treating you decent?"
>
> "C'mon, Frank, they don't treat any of us like we are human. All guards suck—don't you agree?"
>
> "No, Gary. Me, I think *some* guards suck, but I think some prisoners suck too."
>
> "Well, Frank, old buddy, you're wrong. *All* guards suck. In one way or another. But you should know this. You've been in prison. You're a pro too."
>
> "No," I would tell him, "I'm not even an amateur." Then I'd try to change the conversation a bit: "Look, Gary, I don't like to see you in here. I would do whatever I could reasonably do to help you get out. But don't you think you've put yourself in here this last time? Don't you think you *keep* putting yourself in here?"
>
> "Fuck you, Frank. And I don't mean that to be disrespectful. I just mean it. You and no one else can ever understand what I have gone through. So just get fucked. I mean, I get really pissed when people like you start asking me questions and giving me a bunch of bullshit opinions—opinions I don't need and wouldn't use anyway.

"I mean, you don't know what it is like after seven or eight years, do you, asshole? So why don't you tell me, huh, asshole? Tell me. C'mon, tell me."

"Okay, Gary, I'm sorry. Let's talk about something we both know about. Let's talk about what you remember about home."

"That's bullshit, Frank. I mean, I remember that the food was real good, and that Dad sucked. You might think he was a great man, for whatever reason, but to me he was just as big an asshole as you are—except that he was a better man than you are. But that's not saying a whole hell of a lot.

"Say, Frank, I don't mean to be disrespectful, but you are an asshole. Let's face it, Frank, that's what you are. I don't mean to say that you haven't been better than the rest of the family. At least you've remembered that I'm still alive. The rest of the family—if you want to call them a family—has not remembered anything when it comes to me. And as far as being a brother in this family of complete assholes, you are above average. That doesn't mean I really care about you. But then, do you really care what I think?"

"Yeah, Gary. Yeah, I do."

Gary turned and pointed at another prisoner, who was sitting a few seats away in the visitors' room. Then he said: "Don't you think that asshole looks just like Woody Allen? That guy is a real asshole. He thinks all of us are animals, and he thinks that the guards are his buddies. That asshole is going to learn a whole hell of a lot before he does his time."

And then Gary pointed right at one of the guards and said, just as loud as he could: "See that asshole? Well, they say he fucked his sister, and I for one believe it."

The guard walked over to us and said: "One more remark like that, Gilmore, and your visit is over."

Gary just laughed and said: "That asshole never did like me much."

I don't recall one visit when Gary did not tell me at least once about how much he hated Dad and all the times that Dad had beat him. "I cannot remember most of the reasons the old bastard beat me," he said. "All it really taught me was to hate him."

I always hated to leave Gary behind. It bothered me much more than he ever knew. Probably much more than anyone ever knew. I really didn't mind it when he would say all those angry things to me, or when he would call me names. I figured it was better for him to let off steam at my expense, to vent on me, than to get in more trouble at prison.

LATE IN 1973, GARY'S WAR about his teeth flared up again. He renewed his demands for new dentures, and continued to get in fights with guards. He also grew more demanding of his friends on the inside. He would insist that they support each of his protests and each of his demands, and that they should join him in his hell-raising. If they didn't, he considered it a betrayal of loyalty, and Gary was not a man that one could lightly consider offending. There were more fights with dentists, more hammer attacks on enemy inmates. Among the guards, according to one of them, there was an agreement: If Gary ever gave a guard a legitimate reason, the guard should shoot him. "I wish he had fired on me," one guard said, "so I could take him out. But Gilmore was gutless and would wait until your back was turned before he'd hit you."

Gary knew the guards were watching him closely, and he tried to convince some of the other prisoners that they should all kill a guard or two. The other inmates thought this was too extreme. There was no way you could kill a guard and get away with it. It would be suicide.

IN THE FALL OF 1974, GARY FELL IN LOVE with a woman named Becky. She had become familiar with him through another woman who was visiting a friend of Gary's at the prison. Becky started writing Gary, then started visiting him. She talked to him about shaping up and starting his life over—maybe in Canada. She said she would do everything she could to get him released if he would promise to change his life and curb his violence. Gary agreed. Then he asked Becky to marry him. Becky agreed.

First, though, she had to have some surgery—something to do with an ulcerous condition that had been painful for a long time. She died while she was on the operating table.

The night Gary learned of her death, he went to see the prison psychiatrist and asked for some medication. The psychiatrist decided Gary wasn't seriously depressed enough to merit the medication and sent him back to his cell.

Over the next month, Gary grew more outrageous and more violent. One day he got hold of a razor blade and blockaded himself in his cell. He was going to kill himself, he announced, and he would slice anybody who tried to stop him. It took several guards and a can of Mace to get him under control and to get the razor from him.

That was when Dr. Weissert decided to put Gary back on Prolixin. Weissert wrote: "It is my impression that at this time Gilmore is in a paranoid state, so that he is unable to determine what his best interests are. He is totally unable to control his hostile and aggressive impulses, and external controls seem necessary, as he is unable to place internal controls on his own aggressive impulses. He presents a real danger to the physical safety of himself and others, and this, in a structured and closed environment, creates a real physical hazard. It is, therefore, my recommendation he be given intramuscular injections of tranquilizers to help him control his hostility and aggression until such time as he is able to apply the necessary controls . . . In a paranoid psychotic state, medication is the most expedient treatment modality to insure a subsidence of symptoms so that the condition is more manageable. I feel completely justified in giving Gilmore medication against his wishes, as he creates a serious problem to the patient and the entire institution."

When Gary heard of Weissert's recommendation, he wrote the warden, Hoyt Cupp, begging him for any other form of punishment. He said he was more afraid of Prolixin than anything else on earth, and he didn't think he could withstand any more treatment with the drug. He said he would be willing to go for the rest of his life without teeth, rather than submit to Prolixin.

Warden Cupp offered Gary a compromise: a transfer to a maximum security federal penitentiary, in Marion, Illinois. After all, Cupp reasoned, Gary had become a risk to everybody at OSP, including himself. There were several rumors that many of the prisoners who had been his former friends and supporters were now so disgusted or frightened by his behavior, they were talking about killing him themselves.

Gary agreed to Cupp's transfer offer. Then, on the last day, Gary reneged. He told Cupp he thought the transfer was illegal. Besides, he wanted to stay close to his friends and family in Oregon. Cupp told Gary that whether he liked it or not, he was going to Marion.

On the night of January 21, 1975, Gary was sitting in his cell, awaiting the guards. They were supposed to come for him at midnight and take him to his plane to Illinois.

"Man, I don't want to go," Gary told a friend by the name of Roger, in the cell next to him. "At least I don't want to go without a little noise. When they come to get me, do me a favor. Raise some hell. Pound on the bars. I want everybody to know this is going down and how wrong it is."

Roger agreed to Gary's request. No matter what any of the prisoners thought of Gary, he was still an inmate, and inmates had to back each other whenever possible.

When the guards came for Gary, Roger was asleep. Gary asked the guards if he might wake his friend, to say good-bye. They said okay.

Gary called Roger's name. His friend woke up, saw Gary standing with the guards, and started to make some noise, but Gary told him to calm down. "It's all right. I'll go quietly. I just wanted to see if you were still my friend."

Roger offered Gary his hand. "Well, take care of yourself," Roger said.

Gary took his hand. "Yeah," he said. "I'll be seeing you down the road. Right now, I'm going to go get me a couple of Mormons."

Roger thought about Gary's last words for some time. What had he meant?

A little over a year and a half later, Roger said, he had no doubt what Gary meant. By that time, Gary Gilmore was the most famous murderer in America.

CHAPTER 2
DEADLY AND
FAMOUS

WITHIN DAYS OF HIS ARRIVAL AT THE FEDERAL PENITENTIARY at Marion, Illinois, Gary began petitioning Warden Cupp for a return to Oregon State Penitentiary. "I don't want any more trouble," Gary wrote the warden. "I would like to straighten my hand up and repair the mess my life has become. Please reply."

Cupp wrote back, telling Gary that there were no plans to make any changes in his present arrangement. Whether Gary ever returned to Oregon, he indicated, would depend on the nature of the reports that came from Marion.

Gary realized he was in a tight spot. Marion had a reputation as a place that did not abide much crap from its inmates; the guards could be rough, and the isolation techniques were rigid and unpleasant.

I can't say for sure that Gary was anything like a model prisoner at Marion, since the federal prison system would not release his records to me. It's obvious, though, from the reports in his Oregon files that his behavior improved dramatically. There were numerous letters from the federal facility's psychiatrists and officers, stating that Gary was cooperative and friendly. Wrote one doctor: "He does not have a psychiatric illness in the form of pyschosis, organicity or requiring special procedures, or tests. From a psychiatric (neuropsychiatric) point of view, he has probably reached the maximum benefits so far as the United States Penitentiary, Marion, Illinois, is concerned." It was Marion's view that Gary should be returned to Oregon. In addition, there was another matter: The transfer, in all probability, had not been legal, and if Gary could muster the means to press his case, Oregon would probably have to take him back whether the prison wanted him or not.

Cupp, though, remained unmoved. In a June memo to the Oregon corrections deputy administrator, Cupp stated: "I remain adamant in my opinion on the return of Gary Gilmore to Oregon State Penitentiary. We have seen him go this route before, and then revert to his troublemaking patterns. With our present pressure conditions, I would not want to return this man for at least six months more."

Whether he liked it or not, Gary was stuck where he was, a thousand miles from home.

ONE DAY IN EARLY NOVEMBER 1975, my mother and Frank were sitting in the living room of the trailer, talking about ways of bringing Gary back home, when my mother stopped in midsentence. Her face went white immediately, her mouth opened as if to say something, and then she started to spit up blood. It came with such force, it hit the walls of the trailer. She fell from her chair to the floor. Frank ran over to her and tried to cradle her head. "Mom," he said. "Mom! What's wrong?" She couldn't answer, and the blood was still coming. Frank ran over to the landlady's office, told her what happened, and asked her to call an ambulance. By the time he got back, my mother was trying to climb back into her chair. "I don't want an ambulance," she said. "I'll be fine. It was just something I ate. I don't like hospitals. They scare me." Then she collapsed again, in a faint.

When she awoke hours later, she was in a hospital bed. She looked around her. She knew the room. She knew the bed. This was the same room, the same place, in the Oregon City Hospital, where Gaylen had lain as his life slipped away from him. My mother began to scream for a nurse.

FOR YEARS, MY MOTHER HAD BEEN BOTHERED by the progression of arthritis. She had been taking aspirin to help alleviate the pain, but it wasn't helping much. Each time I saw her, I noticed that her hands were becoming more and more crippled. The fingers were starting to curl in on themselves, like a small bird's claws, and her feet had a hard time moving across the floor. My mother's affliction was beginning to slow her down at work, and we all knew it was just a matter of time before she would have to quit her job.

Frank and I tried repeatedly to get her to see a doctor, but it was no use. My mother did not like or trust doctors, and, more to the point, my mother was not a person you could make do anything she did not want to do. In that way, we were all her sons.

So my mother kept taking the aspirin. It was her only defense against the pain. What we didn't know was, she was taking massive amounts of it—sometimes as much as a bottle a day. All that medicine played hell with her stomach, and on the day she had thrown up in front of Frank, it was because a hole had been eating its way through her on the inside, and it chose that time to make its perforation complete. Had Frank not been there, she likely would have died in her own blood on the dirty kitchen floor.

Now, in the hospital, she was in and out of consciousness a lot, and the doctors were nearly certain they would have to operate to save her. They wanted the consent of a relative. Frank was reluctant to give the consent, since the operation would necessitate a blood transfusion—a practice that ran contrary to Frank's beliefs as a Jehovah's Witness. I called my mother's doctor and told him I would take responsibility for the decision. If there was any need to operate, they should do so. They should do whatever was necessary to save her life.

Two days after my mother's arrival at the hospital, the doctors operated. Her stomach was so ruined, they had to remove over half of it and sew the rest up into a small bag. She would have trouble eating; she would have to live according to a certain diet, and if she didn't follow the diet, she would risk reopening the perforation.

The first time I visited my mother in the hospital, she was still in an unconscious state. She had tubes running in and out of her, and she looked dead. I fully expected her to die, even with the surgery. Later, when she was out of the hospital and back home, it was hard for me to relate to her for a while. I had prepared myself for her to be dead—I felt I had already gone through the emotions of grieving for her. Somehow, it didn't seem real that she was still alive. I was glad she was, but I also dreaded the idea that I would have to go through her death all over again someday. Once seemed more than enough.

MY MOTHER'S PHYSICAL COLLAPSE BROUGHT A NEW URGENCY to Gary's situation. He wrote several letters to the Oregon corrections administrators, petitioning a return to Oregon. His mother had almost died, he explained, and he was afraid that if he couldn't get back home soon, he would never again see her alive. He wanted to put his life in order, he said. He wanted to win a parole and help take care of his mother.

This put Oregon in a difficult position. The prison's legal rationale for keeping Gary at Marion was tenuous at best, and now there was a moral matter. Whatever any of the officers or administrators thought of Gary, they did not question the depth of love between him and his mother. Warden Cupp, though, still opposed bringing Gary back. In a letter to the State Corrections Division, Cupp wrote: "The return of Gary Gilmore to Oregon State Penitentiary at the present time is, in my opinion, a calculated risk which contains the elements of unpredictability and portent of danger. I would prefer to avoid the risk. According to the information given to me . . . the Parole Board delegation is to interview Gary this month. We may have some indication for a future move when the evaluation of the Parole Board is presented." The Corrections Division wrote back, telling Cupp that this time he might have no choice. Gary was doing well at Marion, and his mother was now in poor health. If he wasn't returned to OSP, it might be necessary to parole him.

Meantime, Gary had started a correspondence with my cousin Brenda, in Provo, Utah. Brenda was the daughter of my mother's favorite living sister, Ida, as well as the daughter of everybody's favorite uncle, Vernon. From childhood, Brenda and Gary had been each other's preferred cousins, though like many of the rest of us, Brenda had grown distant from Gary over the years. But now, as they began writing each other, she saw a new side of Gary begin to emerge: He was more reflective about his mistakes, and he was starting to long for the sort of family life that his years of incarceration had deprived him of. He was clearly an intelligent man, and, when he wanted to be, seemingly a compassionate one. Brenda thought Gary was probably ready now to grow within the confines of society, and she believed it was the family's obligation to take him in and give him a new start. In a complex series of correspondences between Brenda, Gary, the Oregon Corrections Division, and Marion's administrators, a parole plan was finally worked out. Gary would be paroled into the custody of his family in Utah—my cousin Brenda and her husband Johnny, and Vern and Ida. He was to get a job, stay away from bad habits and crime, and see a parole officer regularly. He was also to stay in the State of Utah. If he lived up to all these agreements for a few months, then he would be allowed a trip to Oregon, to see my mother, and he might even be allowed to move back into the state. In the meantime, my mother was always free to travel to Utah, health permitting, and see her son.

On April 9, 1976, Gary was released from Marion, Illinois, and, after a bus ride to St. Louis, Missouri, he took a plane into Salt Lake City, Utah. Brenda and her husband Johnny met him at the airport and took him to his new home in Provo.

My mother was as surprised by this news as I was. I'd had no idea that there were negotiations underway for Gary's release. When my mother told me that my brother was being paroled into the custody of a family he hadn't known for nearly thirty years, and into the heart of one of Utah's most devout and severe Mormon communities, I remember saying, "This does *not* sound like a great idea." As soon as I'd said it, I felt ungracious. After all, did I want Gary to spend the rest of his life in prison? Didn't he deserve another chance at freedom?

THERE ARE DAYS THAT CHANGE ALL THE POSSIBILITIES OF YOUR LIFE —what you comprehend of your past, what you can expect of your future. Days that tell you, nothing will ever be the same. You will have to live with what has happened for the rest of your life. For my family—and for many others—those days came in late July 1976.

This is how we learned the news:

It was a hot day in Oregon's Willamette Valley. On such days, my mother found the confines of her trailer uncomfortable. A few months before, because of her health problems, she had been forced to quit her job busing dishes at the restaurant in Milwaukie. She was now living off her Social Security benefits, and whatever money Frank brought home from his custodial and day labor jobs. She rarely ventured out of the house. The combined effect of her surgery and arthritis was turning her into something of a recluse—which is probably what she had wanted to be for years.

Still, she was not in bad spirits. Gary was free from prison and was in love with a beautiful young woman in Provo. Only a couple of weeks before, she had received a letter from him. "I didn't know anybody could be this happy," he had written. He also asked, if he sent her the money to cover the costs and arranged for a comfortable mode of travel, would she come visit him in Utah? He badly wanted to see her. On this hot afternoon, my mother had dragged her chair out to the small porch at the front of her trailer and was sitting there fanning herself. She was thinking about Gary's invitation and how much she wanted to see him. She thought she had just about enough strength to make the journey. It would be good to see Utah again.

Then the phone rang.

My mother walked, in her slow, limping way, into the trailer and over to the phone. It always took her many moments to get to the phone, so anybody who called her was accustomed to letting the phone ring for a long time.

When she answered, it was Brenda. Brenda asked to speak with Frank. This struck my mother as odd. "He's not here, Brenda. He's at work. Is something wrong? Has something happened to Gary? What kind of trouble is he in?"

"He's fine, Aunt Bessie. I really think I should wait and talk to Frank."

"Brenda, tell me what's happened."

She heard Brenda take a deep breath. "Bessie, they've got Gary on a Murder One charge. He shot two men in the head, and then he shot one of his thumbs off."

It was Brenda's way to be blunt when she had to be, but this was more bluntness than my mother could bear. "I don't believe you," she told Brenda. "The Gary I know would not do such a thing."

"Well, Bessie, you better believe it. He killed two young Mormon men."

Brenda then handed the phone to Vern. He affirmed to my mother what Brenda had said and gave her a bit more information about the killings. "I think you should brace yourself, Bessie," he said. "They recently restored the death penalty here. People are angry. I think they're going to kill Gary."

My mother hung up and tried calling Gary at the jail in Utah. When a police officer answered, she told him who she was. "Don't kill my boy," she said to the policeman, weeping. "Please don't kill him. We did so much to get him out." The officer was tender with her. Told her that nobody at the jail had any plans to hurt Gary. Then went and told my brother that his mother was on the telephone, wanting to speak to him. "Tell her I'm not here," Gary said.

"Very funny, Gilmore. Are you going to talk to her or not?"

"No, I'm not. I don't know what I would say to her."

"I HAD BEEN WORKING, CUTTING TREES, PAINTING FENCES, THAT WEEK," Frank told me later. "It was hard labor, but it was the kind of work that made me happy.

"I stopped on the way home and got some groceries, so I could fix dinner for me and Mom. I came in with this big sack, and Mom said: 'Why don't you set the groceries down. I have something I have to tell you.' I set the bag down and I turned around and she started crying. At first I thought one of the brothers had been hurt. And so I asked her. I said: 'Man, I hope the brothers are all right.' She said: 'Yes, your brothers are all right, but—but Gary murdered somebody over in Provo.'

"That's how I found out. She told me that, and you know how she would keep crying—you couldn't understand a thing she said. Finally she calmed down enough to tell me what it was that had happened—that he had been arrested for killing two people, one in a gas station and one in a motel, both in armed robberies and apparently both in cold blood. I remember I just sat there. It was a couple of hours before I even got up and moved at all. I just sat there, totally depressed. Finally I fixed something for Mom to eat, then I wrote Gary a letter. The first thing I said was, in real big letters: WHAT HAPPENED, GARY? Then I said something else below it and I sent it over to him. When I heard from him, I remember he didn't tell me what happened. He just wrote a letter saying: 'I'm in jail.' That's all he said."

I asked Frank if he felt as if his life had stopped, after receiving the news.

"For several hours it did, yes. It took a while to reel back from it. It's not something that you want to hear, and we'd had so much bad news from Gary anyway. The other thing is, I remember that I was not just happy because I had some work that I liked for a change, or that I was working with people I liked. I was happy because, for the first time in many years, I had an inner peace. Everybody in the family was out of jail, and that alone was an unusual thing. And when I would come home from work in those days, I'd hear things from Mom like, 'Oh, Gary's working and he's got a girlfriend and they have a little place.' I was thinking: Man, the guy's actually living like a human being, like a normal human being. Everybody in the family is out of jail and doing well and I felt really good about it. Then, when I came in and got that, it was just like everything had gone back. Plus this time it was murder. So I said to myself: Well, there will never be any more times when he'll be out. Not now. Never again will there be a time when I can feel that inner peace that all of us are doing all right on the outside.

"I had felt so strong about him being out—I had really felt good about it. It was something I wanted inside. It was sort of like finding a gold mine and then discovering it was built over a deadly trap. That's the way I felt. To me it was real painful."

I WAS THE LAST TO KNOW. MY MOTHER had not called me to give me the news. She couldn't bring herself to.

Like Frank, I felt these were good days. I had quit my job at the drug clinic—I'd found the work of watching people make bad choices and sometimes dying as a result a depressing career. A couple of years before, I had finally worked up the courage to do something I had been wanting to do for years: I began writing about music. I had been writing for local newspapers, and I was now starting to sell pieces to some national publications. I felt hopeful.

I was also working at a record store in downtown Portland, to help pay the bills. I loved being around the music and most of the customers, but there were sometimes rough aspects to the work. Occasionally we would have to bust shoplifters, and sometimes this obligation made us face the possibility of violence. Just a couple of weeks before, I'd had to confront a whole family of shoplifters who had their coats and purses full of cassette tapes. When I stopped them at the door, they pulled knives on me. Lucky for me, a coworker had called the police, and they arrived at the door at the same moment that the knives came out.

Later, when the matter went to trial, the judge asked one woman who had drawn a knife what she was doing with it in her purse.

"I was on my way to a picnic," she replied.

The judge laughed. "A picnic with a *switchblade?*" he said.

On a Friday night, nine days after Gary's arrest, I came home from work, drained after being on my feet for eight hours on a hot day. Since

I had to open the store the next morning at ten, I passed up a chance to go drinking with some friends and headed for home.

The Wild Bunch, Sam Peckinpah's genuflection to violence and honor, was on TV, and as I settled back on the couch to half-watch it, I picked up the late edition of *The Oregonian.* I almost passed over a page-two item headlined OREGON MAN HELD IN UTAH SLAYINGS, but instinctively I began to read it. "Gary Mark Gilmore, 35, was charged with the murders of two young clerks during the holdup of a service station and a motel . . ." I read on—in a daze—about how Gary had been arrested for killing Max Jensen and Ben Bushnell on two consecutive nights in July. Both men were Mormons, about the same age as I, and both left wives and infant children behind.

I was stunned. I put down the paper, went into the kitchen, and began throwing up in the sink. My girlfriend Andrea came in, alarmed. "What's wrong?" she asked. I told her.

I sat on the couch the rest of the night, rereading the sketchy account. I felt shame, remorse, guilt . . . and rage. It could've been me, I thought, a victim of some senseless robbery.

The next day, I went to visit my mother in Oak Grove, six miles away from my house in Portland. I had no way of knowing whether she had read the news, except to call and ask, which seemed too distant and cold. I was worried about her health. She was now sixty-three, and she had never regained her strength from the surgery of a few months before, and of course she never would. It turned out that she had known of the killings for more than a week but couldn't bring herself to tell me. We sat there in the claustrophobia of her bleak home that day, looking at each other across a gulf of devastated common history, and I finally began to understand that she had always lived much closer to the horror than I had. In tears, she asked: "Can you imagine what it feels like to mother a son whom you love that deprives two other mothers of their sons?

"If I had been there, he never would have killed those two boys. I know I could have stopped him, I could have calmed his heart," she said, and then buried her face in her hands, and all the tears they held.

BETWEEN HIS RELEASE AND THOSE FATEFUL NIGHTS IN JULY, Gary had held a job briefly at his Uncle Vernon's shoe store, and had met and fallen in love with Nicole Barrett, a beautiful young woman with two children. But Gary also had a hard time refusing some old, less-promising appetites. Almost immediately after his release, he started drinking steadily, and he also began taking Fiorinal, a muscle and headache medication that, in sustained doses, can cause severe mood swings and sexual dysfunction. Gary apparently experienced both reactions. He also became violent. Sometimes he would get rough with Nicole over failed sex or what he saw as flirtations on her part. Other times, he would pick fights with the men around him, hitting them from behind, threatening to cave in their faces with a tire iron, which he twirled as handily as a baton. Within a short time, Gary had lost his job, had abused the support of his Utah relatives, and appeared embattled with nearly everyone around him. He drank more; he took more drugs. He took to walking into stores and walking out with whatever he wanted under his arm, glaring at the cashiers, as if they would be crazy to try to stop him. And he took to bringing guns home, where he sat on the back porch, firing them into the trees, the fences, the sunsets. "Hit the sun," he told Nicole. "See if you can make it sink."

When he had hit Nicole with his bare fist once too often, she decided that no man would ever hit her again. She packed up her belongings, grabbed her children, and moved out. Gary tried to get her to come back, but she would not. This went on for a while, until Nicole put herself at a greater distance from Gary. Then Gary told a friend that maybe he was going to kill Nicole.

On a heat-thick night in late July, Gary drove over to Nicole's mother's house and talked his ex-girlfriend's little sister, April, into going for a ride with him in his white pickup truck. He wanted to drive around and talk and drink beer and look for Nicole, he told April. They drove for hours, listening to the radio, talking aimlessly, until Gary pulled up around the corner from a service station in the nearby small town of Orem. He told April to wait in the truck. He walked into the station, where twenty-six-year-old attendant Max Jensen was working alone. There were no other cars. There was only an empty Utah night. Gary pulled a .22 automatic from his jacket and told Jensen to empty the cash from his pockets. He took Jensen's coin changer. Then he led the young attendant around back and forced him to lie down on the lavatory floor. He told Jensen to place his hands under his stomach and press his face to the ground. Jensen did these things, and tried to offer Gary a smile. Gary pointed the gun at the base of Jensen's skull. "This one is for me," Gary said, and pulled the trigger. And then: "This one is for Nicole," and he pulled the trigger again.

Gary walked back to the pickup truck and got in. April had been sitting in the cab with the radio blaring, but she knew something was up. She was spooked.

After driving around for a while, they went to a drive-in to see *One Flew Over the Cuckoo's Nest*. But the movie bothered April—who had spent some time in a psychiatric hospital, following a bad LSD experience that had ended in gang rape—and she forced Gary to leave before it was over. They stopped by his cousin Brenda's, but the visit didn't go too well. Brenda could tell something was wrong. Finally they ended up at a Holiday Inn, where they smoked some dope, and Gary tried to take April's clothes off. She was too freaked, though, and would not have sex with him.

The next night, Gary walked into the office of a motel just a few doors away from his Uncle Vernon's house in Provo. He ordered the man behind the counter, Ben Bushnell—another young Mormon—to lie down on the floor, and then he shot him in the back of the head. He walked out with the motel's cashbox under his arm, and tried to stuff the pistol under a bush outside. But it discharged, blowing a hole in his thumb.

Gary decided it was time to get out of town. First, though, he had to take care of his thumb. He drove over to the house of a friend named Craig and called Brenda. In the meantime, a witness had recognized Gary leaving the site of the second murder, and the police had been in touch with Brenda. She had them on one line, Gary on another. She was trying to stall for time until a roadblock could be set up. After a while, Gary figured out that Brenda wasn't sending any help his way, and he got in his truck and started heading for the local airport. A few miles down the road, just in front of his girlfriend Nicole's house, he was surrounded by police cars and a SWAT team. He was arrested for Bushnell's murder, and within a day or so, he had confessed to the murder of Max Jensen.

GARY WENT ON TRIAL A COUPLE OF MONTHS LATER, but from the start it was an open-and-shut case. Plus, Gary didn't help the case much when he refused to allow his attorneys to call Nicole as a defense witness. (By this time, Nicole and Gary were reconciled; she had felt terrible after his arrest and was now visiting him in jail for hours every day.) Also, Gary didn't help matters by staring menacingly at the jury members and by offering belligerent testimony on his own behalf. Neither the verdict nor the sentence came as a surprise: Gary was found guilty and was sentenced to die. He told the judge he would prefer being shot to being hanged.

My mother called the night of Gary's original sentencing, October 7, to tell me that he had received the death penalty. I found myself echoing my friends' consolations. "Mother," I said, "they haven't executed anybody in this country for ten years and they aren't about to start with Gary."

I hung up the phone and went and sat on the curb outside my house. I sat there a long time, staring at the nearby river, until my girlfriend came out and put her arm around me. "I know it's awful," she said. "But you know they won't kill him. They never put people to death in America anymore."

"No," I said after a moment, "you don't understand. He's going to die. They're going to execute him. He was born for it."

FOR WEEKS AFTER THE KILLINGS AND GARY'S DEATH SENTENCE, I felt grief and anger, and deep and painful humiliation. I could not believe that my brother had left his family with so much horror and shame to live with, and I could not forgive him for what he had done to the families of Max Jensen and Ben Bushnell. I prayed that in some ways the awful episode was over—that Gary would simply rot away the rest of his life in the bitter nothingness of a Utah prison.

Then I tried going on with my life. I had told my close friends about what had happened with Gary—I felt I owed them a chance to decide whether they wanted to be the friend of a murderer's brother—but I hadn't told any of the editors or journalists I worked with. I still thought maybe I could keep enough of this horrible truth buried somewhere, so it would not spill over into the rest of my life and corrupt whatever dreams I might still have.

In the autumn of 1976, I learned that *Rolling Stone* had accepted an article of mine for publication. I was pleased. From the time I began reading the magazine, I had held a dream of someday writing for it. In early November, I went to San Francisco to work on an assignment and to meet the editors at the magazine. We got along okay, and my principal editor, Ben Fong-Torres, indicated that he would like me to do more work for them. I couldn't wait to get home and tell my girlfriend.

When I stepped off the plane at Portland's airport, I heard my name on the loudspeaker: "Mr. Mikal Gilmore: please pick up a red courtesy telephone. There is an emergency phone call for you."

I picked it up. It was Andrea. "I'm sorry I'm late. I've been with your mother all afternoon. She's had an accident—she's fallen down. I think you should come see her right away."

Andrea arranged for a friend of ours, Michael, to pick me up at the airport. I could tell by the way that Michael was acting, as he drove me to my mother's trailer, that he knew more than he was telling me. He was grave and quiet.

When I arrived, my mother showed me a news story on the front page of *The Oregonian:* CONVICTED KILLER ASKS UTAH TO PUT HIM TO DEATH. During the time I had been in San Francisco, Gary had waived all rights of appeal and review and was requesting that his execution be carried out. Fourth District Judge J. Robert Bullock had complied, setting the date for Monday, November 15.

I was shocked and I was furious. I figured Gary was throwing a bluff, but I also figured that if there was one state in the Union that would be happy to oblige his request, it was Utah, with its passion for Blood Atonement. As it turned out, that same day Gary's original attorneys had filed for a stay—against his protests—and the Utah Supreme Court had granted one.

That night, back at my own home, I sat and drank some wine and tried to think about what was happening. I remember thinking that *nothing* would ever be the same. Not for myself, not for my family, maybe not even for the nation around me. I remember thinking that the past and the future were now closed off from each other for me, and all that was left was a terrible *present*: a present that had quickly become the entryway to a nightmare that none of us could ever be delivered from.

THE NEXT DAY I DECIDED IT WAS TIME TO CONFRONT GARY. I put a call through to Draper Prison. To my amazement Gary was on the phone within two minutes.

Our first few exchanges were polite but tentative. Gary grew impatient quickly. "Something on your mind?"

"Gary, are you serious about this?"

"What do you think?"

"I don't know."

"That's right, you don't. You never knew me." Gary had thrown a hurdle I couldn't leap, one he was entitled to. I was at a loss for a reply. "Look," he continued, a softer tone to his voice, "I'm not trying to be mean to you, but this thing's going to happen one way or the other. There's nothing you can do to stop it, and I don't particularly want you to like me. It'll be easier for me if you don't. It seems the only time we ever talk to each other is around the time of somebody's death. And now it's mine."

I hadn't counted on Gary taking the offensive. I felt helpless against it. "What about Mother?" I asked.

"Well, I want to see Mother before all this goes down," Gary said. "I want to see all of you. Maybe that will make it easier. But I am serious about this, and I don't want you or anybody else to interfere. It's totally my affair. I killed two men, the court sentenced me to die, and now I'm accepting that sentence. I don't want to spend the rest of my life on trial or in prison. I've lost my freedom. I lost it a long time ago. Now I'm just going to make them finish the job they started twenty years ago."

I began to form a reply, then stopped. "What's wrong?" asked Gary.

"It's hard to hear this stuff from somebody you love—"

"Hey, I don't need to hear that," Gary broke in. "I won't let anything hurt me anymore, and I don't want you to think I'm some 'sensitive' artist because I drew pictures or wrote poems. I killed—in cold blood." A guard told Gary that his time was up.

The next day, I learned of Gary's successful appearance before the Utah Supreme Court on network news, and I also saw clips of my brother being led from the courtroom in shackles, with that wary, piercing stare in his eyes. I pitied and feared Gary in those moments, and I also hated him for what he was bringing upon himself and our family. I couldn't believe his audacity, the seemingly dispassionate manner with which he sought a state-sanctioned suicide, an act which seemed no less premeditated than murder.

Also, I was reeling from having the most painful and private aspects of my family's history transformed into public news. Overnight, a past that I had tried to escape was everywhere. Gary was now on the national news nearly every evening of the week. He was also on the front page of every American newspaper I saw, and *now* he was staring out at me from the cover of *Newsweek*. Inside the magazine, I found pictures from my family's photo books. There was one from a long-ago Christmas morning, with my father, Gary, Gaylen, and myself, all standing in a line. Nobody in that picture looked very happy. God—was this the same Christmas that Gary came into my room, preaching his philosophy of self-abasement?

The same week as the *Newsweek* story, I received a call at home. "Is this Mikal Gilmore?" asked the voice at the other end. "I'm from the *Los Angeles Times,* and I would like to talk to you about your brother Gary Gilmore." I told him that he had the wrong Gilmore and hung up. That afternoon, I had the number changed. I knew I couldn't escape from what was happening, but I was not going to participate in it. It is unimaginable, the vertigo you can feel when events throw your life to the top of the world.

I resented the way this whole event was being viewed—as something that was inevitable, as a horrible fate that could not be refused or altered. I could not understand modern American courts throwing aside the processes, structure, and logic of law simply to meet a challenge of bravado or to appease a suicidal demand. It was as though everybody was caught up in the novelty, the excitement, the vicarious deadliness of the event, and nothing could stop it.

I decided I'd had enough. Regardless of my brother's wishes, I was going to consult legal authorities in Utah, to learn what the family could do to seek a halt to the execution.

THE NEXT DAY OUTGOING UTAH GOVERNOR Calvin Rampton ordered a stay, referring the matter to the State Board of Pardons and earning the epithet of "moral coward" from Gary. The same night, I received a call from Anthony Amsterdam of Stanford Law School, a longtime and well-versed opponent of the death penalty and a member of the bar of the United States Supreme Court. He outlined possible courses of action for the family. A family member could retain counsel to seek a stay from the U.S. Supreme Court, the duration of which would be determined by the Court's willingness to review the case and the subsequent decision of that review. Realistically, it meant that Gary could be subjected to a new trial.

I passed the information on to my mother, who also spoke with Amsterdam. We agreed it would probably be wise to retain him pending the pardons board decision.

On Tuesday morning, November 16, the day after Gary's scheduled execution, Amsterdam called me with the news that Gary and Nicole had both attempted suicide with an overdose of sedatives. That was my first real indication that any attempts to save Gary's life might prove futile. We can sentence people to die, I thought, but not to live. Gary, though, had an extensive history of suicide attempts, and he had once claimed that few had been in earnest. But that had been years ago, with razor blades and broken lightbulbs. To my knowledge he'd never attempted suicide with drugs.

I had one more phone conversation with Gary in that period, between his hospital release and the pardons board hearing. He had been fasting to protest the hospital's refusal to allow him any communication with Nicole, and he was in a bad temper. I tried to tell him about the toll the whole affair was taking on the family, what a circus it had become, and how that seemed to belie his claims to dignity. "What do I owe you?" he snapped. "I don't even think of you as my brother anymore."

I lost my temper. I was weary from the pressure. "I'm sick of the way you've shoved everybody around," I said. "You're running over a lot of people's lives for you own sake, and you only insult and berate those who don't want to see you die." He hung up on me.

On November 30, the pardons board decided to allow the execution. In anticipation of that decision, I had flown to San Francisco to deliver a retainer to Anthony Amsterdam authorizing him to take action on my mother's behalf.

Events moved rapidly. On December 3, the U.S. Supreme Court granted a stay of execution. But our calls were turned away at the prison, and Gary issued an open letter asking my mother to "butt out." During this time, neither Gary nor any of his legal representatives attempted to contact any member of the family outside of Utah. The only contact in that manner occurred when writer-publisher Lawrence Schiller, who'd bought the publication and motion picture rights to Gary's story from him, asked my mother's sister Ida and her husband, Vernon Damico (who had replaced one of Gary's earlier lawyers, Dennis Boaz, as Gary's agent), to pay my mother a visit, ostensibly to make up for the previous times her counsel and feelings had been bypassed.

But whatever business there was to discuss got put aside once Vern and Ida saw the state of my mother's health and the way she lived in her trailer. Vern went and bought her some groceries while Ida did some cleaning up. There were strains between my mother and these folks now—my mother believed the family in Utah had stolen her son from her and were now using his awful fame to their advantage—but there was also love between them. They remained family. Vern held my mother in his large, strong arms while she cried about Gary's deeds and his fate, and Vern and Ida cried too.

Before leaving, Vern took a thousand dollars from inside his coat and placed it on the table. He told my mother that Gary wanted her to have the money, if she would sign a release. Gary also wanted her to withdraw her opposition to his execution—or at least to stop any further legal action. My mother looked at the money and said, "Well, I could certainly use that," then broke down and cried again. In the end, she refused to sign, and Vernon was forced to take the money back with him. Everybody involved felt bad about the whole deal.

ON THE MORNING OF DECEMBER 13, THE SUPREME COURT lifted its stay, declaring that Gary had made a "knowing and intelligent waiver of his rights." A resignation began to descend on us.

Finally my mother got through to Gary on the phone. "Gary," she said, "do you remember the day when you were a child and you fell into the water off a houseboat in Seattle? I came in the water and got you because I loved you. I loved you no more that day than I do today, so I thought I'd come in the water again to get you. That's what this is all about."

"I wasn't angry with you," Gary replied. "I half-expected it; after all, you are my mother. I knew you would try to stop it because I knew you loved me. I also knew you were doing it for Mikal." Gary asked my mother to withdraw her intervention, and she did.

A day later, Judge Bullock reset the execution for January 17, and Gary was confined to a "strip cell," denying him all visitation rights, including family members.

By Christmas time I told myself, and anybody who asked, that I didn't care anymore about what would happen. I spent the holidays drunk and often drugged. My girlfriend went home to visit her family, and I was with a different woman every night she was gone. I took sleeping pills because I couldn't sleep if I didn't. When I couldn't sleep, I walked around my house, throwing things, breaking mementos. Then one night I dreamed of Gary being tied to a stake and bayoneted repeatedly, while I stood on the other side of a fence, unable to reach him. The next morning I heard of another, nearly fatal suicide attempt.

Suddenly I desperately wanted to see Gary, to reach out for one last time, to achieve whatever reconciliation was possible under the circumstances. And at that same moment, I also realized that I was not yet resigned to the idea of Gary's execution. No matter what had happened, I did not want him to die.

CHAPTER 3

LAST WORDS

IN THE FIRST WEEK OF JANUARY, Anthony Amsterdam, negotiating through Gary's attorneys—Robert Moody and Ronald Stanger—and prison officials, arranged for me and my brother Frank to visit Gary. My mother's physical condition prohibited her traveling. Richard Giauque, a Salt Lake City attorney who had acted on Amsterdam's and the family's behalf in Utah, was to meet us at the airport. As far as we knew, it was a "one time only, no physical contact" visit.

On Tuesday morning, January 11, Frank and I caught a plane into Salt Lake. We tried talking for a while on the flight, but after a bit my brother lapsed into a brooding silence. I could tell he was in deep pain over what would be facing us.

His silence gave me a chance to think about some things I hadn't wanted to think about. I was heading into Utah to confront a man, a blood relative, whom I had never really known, and whom I now had a bitter relationship with. I could tell myself we were very different people—I *had* told myself that for years—and in certain ways, that was true. Gary was a killer, I was not. But in truth, on this day we were both monsters, each determined to get his own way, despite what would likely be mortal consequences for others.

I was prepared and willing to do whatever was necessary to stop Gary's execution. I could tell myself I was doing this for good moral purposes—I did not believe in the death penalty, and certainly Gary's execution would hasten its return—but I had other reasons that were less generous. I did not want Gary to die this way because I did not want his death to ruin my life or what remained of the lives of my family. I did not want to live with the ruin and stigma of being a brother to the man who had brought capital punishment back to America. I had rights to my own hopes, I told myself, and those hopes could never come to be, as long as I was a blood relation to such shame and infamy. I already knew that part of the world would judge me for Gary's actions, and I did not want to share his condemnation. I still had my whole life ahead of me.

To get my way, to win this battle, I would have to impose my will on the situation and on my brother. I would have to take legal action that might forestall his execution, maybe even for years. I knew that if I did so, I would be robbing him of this strange moment he had seized in history. Worse, I would likely be condemning him to another form of suffering—a waiting for a slower death, within the hell of prison—and despite the horrible things Gary had done, I had little doubt that he had suffered much in recent months and that his waiting for the moment of his death could not be an easy thing. But if I didn't make Gary suffer, then the rest of us would have to. I would have to be with my mother and see the look on her face when we heard the news that the execution had been carried out. More than anything else, I did not want to see my mother go through that moment.

Even though I was hoping to save my brother's life in the course of this visit (And what the hell did *that* mean? How could you save the life of a man whose soul was already lost?), I did not feel in any sense like a good person on this morning. In fact, I would never again feel like a good person. That possibility, much less that certainty, got left somewhere up there in the sky during that flight. When the plane landed, I was in a place where people decided who would live and who would have to die. It was both a physical and spiritual place, and it was a place I'd been headed for my entire life, just as Gary had been headed for it. This was the drama we had been assigned to play.

Once you arrived at such a place, the stain of blood would wash upon your hands and would never be cleansed or forgotten.

No, I was not a good person and I never could be again. The momentum of my blood history had taken that possibility away from me.

WHEN WE ARRIVED IN SALT LAKE CITY, Richard Giauque met us at the airport with a Rolls-Royce. He apologized immediately for its "gaudiness"—he'd had to borrow his law partner's car at the last minute, he said. En route to Draper, Giauque explained that it was possible to achieve a stay until the constitutionality of Utah's death penalty had been determined.

Draper Prison is located at a place in the Salt Lake Valley known as the "Point of the Mountain." Because of the heavy pollution in the valley, one doesn't even become aware of the mountains until the final, winding approach to the prison. It rests at the center of a flat basin, surrounded by tall, sharply-inclined snowy slopes. It is perhaps the most beautiful vista in the entire valley.

The car had to stop at a central tower, where a guard gave us clearance to drive down the narrow road to maximum security, a small building surrounded by another tower and two barbed-wire fences. We were told we would be allowed a ninety-minute, uninterrupted visit. Gary was still under maximum restrictions at this point and technically wasn't even allowed visitors, except for his attorneys. This family visit was an "exception." We were led into an open triangular room where no guards were present and informed that we would be allowed a physical contact visit.

Gary strolled in through sliding doors dressed in prison whites and red, white, and blue sneakers, twirling a comb and smiling broadly. For so long, I'd seen only the grim, cold-looking photos and film clips that I'd forgotten how charming he could be. "You're looking as fit as ever," he said to Frank, and to me: "And you're just as damn skinny as ever."

He rearranged the benches in front of the guard-room window. "So those poor fools can keep an eye on me," he said.

For the first few minutes we exchanged small talk, trying to get comfortable with the surroundings and to approach the inevitable subject. Gary's face narrowed as we mentioned the decision of Robert Excell White—a condemned man in Texas whose request for execution had occurred at about the same time as Gary's—to fight for his life. He shrugged. "Yeah, I guess you could say he equivocated. Well, that has nothing to do with me. You see, for a while I felt guilty about this whole capital punishment thing, and that's partially why I tried to kill myself. But I'm tired of everybody pinning that on me. I don't care what happens to all these rapists and torturers. They can take them out and shoot them tomorrow. What happens to me won't affect them; their cases will be judged on their own merits."

I broached the prospect of intervention, but Gary cut it off right away. "Look, I don't want anybody interfering, no outside causes, no lawyers like Amsterdam." He reached out and took hold of my chin, staring me in the eyes. "He's out of this, I hope." Before I had a chance to reply, the visitors' door rolled open and in walked Uncle Vernon and Aunt Ida. We had been assured a private visit. As far as I knew, this was our only time with Gary, and here we were, fifteen minutes into what we expected to be our last conversation with our brother, and in walk Uncle Vernon and Aunt Ida, like it's old folks' week. Uncle Vernon and Aunt Ida, who stood to be richer than they had ever been before if Gary would just sit down in a large wooden chair one week from now and allow five strangers to pump bullets into his heart. *That* Vernon and Ida—our uncle, our aunt. I was so furious, I wanted to rip the cheery, familial smiles off their fucking faces and turn them upside down.

The rest of the visit was aggravating. Gary and Vernon did most of the talking, discussing numerous people Gary wanted to leave some money to and cracking an occasional macabre joke. Vernon had brought along a bag of green T-shirts adorned with the legend GILMORE—DEATH WISH and a computerized photo of Gary. Apparently the shirts had been ordered by either Gary or Vernon. They talked about the possibility of Gary wearing one on the execution morning, and then auctioning it off to the highest bidder. I felt bilious. After the ninety minutes, the visit was terminated.

As we were leaving, Gary offered me a T-shirt. "I'm not sure it would be of much use to me, Gary."

"Well," he drawled, smiling, "it's a little big for you, but I think you can grow into it." I accepted the shirt.

"Is there anything I can do for you while you're in town?" Vernon asked. I replied that I wanted him to arrange a meeting with Gary's attorneys, Ron Stanger and Moody, and with Larry Schiller.

Back in Salt Lake City, I decided to stay for a couple of days and attempt to visit Gary on my own. At Giauque's office, I told him of my ambivalence over the situation—how, on one hand, I was firmly opposed

to capital punishment, no matter the crime or the wishes of the condemned, but also how I felt it was important not to take any action without giving Gary fair warning—that I wasn't prepared to save Gary's life
when it might only result in providing the impetus for a final suicide attempt.

I asked Giauque if he could tell me the names of some of the journalists who were in town covering this affair. I thought that a well-connected
reporter might be able to apprise me of what was going on behind the
scenes in this complex situation. Most of the names he mentioned—
journalists like Geraldo Rivera—were people I had no interest in talking
to. Then he mentioned Bill Moyers, the former press aide to President
Lyndon B. Johnson, and a writer and journalist I had much respect for.

"Can you put me together with Moyers?" I asked.

A couple of hours later I was having dinner and a much-needed drink
or two with Moyers at his hotel. He clearly had some misgivings about
the moral dimensions of covering this story, and he was not glad to see
the death penalty returning to America. He agreed to talk with me and
tell me what he knew, and he assured me that he would never use any of
the information I gave him in his reporting unless he cleared it with me.
He told me that I should be cautious about the advice that any legal,
business, or journalistic people might give me in the days ahead—that
instead, I should try to come to terms with my own conscience and try to
reconcile that with the communications that would go on between me
and Gary. Even now, all these years later, I remain certain that Bill Moyers's gentle concern was a key influence in helping me hold on to my
sanity during that week.

AT NINE O'CLOCK THAT NIGHT I CALLED VERNON to ask if any arrangements had been made for a meeting with Moody and Stanger. The
lawyers were unavailable at the time, but Schiller was flying in from Los
Angeles and was willing to meet me at the Salt Lake Hilton at one in the
morning. I was a little drunk and in need of sleep, but I didn't want to
pass up a meeting with Gary's keeper.

At the Hilton, I recognized Schiller from his picture in the December
20th New West article, "The Merchandising of Gary Gilmore," by Barry
Farrell (who later became one of Schiller's researchers and collaborators);
he recognized me because of my resemblance to Gary. I had wanted to
meet Schiller—who had something of a reputation as a death-minded
entrepreneur for his interviews for Albert Goldman's infamous Lenny

Bruce biography, and for his handling of projects and stories involving Marilyn Monroe, Jack Ruby, and Sharon Tate murderer Susan Atkins— because it occurred to me that he might be trying to exploit this execution for his own ends. Also, I realized that to deal with Gary at this stage, I would also have to deal with the man who owned Gary's story.

Schiller and I talked for nearly two hours. Each of us asked pointed questions about what we were doing in Utah and about our interests in Gary. I spoke frankly of my concerns about Gary's choices and their possible ramifications, and Schiller responded sympathetically to those concerns, but stopped short of professing to share them. Finally I asked Schiller what I considered an inescapable question: Was Gary worth more to him dead than alive?

Schiller hesitated for a few moments, then said: "Many years ago, when I was working as a news photographer, I was sent out to cover a fire. There were firemen carrying a person through a window, and I had to ask myself whether I should take a picture of that moment, or put down my camera and go help them drag that person to safety. I chose to take the picture. I decided then it was my obligation as a journalist to preserve what existed.

"To answer your question, I'm here to record history, not to make it."

At the end of the session, Schiller had impressed me with his forthrightness. Also, I trusted his intentions toward the Bushnell and Jensen families, and felt I could believe him when he promised to keep our conversations confidential. He drove me back to my hotel and, as I was getting out of his rental car, he made a curious comment.

"What's your middle name?" he asked. I told him. He jotted it down in a notebook and then wrote out a phone number and handed it to me. "This is where you can leave a message for me if you need to get in touch and can't find me at either the Hilton or the Travelodge in Orem. But just use your middle name and not your last. That's Stanger's office and you shouldn't tip him off about where you're staying. Gary doesn't have the best attorneys in town, but then I didn't choose them."

I TRIED TO CALL FRANK AT HIS HOTEL the next afternoon, but he had checked out. I called my mother back in Oregon to see if Frank had headed home, but as far as she knew, he was still in the Salt Lake area. This time, I would have to see Gary alone.

When I was signing the visitors log at Draper, I noticed that Moody and Stanger had signed in just before me. I glanced over to the phone cubicle and could see them talking to Gary. I explained to the officer in charge that I wanted to speak with my brother privately. He said he would do his best, and let me in the same triangular room I'd been in the day before. I sat in the far corner, away from the phone cage. Moments later a guard came in and told Stanger that the watch commander wanted to see him for a minute. After Stanger disappeared through the rolling bars, Moody asked Gary how the family visit had been. I couldn't hear my brother's reply. "Listen, Gary," Moody continued, "Schiller met with your brother late last night at the Hilton. He thinks Mikal might try to stop the execution."

I couldn't believe what I was hearing. I moved over to the bench next to the cage. "Did you know that Giauque brought your brothers out here in a Rolls-Royce yesterday?" I couldn't hear the next sentence but it included a mention of the hotel where I was registered.

The guard reentered. "Mr. Moody, will you come with me for a minute?" As he got up to leave, Moody glanced at me, then did a double take. "Who is that?" I heard him ask, farther down the corridor. I had to wait about thirty minutes before Gary came in, spinning a Scotsman's cap on his finger and wearing a black sleeveless sweatshirt. Stanger and Moody were standing behind him. Gary introduced us. "Sorry we have to meet under these circumstances," said Stanger, "but if there's anything we can do for you, just give us a call." I nodded.

"Uh, I'm glad you came back," said Gary, after Moody and Stanger had left. Gary took a seat on the back of the bench.

"Gary, I don't want to play any games with you. I overheard what your lawyers said and, yes, it's true. I did meet with Schiller last night. I am thinking of seeking a stay."

The smile on Gary's face fell away; in its place I saw the stern stare I'd come to know from newspaper and magazine photos. "Is it true that Giauque brought you out here in a Rolls-Royce yesterday?" Schiller had asked me the same question the night before. The Rolls had become a symbol of powerful, outside intervention, I surmised, yet it seemed so trivial. I explained the situation to Gary. He spoke angrily: "Amsterdam and Giauque are cum-sucking nigger-fuckers who are just trying to use you for some cause. Why do they want to meddle with my life? Because they're opposed to capital punishment? Does that make them special, or holy men? I was given a sentence to die. Now is that some kind of joke? I don't want that over my head."

I decided to avoid a discussion of legal ethics or lawyers. "If you want to believe all that shit about Giauque and Amsterdam, then go ahead," I replied, "but it doesn't have anything to do with you and me. I could take action independently that might achieve a stay, that could result in a commutation of your sentence."

Gary shook his head. "That's impossible," he declared. "I couldn't even stop this thing if I wanted to." He paused for several moments. "Could you really do that?"

I replied that I believed I could. Gary stood up and started to walk around the room.

"They'd never let me free, man, and I've spent too much time in jail. I don't have anything left to me." He came face to face. "I killed two men. I don't want to spend the rest of my life in jail. If some fucker gets me set free, then I'm going to go get a gun and kill a few of those damn lawyers who keep interfering. Then I'll say to you, 'See what your meddling accomplished? Are you proud?' "

"Time's up," announced a voice from the guard's nest.

Gary tried to flash a relaxed-looking smile. "Come back and talk to me some more about this tomorrow," he said. As I was passing through the door, he called: "Where were you ten years ago when I needed you?" All the way back to Salt Lake those final words reverberated in my head. I felt confused and broken. An hour earlier, I thought that the only right decision was to argue for a stay, to choose life over death. But I couldn't make that choice for Gary. I wanted to disappear, to fold up into a void where choices and conscience didn't exist. Where I could forget the look in Gary's eyes.

THAT NIGHT I HAD DINNER WITH MOYERS AGAIN. I told him about my conversation with Gary. After listening, Moyers asked me if I thought there was any chance he might be able to visit and speak with Gary. I told him that Schiller had an exclusive deal with my brother, and that no other journalists could talk to him. Moyers said he was willing to assure me and Gary and Schiller that he would not use the conversation for journalistic purposes. He did not want to tape it or film it, and unless he had the appropriate consent of those involved, he would not disclose the contents of the conversation in his report. He just thought that, since both he and Gary were men who had been born in Texas, they might have some common ground for talking. He also thought he might have a philosophical view or two to offer about Gary's situation that my brother might find interesting, maybe even persuasive. I trusted Moyers and told him I would see what could be done.

I went on a long walk around the cold, snow-covered streets of Salt Lake that night. I was walking over by the Mormon Temple when I ran into Frank. At first he didn't see me. He was going along with his hands jammed into his pockets, staring at the ground. I called his name.

I told him I'd been to see Gary, and I told him what we had discussed. I also said that Frank could go back and visit with Gary some more himself, either with or without me. Apparently the prison's stipulation of a one-time visit had been forgotten.

"No," said Frank, "I can't do that. I can't go see him again." And then, as the tears began to fall from his eyes, my brother turned and walked off into the cold night.

Fifteen years later, Frank and I visited Salt Lake together, to try to reestablish some family contacts and to make sense of some of what had happened all those years before. One afternoon, Frank took me over to Liberty Park. It was here, when we were all children and were living with my parents in the haunted house in Salt Lake, that Frank and Gary used to come nearly every afternoon to play. They would run around, play ball, pull pranks on the stodgy Mormons. Frank thought it was maybe the happiest hours the two of them ever spent together. All this was just before Gary began stealing things and hiding them in the garage—before he changed forever into a bad boy.

As we sat there in the park that day, Frank explained to me why he had decided, those years before, not to visit Gary anymore at Draper. After seeing him that one time, Frank said, he came to this park and sat where we were now sitting, and he gave some long thought to what had happened, and what would yet happen.

"I hated what Gary had done," Frank said to me. "What he did was hideous. But I also hate what had been done to him.

"Do you think if Gary hadn't been in prison for twenty-two years, he would have shot that one man in the back of the head in front of his pregnant wife and little kid? What about the other guy? He shot him in the gas station and they say he didn't die for hours. That's the story I heard. That he didn't die for hours and he suffered, suffered to death. I am convinced that the twenty-two years of training that Gary got from the animalistic prison society he had lived in turned him into the animal that brought on those tragedies.

"He'd seen things in prison. He told me about those things. He had seen people maimed—he saw a man get his hands cut off—and he had seen men murdered. He'd seen so fucking many assaults, and when he was younger, he himself had been assaulted. Beaten. Raped. Terrorized.

But he learned to go with it. As he got older and bigger and meaner, he became the assaulter. After that, they had nothing they could scare him with. It was like being in Vietnam for twenty-two years. He'd been the victim and the victimizer of so many hideous things. He could say, 'Yes, I've been destroyed, but now I'm the one who does the destroying.'

"You'll find thousands and thousands of men in this country that lived a similar life, and many of those men would probably make the same kinds of choices as Gary—the same ways of killing and dying. All those years in the horror and brutality of prison changes them. They reach a point of no return. They sort of live a day at a time, and to them, after a while, death starts to look like a way out of life, which is what it is—a way out of everything. They're afraid of almost everything but dying, some of those guys. And they become really dangerous. You can't lock them up, because that's home to them. You can't kill them, because they want that. They are your truly dangerous people, and there are thousands of them in this country walking around, because of our jails and prisons, who are exactly like Gary. Take some kid that has problems— maybe emotional problems, maybe family problems—put him in these outrageous horror house reformatories and prisons, and chances are, eventually, that kid will become like our brother.

"Gary had reached that point of no return. He wanted the release of death. That's one reason I didn't go back and visit him again. I knew he really wanted it, and it bothered me. Not only did he want it, it was like it was a holiday. He was celebrating. He was trying to be set free. It was his exodus.

"That last time I saw him—he was so different from the brooding man I visited throughout the years. This time, he sat there and he was snapping his fingers, he was laughing and he was making jokes. It was like Christmas Eve. He had found the perfect way to beat the system by having them kill him. Then he's out of it. It's over. In his way of thinking, I'm convinced he believed he had won. Most of us couldn't win the way he did. But that was his idea of freedom, and, of course, it was the only freedom he had left. That's the reason I stood back. I know you and Mom wanted to save him, and I never held that against the two of you. But I had to stand back because if I had gone on and done something, if they had kept him locked up in that hell, I would have felt to blame for it.

"I don't think I slept two minutes that night, after seeing him. I knew I wasn't going back anymore. I couldn't watch him suffer, and I couldn't watch him die. I sat here in the park that day and I thought: 'I don't want to see him again. I'm going to try to keep him in my heart and mind as that boy I used to play with here—the little brother that I loved, before he got ruined.' The only thing that bothers me about my decision is, I don't think Gary knew that I actually liked him. I don't think he ever knew in his life that I actually did care about him, that I really felt for him. But there was nothing more that could be done for him. It was all over for Gary. He had no chance. And I think that's what he was trying to tell you."

THE MORNING AFTER I HAD RUN INTO FRANK on the street, I phoned Schiller in Orem. I told him of the remarks I heard Moody make and expressed my disappointment in having any portion of what I'd understood to be a confidential conversation relayed to others.

"I didn't tell Moody or Stanger of our conversation," he replied.

"Who did?"

"Well, I told your Uncle Vernon a couple of things, but just because I assumed he was your main contact here and you would want to stay in touch with him. Now he may have passed some of that along to Moody or Stanger, but anything else you heard was projection on their part." He apologized if he had violated my trust and then offered me some final advice: "Don't call the prison before going out. Information gets passed out of there pretty easily, and a lot of people, including myself, know the minute you enter that maximum-security compound."

After making a couple of calls, though, I learned that visits had to be authorized in advance. I made arrangements for a late-afternoon visit, then sat down and wrote Gary a long letter. It was easy to forget what I wanted to say to him when I was face to face with him and his anger. I wrote him that whatever choice I made, it was a matter of love, an issue between him and me, and not the courts or the newspapers. I told him that I thought redemption was more possible in the choice of life over death, and confessed that for years he'd frightened and confused me because of his violent whims. If time enough existed, I wanted to lift that barrier.

That afternoon at the prison was the first day Gary was officially authorized to have visitors, which meant, ironically, I had to talk to him over the phone. After looking through my letter, a guard gave it to Gary. He read it quietly, pensively. When he was finished he managed a smile. "Well put," he said. "Are you familiar with Nietzsche? He once wrote that a time comes when a man should rise to meet the occasion. That's what I'm trying to do, Mikal . . . Look," he said, suddenly changing the subject, "I was thinking about what I said yesterday, about 'where were you.' I realized that was unfair. I wasn't around much when you were a kid. I don't hate you, although I've tried to act that way lately. You're my brother. I know what that means. I've been angry with you, but I've never hated you."

I forced myself to ask the question I'd been building up to for the last few days: "What would you do if I tried to stop this?"

He winced. "I don't want you to do that," he said evenly.

"That doesn't answer my question."

"Please don't."

"Gary, what would you do? All you've said is that you wanted the sentence of the court carried out. What if that sentence were commuted?"

"I'd kill myself. Look, I'm not watched that closely in this place, no matter what you hear. I could've killed myself any time in the last two weeks, but I don't want to do that. You see, I want some good to come from all this. If I commit suicide, then I can't be a donor—to people who have more right to life than I do—and my whole will could become suspect . . . Besides, if a person's dumb enough to murder and get caught, then, he shouldn't snivel about what he gets."

From there, Gary talked about prison reality, telling me some of the brutality he had witnessed and some that he had fostered. He was terrified of a life in prison, he said. "Maybe you could have my sentence commuted, but you wouldn't have to live that sentence or be around when I killed myself." The fear in his eyes was always most discernible when he spoke about prison, far more than when he spoke about his own impending death. Maybe because one was an ever-present concrete reality and the other an abstraction. "I don't think death will be anything new or frightening for me. I think I've been there before."

We talked for hours, or rather Gary talked. I'd already missed a flight back home and had forgotten about the person waiting out in the parking lot for me. This was the first real communication we'd shared in years; neither of us wanted to let go. Gary asked me to return the next day and, in turn, I asked if he would be willing to meet with Bill Moyers, for the purpose of a conversation, not an interview. Gary readily agreed, as long as it was off the record, because of his deal with Schiller.

Later that night Schiller himself called Moyers and indicated that any communication with Gary was unlikely. I didn't bring up the subject the next day, Friday, but Gary did. "Schiller won't let me see your friend. He wants to guard his 'exclusivity.' Sometimes that son of a bitch acts like he owns me, like he can run my life. He did this to me once before, when I asked him to recover some of my private letters to Nicole. I didn't like seeing that shit in print; the drawings didn't bother me so much, but the letters were nobody's business. And, contrary to my wishes, Schiller read them. I felt like firing him right then, and I probably still should, but it's too late to find anybody else. What I should do, though, is revoke his invitation to the execution." I didn't offer any opinion. I didn't want to get caught up in a feud between Gary and Schiller.

I told Gary that I should leave that night, to go back home and spend the rest of the weekend with Mother.

"Can't you stay one more day?" he asked. "I'd like to see you again, and I have this book Johnny Cash sent me; I want you to give it to Mom."

I agreed to return the next day—Saturday—but before I left he wanted to tell me one more thing. "You know I've said a lot of stuff about how I don't care what people think about me, but that's not completely true. I don't like it when they say I'm jittery and stuff. I've never told anybody this before, but I don't know what Monday's going to be like. Maybe that's why I need Schiller there, so I'll keep cool . . . I know you don't believe this, but I didn't mean for this to become such a big thing. I never expected the books or movies, maybe a few articles."

We pressed our hands against the glass between us and said good-bye.

IMAGINE THE IMPOSSIBLE LEAPS AND BORDERS your heart must cross when you're arguing with a man about his own death. There was a logic, a congruity to Gary's choice, I had to admit, but none of that changed my desire for him to stay alive. But just as you try to convince the lover who no longer loves you to love you nonetheless—because you cannot imagine going on in your life, living it, without the presence or thing that you need and love most—in the same moment that you make your argument, and try to convince the person to stay and love you all over again, you also know that your argument is already lost, and along with it, a version of your future.

When you are arguing with somebody who is hell-bent on dying, you realize that if you lose the argument, there is no more chance for further argument, that you will have seen that person for the last time. I could not believe that I was in that place in my life, that I could possibly be caught up in such an argument. Death is one thing we almost never get to argue with. You can't argue with the disease that takes your loved one or yourself, or the car accident or the killer that snuffs out a life without warning. But a man who *wants* to die . . . When I argued with Gary, I was arguing with death itself—he was death, wanting itself as its only possible fulfillment—and I learned that you cannot win, that this thing which will ruin your heart the most cannot be resisted or stopped, that you will lose this person, and you will have to live with that loss forever. And you will not have lost them to cancer or to the cruelty of another's actions; you will have lost them to the abyss of their own soul, and you will be afraid that maybe their surrender to that abyss is, after all, the only act that makes sense. But mainly, you know that you will never see them again—that you pleaded with them to stay and that there was nothing you could do—it was too late to do anything that would make a difference. Maybe in that moment, you will want to go where they're going, because it can't possibly hurt so much or look so goddamn fucking eternal as the prospect of spending the rest of your life accommodating a loss that no sane heart could ever possibly afford or hope to accommodate without letting ruin so deep inside that it becomes an ineradicable part of your deepest self.

I SPOKE WITH GIAUQUE THE SAME DAY and informed him that I had decided not to intervene. Telling him was almost as hard as making the decision. I could have sought a stay, signed the necessary documents and returned home feeling that I had made the right decision, the moral choice. But I didn't have to bear the weight of that decision. Gary did. Had he chosen suicide, I could rightfully claim that I was not responsible for his choice, only my own. If I could have chosen for Gary to live, I would have.

I had several helpful conversations with Bill Moyers during that week, and at one point he told me that if we are confronted with a choice between life and death and choose anything short of life, then we choose short of humanity. That made it all seem so clear-cut. I wrestled with the decision and finally realized that I couldn't choose life for Gary, and he wouldn't. He had worked out what he reasoned to be some sort of atonement. He wanted death, his final scenario of redemption, his final release from the law. To Gary the greatest irony was that the law—which in his eyes had always sought to break him—finally wanted to save him, when he no longer wanted salvation. In order to beat the law, he had to lose everything—everything except his own unswerving definition of dignity.

I couldn't reason with that, I couldn't change that. And in the end, I couldn't take it away from him.

As a result, I now had a role in this story I had never wanted and had never bargained for: I had become a chooser. I had made decisions that would have consequences. Maybe these consequences wouldn't stop here—maybe other men would now die because we had decided not to challenge history or justice at this point, or maybe there would be numerous other people whose lives would be affected, stopped or turned upside down as a result of these last few days. Maybe the spirit of the nation itself would now be different—bloodier, and more pitiless. The effects, I thought, were incalculable. They could ripple through our lives forever, and into the lives of our children.

What a difference a killing can make.

ON SATURDAY, JANUARY 15, I VISITED GARY FOR THE LAST TIME. By then, camera crews were camped all over the town of Draper, preparing for the finale.

During our previous meetings that week, Gary had always opened with some friendly remarks, a joke or even a handstand. This day, though, he seemed nervous, though he denied it. "Naw, the noise in this place gets to me sometimes, but I'm as cool as a cucumber," he said, holding up a steady hand. The muscles in his wrists and arms, though, were taut and thick as rope.

Gary started to show me letters and pictures he'd received, mostly from children and teenage girls. He said he always tried to answer the ones from kids first, and then he read one from a boy who claimed to be eight years old: "I hope they put you someplace and make you live forever for what you did. You have no right to die. With all the malice in my heart, (name)."

"Man, that one shook me up for a long time," he said.

I asked him if he'd replied to it. "Yeah. I wrote, 'You're too young to have malice in your heart. I had it in mine at a young age and look what it did for me.'"

He had a guard bring the book that Johnny Cash had sent. It was his autobiography, *The Man in Black,* which Gary wanted left with our mother.

"I'd really like to give you something or leave something for you. Why don't you let me leave you some money? Everybody needs money." I declined, suggesting that he give it to the Bushnell and Jensen families instead. "There's no way money can buy back what I did to those people," he said, shaking his head.

Gary's eyes nervously scanned the letters and pictures in front of him, finally falling on one that made him smile. He held it up. A picture of Nicole. "She's pretty, isn't she?" I agreed. "I look at this picture every day. I took it myself. It's the one I made the drawing from. Would you like to have it?"

I said I would be pleased to have it.

Finally I had a last question to ask: "Gary, remember the night you were arrested, when you were on your way to the airport?"

He nodded.

"Where would you have gone had you made it to the airport?"

"Um, Portland."

"But certainly you knew that was the first place they would have looked for you. Why would you want to go there?"

Gary studied the shelf top in front of him for a few seconds. "I don't really want to talk about that night anymore," he said. "There's no *point* in talking about it."

"Please, Gary, I'd like to know: What would you have done in Portland?"

"Mikal, don't."

"Please. I have to know. What would you have done? Would you have come to see me?"

Again, he nodded.

"And . . . ?"

He sighed and looked straight at me, and for a moment his eyes flashed an old anger. "And what would *you* have done if I had come to you?" he asked. "If I had come and said I was in trouble and needed help, needed a place to stay? Would *you* have taken me in? Would you have hidden me?"

I couldn't reply. The question had been turned back on me, and suddenly I could not stand the awfulness of my own answers. Gary sat there for long moments, holding me with his eyes, then said steadily: "I think I was coming to kill you. I think that's what would have happened. There simply may have been no choice for you, and no choice for me." His eyes softened and he gave me a tender smile. It was filled with the sad brokenness of our common history. "Do you understand why?" he asked.

I nodded back. Of course I understood why. I had escaped the family, or at least thought I had. Gary had not.

At that moment, I felt a certain terror. I knew that what Gary had said was true. I knew that death could have been my past, which would mean I would now have no present. In fact, it felt like it had come close to happening, just for the conception of that possibility. And so I felt not just some terror, but also some relief. Jensen's and Bushnell's death, and Gary's own impending death, had added up to my own safety, and as soon as I realized that, my relief was shot through with guilt. And remorse. I thought of all the other things that might have happened in our home or in our love that maybe could have changed this moment, so we would not be sitting here, in this awful place, at this awful time.

Oddly, though, I also felt closer to Gary in that moment than I'd ever felt before. For just that second, I understood completely why he wanted to die.

At that point, Warden Samuel Smith entered Gary's room. They discussed whether Gary would have to wear a hood on Monday morning. I put down the phone. Minutes passed. When I picked up the phone again, Smith was telling Gary that Schiller wouldn't be allowed to visit with Gary in the final hours before the execution.

I rapped on the glass. I would have to leave soon and I asked if the warden would allow us a final handshake. At first Smith refused, but he assented after Gary explained it was our final visit, on the condition I agree to a skin search. I agreed. After the search, conducted by two guards, two other guards brought Gary in. They said I would have to roll up my sleeve past my elbow, and that we could not touch beyond a handshake. Gary grasped my hand, squeezed tight, and said, "Well, I guess this is it." He leaned over and kissed me on the cheek. "See you in the darkness beyond."

I pulled my eyes away from his. I knew I couldn't stop crying at this point, and I didn't want him to see it. "Are you okay?" he asked. I bit my lip and nodded. A guard handed me the book and the picture of Nicole and started to walk with me to the rolling-bar doors. Gary watched me pass through them. "Give my love to Mom," he called. "And put on some weight. You're still too skinny."

The guard walked with me through the two fence gates and patted me on the back as I left. "Take it easy, fella," he said.

I WENT BACK HOME, AND LEFT GARY TO HIS FATE. I hated myself. I felt like I had inadvertently taken sides with the death penalty—a brutal social ethos that I despised. At the same time, I guess I decided that Gary was better off dead. I had little doubt that if he was kept alive, he would kill himself, and perhaps others as well. I didn't want to live with having taken an action that might have resulted in such consequences. I hated living with any of these choices—I hated finding myself in a place where any action or non-action would result in the certainty of death.

The night before Gary's execution, I visited my mother and Frank. I had called the prison earlier in the day and arranged for us all to have a last brief conversation with him on the phone. His last words to my mother were: "Don't cry, Mom. I love you. I want you to go on with your life." And her last words were: "Gary, I'm going to stay brave for you until tomorrow, but I know I'll never stop crying. I'll cry every day for the rest of my life."

She handed the phone to me. Gary told me he had talked with his biggest hero, Johnny Cash, earlier that evening. I asked him what Cash had said. "When I picked up the phone I said, 'Is this the *real* Johnny Cash?' And he said: 'Yes it is.' And I said: 'Well, this is the real Gary Gilmore.' "

Gary told me he had to get off the phone. "I'll miss you, Gary," I said. "We're all proud of you."

"Don't be proud of me," he said. "What's there to be proud of? I'm just going to be shot to death, for something that should never have happened."

Those were our last words.

ON MONDAY MORNING, JANUARY 17, in a cannery warehouse out behind Utah State Prison, Gary met his firing squad. I was with my mother and brother and girlfriend when it happened. Just moments before, we had seen the morning newspaper with the headline EXECUTION STAYED, and turned on the television for more news. *Good Morning America* was on, and there was a press conference: They were announcing that Gary was dead.

There was no way to be braced for that last seesawing of emotion. One moment you're forcing yourself to live through the hell of knowing that somebody you love is going to die in a known way, at a specific time and place, and that not only is there nothing you can do to change that, but that for the rest of your life, you will have to move around in a world that wanted this death to happen. You will have to walk past people every day who were heartened by the killing of somebody in your family— somebody who had long ago been himself murdered emotionally. You will have to live in this world and either hate it or make peace with it, because it is the only world you will have available to live in. It is the only world that *is*.

The next moment, you see a headline that holds the possibility of a reprieve. Maybe, you think, the courts are seizing control of this matter, wresting it from the momentum of this crazy, eerie inevitability. Maybe they will not allow the death penalty to be applied here so hurriedly—and maybe *that* will be enough to break the back of this horror, to diffuse all this madness. Maybe it would prove a reprieve not just for Gary and his indomitable will to die, but also a reprieve for what was left of this family. Maybe now we would not have to live in a world that had killed one of us without any misgiving.

And then, as soon as you've allowed yourself that impossible hope, you turn on the television, and there is Larry Schiller—the only journalist who was allowed to witness the shooting—and he is telling you how the warden put a black hood over Gary's head and pinned a small, circular cloth target above his chest, and then how five men pumped a volley of bullets into that target. He is telling you how the blood flowed from Gary's devastated heart and down his chest, down his legs, staining his white pants scarlet and dripping to the warehouse floor. He is telling you how Gary's arm rose slowly at the moment of the impact, how his fingers seemed to wave, to send a sign of departure as his life left him, as if he were finally trying to bid a gentle good-bye to a hard life.

One moment, hope has come from nowhere. The next moment, you learn that the horror has already happened—and you know you will always have to live with the details of that horror. You will have to try to find a way to live with the sorrow that will now always be at the heart of your heart. You will have to try to find a way to live in this world, in this life, and not hate it—and you will have to try despite the impossibility of such a task.

I thought all this, and then I looked over at my mother, and I saw her face crack, and I heard her wail: "My God, Gary, where are you? Where have you gone to?"

FOLLOWING MY BROTHER'S EXECUTION, an outcry arose in Utah against what many people (including several death penalty advocates) saw as the unnecessarily bloody and "old West" aspect of Utah's mode of capital punishment. Why hold on to such gruesome conventions, the reformists argued, when an increasing number of other states were opting for the comparatively "humane" method of putting the condemned to death by lethal injection? In a fairly brilliant act of legal and moral sleight-of-hand, the Utah legislature managed to accommodate both the traditions of their region and the reformists' pressure for change. As of 1980, hanging—an old West practice if ever there was one—would no longer be an option for execution (nobody ever chose it anyway), and in its place, Utah now offered the alternative of lethal injection. However, under what was rumored to be a tremendous amount of back-room ecclesiastical pressure, the state also retained the firing squad option, in case the man who was going to die wanted his blood to be shed, as a bid for salvation. In the years since, nobody has opted for the choice of being shot, and it is not likely that many will ever again take that course. Chances are, Gary Gilmore will remain the last man to die before a firing squad in America, as well as the last man to pay the Mormons' rigorous cost of Blood Atonement.

YEARS LATER, I would learn what my brother's last words were. They stunned me when I heard them, they haunt me still. Gary Gilmore's final words, before the life was shot out of him, were these: "There will always be a father."

PART SIX
THE VALLEY
OF TEARS

I *want you to take me*
Where I belong
Where hearts has been broken
With a kiss and a song
Spend the rest of my days
Without any cares
Everyone understand me
In the valley of tears

Soft words has been spoken
So sweet and low
But my mind has made up
Love has got to go
Spend the rest of my day
Without any care
Everyone understand me
In the valley of tears

—FATS DOMINO AND
DAVE BARTHOLOMEW,
"Valley of Tears"

CHAPTER 1

FAMILY'S END

SHORTLY AFTER GARY'S EXECUTION, I wrote an article about the turn of events for *Rolling Stone*. I did this because I felt that the experience that I and my family had just gone through had been shattering, and somehow writing about it helped make it bearable. Our lives had overnight exploded in a way that we could never have imagined, and for a long nightmare season, our history, our sins, and our shame had been part of a pageant that was headed inexorably toward a public death. There was no way to withstand that without also trying to purge it, and I think that being able to write about Gary's death helped save an immediate part of my sanity. But the deed wasn't without its cost. I had, of course, blown my cover. People now knew I was Gary's brother, and many of them had comments to offer and questions to ask.

Somewhere during this time, I decided I was tired of the day-to-day costs of my family and its infamy, and so I fled my hometown of Portland, Oregon, and moved to Los Angeles, where I had a job waiting at *Rolling Stone*. Meantime, Frank stayed with our mother, Bessie, in her run-down trailer in Oak Grove, Oregon.

Life in Los Angeles was not easy at first. I drank a pint of whiskey every night, and I took Dalmane, a sleeping medication that interfered with my ability to dream—or at least made it hard for me to remember my dreams. And there were other lapses. I was still living with Andrea but seeing a couple of other women when I could. Plus, for a long season or two, my writing went to hell. I had trouble figuring out what to say and how to say it. I could no longer tell if the things I was writing about were *worth* writing about. I wasn't sure any longer how you made words add up to anything. The editors at *Rolling Stone* were kind enough to keep me on staff and be patient with me. I guess they understood I was shell-shocked, and it would probably take me some time to come around.

Instead of writing, I preferred reading hard-boiled crime fiction—particularly the novels of Ross Macdonald, in which the author tried to solve murders by explicating labyrinthine family histories. I also spent many nights lost in the dark glory of punk rock. I liked the way the music tried to make its listeners accommodate the reality of a merciless world. One of the best punk songs of the period was by a British band, the Adverts. It was called "Gary Gilmore's Eyes." What would it be like, the song asked, to see the world through Gary Gilmore's dead eyes? Would you see through the eyes of somebody who wanted to kill the world, and then kill himself?

All around me I had Gary's notoriety to contend with. For my first few months in L.A.—and throughout the years that would follow—people asked me often about my brother. I met men who wanted to know what Gary was like—men who admired what they saw as his bravado, his hardness. I met women who wanted to sleep with me because I had been close to him. I avoided these people. I would live with being Gary's brother, but I would not live with being one of his fans or supporters.

I also met women who, when they learned who my brother was, would never see me again, never take my calls again. And I got letters from strangers who thought I had no right holding the job I was holding—writing for the attention of young people—since I had been related to a man who had murdered. I also got letters from people who thought I should have been shot alongside my brother.

There was never a season without some reminder of what had happened. In 1979, Norman Mailer's *The Executioner's Song* was published. By this time, Andrea and I had separated and I was seeing another woman—somebody I liked very much. As she read Mailer's book, I could see her begin to wonder about who she was sleeping with, and about what had come into her life. One night a couple of months after the book had been published, we were watching *Saturday Night Live*. Eric Idle was the guest host, and he was doing a routine of flash impersonations. At one point, he tied a bandanna around his eyes and gleefully announced who he was impersonating: "Gary Gilmore!" I was sitting with this woman and a couple of friends, watching the *Saturday Night* episode. After the episode played out, I went and poured a glass of whiskey. Later that night, my girlfriend and I had a difficult talk. She announced that she was leaving me, and within a week she was gone. To be fair to her, she would later insist that her leaving had nothing to do with Gary, that it had to do with me. I'm sure she's right—we had been having trouble for some time, and we both had made many mistakes. But at the time, it felt as though everything that went wrong had to do with who I was—a man who carried the mark of his family.

It was a crushing moment in a long, bad stretch—a period in which almost every few days somebody would ask me: "You were Gary Gilmore's younger brother, weren't you? What did it feel like, having him die like that?"

I was never really sure how to answer that question. I think I wanted to say: I'm no longer sure what it feels like. The emotions of the event, like the details and history of it, were something I could no longer claim as my own. You watch what was once a private and troubling relation of your life become the subject of public sensation and media scrutiny; you watch your brother's life—and therefore, in some way, a part of your own life—become larger than the confines of your sway, and after a while, it doesn't seem much like your life anymore. It doesn't seem like something you should feel too much about, because feeling won't erase the pain or shame or bad memories or unresolved love and hate.

But I hated it every time the questions were asked. I tried for years to be polite or thick-skinned about it. I took comment after comment from people who betrayed their own intelligence and grace with the remarks and jokes they made, and each time, something inside me flinched. I felt that nobody would ever forget or forgive me just for being that dead fucking killer's brother. I learned a bit of what it's like to live on in the aftermath of the punishment: as a living relative, you have to take on some of the burden and legacy of the punishment. People can no longer insult or hurt Gary Gilmore, but because you are his brother—even if you're not much like him—they can aim it at you. It's as if anybody who has emerged from a family that yielded a murderer must also be formed by the same causes, the same evil, must in some way also be responsible for the violence that resulted, must also bear the mark of a frightening and shameful heritage. It's as if there is guilt in the simple fact of the bloodline itself.

I came to realize that Gary meant something different to many people than he meant to me—maybe he even meant more to some. Maybe he was a sign of power, or heroism, or disgust, or an exemplar of fame, or even somebody to be pitied or turned into a cause. Whatever he was, he was something they got to through me, but I knew enough to know that I wasn't what they wanted. I wasn't famous, and I wasn't the criminal. I was a stand-in or substitute target for their reprehension or their fascination, sometimes both at the same time, since many people affect scorn for the killers they secretly admire or envy.

There were days, during this time, that I wanted to kill the world. I suppose that in those moments I was finally like my brother in all respects except one: He was destroyed enough to pull the trigger, and I was not.

AGAIN, I WAS MORE OR LESS LEAVING THE CURRENT-DAY REALITY of my family behind me. I would visit my mother up in Oak Grove, Oregon, a couple of times a year, but it was always disturbing. She had taken to talking incessantly about the past—about her childhood in Utah, about Gary's execution—and her health was in wretched shape. After Gary's death, she refused to leave her trailer, and my brother Frank and I could not convince her to see a doctor. She lived a reclusive existence, in a virtually crippled state, in a dark, closed-up, and dirty cubicle. When I visited there, I felt hemmed in. It was a hard place to breathe; we had the company of bad memories all around us in that space, and the promise of more to come.

There were people, I know, who tried to reach her. Some members of the Mormon church came by to offer their sympathy and help, but she refused them. She would sit in her chair in the trailer, with all the windows and doors shut, and yell at her visitors: "What did *you* do to try to save him? Don't come around now telling me you're sorry, or that you know how I feel. You do *not* know how I feel."

Other times, when people knocked, she would sit there, not moving, not answering. This was something she had done for many years, even during our life on Oatfield. "If you don't open the door to bad news," I remember her saying, "then bad news can't touch you." My mother wasn't about to open the door to anybody anymore, other than her remaining sons.

She had good-enough reason. It was not that hard to figure out where she lived, and sometimes, late at night, about the hours the bars were letting out, she would be sitting in her chair in the kitchen, in the dark, and she would hear a car pull up outside. She would hear voices, whispers, laughs, profanities, threats. Some people yelled horrible things, some people threw bottles or cans at the trailer. She sat there in the dark, not moving, knowing full well that the world outside her walls was a world of no forgiveness.

"Bessie suffered untold things the heart cannot bear," one of her friends remarked later. "That was why she withdrew behind those walls."

I know that in my mother's last few years, my absence hurt her much. I know because Grace McGinnis—who had resumed a telephone relationship with my mother by this time—told me so. I know because, on one of the interview tapes that Larry Schiller and Norman Mailer loaned me, my mother told Mailer: "I miss Mikal. I wish he'd move back up here. He hardly ever calls now, and when he does, he seems so distant, so damn polite. He treats me like something he's afraid to touch."

She was right. I ran away. I couldn't help her, and I couldn't stand watching her die. I wanted to be as far from family as I could.

If I had her now, I would call or see her every day. I would ask her things. I would tell her how much I love her, for what she endured and for trying to save me.

But I don't have her—I have only old photos and her voice on some tapes. I will never talk to her or see her again.

In December 1980, John Lennon, the former leader of the Beatles, was shot to death as he was entering his apartment building in New York City. When I heard the news, I went and visited with a friend of mine, Jim Henke, who was also my editor at *Rolling Stone*. We watched the news coverage, and we talked late into the after-midnight hours. It was hard to comprehend. Lennon's murder seemed such a terrible payoff for a man who had helped form such a wonderful legacy, and who had enriched our lives beyond measure. It was as if a part of our past had been transformed and ruined, finished in bloodshed. Maybe I should have been accustomed to such endings, but I wasn't. When I looked at Lennon's murder, I thought about the horrible murders that Gary had committed, and the terrible, mysterious way that Gaylen had been killed. Murder was a way of ending somebody's—*any*body's—life story. It could come from anywhere, anytime. And it would not only end a life, but could also undermine every good memory or achievement that life had accomplished. I was tired of the ruin that came from killing, but that made no difference. Individual murders could be solved or punished, but murder itself, of course, could never be solved. That could not be done without solving the human heart, and without solving the history that has rendered that heart so dark and desolate.

The day after Lennon was shot, my mother called me at my home in Los Angeles. "I wanted to see how you were doing," she said. "I know you loved this man very much. I know you must be hurting."

She was a remarkable person. I knew it even in the moments when I wanted to be as far away from her as possible. My mother knew what loss was, she knew what it meant. It had destroyed her, but not so much that she couldn't do something like this—calling her son after a hero of his had died, and letting him know she still cared for him and his hurt. On the phone with my mother that day, I was able to do something I wasn't able to do with anyone else: I cried over John Lennon's murder, and the way it had ravaged a certain treasured part of my past.

At the end of our conversation, my mother made an offer. Actually, it was probably more of a plea. "Why don't you come home for Christmas?" she asked. "It's been so long since I've seen you. Sometimes it seems we're hardly a family anymore. Ever since Gary died, it's like it's hard for the three of us to be in the same room together. But there won't be many more Christmases that I get to see any of my sons. Won't you come home this year?"

I went home. I spent that Christmas with my mother and brother. In many ways it was a good visit, in many ways a disheartening one. By now, my mother's health was the worst I'd ever seen it. She sat in her chair at the kitchen table, dressed in her age-old bathrobe. She stayed there the whole time, like a frightened animal that adopts a spot as its safety zone and will not venture from it.

At one point, Frank went out for a long walk, and that was the time my mother told me some of the horrible stories that I would never forget—such as the story about her father forcing her to watch a hanging that had never happened. "You were wise to go away," she told me that day. "I miss you terribly, but you were wise. There is some curse that has devoured us one by one, and before long it will take me too. But living so far away, maybe it will never find you. I want you to be the one of us who is forever safe. I don't want anything ever to get you."

Then she laughed. "Oh, but there I go, prattling like an old woman. You must think I'm awfully silly."

A moment later, she was studying the dark dirt of her floor, as if she were looking for secrets under all its blackened levels. "God, I miss Gary," she said. "*Why* did he want to die? Why did he kill those two boys, and then want to die? I don't think I'll ever understand it." And then she covered her face with her hands, and her sobs filled the darkened space of her trailer.

That was the last time I saw her alive.

YEARS LATER, FRANK TOLD ME ABOUT THE END. He told me about other things as well. He told me about what it had been like to live with my mother in the years after Gary's death.

"She was hurting, obviously," Frank said, "but the combination of all the physical and emotional pain sometimes pushed her toward the irrational. She would sit around and say stuff like, 'Is there anything in the world besides hurt?' She would say that a lot. She became convinced that somehow the renewal of the death penalty had been designed to get Gary—or to get *her* by getting Gary. Sometimes she would go completely off her rocker, screaming: 'Gary's the only one they've killed, the only one who will ever be killed—they'll never kill another person in this country. Those goddamn Mormons did it because they hated me. Those are the people who shot your brother's heart right on the ground.' It would become so bad and so relentless, finally I would get up and leave.

"Part of what made her difficult during this time was her diet. She had to be careful about what she ate, but of course she wasn't. Chocolate became her basic diet, and with her stomach in that terrible shape, you can imagine how healthy that was. One of the few things she would eat was a special kind of bread. I remember one time I went to the store and they didn't have it and she just went hysterical. Accused me of not bringing it home on purpose. The argument between us got so bad, I'm sure the neighbors must have heard it.

"I didn't want to be mean, but she was impossible. She wouldn't do commonsense things, and she wouldn't take anybody's advice. And sometimes I'd forget myself, and I'd get loud—the way you get when you're frustrated. I'd say, 'Man, you've got to start eating better. If you don't, I'm getting a nurse and bringing the nurse here.' Then she just went *completely* hysterical and said, 'You boys, you boys—you want to put me in a rest home.' And then I'd say, 'Oh, come on—please, just calm down. The last thing Mikal or I will ever do is put you in a rest home. We'll *never* put you in a rest home.'

"Mom had this thing in her mind that when I grew up, all I would ever do is care for her—that I would never think of having my own life. But I couldn't stay there all the time. I'd leave—sometimes a week at a time, but usually only a weekend. She considered this a betrayal. I was still, at my age—almost forty—staying there most of the time. That's far more than most sons ever did. But because I couldn't handle it all the time, and I'd get away for a few days, she considered this a betrayal, like I was a Judas. When I'd return after some time away, she'd say: 'You're just like your father.'

"This was the thing I was living under. If I tried to help her I was accused, all the time, of trying to put her in a rest home, and that was not something I was going to do. But I couldn't get that through to her. It was just like getting her to take the right medicine or eat a solid meal—impossible. It was a bigger job than I could handle. I shouldn't have even tried to help because I wasn't qualified. But what else could I do? I tried many times to get her to see doctors or a counselor, but her response was always the same. She would grow frantic. She'd throw things. She'd cry. She did not want to leave her home for anything, and even though I hate to say it, I don't think she really wanted to get better. I think I always had in the back of my mind that someday Mom was just going to get up and change. That was a big weakness I had. I always thought she was going through a phase. But as the years kept rolling by, I began to see it wasn't all that different than things had been with Gary. We always thought, 'Well, the next time he gets out, he'll be different. He'll change.' I felt that way about Mom too. Someday, we're going to get up and magically she's going to change and be the real mother that she should be. When we lost her, I realized that was never going to happen in this world. That was one of the things that hit me real hard.

"I should have done what you did. I should have gone away. Maybe then she would have learned things. She would have learned that she didn't have to be dependent on other people. She could have survived in her own world, in her own life, made her own friends, learned to turn the TV on. She would have learned to overcome some of her other fears. In many ways, it was her fears that just took her right down—so many ridiculous fears that just totally monopolized her health. You could not erase them, no matter how hard you tried or reasoned. She was afraid of everything. Of filth *and* cleanliness. Of water and dirt. Of medicine and illness.

"In the end, she wouldn't accept any help, and the pressure was just too damn much for me. She used to say to me: 'Why am *I* so sick? Why is this happening to *me*?' I felt like saying: 'You're sick because you won't be healthy. You're sick because you want to die.' But I couldn't let go of that last bit of hope, and as angry as I got with her at times, I couldn't bring myself to be that mean to her."

One day it suddenly became apparent to Frank that things had reached a crisis point. For several days, Bessie had been sick. She would lie on her bed for hours, then get up and make her way to her chair in the kitchen. She complained of being exhausted all the time, and she wouldn't eat anything Frank put in front of her. After a couple of days, Frank said: "Mom, I'm getting an ambulance here." She became horribly upset at the suggestion.

"I'd been patient for a long time," Frank said. "Probably too long. It was agonizing to see what she was going through. Finally, after two or three days of her not eating anything, I decided, 'That's it.'"

Frank called the ambulance and Bessie was taken to a hospital in Milwaukie, screaming that her son was trying to kill her. At the hospital, the doctors told her that her son had done the right thing and she should have come sooner. But she wasn't having it. She took almost every dish the nurses brought her and threw it against the wall.

Frank went to see her two or three times every day. He saw the color coming back into her face, saw her becoming more cogent. After two days, the doctors said she was going to be okay.

"I was feeling so good," Frank told me, "I walked all the way back home from the hospital. I got back and I was fixing dinner, and all of a sudden people started banging on the doors. Said, 'They had to put your mother on this machine.' They drove me over there, and when I get there, the doctors had her on a machine that's breathing for her. I'd been there just a short time before and she was talking and looking better. I got upset and I talked to a doctor. He said, 'Well, we put something in there to kill the infection that she has.' She'd gotten some kind of infection from not keeping herself clean for so long. But her body rejected the antibiotic.

"She died on the thirtieth of June 1981, sometime in the afternoon. I remember it was a warm day and there was an eclipse going on. She had always been terrified of eclipses. She used to always say she would die during one. It turned out she did."

———

I DID NOT KNOW THAT MY MOTHER WAS IN THE HOSPITAL. She hadn't written my Los Angeles phone number anywhere that Frank could find. She had been dead for two days when word finally got to me. I had been through several family deaths before, but this was the first time that the news crumpled me up into a weeping wreck.

I went home and helped my brother bury her. He was forty years old, and he seemed lost without her.

The night of her funeral, Frank and I stayed at a friend's house. The next day, I had to fly back to Los Angeles. I told Frank I wanted him to come to California soon and stay with me for a while. We shook hands outside my friend's house, and I watched my brother turn and walk down the road where we had once lived for so many years—a road we had all walked down countless times before.

I wrote Frank as soon as I got back to L.A. Within a few days, the letter came back. It was marked: NO LONGER AT THIS ADDRESS—NO FORWARDING ADDRESS. I tried to find him for a long time, but I couldn't. It was as if, on the morning that we said good-bye to each other on that haunted stretch of Oatfield Road, he just walked into the void with all the other ghosts.

CHAPTER 2
NEW FAMILIES,
OLD GHOSTS

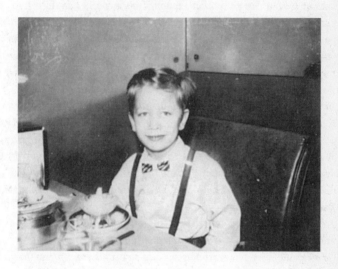

ANOTHER DREAM:

I am living in a single-room apartment in Portland, when one day my father shows up at the door. He tells me that he has recently located my mother, whom we both have lost track of for some time. Apparently she is living somewhere in Seattle, and my father thinks we should go visit her.

We get into his car—an old Pontiac station wagon—and set out for Seattle. My father should know this drive well—he has made it literally hundreds of times—and yet for some reason, every exit he takes turns out to be the wrong one, confusing him and making him increasingly angry. What's worse, all the exits appear the same: They are big, careening loops that encircle vast marshes. After a few wrong turns, after no longer being able to find what should come easily and familiarly for him, my father takes to driving off the loops and onto the marshes, digging his wheels into their softness and turning their turf into muddy tracks. A state policeman sees him doing this and pulls us over. My father explains that somebody has hidden his exit from him, and that he can no longer find what was once as common as home to him. The policeman seems to like my father—he doesn't arrest or ticket him, doesn't even lecture him—and he guides us the rest of the way into Seattle.

When we arrive there, it is early evening, and my father takes me to a small apartment that he has rented for me. It looks just like the desolate firetraps we used to live in when I was a child. The major difference is, this place comes with a live-in woman, whom I am expected to sleep with. My father leaves, saying he will see me later. The woman fixes us some drinks and we begin to make love, when we are interrupted by the arrival of two other women: friends of hers, bearing sleeping bags. They have arrived to spend a few days with her. We all talk for a while, and then they lay out their bags on the floor, at the foot of her bed, and we all go to sleep.

I awaken in the middle of the night, unable to sleep. I get up and fix myself a drink, and then I see the blond woman in the bag at the foot of the bed sitting up, watching me. She also is unable to sleep and invites me to join her on the floor. We begin to kiss. I start to move down on her. "Ah, we don't want to be tacky, do we?" she says, then presses my face between her legs, holding it tight and hard against her, until I can taste her need and my own.

After we have finished, I get back in bed with the woman who is my "girlfriend" and fall asleep with my arm around her.

The next day, my father shows up and says it is time for us to go see my mother. Next thing I know, it is night, and my father and I are seated in a restaurant, sharing drinks with two women; I am with my live-in partner, and my father is with the blond woman I'd gone down on the night before. Everybody is getting along well and having a good time, and there seems implicit in all this the promise of unlimited and uncensored pleasures still to be had.

My father gets up, a little drunk and happy, and says he is going to find my mother. He comes back a little while later and indicates I should follow him. Suddenly, everything feels solemn, as if we are on our way to something ritualistic and unpleasant—like a funeral or execution. To find her, we have to wind our way through the rest of the restaurant, which is like a maze, taking us through rooms and rooms of drunk people. Finally, we round a corner and see my mother sitting at a table, dressed nicely. At a nearby table there is a younger woman, cute and sexy, and she beckons my

*father. He goes over and sits by her. He puts his arm around her and says,
"Here she is, here's your mother."*

*We both know he is wrong, but now that he has found my mother, he is
obviously embarrassed by her and doesn't want to jeopardize his chances with
this younger woman. I turn to my mother. She smiles at me politely, timidly,
an almost fragile smile. She looks old and frail, as if she would crumble if I
put my arm around her, but she also looks happy and grateful that I have
found her. In her eyes I see unimaginable sadness and fear, as if she is afraid
of what I might say, or how I too might reject her. I put my arm around her,
even though I know she'll crumble, and then the dream ends.*

WITH MY MOTHER DEAD AND FRANK DISAPPEARED, I felt like I no
longer had a family. Blues singers will tell you about what an awful condition it can be to end up as a motherless child in this world—how devastating it can feel to be cut off from not just the love and solace that a mother
can give, but also the wellsprings of your own history. To lose your
mother, the singer says, is to lose your anchor in this world. Everything
that made and protected you is now gone. You are adrift, and even if you
find your place, you will have forever lost your most vital link to your
ancestry. You will have lost something sacred.

I always liked those songs, but I don't think that's how I felt. Yes, I
mourned my mother. I felt heartbroken and outraged for the pains she had
suffered in her life, and it is true that in experiencing the knowledge of her
death, I felt a sense of loss and severance—a feeling of absolutely piercing
and inconsolable pain—that I did not feel with any of the other deaths in
my family. In the seasons to come, I would miss talking to her and I'd miss
the hope that someday I might be able to bring her good news that could
help make up for all the decades of bad news that she had endured. In
addition, I had now lost track of Frank, and I worried what might become
of him, with his shyness and depression, in such an unkind land.

But the truth is, I did not feel lost in the world when I lost my family.
If anything, I felt a relief: I was no longer tied to the wreckage that had
been my family's spirit, and whatever undoing might come in my life, at
least now it would be my own. I would no longer have to sit around and
dread the next kindred disaster.

A FEW MONTHS AFTER MY MOTHER'S DEATH, I met a young woman
with eyes that I thought needed loving. Her name was Erin.

Like me, Erin had come from a family with a history of death and other troubles, and we each believed we might be able to help make up for some of the losses in the other person's life. We fell in love, and in August 1982 we were married in Tucson, Arizona.

Around this same time, I learned that Larry Schiller was finishing a four-hour TV-film adaptation of *The Executioner's Song*, for broadcast in November 1982. Schiller and I had not been on good terms in a long time. In 1977, right before Gary's execution, I left Utah without talking to Schiller again or taking his calls. I had come to feel that his involvement in the whole affair had helped turn Gary's execution into a media commodity and an invasive reality in my family's life.

Later, after I'd moved to L.A., Schiller called me to say that he had convinced Norman Mailer to write a book about Gary's life and death, and he asked me to contribute an interview to the work in progress. I declined. I respected Mailer, but I had too many doubts about Schiller's credibility to participate in such a project. Also, I simply did not want to keep retelling and reliving the tragedy of my family.

When *The Executioner's Song* was published in 1979, I realized that Schiller—who had conducted most of the interviews for Mailer's book—had served his material more scrupulously than I might have imagined. Mailer did not attempt to make myth or discourse of Gary's story, but instead seemed interested in the truths revealed through the unfolding of surface details: the interplay of characters and incidents that propelled the event with such fateful force. Just the same, I still felt that Schiller's stance as a recorder of history might amount to a kind of moral ruse designed to let the record keeper off the hook.

Once, after the book's publication, Mailer asked me why I had refused to be involved with *The Executioner's Song*, and I said, "Because of Larry Schiller." Mailer thought for a moment and replied: "I know what you mean. You know, Larry and I have had our disagreements over the years. But I have to say, I think there was something about this experience that deepened Larry."

Now, Schiller had made a film of this story, and I knew that I would once more have to witness the re-creation of painful parts of my family's past. In addition, I knew that filmic accounts often seem to have an authority which written accounts do not; because films have real faces and real voices, people often believe that they are telling real stories. But I knew too well that the truth of what had happened in Gary's life could not easily be conveyed in a television drama, and I wanted to say so. This time, I decided, I should not hide. The editors at *Rolling Stone* agreed, and gave me an assignment to cover the film of Gary's life.

Soon enough, Schiller learned about this assignment and called to invite me to see the film, and to offer his cooperation. It seemed a surprisingly gracious (not to mention shrewd) offer, considering that I had turned down his numerous requests for me to participate in Mailer's efforts.

A few days later I saw the film and found it in many ways unsparingly true to its subject. It presented, with little embroidery and no sentimentality, a fast-moving narrative account of Gary's life in Provo, Utah, and it showed the mounting of his rage and the venting of it in two senseless murders. And it showed his subsequent, relentless pursuit of his own negation, culminating in execution. But I felt the film also missed plenty: It missed Gary, and in doing so, it missed its one opportunity at re-creating or salvaging a soul. There simply wasn't much in the manner of actor Tommy Lee Jones that suggested Gary as he really was, nor was there much that showed the real reach of Gary's deadliness or the range of his intelligence. Perhaps most problematically, there was also little attempt to animate the promptings behind Gary's pursuit of his own death, and without an understanding of that, I felt, the other details and actions of his story fell flat.

On a summer evening a week or so after seeing the film, I sat in Schiller's backyard with him and shared my reactions to his movie. "Well," he replied, "you're right. This Gary is certainly not the Gary I met or the Gary that you knew as a blood relative . . . But I also think this Gary takes you to the same end result as the real one."

Schiller regarded me quietly for a moment and then said: "Now I want to ask you a question. Why have you waited until now to have anything to do with this story? Why didn't you give me an interview for Norman's book when I asked you for one?"

Because, I told him, more than anything else I simply wanted to retain my own voice about matters concerning Gary. I didn't want to give somebody an interview and then later feel I had forfeited control over my own words.

Schiller nodded. "Retaining your own voice. I think I might have understood had you explained it to me the way you did just now. You see, I looked upon you as a crucial spoke in the wheel of this story that I could never get."

Also, I went on, it seemed clear to me in Utah that the most important part of Gary's worth as news item or literary property was the event—in effect, the staging—of his death. That it seemed clear that Gary was prob-ably worth more to Schiller . . .

Schiller finished the thought for me ". . . dead than alive. Which, in fact, he wasn't."

"You don't think so?"

"Nah. Gary Gilmore wasn't worth anything dead. His story would have had more social significance if he had just disappeared back on death row again."

"In what way?"

"Because then, truly, we would have seen how the public can give an event its importance, but how they can do away with that importance, too. I wish my film had that ending."

"But didn't you ever ask yourself whether your involvement was go-ing to help determine the execution?"

"I don't think our actions actually determined Gary's death," Schiller replied, "but I think they determined the entire size of his death. If the media, myself included, had decided to move out of town two weeks before the execution, Gary's death would not have been as important as our coverage made it seem.

"You see, regardless of what you may think, I did not want to see Gary executed. I certainly had deep feelings about the value of a life, but I also understood that Gary had the right—the *inalienable* right—to choose his own destiny. I wasn't necessarily convinced he was bringing harm to anybody else by choosing to die that way."

It was late on a hot summer night. The only noise around us was the rustle of trees as the night air shifted and began to slough off some of its heat. I found that I was sitting across a table from a man for whom I once felt the strongest dislike, and I discovered, to my surprise, that I could no longer summon up that rancor.

TOWARD THE END OF MY DISCUSSIONS with Larry Schiller, I asked him about getting in touch with Nicole Barrett Baker, the girlfriend whom Gary had left behind. I had, in fact, never met or spoken with Nicole. When I visited Gary in Utah the week before his execution, she was still hospitalized following a joint suicide attempt with Gary. I tried to find some way to establish communication with her—in part, because Gary had asked me to, and also because the pain and confusion of the moment seemed to suggest reaching out to someone—but I could find no way around the strict confinement of her hospital. The closest I came to getting any message to her was by calling a Salt Lake radio station and asking them to play a song for her at Gary's request. It was Gary's favorite old rhythm & blues song, Fats Domino's "Valley of Tears."

In the years that followed, there wasn't a month that passed that I didn't think of making some belated contact — in part, because something about the events surrounding Gary's death had always seemed unresolved to me. But the only way I knew to find her was through Larry Schiller and, by my own choice, I had shut off that course. Also, I probably wasn't ready. Meeting Nicole would be something like confronting a living reminder of Gary's losses, and there were times when that would have been too much.

Now, though, with the address that Schiller had furnished me, I sat down and wrote Nicole a letter, telling her about what I was doing and asking her if she would be willing to meet and talk. A few weeks later, I flew up to the small town where she was living in Oregon. The Nicole who met me at the airport seemed every bit as lovely as the Nicole played by Rosanna Arquette in the film, though also a good deal shyer and more self-possessed. Apparently, the last couple of years had worked some well-deserved kindly changes: Nicole was now a happily married, born-again Christian and the mother of a new baby boy. We greeted each other with a little uncertainty and headed out to an all-night restaurant for dinner.

We talked for hours, but it took us a while to get around to Gary. She told me about her marriage and her Christianity; I told her about my marriage, and why I loved rock & roll so much. We talked a lot for the next few days, and in time we could talk about Gary and what had happened. The funny thing was, it took us a while to sort through all our own, real memories and the written and filmed accounts of what had happened in our lives. Somewhere in the midst of all the interpretations of real life, we realized, it was far too easy to lose part of the elements of our real selves.

During the last night I saw Nicole, we went for a long drive in the Oregon coastal woods. We talked about our memories of the time around Gary's execution. I told her about my last visits with Gary — how, despite all the distance and difficulty between us, we found a way to say good-bye with a bit of hard-earned mutual regard.

"You know," said Nicole, "I never got to say good-bye to Gary." She fell quiet for a few moments and stared into the dark as we sped down the highway. "One night," she continued, "when I was staying at a house Larry had rented for me in Malibu after the execution, I had this dream about Gary. He came up to the house on this big motorcycle. He didn't say much, but I knew he wanted me to go with him. I climbed on behind him and just held on tight, and we rode a long, long way. Finally, we came to a strip of land that stuck out into the sea. Out at the end of it stood this prison—but not the kind with guards or gates. More like a place where people go before leaving for somewhere else.

"On the inside, there were walls of white stone. Gary got off the motorcycle and said 'Good-bye.' I said, 'I can't go with you?' And he said, 'No, you don't understand. You won't be seeing me again.' I started to cry then, just as hard as I had ever cried in real life. Then I looked around and saw another woman sitting close by, crying. It was your mother. I went over and held her close, and we cried together."

We were both quiet for a long time, and then I asked Nicole: "Do you find yourself still thinking about him much?"

She looked at me a moment, smiled, and looked back out the window. "Oh," she said, "the way the sun will set at night—sometimes that will remind me of Gary." I thought about her words for a moment and realized what she was saying: Always.

Outside, the hill ranges of the small coastal town glided by, black silhouettes against the starlit sky. I came to understand that meeting Nicole had been a powerful experience, and a nice one. It reminded me that in real life, the truths of our hearts and memories never finish running their risks. Also, it felt a little like being part of a family—and that was something I hadn't felt for a long while.

A few minutes later, Nicole dropped me back at my motel. "I hate good-byes," she said, flashing a timid smile.

"I'm not good at them myself," I replied.

I gave her a kiss, then watched her back her car out, turn and wave, and drive away. She went back to her life, and I went back to mine. It was all we could do.

MAYBE THAT SEEMS LIKE WHERE THIS STORY SHOULD END. Maybe it feels like a closure of sorts. Maybe it even carries a hint of redemption about it. At least, that's the way it felt back in the autumn of 1982, when I wrote about meeting Nicole at the end of my article about *The Executioner's Song* for *Rolling Stone*. I thought: Here is what I have to learn—what we all have had to learn: Our lives go on. We have to imbibe the pain, face the memories, and forgive what we can. All in all, not the worst truth to learn.

But the problem is, our lives *do* go on, and life has no real closure, except death. It is death that tells us that a story's ended—that it is now time to evaluate the life that is finished, to reckon its plot and its drama, and to tell its stories. Gary and all those others who had joined the dead—the members of my family, the men Gary murdered—they were the only ones in this story who had any claims to closure, the only ones who had completed their parts, who had finished paying for or escaping the legacy. The rest of us were still living the lives that had to go beyond final pages, lives in which the bequests of the dead have never ended.

MY LIFE DID NOT ALWAYS GO IN GOOD PLACES, though on one level it probably seemed to. My career as a music journalist was a fairly fortunate one. I left *Rolling Stone* in 1980 for a few years, though I continued to write for the magazine. I went on to become the music editor at *L.A. Weekly* for a while, and then worked for five years as the pop music critic at the now-defunct, much-missed Los Angeles *Herald Examiner.* I did some of my favorite work as a writer during this period—I felt, for the first time in years, that I had found a critical voice that I was confident with. I also had the chance to meet and interview some of the people whose music had affected me most deeply over the years, including Bob Dylan, Miles Davis, Mick Jagger, Keith Richards, Johnny Rotten, Bruce Springsteen, and my favorite music hero of all, Lou Reed.

I do not mention this information to boast, though I am proud of much of the music journalism I have done, and grateful to the various editors who gave me the opportunity to grow as a writer. I mention my work because, although I had a true and constant passion for rock & roll and other forms of popular music and culture, my work was not really where I lived the most important part of my life, nor for that matter did it always give me a sense that my life had amounted to much. When the day's writing was done, I still had to go home and face the real life I was living. My marriage had been in trouble more or less from the start. I think we both had brought too many family demons to live together in one house, and to be honest, I wasn't understanding or supportive enough of the fears and damage that had driven my wife into her troubled space. The union was probably fated the moment I realized that I hadn't so much loved my wife as I'd tried to save her, maybe as a way of atoning of how I had *not* tried to save my brother. That didn't make for a well-balanced marriage, and when, at the end of one of our particularly painful arguments, Erin said to me, "You don't *need* me the way I need you," I saw that she was right, and I understood how unfair I had been. We separated a little over two years after we were married, and were divorced in 1985. We remained good if troubled friends afterward, and once or twice over the years we tried to find ways back to each other, but I'm afraid too much damage had been done by that time. She remains somebody I love, and somebody I still hope the best for.

After that, it was pretty much one feverish relationship after another. I was getting older, and I desperately wanted to find somebody I could build a family and home with. And then, for far too long, I simply stopped wanting *any* home or family, because it hurt too much, felt too much like irredeemable failure, to want those things and yet feel I would never have them or might damage them once I did. Then, perhaps not surprisingly, I fell into a bout of clinical depression. I would be sitting doing my work, or listening to music, or reading a book, when sudden fear would grip me. I would go and lie on my bed and curl up for hours at a time, waiting for the darkness to pass, waiting for a chance to breathe normally. I found myself doing the same thing I had done as a child during those hours of my odd spells of illness: I'd grip my hands tight, concentrating on my palms. It felt as if at the center of them there was some relief or answer to be found, if I could just press them hard enough.

I knew enough about depression to know that it could get worse, or possibly turn fatal. I went into therapy with a good doctor, and in time the fear and other symptoms began to lift. Life began to regain some of its fundamental pleasures and purposes. The entire bout probably only lasted a few months but it felt like an eternity. Depression is a hard experience to communicate, and perhaps a hard one to understand, but once you've had it you don't forget it. It makes you look on the rest of the world with a bit more compassion, and it also causes you to watch the corners of your life more closely, so you can spot the darkness rapidly if it begins to creep back in.

DURING THIS TIME, I SIGNED A CONTRACT to write a book about a musical group. I shouldn't have done this—I didn't have enough real feeling for the subject at the time—but I thought I wanted to change some things in my life, and I thought I knew enough about writing and music that I could summon the passion. After nearly a year, I hadn't written anything, and I knew I wasn't going to. Instead, I came up with an idea to do a different book about another music group, the Grateful Dead. It was a good idea. The Dead is a fascinating group with a remarkable history, and by telling the band's story, one could examine an important period in modern American culture. Maybe I would actually have risen to the task this time, but I made a near-fatal mistake: I fell in love.

This is not a proud story that I am about to relate. It involved the betrayal of one or two people who loved and trusted me, and it involved embarrassing ruin. I met a woman—whom I'll call Roxanne—during a vacation to Portland, while I was researching the Grateful Dead project. Actually, I'd known her casually for years. She was the younger sister of an old girlfriend. At the time, she was recently divorced and the mother of a four-year-old boy. She was looking for a change in her life, and of course I was too. It was an affair like many others. At first it was a secret, and as a result the passion that we brought to our meetings and couplings took on a special intensity—the sort of passion that makes love feel imperative. But there was more to it than that. I had told Roxanne a bit about my dream of having my own family, and she told me that she hoped someday to have more children. We talked about whether we could someday merge our dreams, and it seemed that maybe we could.

I moved up to Portland for a while to do some of the writing of my book, and also to see what might come of this love affair. I went there with the conviction that I'd finally won a real shot at happiness—that I could now build a family of my own. I even told myself that I was redeeming not only my own history, but perhaps my family's as well, by building life back in the place where once so much had ended in death and loss.

Well, it didn't work. Within two days of my arrival in Portland, I could tell something was dreadfully wrong between us. As it turned out, Roxanne had met somebody whom she had a stronger interest in. We fought, we parted, and she went on to marry the other person and have a child with him. These things happen. There was really nobody to blame but myself, and there was nobody to forgive but myself. But this time, self-forgiveness did not come easy.

It was not a pretty time. I sat around in my apartment in Portland and wept uncontrollably. I drank myself to sleep most nights, and I couldn't concentrate on the work I had to do. Finally I gave up on the book.

I probably came as close to self-destruction as I have ever come, or at least as close as I knew how to come. And when I understood I didn't have whatever it took to finish it all, or didn't even have the ability to fall apart entirely, the realization didn't make me feel any better. It made me feel like there was simply no relief, no deliverance for what my life had become, and that I would have to live with that awareness whether I wanted to or not.

———

THAT WAS WHEN I SAW THE GHOST.

It was late at night, about 3 A.M. I had fallen asleep drunk, but it was fitful sleep. I was living in a loft apartment near downtown, and lights from the street bounced off the walls throughout the night, making for a steady sense of motion in the place. I opened my eyes and saw something moving. Lights, I thought, and closed my eyes. Then I heard a floorboard creak. I opened my eyes, and across the room from me I saw a woman. She was lambent—she had an amber glow about her—and I could see that she was tall and blond, dressed in white. She walked back and forth at the foot of my bed, talking, saying things in a lulling, attractive voice. She moved onto the bed and straddled me, riding up to my chest. She gripped me by the wrists and twisted the upper part of my body, until she had forced my hands and arms against the wall in a painful arrangement. She bent over and kissed my ear, and said: "I know you. You're the last one. I've taken everything from all of them, and now I've come for you."

I woke up, my wrists pressed against the wall, hard enough to hurt. I looked around in the neon-lit dark. There was nobody there. I got up and made my way through the apartment. I was alone.

Had I seen a real ghost? No, of course not. It was likely the sort of dream that some doctors call a night terror: a dream that occurs in a certain state of sleep consciousness and has a sense of physical reality and threat about it. Such dreams are common in some cultures, and many people, it is believed, have died in their sleep from them, frightened into heart failure.

No, it wasn't a real ghost. I knew that. But for days after, I couldn't shake the memory of how it had *felt* real—like a messenger that had come from another realm, or from my own subconscious, to remind me how much my loss was part of a chain that connected me to a history beyond my own isolated pain. That was the night I began to understand that I had never really escaped my family after all, but that instead I'd carried their ruin deep inside me, maybe from the very beginning. Realizing that was enough to drive me from the land where they were all buried, back to my friends and life in Los Angeles.

I HAD BEEN BACK IN LOS ANGELES A FEW MONTHS when a friend, singer Victoria Williams, called to tell me that *A Current Affair*—a nationally syndicated program that takes real-life scandal and repackages it into a news-entertainment format—had announced it would be running a segment that night on my brother. The show's producers had tracked down Nicole Baker and talked her into granting an on-camera interview about Gary and his murders and execution—the first lengthy television interview she had ever granted on the subject.

It came as a bit of a surprise to me that, well over a decade after the fact, Gary's relationship with Nicole and his death would still be fodder for hot news, but maybe it was just a slow day for topical scandal-mongering. I tuned in the program, expecting something tasteless, and what I saw was certainly that—indeed, it was (at least for me) flat-out enraging. But it was also strangely affecting in ways I had not expected. There was news footage of Gary being led to and from court during the many hearings of those last few months, handcuffed and dressed in prison whites, his wary, appraising eyes scanning the cameras that now surrounded and documented him at every possible opportunity. I remembered watching this footage back in the daze and fury of 1976 and thinking he looked exactly how people thought he looked then: cold-blooded, arrogant, deadly. Seeing these images now, so many years and experiences later, I also saw a couple of things I'm not sure I'd seen very accurately back in those days: namely, that Gary looked plain scared, and he also looked like my brother. That is, he looked like somebody I both loved and hated, somebody who had transformed my life in ways that could never be truly repaired. Mostly, he looked like somebody I had missed very much in the years since his death—somebody I wished I could still sit and talk with, no matter how painful the talking might be.

By and large, though, the segment was sordid and mean-spirited. The point, it seemed, was to try to hang much of the blame for Gary's murders on Nicole. Nicole described the last time Gary had hit her. She said that she knew right then that she was leaving. "I had been hit before by men," she said, "and I told myself, 'I'm leaving.' No matter what I did, I did not deserve that. He knew that was how I felt. And when I looked at him, I knew that when I go, he will kill someone. I knew that if I left him, somebody would die for it."

"And yet you left anyway?" the interviewer asked.

Nicole looked off camera for a moment, and I saw that familiar twinge around her eyes, and the start of a broken smile. "One of the greater regrets of my life," she finally answered.

The interviewer's implication couldn't have been plainer: Nicole shared in the blame. Because Gary had lost her, and could not cope with that loss, he killed Max Jensen and Ben Bushnell, rather than turning the murder onto the woman who had left him. And beyond this question and conclusion lay an even more insidious implication: that, somehow, it had been Nicole's obligation to stay with Gary—to continue to absorb his violence so he would never turn that violence outward, against an innocent world. In other words, the interviewer was saying that Nicole was guilty because she had refused to abide the violence of the man in her life.

Just in case that point wasn't plain, at the segment's end the interviewer set up another combination punch. "How could you say you loved somebody so cold-blooded?" he asked.

"There isn't a day goes by," said Nicole, "his name doesn't go through my head. He came into my life, he loved me, and he destroyed all the good that was there."

"If you could erase Gary Gilmore from your life, would you?"

Again, another broken smile, another glance away, and she shook her head.

"And you say that," the interviewer asked, "knowing that if you erased Gary those two men would still be alive, those men's children would still have their fathers . . ."

Finally Nicole closed off the question. "Yeah," she said, nodding. "Yeah, then I would."

After that, the camera cut to host Maury Povich, wearing an expression of smug disgust. "Tough to shed a tear for her," he said.

I think it was the closest I have ever come to smashing my television.

I sat there looking at Povich's face, and I thought: Nicole never asked for your fucking tears. None of us did: not Gary, not her, not me. Yes, if anybody deserves tears, it is the families of Max Jensen and Ben Bushnell; they deserve not just tears but compassion and support and prayer. But they aren't the only ones. While you're at it, I thought, you might try crying for all the people who never really cared to examine how and why these murders happened, and how they might have been prevented. You might try crying for your*self*, you fucking self-righteous prick, because in a way, just like me, you are a part of the context that helps breed murder in our daily world. And, Mr. Povich, if you cannot feel compassion for Nicole—whom you had no compunction about exploiting in order to draw an audience for your show—you might try showing some compassion, or at least some understanding, for those people who had the possibility of murder jammed deep inside their hearts at an early age, because sometimes murder is the only vintage that can come from an annihilated heart.

I admit that not everything I was thinking in these moments was very gracious, much less terribly rational. I was angry and I was hurting, and I was tired of all the world's merciless judgments.

I turned off the TV and the lights in my front room and sat there in the dark for hours, thinking. Only a few months before, I had gone through one of the worst chapters of my life—my brief move to Portland and back—and as I reflected on it now, from a little distance, I realized that what had gone wrong had occurred in large part as a result of my past. It was an echo of a ravage that was already in motion long before I was born and, in effect, formed as much my true bond with Gary as any blood tie we might share: that is, we both had been heirs to a legacy of negation that was beyond our sway, maybe even beyond our understanding. Obviously, we each had different ways of dealing with that legacy: Gary ended up turning the nullification outward—in fact, turned it anywhere he could: on innocents, on Nicole, on his family, on me, on the world and its ideas of justice, finally on himself. I had turned the ruin inward, because I had not been allowed—and would not allow myself—to turn it outward. Outward or inward—either way, it was powerfully destructive, and for the first time in my life I came to see that it was not really finished. My family's ruin did not end with Gary, because it had not started with him.

Sitting there that night, I realized I had grown up in a family that would not continue. There were four sons, and none of us went on to have our own families. We did not go on to spread *any* legacy or dynasty, to extend or fulfill any of our needs, kind or cruel, damaged or conscientious, through children. We didn't even have kids in order to beat or ruin them as we had once been beaten or ruined. And though I may have spent years telling everybody that I wanted a family, in part so I could redeem some of the destruction I'd seen in my own home, the simple truth is, I never had that family. I never made the right choices that could have made that dream real, and now I had to wonder if I'd ever really wanted it in the first place. It's as if what had happened in our family was so awful that it had to end with us, it had to stop, and that to have children was to risk the perpetuation of that ruin. The only way you can kill that ruin truly is to kill yourself. In a way, that's precisely what Gary and Gaylen did: They ended the family by ending themselves before they could continue the family.

It is not easy to come to such a place—to feel as if there is something in you that should not continue on the face of this earth, something about yourself that should not survive your own life. Coming to that place, and to that sense of myself and my future, changed my life. I have not been the same since, and I sometimes suspect I will not be the same again.

CHAPTER 3

SECRETS AND

BONES

I DECIDED TO GO BACK TO PORTLAND ONCE MORE—this time to find my brother.

Frank was the last family I had, and I had relinquished him. I had no idea whether he was happy these days or living homeless, whether he was sane or crippled. Too often in my life I had lost those I loved or cared about—sometimes because death took them, sometimes because they gave up their love for me, and sometimes because something in me made it easy to walk away, to withdraw in some irrevocable way from those who might love or need me the most. There were times when it was a frighteningly easy thing to do—something I did almost without thinking—just one of those shameful secrets about myself that I did not fully understand, but now wanted access to.

But the truth is, I missed Frank terribly. I had tried to find him from time to time over the years. I'd get reports that somebody had seen him working someplace, or walking down one road or another in Portland, but I could never track him down anyplace. The last I had heard about him had been a couple of years before. A friend had seen him doing some custodial work. By the time I called the employer, Frank had quit and was gone.

I had no idea what I would find when I found my brother, but I did know I wanted to see him. I wanted to talk to him, touch him, see that he was okay and attempt to be fair with him, even if it only resulted in his casting me out of his life for good.

I HAD BEEN IN PORTLAND A SEASON BEFORE I FINALLY FOUND FRANK. I had done everything I knew how to locate him, yet despite a lifetime of reading mystery novels, I wasn't proving very good at the missing person business. I searched death certificates, I went to homeless shelters, I looked at the face of every man I passed on the street who could possibly be my brother. Then one night not long before Christmas, I was having dinner with Jim Redden, a friend who was a journalist and crime reporter. He offered to make some calls for me. The next morning, when I got up, Redden had left a message on my answering machine. He had found where Frank was living. It was ten blocks from where I was living, in northwest Portland.

I got dressed and walked over to Frank's address. It may have been only ten blocks, but in those few blocks one walked from one world into another. The area of northwest Portland I lived in was an old part of town, filled with Victorian houses that had been refurbished. It was now an upscale district with shops, cafés, and bars—just another of those self-conscious, affluent bohemian neighborhoods that have sprung up in most American cities over the last decade or two. But as you walk north along 23rd Avenue, you begin to move into the area where the Victorians have not been refurbished—where old homes look simply like old homes, and you come closer to the fringes of northwest Portland's industrial district. It was a part of town that had stood largely untouched and unloved since the 1940s, and where many older folks and several down-and-outers now congregated, hanging around corner grocery stores that had iron bars across their windows, and guard dogs or guns behind the counters. There were several taverns in the area, and most of them were rough laborers' hangouts.

Frank lived in the middle of all this, in an old rooming house, situated above a noisy tavern. I had seen places like this before; it was like the places my father had taken me as a child, when he went to find his salesmen. It was the sort of place where new light or fresh air rarely entered. Instead, you found the accrued smells of old men who had come to bide out their time, watching TV, drinking, brooding. The place had a depressing impact on me that felt unexpectedly primal. For a moment, I wanted to run.

I climbed the stairs and knocked on the door that I'd been told was Frank's. There was no answer. I knocked again, which brought the apartment manager's attention. He told me that the man who lived there had gone to work and wouldn't be back until mid evening.

WAITING UNTIL NIGHT TURNED OUT TO BE one of the longest waits of my life. I kept thinking about the place where Frank was living. I tried to imagine the reality of his life. Whatever problems I felt I had, I'd known comfort and social interaction. Life had been good to me in many ways—better than to anyone else in my family.

It seemed amazing to me that the lives of two brothers had taken such different courses. It also seemed terribly unfair. Frank had stayed home and taken care of my mother. Indeed, he was the only one of the brothers who had ever really tried to do the right thing. By contrast, I had simply escaped and looked after myself. I had never thought about taking on the burden of my mother and her problems. For his devotion, Frank had ended up with what looked to me like a devastated life, spent in the company of vagrants and other outsiders. Though I may not have ended up with some of the things I claimed to want in life, the truth is, I had not ended up with nothing. I went places, I did things, I had money in the bank. I was not about to end up in a rooming house.

There's no point in flogging myself too much here, or apologizing. I don't believe even now that I would have done anything differently in my life. I think I *had* to run away from my family in order not to be dragged down by its claims. Still, seeing where Frank lived gave me an idea of what his life must have been like in the last decade, and it did not make me feel good about the distance between us. Nor did it make me feel any better about the prospect of walking back into his life.

I SPENT THE REST OF THE DAY DRIVING AROUND, thinking about these things. I wondered what the two of us would have to say to each other after such a long time.

At about nine that night, I returned to the place where Frank lived. At the top of the stairs I nearly bumped into a man who was zipping up a parka jacket and pulling a stocking cap down over his ears in preparation for the cold outside. I studied the face quickly—a habit I'd picked up in recent months—and I saw something I'd seen so many times in my mind's eye over the years: a face deep-cut with the lines that come from bad history. I saw the face of my brother.

"Frank," I said. He looked up. I could tell he didn't know who I was. "Frank, it's me, Mikal." He stood there, staring at me, his face pulled into a questioning look, as if he didn't believe what I said. I think if he had reached out and shoved me down the stairs I probably would not have resisted him. I would have thought it was okay.

Instead, he reached out and took me in his arms, and held me. In that moment, the squalor around us didn't matter. In that moment, I felt like I was in the embrace of home.

A HALF HOUR LATER WE WERE SEATED in the warmth of my apartment. Frank hadn't wanted me to see the room where he lived.

As he entered my place, Frank looked around, taking in the clutter of books and CDs, and the electronic and computer equipment. "Man," he said, smiling, "you're kind of like Mom. It looks like you don't ever throw *any*thing away."

We sat on my sofa, sipping warm drinks, talking. Frank said he had heard I was married, and he wanted to know about my wife. I explained to him that the marriage had been over for a long time, and that it had been one of those honest but sad mistakes that people make. "Geez, man," Frank said, stirring his coffee, "I'm really sorry to hear that. No children?" I said no, and he lapsed momentarily into silence.

I asked what had happened to him since I had last seen him. He shrugged and cleared his throat. "Oh, I've just sort of drifted around for the most part, spending a few months here, then there. For a few years after Mom's death, I got into drinking a lot. I felt pretty bad about her dying. I felt responsible in some ways, and I couldn't get it out of my mind. She had hated and feared hospitals. I sent her to one and she died. Maybe if I hadn't, I thought, she would have had a chance. I sold the trailer afterward and just took off. I guess I spent years that way— traveling, working, drinking. I spent a lot of time on the streets. Got into a couple of fights. Had my arms broken twice. Got jumped on once by a bunch of fucking skinheads. They took everything I had."

Frank paused and smiled a gentle smile that was in startling contrast to the litany of horror he had just recited. "I guess I simply went a little crazy during those years. Then I got to thinking about all the other stuff, about Gaylen dying as such a young man, and Gary doing all those horrible things he did . . . I had people I barely knew come up to me and ask the most terrible questions. 'Is it true that your brother did those awful things? How could you have lived in the same home with a man like that?' A couple of times, when I was working at a job, somebody would figure out I was Gary's brother. They would want to get in fights with me, like somehow beating me made them bigger or tougher than Gary, or punished him more. A few months ago, I was working a job over in Salt Lake City, and when somebody figured out I was related to Gary, they fired me."

As Frank talked, I felt the past sitting in the room with us. Maybe he felt it too, because he got up and started to move around. He walked around my apartment looking at things, until he came to the dining table, where I had sprawled several of the photos from our family albums. For some reason, I'd become the caretaker of these pictures. They were all I had left of the family's possessions. I'd spent a lot of time recently studying these photos, trying to read them for clues to the riddles of our lives.

"I'd wondered what happened to these," said Frank, picking up one of the pictures and looking at it. "I don't have many of these left. I've traveled so much, had so much stolen or lost. I think about all I have left is a picture of you as a baby, in your playpen with your rubber toad. Do you remember that?"

Frank put down one photo and picked up another. "Do you mind if I sit here and look through these?"

I said he was welcome to look as long as he liked, and I'd have copies made of any of the pictures he wanted. "That's okay," he said, pulling a chair up to the table. "I don't really want to carry this stuff around with me. It might be fun to look at it, though."

We sat together at the table, poring over the old photos. Frank looked at them as somebody who knew a different story about every picture. I looked at them as an outsider. These photos described a certain world, and I had been born at the end of that world.

Frank picked up one of the only color pictures from the batch. It was a picture of a Thanksgiving turkey, of all things. Just the cooked bird itself. No people, no smiling holiday faces.

"I remember that turkey," Frank said. "I remember how good it looked sitting on the table while we waited for what seemed like hours to sit down and eat it. I remember Mom and Dad getting into a fight immediately. I remember Mom picking the turkey up and throwing it across the room, and I remember it hitting the floor—*SPLAT!*—and the dressing bouncing out all over the place. I remember that bird sitting there on the floor the rest of the day, because nobody would pick it up, because they were too busy calling each other filthy names. I remember never getting to taste it." Frank put the photo down and sighed. "It had looked like such a nice turkey."

A few photos later, Frank came across the only picture I have of my father and Gary alone together. In the picture, Gary is wearing a sailor's cap. He has his arms wrapped tight around my father's neck, his cheek pressed close against my father's, a look of broken need on his face. It is heartbreaking to look at this picture—not just for the look on Gary's face, the look that would become the visage of his future, but also for my father's expression. In that moment, my father is pulling away from Gary's cheek, and he is wearing a look of barely disguised distaste.

Frank studied the picture quietly for several seconds, then he looked up at me. "Did you know," he said, speaking carefully, "that Gary had a son?"

I told him I had recently learned as much from one of Larry Schiller's last taped interviews with Gary. I told him I had also heard on one of my mother's tapes that the boy hadn't died after all, as Gary thought.

"That's right," Frank said. "The baby never died. That was just something Mom and Dad told Gary. In fact, I think I might have run into Gary's son a couple of years back. It wasn't a very pleasant meeting.

"It was a late summer afternoon. I was walking along Burnside, not far from the park where a lot of the homeless people hang out. There's a little tavern up the street. I was coming from work, and I was heading for the tavern to get a pitcher of beer. Just as I got to the place, this guy comes running up and starts talking to me. He asked me if I was Frank Gilmore, and I said I was. He said, 'Your brother Gary was my father.' I looked at him and said, 'I don't know what you're talking about,' and then I tried to walk on.

"He stopped me. He said, 'Yes, you do. Your brother was my father. Your family fucked me up real good, and now I'm going to fuck you up.' Then he tried to lay me out with a punch. I ducked and grabbed him and slammed his back up against a building. Then I saw a dummy stick fall from one of his hands. Those things can hurt you real bad. I kicked it into the street and said, 'Jesus, can't you even fight like a man?' I let go of him and backed off. When I saw that he wasn't going to move on me,

I made my way into the tavern and told the bartender what had happened. He said he noticed that the guy had been hanging around there off and on for a few days, like he was waiting for somebody. I sat there and had a beer, and after a while I looked up, and the guy was standing outside, looking at me through the window. I decided I should go out and try to have a talk with him. By the time I got out there he was gone, and I never saw him again."

I asked Frank: "Do you think the man might actually have been Gary's son? Did he look anything like Gary?"

Frank watched me quietly for a moment, then said: "He looked *just* like Gary."

Fucking hell, I thought. If this were true, if the young man Frank faced had in fact been Gary's son, then it might mean something worse than I'd ever imagined. Maybe there was simply no end to a violent lineage or bad legacy. Maybe it just kept spilling over into history, into the world, into our children, into everything that came of our blood.

As I was thinking this, Frank leaned across the table and said to me: "I'm sorry I didn't get in touch with you for all these years. It's not like I didn't know where you were, or didn't know how to find you. I could always have called or written you at the magazine where you worked.

"It's just that . . . I don't know. I thought you were doing fine. Sometimes, I'd be out there, working some dirt job somewhere, or sleeping under a bridge, and I'd think: 'Somewhere, I've got this brother who's doing well. He's a writer, he talks to famous people and people respect him, and he's married and probably has kids now. Yeah, I'm probably an uncle by this time.' And I'd wonder if it was a boy or girl, if it had blond hair and blue eyes like you had when you were a baby. I'd think about all that, and sometimes it would help. Like I said, I was a lost man after Mom died. But I'd think about you and I'd feel proud. And I kind of decided I would never bother you, I wouldn't look you up and embarrass you by making you acknowledge me. I wouldn't be a reminder of the past that I thought was safely behind you. I thought: 'There's one of us—*one*—who has come out all right, who has made it. I think I owe it to him to leave him alone and let him have his happiness. It's good to let him go. There's no reason he should have to stay tied to this family.'"

I didn't say a word. I don't think I could have. I sat there, looking at my brother and thinking: This may be all the family I have left in the world, but it is family enough. I had never truly understood the depths of this man's heart or the expanse of his loneliness, but maybe it wasn't too late. Maybe, just maybe, I was ready to learn something worthwhile about the fidelity born of blood.

FOR THE NEXT YEAR, FRANK AND I GOT TOGETHER at my apartment a few times each week and talked about our past. Frank told me many of the stories that I have repeated here, and through him, I managed to come to a fuller and more balanced understanding of our family. As it turned out, Frank has a remarkable memory, and an impressive knack for recalling vivid details. Time and again, he steered me to elements of the family's story that I had never suspected, and when he couldn't answer my questions or didn't know the solutions to all the various mysteries, he simply told me so. In the course of all this, I got to know my brother in a way I had never known him before, and we each found a chance to talk about difficult experiences and legacies in the sort of candid way that probably too few siblings ever get with one another.

I also came to understand, more indelibly than ever, how much Frank had paid over the years for being a son and brother in our family. One day Frank showed up at my door, looking terribly wrought up. He could barely speak for the first half hour or so. As he began to talk, he told me about a phobia that he had been afflicted with for years. It's a complex phobia—in part, a fear of blushing or self-consciousness, the sort of fear that inevitably only feeds on itself and becomes worse. But it is also a fear of guilt or judgment. On this particular occasion, the phobia had been activated by an incident that had occurred in a grocery store a short while before. The woman behind the counter had said something that caused Frank to suspect that she thought he might be a shoplifter. Apparently he had felt he was being watched by the woman during other visits to the store. "I'm afraid of being judged guilty for things I haven't done," he told me. "I'm afraid that people think I'm a thief or a killer. Sometimes I feel like I'm just alone in this fucking life—it's me against the world."

This is not a small fear. In part, Frank believes that the phobia derives from his having been the brother of a murderer. I think it probably goes beyond that. From the time he was a child, Frank—like some of the rest of us—believed he was responsible for the unhappiness in our parents' marriage. That's a big thing for a child to feel guilty about. Then, as he grew older, every time that Gary got punished by my father for something that he *did* do, Frank got punished along with him, whether he was innocent or not. Such treatment—especially when administered consistently and brutally over the years—would be enough to give anyone a deep fear of being thought guilty.

As I sat and watched my brother cry that day, I realized how deeply the world's judgments had been embedded in him. More than any of us, Frank has never stopped paying for what happened in our family. He pays for Gary and my mother and my father every day of his life, and that payment has driven him into a fearful and private place.

IN THE MIDDLE OF 1991, FRANK AND I TOOK A TRIP TO UTAH. I wanted to see firsthand the places where my mother had grown up and where my parents had met, and to see, also, the places where Gary had done all his damage. I also wanted to make a peace with what remained of the family there. Years before, during the events that surrounded Gary, I had judged these people harshly and probably unfairly. I held them responsible for much of what happened, but then, that was an awful time, and it was as easy for me to come to bad judgments as it was for everybody else. I now understood that my uncle and aunt and cousins had done the best they knew how with a horrible, bigger-than-life situation. They had not asked Gary to come into their world and turn it upside down, to murder their neighbors and then go out in a self-appointed blaze of glory. He had ruined many lives during those few months. The time had come for me to remember that these people were family too.

Frank and I traveled separately. He wanted to stop and see some friends along the way, and I wanted to drive straight through. Shortly after midnight one night in July, I pulled into Ogden, Utah, and checked into a motel. I turned on the TV to catch up with the news as I was unpacking, just in time to hear a reporter say: "The execution went off smoothly, without any hitches, without any scenes." I sat down on the bed, dumbfounded. William Andrews, one of the two men who had been known in the state as the Hi-Fi Killers (because they had tortured and murdered people in a stereo store), and who had been on death row at the same time that Gary was there, had been put to death by lethal injection. I had not known that his execution was planned, or I would not have come to Utah. I've become like my mother that way: When executions happen now, I run and hide. I can't stand knowing about them.

Well, I'm truly back in Utah, I thought, and then went in the bathroom and threw up.

IF I REMEMBER RIGHT, I ALSO THREW UP THE NEXT NIGHT. I had driven down to Orem—the town right next to my mother's birthplace, Provo—to visit the Sinclair service station where Gary had committed his first murder. The old station has been long since torn down, and in its place is a self-serve facility, with a cashier's booth, a couple of islands of gas tanks, and a rest room building. I was relieved to see this—it meant I wouldn't have to stand in the actual tiny lavatory where my brother had forced the young Max Jensen down on the floor and fired two bullets into the back of his head. Still, I found something haunting and unbearable about the place. It was one of those spots where history had ended up spilling onto the earth and taking lives. I sat in my car, studying the place, thinking what my mother had thought all those years before: How *could* you, Gary? How could you have done this to that man? I think I understand well enough what ruined my brother, what made him murderous, but I have never been able to make a certain leap—to imagine putting a stranger with a kind face on a cold floor and shooting him.

I sat there and thought about it until I couldn't think about it anymore. I felt all the old shame and all the old shock. I drove into Provo and found a place that served good stiff drinks—which is not an easy thing to find in Provo. Then I went back to my motel and threw up.

A DAY OR TWO LATER I MET UP WITH FRANK and we went to see our Uncle Vernon at his home outside Provo. We also saw his daughters, Brenda and Toni. Ida had died years before, and Vernon was now remarried, to a gracious and caring Mormon woman. Brenda had lost her mate as well: John had died of cancer some time ago and was buried next to Ida in the Provo cemetery, not far from where my grandparents and George and Alta lie buried.

For me, the visit was like getting to discover people—people I had never really been close to before, whom I had not really spent any time with since the time I'd visited the farm when my mother brought me back to Utah for her father's funeral. For Frank, though, it was something else. He knew these people well. He had grown up with them. Watching him talk with Brenda and Toni, I realized that he felt toward them as if they were his sisters. All these people liked each other, and I was glad to see it.

Afterward, driving Frank back to Salt Lake City, we got lost in Provo, and drove in circles for a while, trying to find a main street to take us up to the freeway. I pulled over to look at my map, and after a moment Frank said: "There it is." I looked up. We were parked just outside the

City Center Motel, where, on the night after he had killed Max Jensen, Gary forced Ben Bushnell to lie on the floor and shot him as well. Frank and I sat there in silence for what felt like a long time. Finally I took a deep breath and said: "Do you feel like we should go in the office and take a look around?"

"No," Frank said. "I don't want to see it."

I felt relieved. "Neither do I," I said, and we drove off into the night.

AT VERN'S THAT NIGHT, MY UNCLE HAD TAKEN ME aside at one point and said: "I have Gary's clothes here in the house with me. There's something about them I want to show you. Would you like to see them?"

I said I would be willing to see them another time, but I didn't think it would be appropriate to do so in front of Frank.

I went back another night and sat at Vern's kitchen table, on which he placed a large plastic bag. From the bag he pulled out a sleeveless black sweatshirt, white pants, and tennis shoes with red, white, and blue shoestrings, and spread them before me. These were the clothes that Gary was wearing when he was executed. I had expected them to be bloodied and ravaged, but they weren't. All the blood had since been washed out. I sat there and ran my hands over the clothes. They felt soft to me, and for some reason it did not make me sad to touch them. There was almost something comforting about it.

Vern picked up the shirt and pointed out the pattern of perforations that the bullets had made as they pierced the cloth and ripped through Gary's heart. Four neat holes, each about the size you could put your finger through.

"Look at this," Vern said, and pointed out another hole, a little farther apart from the others. "That, too," he said, "is a bullet hole."

According to Utah's tradition—and perhaps its law as well—there are five men on a firing squad, but only four of them have loaded rifles. One of them has a gun with a blank in it. This is done so that if any man is bothered by his conscience, he can always entertain a reasonable doubt that he ever actually fired a bullet into the condemned man.

There should have been four holes in the shirt. Instead, there were five. The State of Utah, apparently, had taken no chances on the morning that it put my brother to death.

———

I SPENT A LOT OF TIME VISITING MY COUSIN BRENDA during my Utah stay, and I also came to know and like the man she was about to marry, a strong, smart, good-tempered guy named Jack. It didn't take me long to realize what all my brothers had loved about Brenda. She was funny, earthy, dead-honest, terribly bright and loving. She also had a conscience that she could not violate, and it was in misjudging that aspect of her that Gary had made his most fatal mistake. Brenda loved Gary and felt bad for him, but when he started to kill people, she would not harbor or protect him. She knew that if she did, he would kill others. I knew exactly how she felt, and I knew that when she told the police where they could find him, she had done the right thing.

On the last night I spent in Utah, Brenda brought me an opaque green jar, with a sealed lid on it. Through the cloudy greenishness, you could make out the contents: They were chips of bone that had been sifted out from the ashes of a cremation.

"I've lived with this a long time," Brenda said. "I think it more rightly belongs with you."

I now own all that is left in this world of Gary Mark Gilmore. It sits in my office, and it has been close to me as I have written every word these last few months.

BUT BONES AREN'T THE ONLY THING I brought back from Utah. I also brought back the knowledge of a secret that I found truly devastating and that I did not know what to do with.

I had first learned about this secret from the taped interviews that Larry Schiller and Norman Mailer loaned me. In a conversation between Schiller and my Aunt Ida, Ida had told him about something that had happened a long time before. It was during the time when my father had been in prison, and my mother had taken Frankie and Gary back to her parents' farm, to live in the house out back. One day my mother was showing Ida some photos, when she came across a picture of Robert Ingram. "Isn't he about the most handsome man you've ever seen?" Bessie asked Ida. "I sure miss that boy. You know, he's Frank Jr.'s real father."

Bessie went on to tell Ida that she and Robert had a brief affair shortly after she had married my father, during one of the times when Frank Sr. had left her alone in Sacramento with his mother and estranged son. Bessie had liked Robert, and Robert had liked her, plus the affair had been a way of paying Frank Sr. back for all his abandonments. Bessie had not meant to become pregnant, but when she did, she knew it would be easy enough to convince Frank Sr. that the child was his. Still, my father had always suspected something. Ironically, he thought that Gary might have been Robert's son, and perhaps that played into his later special dislike for Gary, and the intensity with which he beat him. Perhaps the secret also figured into why Bessie used to beat Frankie when he was a little boy. Maybe every time she looked at him, she remembered the affair. Maybe she felt guilt or shame, maybe she blamed the child. In any event, Frank Jr. was the only one of us that my mother ever beat regularly. Between her and my father, Frank Jr. and Gary paid a lot for that secret.

I had known about this story for some time, but I wanted to try to confirm it with the family in Utah, if possible. I had not yet told my brother Frank. I didn't know how to. At the same time, Frank and I had made a deal to tell each other whatever truths or rumors we learned. He had told me things that had troubled him deeply to tell me. After Utah—where Vern and Brenda confirmed the rumor as much as possible and filled in some of the details—I realized I had to tell Frank what I knew.

During one of our last visits, I told Frank I had something to tell him.

He took a seat. "Is it a shocker?"

I said yes, it was. And then I told him. He took it in quietly for a while. When he spoke, it was in a low voice. "I'd heard Dad insinuate something like that once or twice with Mom. He was screaming it at her at the time, saying that she and Robert had this thing, and that he had always known about it. I'd heard him, but I thought he was just shooting his mouth off, trying to get at her.

"I guess that explains a few things. I guess it explains why I'm kind of fucked up emotionally. And I guess it explains why Mom was always so hard on me. I mean, after Dad died, Gary and Gaylen were in trouble constantly. They were ruining her. But she always had a lot of love for them. I was the one that had to bust my ass to try and keep her going as best I could and in turn I got nothing but just hatred, hatred, hatred."

Frank paused and looked at me, his face in pain. "So this means Dad wasn't my father. It means my half brother was my father, and Dad was my grandfather. But what I want to know is, since you and I don't have the same father, does it mean that you're still my brother?"

"I will always be your brother," I said, "and you will always be my brother. Nothing will change that. I'm sorry I had to tell you this. I wondered for a long time whether I should. It's kind of a hard thing to talk about."

Frank looked down, trying to blink back his tears. "Everything in our family," he said, "is hard to talk about."

CHAPTER 4
A LETTER
FROM HOME

I HAVEN'T SEEN FRANK SINCE THAT LAST VISIT. I had to go back to Los Angeles to finish my work, and he preferred to stay in Portland. We rarely talk on the phone, because Frank doesn't have one. We write each other now and then, though. Frank is the better letter writer.

A while back he sent me a letter in which he tried to fill in some of the things about our family life that he had never gotten around to telling me. I read this letter over and over.

Here is some of what it says:

> During the time before you were born, when we lived on Crystal Springs Boulevard, Gary and I were attending school not far away. It's always hard for me to think of that school because it reminds me of the time that I saw a young schoolmate killed while he was trying to cross a street called Flavel.

His name was Paul, and he was walking with his father. The next thing I knew, I saw Paul running across the street and then he was hit by a large black car. I remember his father panicking, and I remembered just then that I had forgotten to get my brother Gary at school. I was supposed to bring him home with me but for some reason that I can't remember, I did not.

Seeing Paul get hit by the car shocked me and confused me. I thought that it was Gary. I ran all the way back to the school screaming that my brother had been killed by a car. I remember some lady with dark hair in her front yard, looking at me with sadness. I found Gary and I was still upset. I told him what happened and we both went home together. I told Mom what had happened. She just looked at me with disgust. She said: "Clean up for dinner. And *don't* forget your brother again." I learned then that when you have something that is bothering you, you never tell your parents about it . . .

Around this same time Gary and I both had newspaper routes. It lasted for a while, but then Gary got tired of his route, and so one day instead of delivering his papers he just threw them away. That was the end of his route. He got fired, and I remember that Dad was so upset, he beat Gary terribly, for a long time. None of us kids were perfect. But poor Gary, he just seemed to be a little less perfect . . .

My brother Mikal came into our lives when we were living on Crystal Springs Boulevard. It was before we moved to Utah. Gary and I were listening to the radio when the telephone rang. Dad answered it. A couple of minutes later he came into the room and said, "Well, boys, I don't know how you're going to take this, but you have a new brother." Gary and I were both old enough to know there was a baby on the way, so it was no surprise, but we were still both happy about it.

I remember that a few days later we went somewhere up above 23rd Avenue in northwest Portland, where we picked up both Mom and our new brother, Mikal. I remember that the baby was a lot smaller than I expected, and he was kind of pruned up, but I took a real liking to him. And Dad had found somebody he really loved. Dad really liked Mike, and so did I. I can remember one time when Mike got sick and Dad called the doctor. When the doctor got there he said it was nothing bad, which made us happy. After all, Mike was the family's baby. However, the doctor did say that he was going to have to give Mike a shot. I remember that it bothered me so much that I had to go outside while he gave him the shot.

I also remember that Mikal used to have a little crib with real high walls around it, so that he could not get out. And no one would ever let him out except me. Every time he would see me he used to get all excited and reach up for me to take him out. As soon as I would lift him up, I remember that his legs would start to go a million miles a minute. By the time he reached the floor, *zip,* he was gone. I mean everywhere, all over the house, in a flash. It was like he wanted everyone in the family to know that he was free.

EPILOGUE

11. *My days are past, my purposes are broken off, even the thoughts of my heart.*
12. *They change the night into day: the light is short because of darkness.*
13. *If I wait, the grave is mine house: I have made my bed in the darkness.*
14. *I have said to corruption, Thou art my father: to the worm, Thou art my mother, and my sister.*
15. *And where is now my hope? As for my hope, who shall see it?*
16. *They shall go down to the bars of the pit, when our rest together is in the dust.*

—BOOK OF JOB, CHAPTER 17

THE TRIAL

A LAST DREAM:

I am attending Gary's trial. We are in a small, stately chamber in a Utah courthouse, and the room is full of grim, unforgiving faces. They are judges. They are asking Gary—who, in this dream as in real life, is requesting to be put to death—why he committed his crimes, why he was so violent. He seems bemused by the questions, and is unwilling to mount a defense. I am part of his defense team—either an assistant attorney or a witness—and I pass a note to Gary's main lawyer. "I can tell the truth about this," I write. "Put me on the stand."

I go on and I tell what I think will make a difference: I tell the judges how Gary was beaten as a child, how he was forced to watch his mother being beaten, how he was abandoned and abused a thousand times.

Nobody seems to think that what I'm disclosing matters. Gary himself shrugs it off. The judges rule that my testimony is irrelevant. "What happens to the child doesn't absolve the man," says one judge.

But then there is a curious flaw in the dream's logic—or at least in the judges' logic. The judges learn that Gary has a dark-haired daughter, about three years old. They decide that, as Gary's offspring, the girl has been too contaminated by him to survive. If Gary wants to die, the judges rule, then his child must die alongside him. Gary accepts this.

I am livid at this decision. I am so angry, I am dragged from the courtroom. I try prevailing on everybody I encounter to see the injustice, the cruelty and the waste of this judgment. But nobody seems unduly bothered by it. Gary is willing to accept the cost of the child's death to win his own end.

I now no longer care about what happens to my brother. I want to save this child. I try to fight it until the last moment—until somebody comes to me, standing outside the prison in the dark, and tells me: "The child is dead."

When I learn this, I break down in a crushed, insatiable grief. I cannot believe that this has happened. I cannot imagine life going on or being tolerable in the face of this loss. I can't live with something this unbearable.

I AWAKEN THEN, MY INSIDES RACKED in a sharp pain. I find I am truly crying. I lie there in the dark sobbing, and though I know no child has actually died, I can't stop crying. It feels like a real loss, and it feels like I *can't* live with it.

I get up and look at the clock. It is four-thirty in the morning. I go into the kitchen and pour myself a glass of whiskey. I go back and sit up in bed in the darkness. I sit there a long time. I finish my whiskey, slip under the covers, pull a pillow over my head to keep out the horrible morning light I hate so much. I curl up and I tell myself: "It will never be all right. Never. It will *never* be all right." I say this to myself over and over, until I find enough comfort in the words that I am able to fall asleep again.

ACKNOWLEDGMENTS

MANY PEOPLE HELPED ME DURING THE PROCESS OF DISCOVERING and telling this story.

Chief among them were my brother, Frank Gilmore, Jr., and Lawrence Schiller and Norman Mailer.

When I went looking for my brother at the end of 1991, after ten years of absence from each other's lives, I had no idea what his state of heart or mind might be, and I couldn't begin to guess how he might feel about the prospect of me writing a book about our family past, which we had both done our best to distance ourselves from. Though Frank had some real misgivings about exhuming that past and putting some of its less pleasant aspects forward for public scrutiny, he was amazingly gracious in his willingness to share with me everything he knew about that difficult history. In the end, Frank and I did something like a hundred hours of interviews—if *interviews* is the right word to apply to two brothers' intimate conversations—and over the course of those discussions, my own sense of the story I was telling underwent a dramatic change. Frank had no desire to condemn or rehabilitate anybody in our family's history—himself included; he simply wanted to tell his stories as plainly and evenhandedly as he remembered them. Time and again, I was astonished at his ability for vivid, detailed recall, and I was constantly humbled by his depth and unaffected eloquence.

This book is dedicated to Frank, as it should be. Without his help, I would have told a different, less accurate, and less meaningful story. More important, without his concern, I would not have regained the last bit of family I should never have lost. I am fortunate and proud to call Frank my brother.

Schiller and Mailer's contribution was also immense, and even more unexpected. In 1977, when Schiller was conducting and compiling interviews and research material for Mailer's *The Executioner's Song,* he contacted me on a few occasions, requesting that I sit for an interview with himself and the author. I always declined those requests—and not always politely. In part, I did so for reasons already discussed elsewhere in this book: Larry and I had some bad communications in Utah in the week prior to Gary's death, and the simple truth is, I chose to hold a grudge. Also, I questioned the merits of an exhaustive look at my brother's pathology (in fact, I wasn't yet ready to face examining the sources of all that tragedy). Later, when I read the finished book, I was greatly impressed. Mailer had told a complex and troubling story without imposing a voice or judgment of his own, and Schiller had done a scrupulous job of research. Later, when Schiller's film version of the book was finished, he offered me an early glimpse of it, and granted me an interview for an article I was writing about the movie for *Rolling Stone.* In a way, I regretted my earlier decision not to give him an interview for *The Executioner's Song*—given his helpfulness, I felt churlish about withholding what I knew about my brother's life. At the same time, I came to respect Schiller in ways I had not expected to respect him—he served his material truthfully and honorably, and he and Mailer created something monumental from that effort.

In the autumn of 1991, I was discussing with Schiller some of the problems of trying to find the more hidden aspects of my family's story, when Larry made a remarkable and unsolicited offer: He proposed to let me borrow the original interview tapes of the discussions that he had recorded with both Gary and my mother. He thought such a listening experience might expand my emotional sense of the story, plus it might explain a few of the more bothersome puzzles. Obviously, I was somewhat embarrassed by this offer—after all, I had once declined all of his and Mailer's requests for help—but I wasn't so embarrassed that I didn't jump on the chance. Merely hearing my mother's and brother's voices again after so many years, like hearing Frank's astonishing stories, not only changed how I thought and felt about the people I was trying to rediscover, it also deepened my relationship to them. Additionally, of course, I gathered many significant details and accounts from the tapes, and I have tried to acknowledge those boons at several points in the course of this text. (As much as possible, I have tried not to cover the same ground that Mailer covered in his work, though some shared stories were unavoidable. At the same time, if you want a meticulous and revealing examination of Gary's misadventures in Utah, *The Executioner's Song* is the place to go; it tells a different story than I have told, and it tells it remarkably.)

In addition, both Schiller and Mailer—as well as Mailer's personal assistant, Judith McNally—remained patient when I wrote and called them at various points, asking if they could help me figure out some of the various perplexing mysteries of my parents' past. They helped when they could, but sometimes they were as stumped as I was. "Your questions were once my questions," Mailer replied at one point, and in the end, many of those questions could not be answered. My father and my mother had done a good job of covering their tracks. Whatever Frank and Bessie Gilmore's best or worst secrets were, they managed to keep them hidden long past their own deaths. I doubt I'll ever be so lucky.

SEVERAL OTHERS HELPED IN THE HARD AND TEDIOUS WORK of researching this history of lost lives. The following people spent hours helping me dig through files and records and state and institutional bureaucracies for essential materials: Paula Jean Brown, Jennifer Kriegh-Lobianco, Jim Redden, Sheila Rogers, Neil Thompson, and Ewa Wojciak.

Karen Essex organized, read through, and annotated my interviews with my brother Frank. Her comments and observations were always insightful and helped me think about Frank's stories in new and substantial ways. Karen also helped with many other acts of love and kindness as well.

In addition to my brother Frank, the following people were willing to sit with me and share their remembrances of various people and events in my family's history: Steve Bekins, Craig Esplin, Duane Fulmer, Tom Lyden, Grace McGinnis, Robert Moody, Larry Olstad, Rich Parker, Norm Rieter, and Roger Shirley. There were others who also gave interviews, but for various reasons, they cannot be identified here. My thanks to all these people for sharing their time and memories.

EARLY ON, WHEN I WAS STILL DEBATING WITH MYSELF about writing this book, several folks offered kind and crucial encouragement and guidance. Among them were: Nancy Clark, James Ellroy, Karen Hall, and Victoria Williams. A dear friend, Helen Knode, suggested this book's title. The moment she did, I realized I had found something valuable. For two years now, knowing that title has helped me draw a center on this story.

SEVERAL YEARS AGO, I WROTE about the events surrounding my brother's execution, and the later film version of his life, for *Rolling Stone*. Portions of those articles appear in revised form in the fifth section of this book, "Blood History." I would like to thank the following current and former *Rolling Stone* staffers who helped me in crucial ways with those articles: Barbara Downey, Ben Fong-Torres, James Henke, Sarah Lazin, Terry McDonnell, Susan Murcko, Steve Pond, Bob Wallace, and Jann Wenner.

Rolling Stone helped me keep writing at a time in my life when all I really wanted to do was disappear. My thanks to the folks I have worked with at the magazine for their long-standing patience and support.

I WOULD ALSO LIKE TO GIVE THANKS TO THE FOLLOWING: Lee Youngman, for her tour of MacLaren's School for Boys and her edifying comments about youth violence; Charles Crookham and Jeff Van Valkenburgh at the Oregon State Attorney General's office, and Robey D. Eldridge at the Oregon Department of Corrections, for their help in obtaining my brother Gary's prison and medical and psychiatric records; William Drucker, M.D., for sharing with me his knowledge about the complex subject of antipsychotic drug treatment; David Copperfield and Kreskin, for helping me sort out the truth behind the Houdini rumor; L. Kay Gillespie, at Weber State University in Utah, for helping me to understand Mormon Utah's history of capital punishment (Gillespie is the author of a much recommended volume, *The Unforgiven: Utah's Executed Men*); Harry Crews, for his terrific story, "Fathers, Sons, Blood" (in *classic crews: a Harry Crews Reader*), from which I lifted the title for this volume's fifth section, as well as a Goethe quote that I probably would not have found otherwise; and Virginia Campbell, Katherine Dunn, Steve Erickson, Neil Gaiman, Dr. Leonard Lewenstein, Bernadette Megowan, Shannon Riske, Dr. Larry Ryan, and Michael Sugg, for many invaluable hours of conversation, counseling, and perspective. I would also like to thank Alan Pakula, for his early faith and support in this venture.

SEVERAL OTHERS GAVE ME INVALUABLE PERSONAL HELP: my New York cousins, Peter Lancton and his late father, Clarence Lancton, for filling in parts of my grandmother Fay's history; and in Utah, my uncle Vernon Damico and his daughters (and my cousins) Brenda Wagstaff and Toni Gurney. Vern, Brenda, and Toni gave freely of their time and their memories — memories that still held much real pain for them — and they also made me feel love in a land that my legacy had taught me to hate. I would also like to give special thanks to Nicole Barrett. She gave me a tremendous amount of help and understanding during a difficult period in her life, and her friendship has become irreplaceable. Thanks, Nicole, for putting up with all the trouble and the bad reminders. I owe you love, and more.

Finally, I would like to thank my editor, David Gernert, his editorial assistant, Amy Williams, and my agent, Richard Pine. These folks were all patient and generous beyond the reason of duty. In particular, I owe Richard deep thanks for his forebearance and stimulus through several difficult years and too many false starts. This book would not have happened without his unswerving faith in my ability to take on the past.

I began the full-time research for this book in Portland, Oregon, in October 1991, and finished it in Los Angeles, in January 1993. The text was written from February to October 1993.

LIST OF PHOTOGRAPHS AND PHOTO CREDITS

Unless otherwise noted, all photographs are courtesy of Mikal Gilmore.